Using

Lacanian Clinical Technique

-an introduction-

Philip H F Hill

Press for the Habilitation of Psychoanalysis

This book is intended to help those who work —or wish to work— privately, in multidisciplinary teams, general practices and schools, and addresses two different sorts of reader: the complete beginner, who has very little clinical experience or training —or none at all— and the experienced clinician who is interested in finding out how Lacanian ideas work in the clinic. Contrasts and comparisons are made with the theories and techniques of other influential schools such the Kleinians, Rogerians and object relations theorists through discussions of their clinical cases.

The book assumes no specialist knowledge and is accessible with clear explanations, clinical examples and the minimum of jargon. Some connections are made with the theory of the clinic, culture, literature, science and logic, demonstrating the clarity, theoretical rigour and benefits of Lacanian clinical practice.

There are diagrams, cartoons, an index, and a helpful list of books and articles. For those with visual difficulties this book is also available on a CD, for PC or Mac in rich text format for text to speech programmes.

The emphasis throughout is on understanding how the client's speech uniquely marks out their suffering and desire. Freud was the first clinician to use techniques that rely on this radical theory, and to listen carefully to what clients say. Lacanian practice and theory develop this central theme in Freud's work. If your work is helping transform their suffering, by listening and studying what they say, then you are interested in Lacan's Freudian project.

Philip Hill is a registered psychoanalyst in private practice, a member of the Centre for Freudian Analysis and Research, and has worked in the National Health Service and for charities and schools. He has written *Lacan for Beginners* for Writers and Readers Inc. and is currently writing two books: *Structure in the Clinic and Theory of Immunology and Psychoanalysis: Freud's and Lacan's contribution to Psychoneuroimmunology,* and *Psychoanalysis as a History of Science and Ideas: Feminine Sexuality as essentially indeterminate.* Philip Hill can be contacted on: phfh@philiphill.com

This is not a comprehensive instruction manual. Clinical work requires training, supervision and an analysis of one's own.

CONTENTS

4 CONTENTS

ACKNOWLEDGEMENTS

In reading this you have parted with both your limited time and perhaps with your money too, so the question of a debt is raised: what exactly do I owe you? It is traditional in this part of a book for the author to acknowledge his debt —not to the reader— but towards an infinite regress, to another set of people or institutions!

In order to devote myself to writing this book for you I have neglected those I love. My children no longer recognise me, my wife is having an affair, my friends have deserted me and my dog growls at me. My esteemed and gifted colleagues have contributed more to this book than I could begin to hint at, over the decades that I have laboured on it. You, my reader, are getting more than my life is worth.

Presumably this kind of offering might placate the reader in the same way that a bankrupt individual or country, unable to make any one particular payment of interest that it owes, instead proposes to 'reschedule all interest payments', swallowing up the one particular debt in the universe of its indebtedness.

The truth is that many people have unwittingly and wittingly contributed to this book. If you feel short changed, or that your time would have been better spent, please feel free to contribute or to complain. E-mail me at: phfh@philiphill.com

Most of the artwork is by David Arnold Leach —cartoonist, animator and web designer— who can be contacted at: animatt@globalnet.co.uk Thank you Steven Appleby for your revelations about nudists on page 54, and Bud Light for permission to use your advertisement on page 173. Min Cooper kindly contributed 'Him and Her Discuss Fashion' on page 322. Debbie Daniels influenced the section on The Child's Right to Confidentiality in Chapter Thirteen. Katie Hunter, Oliver Rathbone, Kirsty Hall, Jim Grotstein, Dany Nobus and Rik Loose made helpful comments on drafts of this text. Tim Haigh (haightim@aol.com) and Jolyon Jenkins edited the text, and Cormac Gallagher generously supplied his own translations of many of Lacan's seminars.

PREFACE

Why another book introducing Lacanian clinical techniques?

A few Lacanian clinical texts have been published. All of them are good in different ways. Some are informal while others assume prior familiarity with Lacan's ideas: I hope this book is both accessible to those with little or no experience of clinical work or psychoanalytic theory, *and* that it shows the rigour and clinical value of clear theoretical ideas. There is a live debate about the value of Lacanian theory and its relevance to clinical practice. Many clinicians claim to be:

'. . . troubled by . . . theoretical papers on Lacanian themes which have little to do with clinical psychoanalysis. How can we persuade academics that playing . . . games with Lacanian ideas has nothing to offer to the ordinary steam psychoanalyst in his consulting room?' [1]

Another writer has slandered Lacan and Lacanian psychoanalysis with the lie that:

'Lacan . . . has had little effect on the practice of psychoanalysis.' [2]

The truth is that there are some 15,000 to 20,000 psychoanalysts worldwide and approximately half use Lacan's ideas in their clinical work[3]. Fifty per cent is not a 'little effect'. I hope that this book will introduce readers to the writing of Lacan, and perhaps encourage the reading and re-reading of Freud's work.

In trying to understand Lacan's work it is helpful to look at some of the alternative theories studied by Lacan in developing his own; I refer to a selection of non-Lacanian clinical theories and cases for the perspective they provide on Lacan's work.

I hope that this book is a proper reply to some of the critical and often emotional responses to the theories and techniques of Freud and Lacan. Anti-Lacanian and anti-Freudian sentiment is found amongst some clinicians as well as the views of those who are simply 'anti-psychoanalysis'. Compare these similar emotional reactions:

---

[1] Anonymous reader for the International Journal of Psycho-Analysis, 1992, in a letter to the author.
[2] *Hutchinson Multimedia Encyclopaedia,* on CD, Helicon Publishing Ltd, 1996.
[3] E Roudinescu *Jacques Lacan & Co, A History of Psychoanalysis in France,* 1928-1985, FAB, 1990, p705-712.

'Freud's theories are thoroughly unoriginal . . . Numerous psychoanalytic observations are faked . . . No psychoanalytic interpretation is supported by any clinical observations. It is simply not possible that any pattern of observations could be encountered in the real world, which would supply evidence for any psychoanalytic interpretation or proposition . . . As for psychoanalytic propaganda . . . Freud was perfectly aware of the fact that he had never discovered anything, nor ever cured any patient . . . Concerning the personality of psychoanalysts . . . All psychoanalytic writers reveal an unusually low degree of knowledge of human nature . . . , empathy or capacity for clinical observation . . . ' [4]

'Future historians trying to account for the institutionalised fraud that goes under the name of 'theory' will surely accord a central place to the influence of the French psychoanalyst Jacques Lacan. He is surely one of the fattest spiders at the heart of the web of muddled not-quite-thinkable-thoughts and evidence free assertions of limitless scope, which practitioners of theorhoea have woven into their version of the humanities.///// His lunatic legacy still lives on.' [5]

Freud had observed that:

'What people seem to demand of . . . [psychoanalysis] is not progress in knowledge, but satisfactions of some other sort; every unsolved problem, every admitted uncertainty is made into a reproach against it.' [6]

While this book was inspired by Freud's and Lacan's clinical work and theories, I have no guarantee that the ideas here represent Freud's or Lacan's work: some ideas here are my speculations, hypotheses and guesswork. This is not a 'pure vision' of Lacan's clinical technique and theory; one consequence of Lacan's theory of language is that meanings are liable to change whenever there is an attempt to transmit or transfer them.

What exactly is 'psychoanalysis'?
Psychoanalysis is the practice of Freud's clinical theory. This true but trivial claim leaves unanswered a key question: which of the many interpretations of Freud's theory —some of which he changed over time— should be relied on? What about the diverse schools of psychoanalytic thought? There are many

---

[4] M Scharnberg, The Non-Authentic Nature of Freud's Observations. *Uppsala Studies in Education*, Vols. 47-48. 1993, Uppsala: University of Uppsala, Vol II, p64-5.
[5] R Tallis, *The Times Higher*, October 31, 1997.
[6] S Freud, *The Standard Edition of the Complete Psychological Works of Sigmund Freud*, 24 Volumes, trans and ed Strachey et al, London, Hogarth Press. References to this work will be marked 'SE', followed by the volume. In this case: New Introductory Lectures, *SE 22*, [1932], 1976, p6.

debates about including: 'What Freud really meant', as to 'Who speaks for Freud?', 'Who speaks for psychoanalysis?', 'What is the status of counselling versus psychoanalysis?' One thing remains clear: the essence of Freud's work is an understanding of the human condition that relies on a study of speech and language. This suggests a clinical question: what techniques should be used to study speech? We will return to this question, first we should get clearer about the importance of technique. The truth is that clients are often able to make important changes in their lives, whatever the professional label for their clinical work, once they have been able to talk freely. Freud's and Lacan's work privilege the client's speech as the central variable that explains the human condition and these changes.

How important is technique?

'Technique in analysis is never a matter of course. Although there may perhaps be more than one good road to follow, still there are very many bad ones, and a comparison of the various methods cannot fail to be illuminating . . .' [7]

'Psychoanalytic writings swarm with improprieties of method.' [8]

'The inadequacy of psychoanalytic teaching had to be publicly exposed for me to become engaged in the task.' [9]

If you think that variations in clinical technique are unimportant then this book will probably make no sense to you. Supporting this sceptical view of the importance of technique are a number of medically orientated 'outcome studies'. Outcome studies compare the supposedly measurable 'outcomes' of different therapies, and always have as an ideal, the elimination of a symptom or set of symptoms in the style of medical cures. [10]

---

[7] S Freud, The Handling of Dream Interpretation in Psychoanalysis, *SE 12*, [1912], 1976, p91.

[8] J Lacan, *Book One, Freud's Papers on Technique of Psychoanalysis, 1953-1954*, ed Miller, trans Forrester, Cambridge University Press, Cambridge, England, 1988, p24.

[9] J Lacan, Presentation of the Memoirs of President Schreber, (1975), trans Lewis, *Analysis* no 7, 1996, p3.

[10] *'[The] therapeutic success [of psychoanalysis] give grounds neither for boasting nor for being ashamed but statistics . . . are in general uninstructive . . . It is wiser to examine one's individual differences . . . I do not think our cures can compete with those of Lourdes. There are so many more people who believe in the miracles of the Blessed Virgin than in the existence of the unconscious.'* S Freud, New Introductory Lectures, *SE 22*, [1932], 1973, p152.

Clinicians who work with their eye on a specific behavioural or emotional
outcome aim for a 'normalisation' or for some kind of predetermined outcome
for all their clients, regardless of their individual client's desire. Typically such
clinicians arrogantly think that they know just what 'a cure' will mean to their
client, just through a knowledge of their obvious symptoms. It is not surprising
that many outcome studies conclude with a claim along the lines that: *The use
of one therapeutic technique rather than another makes little or no difference
to the outcome.'* Whatever we may think of medicine and outcome studies in
the arena of social and psychological suffering, medical approaches remain
important, influential and sometimes useful, so I suggest some possible ways of
working alongside colleagues who rely on such medical and psychiatric
approaches, within multidisciplinary teams, GPs' practices and schools in
Chapter Thirteen.

Professional status
There are many competent and well-trained clinicians who do good work, who
dare not call themselves 'psychoanalyst' even though they rely heavily on
Freud's psychoanalytic ideas when they practice. Why? Because the
International Psychoanalytic Association in Britain and elsewhere decided that
it ought to govern and regulate psychoanalytic practice: other trainings would
have different status. The graduates of other trainings would not be allowed to
use the title 'psychoanalyst', instead they could use titles such as 'counsellor',
'psychotherapist', or for the most worthy, 'psychoanalytic psychotherapist'.[11]

Lacan argued that this situation is rather like a single company having a total
monopoly on the manufacture of cars, and on driving tuition, on the issuing of
driving licences, as well as being in charge of every traffic warden and all road

---

[11] This attitude is clearly demonstrated by a letter (9th December 1999) by Donald
Campbell, President of the British Psycho-analytical Society. Campbell sets out a
system of segregation reminiscent of the Hindu caste system, early Nazi policy and
South African apartheid: *'It has recently come to my attention . . . that the
Psychoanalytic and Psychodynamic Psychotherapy Section of the United Kingdom
Council for Psychotherapy decided: 'That Psychoanalytic and Psychodynamic
Psychotherapy registering organisations may choose to use the title 'psychoanalyst'. .
. ' Under Rule 13 of our Society: 'No Honorary Member, Member or Associate
Member shall take part in any training activity, whether individually or as part of an
organisation, outside the official training organised by the Society or any Component
Society or Study Group of The International Psychoanalytical Association if the
organisation or psycho-analyst concerned claims to train persons to be psychoanalysts.
This means that if any of our members are involved in a training activity of a United
Kingdom Council for Psychotherapy organisation which decides to allow its members
to call themselves psychoanalysts, our members would have to withdraw, including
participation as teachers, training therapists and supervisors.'* Rule 13 appears to be a
simple attempt at protectionism, at procuring jobs for the boys. This issue is explored
by Robert Young's *The Culture of British Psychoanalysis* www.human-nature.com

works. Unravelling this analogy: there are many interpretations and developments of Freud's work; the approach of the International Psychoanalytic Association is only one of many: they have no monopoly. Lacan had argued —to his cost— that many of the central ideas and practices of the International Psychoanalytic Association were not only wrong but that they were also opposed to Freudian theory and practice! It is easy to understand why the International Psychoanalytic Association expelled Lacan and censored his work in Britain.

These questions of affiliation are often raised alongside questions of professional status. Hence the questions: 'How Freudian is Lacan?' and 'What are the differences between counselling, psychotherapy and psychoanalysis?' This last question often generates heated debate from those with careers, as well as many years of their own personal therapeutic work invested in a particular position.

How Freudian is Lacan?

Any answer to this question should be prefaced with a comment on their texts and writing styles. Much of Freud, for instance his 'Introductory Lectures' is deceptively clear; it is not difficult to read such texts, but try explaining the ideas to someone else! It is not so easy: Lacan is often deceptively difficult, while his texts are hard to read the ideas are on the whole no more complex than those found in Freud's work, and sometimes they are simpler.

If psychoanalysis does properly refer to that which is essentially human then psychoanalysis can legitimately make reference to the sciences and arts because they are products of the human condition. But some of Freud's fans complain that Lacan's work has 'too many intellectual references' (see the top of page 11 for an example). I have been surprised by this complaint because I have never heard the same criticism made of Freud's work, which is often unashamedly intellectual. The fact is that many 'intellectual Lacanian references' are exactly the same as those referred to earlier by Freud, and are only developed later by Lacan.[12]

---

[12] Here is a brief selection of some of Freud's references to intellectual topics: Topological theories of space: *SE 21*, p70, Logic: *SE 19*, p435, Theories of language, *SE 14*, Theories of evolution: *SE 19*, p221, Kant's moral philosophy and theory of the 'Categorical Imperative': *SE 19*, p167, Anthropological theories: *SE 13*, Genetics: *SE 18*, p50, Immunology: *SE 2*, p290, Embryology: *SE 18*, p26.

How Freudian was Freud?

Most of the literature mistakes Freudian technique as a complete set of rules written in stone. But the truth is just as Lohser and Newton [13] write:

'We find that that the contemporary ideal of mainstream analytic treatment, which is called "classical" and attributed to Freud, is actually a post World War II invention [that is after Freud's death].'

Freud himself was quite clear on this idea of providing a full and clear set of rules for technique: *'. . . nearly everything still awaits definitive settlement [in the field of technique]* '[14]; and: *'The answer to the questions of technique in analysis is never a matter of course. Although there may perhaps be more than one good road to follow, still there are very many bad ones, and a comparison of the various methods cannot fail to be illuminating, even if it should not lead to a decision in favour of any particular one.'* [15]. He also wrote: *'I do not believe that one can give the methods of technique through papers. It must be done by personal teaching. Of course, beginners probably need something to start with . . . But if they followed the directions conscientiously, they will soon find themselves in trouble. Then they must learn to develop their own technique.'* [16]

There is much freedom with some aspects of technique while others are fixed. We will return to this issue when we look at Lacan's development of Freud's idea of 'warfare in the clinic', with Lacan's distinctions of the 'clinician's tactics, strategy, and policy'.

The differences between Freud and Lacan arise mostly through Lacan taking some of Freud's ideas more seriously than Freud himself. Freud was a genius and a great pioneer but a century later it would be surprising if some developments and advances had not been made within Freud's field. Lacan — who is widely regarded as having made a return to Freud— claimed:

'All I've done is re-release what Freud states . . .' And: *'My own work is to understand what Freud did. Consequently, to interpret even what is implicit in Freud is legitimate in my eyes'.* [17]

---

[13] Lohser and Newton, Unorthodox Freud, New York, Hawthorn Books 1996, p1.

[14] S Freud, The Future Prospects of Psychoanalytic Therapy, *SE 11,* [1910], 1976, p144.

[15] S Freud, The Handling of Dream Interpretation in Psychoanalysis, *SE 12,* [1912], 1976, p91.

[16] S Blanton, quoting Freud in Diary of My Analysis with Sigmund Freud, p48, New York, Hawthorn Books, quoted on p130 of Lohser and Newton *Unorthodox Freud.*

[17] J Lacan, *The Psychoses,* ed Miller, trans Grigg, Routledge, London, 1993, p180.

There is a lot of truth to these claims: much of Lacan's work details and elaborates ideas that are implicit or explicit in Freud's writings, but Lacan is not straightforwardly Freudian, there are some differences and even contradictions between the two sets of theory that we won't be concerned with. What is important here are the advances in clinical technique found in Lacan's work. If no clinical advances were to be found in Lacan's work over Freud's then there would be no justification for a book like this. Here is a brief list of some of Lacan's important clinical advances:

• The possibility of reducing the number of sessions from four or ten per week, to typically between one and three per week.

• The increased average length of time taken to go to 'The End of Analysis', from perhaps six months to three years, to typically, some ten to fifteen years.

• A new theory of 'The End of Analysis'.

• An elaborated version of Freud's theory of psychosis, along with a set of techniques for working with psychotics [18]: Freud preferred not to work with psychotics.[19]

• The use of variable length sessions that may be as short as a fifteen minutes or as long as two hours, rather than fixed fifty minute sessions.

• In the early years of his clinical work Freud sometimes played the role of the professor or master, and assumed that he had a privileged knowledge, and told his clients so, for instance in the tragic case of 'Dora'. Later Freud became critical of this masterful approach and instead stressed the importance of an ignorance that the clinician relies on to inform his interpretations and questions. Lacan developed this later thinking of Freud's in his theory of the four discourses, explored in Chapter Thirteen. Lacanians rarely, if ever, make interpretations that assume that they know the truth about the private associations connected with their client's speech.

It is worth mentioning that Lacan's theories and techniques also changed during his career —just as Freud's did— and that different Lacanians use

---

[18] J Lacan, On the Possible Treatment of Psychosis, *Ecrits*, trans Sheridan, Tavistock Routledge, London, [1966], 1980.
[19] *'[A] . . . limitation upon analytic success is given by the form of the illness . . . the field [of] application of analytic therapy lies in the . . . neuroses — phobias, hysteria, obsessional neurosis . . . Everything differing from these, narcissistic and psychotic conditions, is unsuitable to greater or less extent. It would be entirely legitimate to guard against failures by carefully excluding such cases.'* S Freud, New Introductory Lectures in Psychoanalysis, Explanations and Applications, *SE 22* [1933], 1976, p155.

different techniques. For simplicity's sake I will present 'Lacanian techniques' as a single set.

When exploring Lacan's ideas and techniques I often rely on Freud's texts because Lacan's ideas are often Freud's. It is ironic that in order to understand Lacan, we first study Freud, then return to Lacan, so as to *'re-release what Freud states'* [20]

Why do I use parallel columns?
When different texts are placed in parallel columns the supposition is that there is some kind of relation between the two texts. Establishing such a relation calls for the texts to be read with a method invented more or less by the reader, through the demands and desires of the texts. Parallel columns compare different texts but they also demonstrate something important about clinical technique: when the client speaks the supposition is that that is some relation between his words, and his suffering, symptoms and fantasy. But suffering, symptoms and fantasy often appear remote from such popular topics that turn up in the clinic as fashion, football and food. Establishing relations between what the client says, and his suffering, symptoms and fantasy demands that his speech be listened to in a non-standard way that cannot be set out in advance. What is said should be compared with what has been said before, and connections made, with a method invented more or less by the clinician, through the demands and desires of the client.

Why is this book so long?
Because genuinely introductory books on technique are inevitably lengthy, whether they are on cooking, bricklaying, osteopathy or psychoanalysis; I wanted both those without knowledge of Freud or Lacan as well as loyal Lacanians to enjoy this.

---

20 This idea of meaning being attributed afterwards, by Lacan, after Freud, retrospectively, refers to a piece of Freudian and Lacanian theory. When clients present their problems early on in the clinical work it is just like being told the punch line of a joke —in isolation from the rest of the main body of the joke— that may be some years in the telling. Freud's German for this phenomenon is *'nächtraglichkeit'*, which is sometimes translated as 'afterwardness' (see *Essays on Otherness*, J Laplanche, ed Fletcher, Routledge, 1999, p263,) or 'deferred action'. Lacan developed this idea with his theory of time and word meaning in his 'Graph of Desire' (*Ecrits*, Tavistock Routledge, London).[1966], 1989, p315).

CHAPTER ONE

Introduction

Every practice is theoretical

'However panoramic our comments may be, you must be aware that they have the most precise repercussions, not only for the understanding of cases, but for technique.' [21]

'It is the theory which decides what we can observe' [22]

'We have often heard it maintained that sciences should be built up on clear and sharply defined basic concepts. In actual fact no science, not even the most exact, begins with such definitions. The true beginning of scientific activity consists rather in describing phenomena and then in proceeding to group, classify and correlate them. Even at this stage of description it is not possible to avoid applying certain abstract ideas to the material in hand, ideas derived from somewhere or other but certainly not from new observations alone. Such ideas —which will become the basic concepts of science— are still more indispensable as the material is further worked over. They must at first necessarily possess some degree of indefiniteness; there can be no questions of any clear delimitation of their content.' [23]

'Insistence on complete logical clarification would make science impossible.' [24]

H ow do you play the flute? *'Blow in one end and move your fingers up and down the outside'*, says Monty Python [25]. Similarly in psychoanalysis the clinician simply listens to clients, occasionally making comments. On the face

---

[21] J Lacan, *The Seminar of Jacques Lacan, Book Two, The Ego in Freud's theory and in the Technique of Psychoanalysis 1954-1955*, ed Miller, trans Tomaselli, Cambridge University Press, England, 1988, p273.

[22] A Einstein, *Physics and Beyond: Encounters and Conversations*, New York: Harper and Row, 1971, p63.

[23] S Freud, Drives and their Vicissitudes, mistranslated as 'Instincts and their Vicissitudes', *SE 14*, 1915c, p117.

[24] W Heisenberg, *Physics and Philosophy,* Harper, 1958, p86.

[25] *Monty Python's Previous Record,* The Famous Charisma Label, 1973, Phonogram Ltd.

of it psychoanalytic work appears absurdly easy, as a variation on ordinary conversation, surely a skill possessed by almost everyone?

The truth is that clinical work in the psychoanalytic tradition is difficult. This difficulty is necessary because life itself is necessarily difficult and clients present their problems with love and work. Hence psychoanalytic work has to endure special impossibilities and difficulties. One difficulty is the question of the clinician's responsibility for the client's suffering. What should the clinician do about it? The question for the clinician carrying out Lacanian work is **not**: *'How can I reduce or eliminate my client's suffering',* but instead: *'How can I help the client find a new position in relation to his suffering?'*

As a writer rather than as a psychoanalyst I can assume that you —as a reader— have a more specific question, along the following lines: How can Lacan's ideas be used to help clients find a new position in relation to their suffering? Before looking at Lacan's approach to this clinical problem let's broaden the scale of the question so as to include the approach of every psychotherapeutic school: *'How, in general, can **any** clinician help any client find a new position in relation to his suffering?'*

Any adequate answer to this question must necessarily be phrased in theoretical terms, not in any theoretical terms but in the terms of the clinical theory of the particular school. So for example, from the practice of the behaviourist clinician who electrocutes his homosexual male clients when they become sexually excited, appeals to 'learning theory' along the following lines: *'Behaviourist theory says that in order to learn anything there must be either punishment or reward; so for my client to learn the proper sexual behaviour for a man, I must punish what he has mistakenly learnt so that he can relearn the right way to behave sexually.'*

Every clinical practice —of whatever school— has an attached theory. It is not possible to use a clinical technique without there first existing a specific theory that the clinician actively relies on, even if that theory is hidden, intuitive or unconscious. By analogy think of the English language, which you probably read and speak without having to consciously worry about our highly complex rules of grammar. If you try explaining to someone who only speaks a little English exactly what the rules of grammar are, you will almost certainly find that you can't, unless you have made a special study of the theory of grammar because the rules for grammar —the theory of language that each English speaker uses— are hidden away and work in the background. We could not speak without them, yet we can't say what they are!

Some clinicians try to hide away their theory so as to gain immunity from criticism. Others try to rely on their 'feelings' rather than 'theories' in their clinical work. This is a misguided and potentially problem making approach, and in any case, is itself a theory! It is a theory that says that *'your feelings inform your clinical interpretations and interventions'*. We will look at some arguments for and against this popular view later, when we will also discuss the importance of 'intuitions', which are very different from both 'feelings' and 'instincts'.

Every single practice is theoretical, whether it is the practice of clinical psychoanalysis, driving a car or just speaking a sentence, even if you can't specify exactly what the relevant theory says. This point has implications for those clinicians who describe themselves as 'eclectic', claiming that they use different bits of different theories, depending on the circumstances. This sounds flexible and more likely to meet with success than relying on a rigidly fixed scheme: I disagree with eclectic approaches on principle. Why? Because different theories are often incompatible with one another. Clinical techniques are not just like any old set of tools in someone's tool box, collected over the years, more or less at random: a set of clinical techniques have to work together. Just as many theories are incompatible with one another so too many clinical techniques are incompatible with one another.

Often eclectic clinicians do not have a full set of skills in any one school of clinical technique or theory, and they muddle along, just like some tradesmen who are content to bodge a job because they haven't got the right tools. A Jack or Jacqueline of all trades is rarely skilful or even competent at any one trade. It is hard enough doing clinical work with just one approach, without complicating matters by using two incompatible approaches. The analogy of a musician trying to play more than one instrument at the same time, each tuned to different scale, gives a picture of the problem: if you want to play well you would do better to focus your attention on one instrument at a time, and become skilled with that one instrument, rather than dividing your resources and torturing ears.

Developing this analogy, I believe that some musical instruments, all things considered, are better than others; a guitar, piano or violin are individually better than a triangle. I want to claim that some therapeutic techniques are better than others for two reasons: some techniques are more effective than others, and some theories are better than others because they explain more and predict more than worse theories. For example the theory that 'the stork brings babies' is a worse theory than the currently popular biological theory. Better clinical theories have associated techniques that help clients to find new positions —in relation to their suffering— more easily or quickly than worse theories. I aim to demonstrate the important advantages that Lacanian techniques provide to both clients and clinicians.

If every practice is theoretical, whether it is playing a musical instrument, catching a ball[26], speaking an ordinary sentence, or a using a clinical technique, the next step is to introduce the relevant Lacanian theory, because: *'There is nothing as practical as a good theory.'*

Introducing Freud's and Lacan's five modest beliefs

There are five central beliefs in the theory of Freudian and Lacanian clinical practice. These beliefs are not bizarre or outlandish. Ordinary people would probably agree with most or all of them, but what follows logically from the beliefs, as Lacanian clinical technique, is neither obvious or 'common sense'. It does not matter at this point whether you believe that any of the five beliefs are true or false, or if you are undecided. We will spend some time exploring the consequences of each, and what some of the alternatives look like.

1. A word's meaning is not absolutely fixed but varies according to its use. Each person has had a unique 'language history' and use for any particular word, such as 'blue', so the meaning that any one word or phrase has for them is often unique. But there is a special kind of exception: proper names. Proper names like 'Fred Smith' have very important clinical consequences because they rigidly refer to specific people and special relations in between them.

2. Suffering is the human condition; life is generally conflictual and difficult, rather than harmonious and easy.

3. People often avoid the truth about themselves whenever recognising the truth and acting on it seems likely to cause conflict and difficulty.

4. People typically both perceive and remember change, interruptions or 'discontinuity' much better than continuity or the lack of change. The more dramatic the change, the better it is usually remembered. Sometimes the most dramatic changes or interruptions are 'remembered' very well but are deeply buried in the unconscious. These memories are called 'traumas', from the Greek for a 'wound' that scars, leaving a mark, like strange writing or graffiti that might be read, but only with difficulty.

5. Love and desire are to be distinguished — and are fundamental in explaining the human condition. For Lacan, love and desire are what makes the psyche go around. The unique lifestyle and symptoms that each of us has chosen is a kind of solution to the particular problems, difficulties and traumas that each of us have had in acting on our love and desire.

It is surprising that Lacan's innovative clinical techniques arise almost completely from these five ordinary and simple beliefs. Freud —the main

---

[26] If you are sceptical read E Masood's 'Howzat! Why the best players don't always watch the ball', *New Scientist,* 25th November, 2000, p22.

influence on Lacan—was also convinced of the truth of each of these five beliefs. There are some other beliefs on which Lacan relies, and which he also goes some way towards justifying. The five sections of the next chapter briefly explore each of these five beliefs and their relation to clinical practice.

CHAPTER TWO

Elaborating Freud's and Lacan's five modest beliefs

BELIEF 1: Word meaning varies according to use and is not fixed, with the special exception of proper names.

'Words, since they are the nodal points of numerous ideas, may be regarded as pre-destined to ambiguity.' [27]

'The very foundation of interhuman discourse is misunderstanding.' [28]

'We didn't talk about this because we didn't have much of a vocabulary then. A penis was a tinkler, a dick, or a boner if it was hard, and my mother's breasts we called pontoons. That was about it, at eleven years old. Then one day Mrs Tarbox caught us changing into our bathing suits to go for a swim. We were all naked, Patrick, Scott, and me, and we clutched our suits over our tinklers and Mrs Tarbox said, "What, are you modest?. And we didn't know what that meant and we weren't the kind to go look it up. But all of us were stamp collectors, and we each had something called "The Modern Stamp Album". So we equated the word modest with modern. It became the key sexy phrase —kind of a catchall— that we used whenever we wanted to talk about something dirty. We'd giggle and ask, "Is that a Modern Stamp Album picture?" "Is that a Modern Stamp Album movie?" Then we burst into hysterics and laughed until we fell down.' [29]

Lacan, along with many of other theorists of language, including Freud, had argued that the meaning of a word depends on how that word has actually been used and contrasted with other words, rather than on a meaning that is somehow rigidly fixed beforehand. So the word 'house' might refer to an igloo, to a kind of music or even function as a password. 'House' is likely to have quite different associations and meanings for a builder, a musician and for someone who is homeless. 'Blue' can refer to a depressed mood, to a period of Picasso's work, to pornography, a colour or a kind of jazz. Whenever people speak they demonstrate, often obliquely, the particular associations and meanings that certain words have for them.

Lacanian work sets out to observe some of the idiosyncratic language functions of each client: for one woman 'father' and 'husband' turned out to mean something like: 'a man who hits a woman he loves'; this client had frequently

---

[27] S Freud, The Interpretation of Dreams, *SE 5* [1900], 1973, p340.
[28] J Lacan, *The Seminar of Jacque Lacan, The Psychoses*, trans Grigg, ed Miller, Routledge, London, 1993, p163.
[29] S Grey, *Swimming to Cambodia*, Theatre Communication Group, 1988.

witnessed her father striking her mother, and the client repeatedly found herself in relationships with men who beat her.

Often these associations or meanings are not conscious, but by studying a client's use of words and carefully reminding them of their earlier associations and speech, clinicians help their clients explore their unique and often difficult meanings.

One client described his father as 'grumpy and aggressive' and, in another session, used exactly the same words to describe himself. Simply pointing out that he had used the same words to describe himself and his father —without making any other comment— allowed the client to start re-evaluating his difficult relationship with his father, and changing it.

This type of intervention —simple quotation— is a very important and much used Lacanian technique. It relies principally on a careful use of memory. Clients are often unaware of many similarities, connections and contradictions in their speech. Sharing your observations of some of similarities and inconsistencies in their speech —through quotation— is probably one of the two most valuable types of clinical intervention that can be made.

Quotation also has the merit of being objectively true; if you remember correctly —when you quote— you are simply reporting what the client said, without making speculative interpretations as to its significance or meaning. The question of meaning is therefore left open for the client to explore. If you are not sure if you remember correctly it might help to say so. So when you quote a client's speech you avoid confusing and complicating the picture by keeping many of your own ideas —some of which are likely to be wrong— on one side. This strategy of working very closely with what the client has actually said ensures that most interpretations will be objectively true, such as in the example of simple quotation above, rather than being based on what the clinician speculates or imagines the client's thoughts, feelings or meanings. Clients are often startled and surprised to hear their own words. Later we will look at more complicated kinds of quotation such as 'quotation by category'.

Early on in the work clients often demand to be told *'the meaning of my contradictions'*, or the meaning of having said a particular thing, or *'the meaning of anorexia'*, *'the meaning of depression'*, or *'the meaning of alcoholism'*. The fact is you don't actually *know* the private associations of your client's speech or symptoms. And even if you did know, it is crucial that you recognise that it is *not* your job to feed clients your idiosyncratic beliefs or knowledge. As Freud put it: *'Our knowledge about the unconscious is not equivalent to his knowledge; if we communicate our knowledge to him, he does not receive it instead of his unconscious material but beside it; and that makes very little change in it.'* [30]

This Freudian and Lacanian position stands in opposition to many other clinical practices where the emphasis instead is on the clinician producing a knowledge the client is directed to use to understand his suffering and symptoms. But your client's problems arise from their unconscious beliefs, demands and desires, not from some missing bit of knowledge that you can provide them with: saying *'I don't know'*, asking questions, remaining silent, or ending the session are far more likely to help your client gradually uncover his own beliefs, instead of impressing him with yours. The emphasis in Lacanian work is on the clinician being taught by the client rather than on the clinician teaching the client.

Returning to the theme of fixed and fluid meanings: there is a very important exception to the flux of meanings found in most types of words: proper names. 'Fred Blogs' refers to a particular individual, or set of individuals, each called 'Fred Blogs', who lived in a particular time and place. Whatever happens to vary the meanings of words like 'house' and 'blue', proper names seem to stick like glue —without variation— to the objects they name. Proper names are important because their special functions both cause and prevent psychosis.

Alternative theories that claim that all word meaning is not variable but fixed

Lacan's theories of language have profound consequences for clinical practice; imagine the situation for a clinician in which he judged that a client 'misused' a particular word. Such a clinician, believing that word meaning was not variable but fixed, would be duty bound to impress his knowledge of the 'proper meaning' and use of the word on the ignorant client, and so educate the poor client out of his suffering and confusion. This sounds like a bizarre and unlikely situation but actually it is just what many clinicians set out to do.

There are a number of influential clinical theories and practices that involve the clinician instructing, schooling and correcting the client's use of words, actions and emotions. These clinicians set themselves up in a masterful or authoritative position. Sometimes clients collude with this approach and adopt a complementary position that supposes their own ignorance and submission. We will return to the idea of authority in Lacan's ideas about the 'the slave and master relationship' in Chapter Thirteen on the clinic and the institution. To illustrate this problem of fixed and fluid word meaning, imagine a client who complains of being plagued by a question of sexual orientation: *'I don't know if I am gay or straight'*. Now if word meaning was fixed, and if —by virtue of your superior clinical education— you truly had the measure of word meaning, you

---

[30] S Freud, Introductory Lectures on Psychoanalysis, Transference, *SE 16*, [1916], 1973, p436.

could teach your client: *'Having a penis means that you are a man, and being a man means that you desire women, not men'.*

An attempt to educate your client (with special exceptions discussed in Chapter Fifteen) is an attempt to situate yourself in the position of a master or teacher. Freud claimed that this sort of approach —from a position of knowledge— is typically medical and completely inappropriate for psychoanalysis.[31]

Lacan's theory of meaning and sexual identity disregards common beliefs or what passes as 'knowledge' to the extent that Lacan argued that it is possible for a person with a penis to be a woman and that someone with a womb can be a man.[32] For Lacan being a man or a woman is not determined by the type of your reproductive organs but by your psychic structure, by the way your language and unconscious function.

The variation of meaning in language might help explain why sexual identity is such a common problem for most people, and why for example there is so much variation regarding sexual identity; why there are transvestites, transsexuals, homosexuals, heterosexuals, bisexuals, bestialists, paedophiles, and all sorts of other variations. Most of those who regard themselves as men and women are burdened, to varying degrees, with the question: 'What exactly does it mean for me to be a wo/man?'

In stark contrast Jung and Klein have produced influential clinical theories that are similar: both claim that some meanings are rigidly fixed and cannot be moved. Klein claims to know beforehand what the 'proper meaning' of 'man' and 'woman' is, along with the rest of language. In Klein's theory there are a series of privileged and fixed ideas that she calls 'objects', such as the *'good breast'* and the *'bad penis'*. Incredibly, she also wrote that infants are actually born with knowledge of both male and female genitals: *'my belief that in both sexes there is an inherent unconscious knowledge of the existence of the penis as well as of the vagina.'* [33]

Are we all born with a comprehensive knowledge of the Fallopian tubes and the prostate gland too? Maybe if every would be gynaecologist completed a

---

[31] *'In his medical school a doctor receives a training which is more or less the opposite of what he would need as a preparation for psychoanalysis'. ,: 'It would be tolerable if medical education merely failed to give doctors any orientation in the field of the neuroses. But it does more: it gives them a false and detrimental attitude . . . The less such doctors understand about the matter, the more venturesome they become. Only a man who really knows is modest, for he knows how insufficient his knowledge is.'* (S Freud, On the Question of Lay Analysis, *SE 20,* [1926], 1976, p230 & 232.

[32] J Lacan, *On Feminine Sexuality, The Limits of Love and Knowledge,* Book XX, Encore 1972-1973, 1998, Norton & Co, p15.

[33] M Klein, The Oedipus Complex in the Light of Early Anxieties, 1945, *Love, Guilt and Reparation,* Virago, 1975, p409.

Kleinian analysis they would not have to bother studying anatomy at all? Kleinians argue that because their clients have 'forgotten' this kind of crucial 'unconscious knowledge', they must be reminded of it by the knowledgeable clinician. Then, when they eventually remember properly —by being educated— their problem will be put right. Kleinians who use this technique are relying on Plato's unbelievable theory of memory. In his *Republic* he argues that each of us knows everything, but that most of us have forgotten bits of this comprehensive and universal knowledge. However (he claims) we just need reminding in order to sort ourselves out and clearly see the truth. By contrast, Lacan argued that the purpose of psychoanalysis is to produce a unique knowledge about a unique individual's life.

Jung thought that whatever our experiences, and however different our backgrounds and cultures, we can only conceptualise and experience the world, each other and language through a fixed number of universal ideas that he called 'archetypes', such as the 'Earth Mother' or the 'Trickster'[34]. In these schemes there are no possible alternatives to understanding and expression other than through the authorised and fixed meanings of the licensed clinicians who have a supposed monopoly on knowing the truth. Such clinicians believe that their scheme is The Exclusive representation of The Truth which grants them their licence to work as language policemen. As such they tell clients when they have gone wrong and which is the right way.

But there is a problem with all these theories that insist on having fixed meanings, where one word or phrase always has a corresponding 'fundamental meaning'. They all run into trouble when it comes to justifying their fixed categories, archetypes and objects. How exactly did Melanie Klein suppose herself to have knowledge of the existence of the 'good breast' or 'bad penis'? Or that infants are born equipped with knowledge of both male and female genitals? How was it revealed to her? And how did Jung justify his archetypes? There is not a single example of a theory of fixed meanings —such as Jung's, Klein's or Plato's— that can justify privileging its own favourite set of fixed meanings. They are all arbitrary in their selection. It is very easy to invent any number of new arbitrary theories of fixed meaning that relies on privileging a particular set of objects, such as 'The Thumb and Ear', or 'The Pink and the Blue'.

But beware; many clients, especially those who demand a quick fix, are delighted to be authoritatively told the meaning of their speech, dreams or symptoms, and will even demand to be told or referred to a book, with the

---

[34] The extent to which this is not true for a particular Jungian is the extent to which the clinician is not committed to Jung's theories. Either meaning is prior and fixed, or it is not. Either a particular archetype of the 'collective unconscious' exists, that is, is universal, or it does not exist as an archetype.

expectation that they will find the comprehensive description of their unique problem and a cure. If a clinician imposes his own meanings on a client's symptoms there may be 'therapeutic effects': that is, symptoms can shift if the clinician is assumed by the client to be in a position of knowledge or authority. Hypnosis is a popular example of such a practice: the hypnotist suggests prearranged values and meanings to his client and the client drinks in every word. In this sense hypnosis is the opposite of psychoanalysis. The client being hypnotised often makes more effort to learn and take in what the clinician is trying to teaching them than they do learning what it is that they want in their own life, and what their values and their problems are, and how they hide from them.

Freud was generally opposed to standard and fixed interpretations of the Platonic, Jungian and Kleinian varieties because they often stop clients exploring their own non-standard values. Early in his career Freud found when he experimented with hypnosis and made standard or fixed interpretations, that symptoms sometimes disappeared after hypnosis, only to reappear later or to be replaced by others.

Dreams and fixed meanings

When a client tells us a dream, we usually ask the client what associations he has with the dream, what the dream reminds him of. If we were to instead instruct the client as to the 'definitive meaning' of his dream, from one of the many bogus dictionaries of 'Dream Symbols', then we would be foisting our own or the book's values on the client's speech rather than helping him to explore his unique associations and desires.

Such a dictionary —whose existence is implied by Jung's and Klein's theories— would allow you look up 'the definitive meaning' of a dream symbol such as 'dog'. But if I dream of my dog barking, my dream might have a particular meaning. But if a veterinary surgeon, or perhaps someone with a phobia of dogs, had the same dream, 'dog' would probably have a different meaning. There is no authority who 'knows the truth about associations or meanings' on whom we can rely authoritatively to interpret the meaning of all our unique unconscious ideas as if they were one. Freud's position is clearly opposed to Plato's, Jung's and Klein's theory of fixed word meaning. *'My procedure is not so convenient as the popular decoding method which translates the given piece of a dream's content by a fixed key. I, on the contrary, am prepared to find that the same piece of content may conceal different meaning when it occurs in various people or in various contexts'.*[35]

---

[35] S Freud, The Interpretation of Dreams, *SE 4*, [1900], 1976, p97.

Ignorance and language as a universal curse or wound, and authority

So psychoanalysts are not in a position of authority regarding word meaning, argues Lacan. In what position exactly *are* psychoanalytic clinicians, relative to their clients? Ignorance. This situation is similar to one in which you, as a clinician, are called on to provide a special translation service. But there is a problem, because you don't speak his language or dialect he has offered to teach it to you, as the teaching progresses so does your client's translation of his own dialect into English.

Translations are strange things. There is no single definitive translation of any single sentence, but always a number of translations that compete on more or less equal terms. For example, does the German word *'gemütlich'* mean *'cosy'*, or is *'comfortable'* better? Is *'mental state'* a good translation of *'intellectual nation'*?

It is always possible to offer a number of different but equally worthy translations or substitutions for any sentence, even in context, and of many individual words too, so it is impossible to decide on any objective basis which is 'the best' or 'the definitive translation'. Importantly for clinical work, exactly the same problem found in translation applies equally to any interpretation within the same language[36].

There is an important sense too in which we are all in this situation when we listen to each other, even when we speak the same dialect. Often, at the start of listening to someone we get the wrong idea, and only later when we have heard more do we get a better idea of what the speaker's desire is. Translators —as well as ordinary listeners— usually do not understand the beginning of a sentence until they have heard more. These kinds of necessary confusions form the basis of many jokes. On hearing the punch line the meaning of the words that came before it are revised. In the best of conditions, even when we know someone else very well, and listen carefully to what they say, we will still misunderstand them at times. We are frequently forced to revise our beliefs about what someone means because language is such an inefficient technique of communication, yet it is the best we have.

Ambiguities and misunderstanding are necessary qualities of language because meanings are in flux; yet language is all clinicians have to work with. In Lacanian work it is crucial that the clinician uses some of the ambiguities in his client's speech to help the client re-evaluate his relation to his own questions, answers, misunderstandings, and, above all, his relation to language.

---

[36] This view is famously argued by the philosopher Quine, for instance in his 'Three Indeterminancies', *Perspectives on Quine*, ed Barratt and Gibson, Blackwell, 1990.

Introducing Mr Unique Dialect

Imagine the following dialogue between a client and clinician:

Client: I would like you to help me; I am from a unique and strange culture. I have long become separated from my people, from the few I loved and grew up with. This I believe is the cause of my suffering. It is so long since I have spoken my family's language that I am fast forgetting it. Will you help me, by listening to me trying to speak my old language, so that I can remember it?

Clinician: Would I just listen?

Client: The main thing is that you help me to remember what I have forgotten. Perhaps you would sometimes ask me questions and make comments to help me think and remind me?

Clinician: Let's try now, will you speak some of your language?

Client: OK, I am now speaking it now.

Clinician: But that is extraordinary, it sounds just like English!

Client: The words are mostly the same as English, but the way we used them was often different, sometimes only subtly. Perhaps it would be for the best if you used some of the following techniques to help me. If you notice that I use a word or phrase in a way that surprises you, let me know, because I might be taking a family meaning for granted, without being aware of it. This sort of thing might be an example:

Whenever you have spoken of "your father", it has *always* been in relation to your mother. That is in all the times you have spoken of your father, you have not mentioned him without speaking of her.'

If I seem to use a word or phrase in an inconsistent or contradictory way then please point it out. I might be completely unaware of the contradiction. By showing me the contradiction in my speech you might help me remember my language and its history better, and to understand how it has influenced my life today.

Sometimes when I am trying hard to remember or explain something complicated I lose track of what I have said and get a bit stranded. A simple one sentence summary of what you have understood me to say will help me find my place and then to move on, even if I have to correct you.

But it is important that you do not pressure me! I don't want you to tell me what you want, that things ought to be like this or like that! Our relationship will have my language as its focus, we will concentrate on my words. If I end up talking about you, or about stuff that you don't approve of —that has to be OK— I don't want you to take offence, defend yourself, or talk about anything except my language.

Clinician: So you don't want me to guess what you might be feeling, or for me to tell you my feelings?

Client: That is right. My feelings are my problem: your feelings are your problem. I can only go ahead with this if you study my speech alone, without your guessing about my feelings. The only way for me to get clear about my problems is for me to understand my mother tongue. So you will have to study it and not add in your own stuff. You might get tired sometimes or fed up. That will be tough, but that's the job. I may even make believe that you are my mother, sister or father, or a lover or anyone else who has been important to me, if it helps me to remember. And you should not challenge this make believe, or even distract me by pointing it out. I want to find out the truth, I might have to fantasise, using you as a kind of dummy to do it. If, in the middle, you start telling me what *you* imagine I am imagining you are . . . then I will have to stop my make believe experiment, and start listening to your complicated confusion, instead of working through mine at my own pace, with my own method.

Eventually, when I have completed this re-search into my past meanings I may stop pretending that you are someone else: I will have learnt something crucial about what my speech means to me. When that happens I will also have got clearer about what my family and the other people in my life mean to me, and we will have finished our work'.

BELIEF 2: Life is conflictual and difficult rather than harmonious and easy

'Life, as we find it, is too hard for us; it brings us too many pains, disappointments and impossible tasks' [37]

'The Freudian discovery teaches us that all natural harmony in man is profoundly disconcerted.' [38]

'But I know that people do not want to live in a state of harmony with one another, and quite frankly, I don't think it is desirable either as living or as harmony.' [39]

If you think that life in general is harmonious and easy, then you are just wrong. Wake up and look around. Empedocles, Darwin, Nietzsche, Freud, Jagger — *'I can't got no satisfaction'*— and Lacan believed that life was characterised by

---

[37] S Freud, Civilisation and its Discontents, *SE 21*, [1929], 1976, p75.

[38] J Lacan, *The Seminar of Jacque Lacan, The Psychoses*, trans Grigg, Routledge, London, 1993, p163.

[39] F Nietzsche, *My Sister and I*, Amok Books, Los Angeles, 1990, p140. Note Nietzsche's Lacanian notion that desire and 'harmony' are incompatible.

conflict. However you live, life has to be difficult, by necessity. For Lacan: *'There is not the slightest idea of progress in anything I articulate, in the sense that this term would imply a happy solution.'* [40]

Psychoanalysis does not lead directly to happiness but its opposite, unhappiness. Freud declared that the work of analysis was: *'transforming your hysterical misery into common unhappiness. With a mental life that has been restored to health you will be better armed against that unhappiness.'* [41]. We will return to the idea of The End of Analysis as a sad realisation in the Chapter Sixteen. For Freud and Lacan the necessary conflicts of life can be found both between one individual and another, and within each and every individual. For some of us it is better to be unhappy, and to know the cause of our suffering, and so have a chance of changing it, rather than suffering, remaining unaware of the causes of our suffering, its consequences and its domination of our lives.

If peace and harmony were as easy to organise as strife and war, then war, lawsuits and divorce would become very unpopular. But the fact is that there are hundreds of wars, and hundreds of thousands of divorces and lawsuits being pursued. Why have war and conflict always been popular with humanity? Because life *is* conflict. It is easy to pretend instead that life is easy or that all we have to do is 'just love each other', but it is hard to realise the truth about the ways in which life is and has been uniquely hard for each one of us, how love and conflict have often become tightly knotted together.

For both Freud and Lacan, so-called 'harmony', 'peace' or 'integration' are a kind of conflict that is hidden underneath the 'harmonious' surface. This is why Freud and Lacan so often used the language of warfare to describe clinical work; clinical work engages and identifies conflict. Of course many particular conflicts can be changed, especially once they have been carefully identified, but conflict cannot, in general, be eliminated. Life and conflict are the same. Suffering is the human condition. That is not to say that life cannot be rewarding or good — whatever that means— but only that a minimum of suffering and tragedy are necessary in every human life.

There is a cure for suffering and conflict —death— but most of us are not prepared to knowingly pay this price prematurely. Death is also one of the essential conditions of desire. Without death we could not desire. This is because desire relies on repression, and death is an extreme and fundamental form of repression: if we were immortal it would almost certainly become impossible to desire, because the profound repression that death constitutes would be absent. If you could not die you would have nothing to live for. If genetic engineering could create immortals, it would also be likely to produce psychotics who could not sustain desire. The expression of desire and its repression are two sides of

---

[40] J Lacan, The Inverse of Psychoanalysis, unpublished, trans Gallagher.
[41] S Freud, Studies on Hysteria, *SE 2*, [1893], 1973, p305.

the same coin. So it is not surprising that death is a common topic for many people in their clinical work as they struggle to come to terms with the expression and consequences of their desire.

We all have our own recipes for surviving and avoiding, escaping or ignoring conflict. None of them work without cost, and some are more expensive than others. Amongst our armoury of devices for living with conflict are the fantasy and the symptom, and a belief in some 'other' or 'others', that is some figure, ideal, lover or institution that is imagined to possess the power of protection, support, salvation and even of meaning. 'Armoury' is a term for a collection of objects that we use to pursue our love such as Saddam Hussein used to pursue his love of Kuwait's oil.

A popular choice within this category of methods of conflict management is an idealised relationship with 'the right lover or sexual partner', or an idealised relationship with God in one of the religious traditions. Many people complain that if only they could 'find the right partner', or find 'enough faith to truly have an intimate relationship with God', then, and only then, life would be good, and without conflict. Nuns for instance regard themselves as 'brides of Christ', and mystics have reported sexual ecstasy in their mystical union with God. Sometimes salvation is thought to consist in the right form of recognition by others. For instance, a mother might seek recognition from her loving child; or an employee from his boss; or one might think: 'if only my work or talent was properly recognised by my other, then my problems would be solved'.

The client's suffering and desire is addressed to their other. Because of the belief that the other holds the solution to his suffering, clients typically complain to their clinician that they are not getting what they want from their other. Such complaints are a working through of demand. Freud and Lacan argued that suffering is necessary because of our impossible demands for love and recognition.

It is probably true to say, as Freud did, that we are all fundamentally bisexual. If this is the case then there must have been some kind of deep struggle in most or perhaps all of us who end up physically making love either to men, or to women, but typically not to both: most of us have uniquely eliminated either all 'men', or all 'women' as potential lovers.

People have demonstrated that they are able to have sexual or love relations with an extraordinary variety of things, including men, women, children, chairs, as well as ideals such as 'science', a nation, 'justice', works of art, 'revenge', and favourite of all, themselves. Given this enormous and potentially infinite universe of objects of love and lust, how is it that such a high percentage of men end up loving women, and so many women end up loving men?

The popularity of heterosexuality suggests that forces exist which lead our sexuality to converge on the same points. We will return to this phenomenon and to the myth that finding the correct or ideal lover is the solution to all of a person's problems when we explore the origins of conflict in the mother-child relation, in language and in the myths of the Primal Horde and Oedipus in Chapter Five.

What exactly falls into the category of 'sexual experience and behaviour' for humans? How does what-is-sexual for people compare with what-is-sexual for other animals? It seems that for all (or almost all) non-human animals, sexual behaviour and experience usually refers to specific activities that focus closely on reproduction. The aim of animal sex is mostly reproduction. But people are more complicated; unlike sticklebacks and crocodiles, people's sexual behaviour is not uniform: people can have sex all the year round; there is no 'mating season'. Some people use contraceptives and have 'recreational sex', while others become nuns or monks, some have sex with lampposts, sheep or children. Animals do not display this extraordinary variety of sexual objects and behaviours.[42]

Language or symbols —as distinct from 'communication'— seems to explain this important difference between people and animals: Animals communicate with signs. These are a bit like traffic lights: the signs have fixed meanings for the animals. But there is very little, if anything that has a fixed meaning for people. As Lacan put it: *'The two sides, male and female, of sexuality, are not given data, [and] are nothing that could be deduced from experience.'*[43]

So sexual identity for people is not 'given' or fixed as it is with animals because word meaning is not fixed, and words or language are unique to people. This leaves us with the difficult question: What is sexual for people, and what is not? 'Sex' for Freud and Lacan is a very general term, not unlike the term 'force' in physics or engineering. A physicist would probably tell you that 'force means twenty or thirty different things to me, which one do you mean?' So it is with people and sex. Sex in psychoanalysis is certainly not to be comprehensively equated with sexual intercourse. According to Freud: *'[W]hat psychoanalysis called "sexuality" was by no means identical with the drive towards a union of the two sexes or towards producing a pleasurable sensation in the genitals . . . '*[44]

---

[42] Although Bagemihl's *Biological Exuberance: Animal Homosexuality and Natural Diversity*, 1999, St Martins Press, New York) challenges the idea that animals' sexual activity is exclusively reproductive, marshalling evidence from many sources of animal homosexuality and masturbation. However it remains true to say that human sexual behaviour remains far more diverse than animal sexual behaviour.

[43] J Lacan, *The Seminar of Jacque Lacan, The Psychoses,* trans Grigg, Routledge, London, [1981], 1993, p248.

[44] S Freud, Resistances to Psychoanalysis, *SE 19,* [1924], 1973, p218.

The infant, according to Freud, is 'polymorphously perverse'; that is, the ways in which the infant can derive a kind of sexual satisfaction are not fixed by an ideal of genital intercourse, but vary enormously. For people there are infinitely many forms and actions that can provide pleasure and satisfaction, but as the child ages, the sources of his pleasure and satisfaction become increasingly fixed.

Adults too have an extraordinary range of sources of sexual satisfaction including words, breasts, specific smells, hair, genitals, rubber, animals, a particular voice or a kind of look. But as time passes for the human subject the source of enjoyment, the object of desire becomes increasingly fixed.

The meaning of sex is not fixed by the seasons or reproduction. In fact, it is often very difficult to properly separate meaning and sexuality when people are concerned, but not so with the other animals. In the whole of the animal kingdom human infants are the most disorganised and most helpless for the longest period. If you compare a human baby with a dog, an ant or an elephant at any time up to three years, it is the human who is the most helpless and the most dependent. The world is a very chaotic place for infants because meanings are not fixed by instincts.

BELIEF 3: People usually avoid the truth about themselves when acknowledging the truth would imply that conflict and difficulty would have to be recognised.

Is this claim true? We have all had experience of people of all ages and intelligence kidding themselves that a particular belief —especially about themselves and their love relations —is true, while we have had good reasons for thinking that their belief is false. This approach of Freud's and Lacan's is very different from the Rogerian position which makes the claim that *'persons are motivated to seek the truth'* [45] Freud and Lacan argued that neurotics —that is, ordinary people— work hard to deceive themselves and others about those truths that might cause them trouble or upset.

Why do people deceive themselves?

What is at the heart of these self-deceptions? Why and how do people do it? Freud's and Lacan's answer is that people deceive themselves to solve a problem. Deception is carried out in order to avoid facing life's many conflicts. Swept under the carpet, the problem is 'out of sight and out of mind'. It is often much easier for people to pretend to themselves and others that a problem does

---

[45] D Mearns and B Thorne, *Person Centred Counselling in Action*, Sage, London, 1988, p18.

not really exist, than to take responsibility for a difficult situation and to find an approach to the problem that they can consciously live with.

For example a married man explained that his problem was *'alcoholism'*. He would also tell his wife: *'I can't make love to you because I've been drinking'*. In his analysis this man discovered his unconscious desire to be homosexual; he had used drink as a way of avoiding sex with his wife. His explanation of alcoholism had effectively convinced him and his wife, and did not betray his unconscious desire to love men rather than women.

How exactly do people deceive themselves?

This question is difficult to answer properly in detail because no one seems to know for sure, but Freud and Lacan have produced some theoretical ideas that fit clinical and everyday experience. Freud called the part of the mind that hides the truth and deceives 'the ego'. The main job of the ego is to manage conflict by making things look all right, whatever that means!

The ego does this by taking two criteria: something judged 'true', and also judged to produce a difficulty, problem or conflict. When the ego has identified something in this category of 'the true and the difficult' it hides it away by connecting the true and difficult idea to another idea, sometimes one that is false, or one remote from the true and the difficult idea. So the work of the ego is establishing 'false connections' [46] or false trails that cannot easily be followed. These often take the form of denials —where the truth is negated— or of rationalisations, that is 'understandings' that have been misdirected, misconstructed or misunderstood.

For the homosexual man heavy drinking was used by his ego as a false connection, connecting the true and difficult idea —his unconscious desire to love men— with his impotence in relation to his wife. All his wife saw was his drunkenness and his impotence, not his homosexual desire. The impotence and drunkenness were easier to bear than the truth of his desire and its consequences.

In another example a Mr Brown loved Mrs Jones, who was married to Mr Jones. If Mr Brown were to openly admit his love for Mrs Jones, then there would be a difficult situation. What would Mrs Jones do? What would Mr Jones do? Would he have to suffer his unreciprocated love, would he go and live somewhere else, would there be a messy divorce between Mr and Mrs Jones? Whatever the outcome, someone would have to lose out, and, even if Mr Brown happened to come out of the difficult situation well, he would have had to endure big risks, and live with the uncertain consequences of having acted on his desire.

---

[46] S Freud, The Psychotherapy of Hysteria, *SE 2*, [1895], 1973, p302.

Mr Brown did not admit to anyone (including himself) his love for Mrs Jones. Instead he connected his true and difficult love for Mrs Jones with a false connection —an invented set of malicious rumours regarding Mr Jones— whom he slandered. Establishing a bad reputation for Mr Jones was a false connection, designed to distract attention from the true and difficult love that Mr Brown had for Mrs Jones.

So the ego makes false connections in order to hide away conflicts and difficulties. Sometimes the conflict is on such a big scale that keeping the truth secret and hidden away takes a huge amount of energy, like trying to keep a door shut while someone else is trying to push it open from the other side. The ego is like Basil Fawlty in the BBC TV series *Fawlty Towers*. His job is to hide away the terrible truth at all costs, and pretend that everything is fine; and just like the ego, Fawlty has a management position.

So in Freud's theory there is —very roughly— the unconscious where unconscious desires live. Consciousness, by contrast, is that part of the mind to which we have access, the images, feelings and ideas that we can simply introspect and see. This, very roughly, Freud called the 'ego'.[47]

Basil Fawlty may appear — to those who don't know his place in the business — to be in the position of autonomy and authority but it is clear to all those who know how Fawlty Towers operates that he is not. Freud describes the restrictions under which the ego operates like this: *'In its relations to the id, therefore, the ego is paralysed by its restrictions or blinded by its errors; and the result of this in the sphere of psychical events can only be compared to being out walking in a country one does not know, and without having a good pair of legs.'* [48]

So for Lacan, following Freud, the primary function of the ego and of consciousness is deception. This means that whatever the circumstances, and

---

[47] Freud's theory is actually more sophisticated than this crude account: *'It is certain that much of the ego is itself unconscious . . . '* (Beyond the Pleasure Principle, *SE 18*, p19) Freud thought of the ego as the surface or façade that negotiates between the unconscious and the world. There is a complication, a third entity that the ego must struggle and compromise with, the 'superego'. He described the compromised and difficult position of the ego: *'We see this . . . ego as a poor creature owing service to three masters and consequently menaced by three dangers: from the external world, from the libido of the id [which very roughly is the unconscious], and from the severity of the superego . . . As a frontier creature the ego tries to mediate . . . ; it is also a submissive slave who courts his master's love. Whenever possible, it tries to remain on good terms with the id, it clothes the id's unconscious commands with its preconscious rationalisations . . . ; it disguises the id's conflicts with reality and, if possible, its conflicts with the superego too . . . it . . . often yields to the temptation to become sycophantic, opportunist and lying, like a politician who sees the truth but wants to keep his place in popular favour.'* S Freud, The Ego and the Id, *SE 19*, [1923], 1976, p56.

[48] S Freud, Analysis Terminable and Interminable, *SE, 23*, [1937], 1976, p37.

however much psychoanalysis a person has had —in matters of consciousness and judgement, especially reflexive ones in which people make judgements of themselves —the productions of the ego are suspect.

The deceptive function of the ego is something that we are all stuck with. A deceptive ego that tells lies is a necessary part of our mental structure. This Freudian model of the 'ego as deceptive' has been confirmed by hundreds of experiments carried out by psychologists with the techniques of mainstream science over the last forty years. But, surprisingly, this Freudian and Lacanian view contradicts what has become the predominant view in American culture and 'therapy' that is known as 'Ego Psychology'.

What is called 'therapy' in America usually has very little if anything to do with either Freud's or Lacan's ideas. Ego Psychologists argue that the ego can be 'strengthened', by the construction of a *'conflict-free zone'* within it, and thus have the ego 'accord with reality', instead of lying compulsively.

There are many problems with this view: for Lacan and Freud, the ego works to negotiate between reality and unconscious desire by covering up the necessary conflicts that life entails. In other words, it bullshits, like any public relations department or government. It must do so because of the conflicts we necessarily endure. Life is tough; we are divided in many ways, for instance as men and women. In our state of division it is far from obvious which is the best way to live. What should we do? Where should we do it? Who should we love? What work should we do? How do we live with our desire? Whatever position we take life is a series of conflicts.

What are the consequences for supervision?

'Supervision' for psychoanalytic work is very different from 'supervision' in other contexts, such as a manager in industry might ordinarily carry out. There the supervisor's job is to make sure that his supervisee is doing his job correctly, by smoothing over conflicts, giving new orders and in general acting like an ego: in contrast, a supervisor of Lacanian clinical work has different functions.

The most important function of a supervisor is to help the clinician to get clearer about his own position in relation to his client. So for example, a supervisor might help a clinician to realise that he is repelled or strongly attracted to a particular client. It would be strange if at some point, with one or another client, clinicians were not. Being sexually attracted to a client, or hating a client, might make it harder for the client to do any therapeutic work. Keeping an eye on this aspect of your work —your desire and its ethical consequences— is the most important function of a supervisor. If you are a client yourself you will probably find that your demands and desires regarding your own clients comes up in your own therapeutic work.

Another related function of supervision is to point out connections, themes and topics in the client's material that the clinician has missed. Furthermore, a supervisor should suggest a variety of techniques that might be used to overcome specific 'practical' difficulties, such as late attendance, aggression, seductive behaviour, non-payment and others. These issues come under the heading of 'strategy' and 'tactics', which we will return to. Last and least, a supervisor should be able to refer you to useful articles and books.

It is important that your supervisor is someone with whom you do not have other important relations of love or power; if your supervisor is also your manager or lover it will probably be impossible for him to properly supervise your work.[49]

According to Lacan *'There is one point, however, at which the problem of desire cannot be eluded —when what is at stake is the desire of the psychoanalyst himself.'*[50] In general, clinical work should be carried out in a situation that is as far as possible free from conflicts of interest, from love, power and all practical issues. Nothing of practical value should occur in the clinic. It is the absence of practical issues that allows the client to freely associate and discuss any topic with liberty, and so approach more efficiently the fundamental underlying issues. The principal purpose of supervision is for the clinician to pursue The Ethics of psychoanalysis, a topic that we will turn to in the final chapter.

If you have an unconscious, as most of us do —that is, all neurotics and perverts— then it doesn't matter how much clinical work you do on yourself as a client: you will still have an unconscious, although in the course of an analysis some of the contents of the unconscious change. You cannot be cured of having an unconscious; you will always find ways of avoiding the truth about yourself when it means facing a difficult conflict. This means that however much experience you have as a clinician, however old or clever you are, you will still have to have supervision in order to be an effective clinician. There is never a time at which a clinician can justifiably say: *'I don't have an ego; I never deceive myself, so I don't need supervision.'* It can be helpful to have supervision from a number of different supervisors, especially regarding the

---

[49] Having a supervisor with whom you have the minimum possible conflicts of interest is crucial. Good clinical work insists on it. Yet in the National Health Service and other institutions in the UK it is common for managers within a multidisciplinary team to also be responsible for the clinical supervision of those they manage. If such a manager refuses your request for external or independent supervision on the following grounds: 'It would be too expensive for us to provide you with supervision from someone external to our organisation; we don't have the funding for it', you might reply that it is not unusual for organisations to temporarily swap supervisors with another organisation, so that no money has to change hands. This solution works well in avoiding the power relations that all managers —as managers— cannot fail to become entangled with.

[50] Television, *October* 40, trans Mehlman et al, MIT Press, 1987, p104.

same client. The greater the variety of views and ideas you hear, the more quickly you will find your own style.

BELIEF 4: People both perceive and remember interruptions or discontinuity in time far better than continuity or the lack of change.

Before we look at the evidence for this belief, let's ask 'What is time?' Time is the measure of change. You can only tell that time has passed because something has changed, even if it is only the position of clock hands. What has this got to do with psychoanalysis?

Psychoanalysis is a theory of psychic change, of the ways in which people change, so it is not surprising that psychoanalysis has something to say about the ways in which those changes are perceived and conceived; and how people experience and remember change. The more dramatic the change, the better it is usually remembered. Sometimes the most dramatic changes or interruptions are remembered very well, but are deeply buried in the unconscious. These memories are called 'traumas', from the Greek for a 'wound', one that leaves a scar. Trauma is a discontinuity within the subject's perception of time. Repetition or returns are symptoms of trauma (but not the only ones) because they form a continuity in their return, taking the place of remembering, of the subject's failure to remember their trauma/s.

The evidence

There are three sorts of evidence for Freud's and Lacan's claim that people remember interruptions or discontinuity in time far better than continuity. First, there are formal scientific studies of large numbers of people by psychologists. Second, there are studies carried out by psychoanalysts on individual clients. And finally, there are investigations that each of us can carry out on ourselves, by self-observation and introspection.

Looking at the first of these, consider 'The Zeigarnik Effect'[51]. This is named after the psychologist who claimed, after hundreds of hours of experiments, that people remember interrupted tasks far better than completed tasks. Hundreds of researchers in different fields have supported this view. For instance the educationalists Bigge and Hunt write that *'allowing students to leave each class with some unanswered questions . . . is much more effective than passive reception'* [52]

---

[51] B Zeigarnik, 'Das Behalten erledigter und unerledigter Handlungen', *Psychol. Forsch.*, Vol. 9, p1-85.
[52] M Bigge and M Hunt, *Psychological Foundations of Education*, 2nd ed., New York, Harper & Row, 1968, p244.

The second kind of evidence —the less formal studies carried out by individual psychoanalyst— is typified by individual case studies such as Freud's famous case known as 'Dora'. There are also more recent reports of traumas in the literature that are often classified as 'post traumatic stress disorder'. In such cases the traumatic episode can be seen as an interruption, a discontinuity in the events that preceded it. Interestingly, clinical work with clients who have experienced some obvious trauma such as a train accident or rape will always lead, if the work progresses well, to a revaluation of events *prior* to the trauma that they first complained of, and which had not been consciously judged as traumatic or even important by the client. What is going on here is recalibration of 'repression', a technical term that Freud used to explain the ways in which people learn. A trauma is a discontinuous repression, that is a repression that is 'too much' or 'too little' relative to the other repressions. There are though, minimum and maximum levels of repression which will no doubt be different for many of us.[53] Traumas, as the real or unspeakable are typically marked, not by an unambiguous reference but by a discontinuity or cut in time, such as an anniversaries, which invite a return of the repressed, such as '*11th September*'. Baptising a trauma thus provides a program: the annual prospect of revising and working through the trauma by returning to find more symbols or signifiers to take the place of what could not be said.

Finally, consider the informal investigations that each of us can carry out on himself by introspection. Recall some of the most memorable events in your life. Generally, people report that it is the points of radical difference and change that are the most memorable. Interruptions are conspicuous points of arrest in the perceived flow of time. Lacan had also noticed that if you want something a lot, it seems to takes ages before you get it —the watched pot that never boils— and if you don't want something, it typically happens all too quickly. He was talking about a kind of 'subjective time', which is the subject's perception of the passage of time. 'Subjective time' is not the same as the passing of time indicated on a clock, which is also known as 'chronological time' or 'objective time'. Clock time goes on ticking away, and it provides a reference, something with which we can compare subjective time.

---

[53] Freud's theory of trauma can be found in his Introductory Lectures to Psychoanalysis, under 'Fixation to Traumas', *SE 16*, [1915], 1973, p273. See also p22 of Lacan's Seminar Three, Routledge, London, *The Psychoses*, [1981], 1993.

What is the relevance of time to clinical work?

'Discontinuity, then, is the essential form in which the unconscious first appears to us as a phenomenon —discontinuity— in which something is manifested as a vacillation' [54]

'The ideal of analysis is . . . to render the subject capable of sustaining the analytic dialogue, to speak neither too early, nor too late' [55]

There are many important consequences for clinical work that follow from the belief that the perception of time is not uniform for everyone all of the time. One important clinical consequence of this appreciation of subjective time is the ending of a session on a question, ambiguity or important point, rather than at the arbitrary point of fifty minutes duration.

Just about the only things in life that take a precisely fixed length of time —in the field of negotiated social activities— are school lessons and fixed length clinical sessions: almost all other human activities are not of fixed chronological length: making love, seeing a doctor, a dentist, making meals and arguments are all, fortunately, of variable length. This fact is closely connected with complex shifts and changes in meanings and language; the meaning of an act is not generally determined by its taking a standard period of time to carry it out.

Lacan's radical practice involved ending a session at the point when an important question or ambiguity has been made clear in the client's speech. This might take fifteen minutes, twenty-five minutes, or an hour and a half. Choosing to end on a question means that everything a client says must be listened to carefully by both the analyst and the client, and that the client will leave the session with some important loose ends to consider and do some homework on. Ending a session on a client's question also emphasises a fundamental truth: the analyst really does not have the answers to his client's crucial questions, only the client might possess those through reflecting on his own questions, and on his symptom as a impulsive and hasty answer to his questions.

Alternatively, fixed length sessions mean that a client's speech will be interrupted regardless of what they are actually saying at the time. So fixed length sessions are a way of not listening to what the client is saying; their speech is systematically ignored when sessions are arbitrarily ended.

---

[54] J Lacan, *The Four Fundamental Concepts of Psychoanalysis*, trans Sheridan, Pelican, London, 1979, p25.
[55] J Lacan, *The Seminar of Jacques Lacan, Book One, Freud's Papers on Technique of Psychoanalysis*, 1953-1954, ed Miller, trans Forrester, Cambridge University Press, Cambridge, England, 1988, p3.

Meaning as retrospective

In essential part it is differences of timing that allow sounds or words to have variable meanings. For example it is often necessary to wait for some *time* after a word has *first* been used, in order to begin to understand the meaning, to grasp the context. Here is an example: *'I am going to the bar'*. Does this mean that the speaker is going to have a drink, or that he has reached the point in his legal training where he is to become a barrister? The passage of time might allow you to find out the answer to these or other questions. Perhaps the speaker, if listened to for just a moment longer would have been heard to say: *'I am going to the barn'*.

Waiting longer still might have allowed the discovery that *'I am going to the barn'* was actually used as a password, and that it had a wholly different meaning from the one you had understood earlier. Jokes are another example of this phenomenon; jokes are not usually understood until the punch line has been delivered. The punch line has the effect of giving a meaning to the whole of the joke. So meaning operates retrospectively, that is, with the passage of time.

But it is not only jokes that get their meaning retrospectively. All the words that have ever been spoken or written have their meanings changed continually. You can see this for instance in the work of scientists, where the word 'mass', for example takes on a new meaning in Einstein's theory, which came after Newton's theory. The work of historians is also to find and refind new meanings in old words.

Psychoanalytic work aims at helping clients find meanings in their words and symptoms. Typically clients repeat certain words, phrases and stories that have special hidden importance for them. It can take many years to explore the shifting meanings of these special phrases. So every session is the discovery or questioning of new meanings in old words, like an archaeological investigation of an ancient site with many layers, each one overlaid by a different but related culture that took over the one before it.

BELIEF 5: Love and desire are fundamental in explaining the human condition

Lacan argued that love and desire are what makes psyche go around. The unique lifestyle that each of us chooses is a kind of solution to the particular problems, difficulties and traumas that each of us have had loving and desiring. How plausible is this idea? If you don't believe it then try having a love affair, or start being psychoanalysed! People often devote their lives for their love of someone or for the love of an ideal such as *'my country'*. Dying for love is probably unusual: living for it is not.

A large proportion of clients initially present their problems with love and desire. Their desire is often knotted and hidden away. Some clients complain of suffering the wrong kind of lover or spouse, and imagine that the ideal partner will solve all their problems. Sometimes a client will infer that he is depressed because he has difficulty loving someone else [56].

Love is a synthesis, the making of something new. Clients come for analysis because of their problems with their syntheses, with their love and its consequences. Many clients insist on having relationships that repeat problematic features of an earlier love, often with a sibling or parent. Successful analysis identifies the client's investments in their love relations, and their often impossible consequences.

If a woman has unconsciously chosen all her lovers on the model of her beloved brother, and has been bitterly disappointed with each of them, then psychoanalysis may allow her to identify her beliefs, and perhaps the high cost or impossibility of having a love affair with her brother, or even with men who resemble him. Psychoanalysis then is a set of methods of persuasion for helping clients to give up certain beliefs. Which beliefs? Neither the clinician nor the client know in advance but in general such beliefs seem to be profoundly rooted in the idea of sexuality and gender, of being a man or a woman and their place within the client's economy of love.

To get clearer about the relation between 'love' and 'desire' —which are very different, although related— calls for an understanding of Lacan's distinctions between 'need, 'demand' and 'desire', which we will look at next.

---

[56] While broadly speaking the 'depression' of ordinary language and psychiatry is too vague a term, covering every Freudian and Lacanian diagnostic category, the problem of those who suffer with what Freud called 'melancholia' (Mourning and Melancholia, *SE 14*, [1915], 1976) is that they love themselves too much.

CHAPTER THREE

Need, demand and desire

'Need', *'demand'* and *'desire'* are radically different clinical categories for Lacan but they are frequently confused and confusing in the approaches of other schools. How can a clinician tell the crucial differences between a client's 'needs', 'demands' and 'desires'? What has love got to do with it? To answer these questions we have to introduce an idea that Lacan developed from Freud: the *'symbolic father'*.

The 'symbolic father'

The symbolic father [57] is not the same as the biological father, whose sperm helped create the client: nor is the symbolic father necessarily the man who lived with him and played football with him. The symbolic father is any agency that has separated the young subject from the mother. So for example, if the

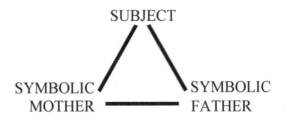

mother leaves her child to go to work, then the mother's work is the symbolic father. If a lesbian lover spends time with the mother, separating the mother from the child, then the lover is the symbolic father. The symbolic father can be a sibling, or even be the mother, or perhaps her illness.

To be consistent we should really not use the term 'mother' but 'symbolic mother' because the actual mothering that we are talking about here can be

---

[57] J Lacan, Seminar on Transference, unpublished, trans Gallagher, 22 March 1961.

carried out by all sorts of different people such as a father, a brother, sister or aunt. So there is the person who does the mothering —who for ease of reading I will call 'mother'— and there is the agent that separates the baby from the mother who is the 'symbolic father'. Now we are ready to distinguish between 'needs', 'demands' and 'desires'.

Need

'Need' is something physiological such as the need for food or for warmth. Not much about people is simple, but if you could imagine a need on its own —which would never happen— it would be something that could be completely satisfied. If someone is cold, he can be warmed, and if he is hungry, he can be fed. Need in this sense can be eliminated, temporarily. In this sense people are no different from animals.

A newly born infant is often in a state of need. He has sensations of pain and pleasure that are more or less managed by whoever mothers him. So the mother is the sensation manager of the infant. She feeds and changes him, keeping him neither too hot nor too cold, and appearing to the infant to be very much in control of his pain and pleasure. The mother is powerful in relation to the powerlessness of the baby.

Note that this relation of 'power over sensations', of one person's mastery over another's pain and pleasure is one definition of sexuality or the erotic. Lovers often say to each other: *'You make me feel . . . '*

This seems surprising, since pain and pleasure are the measure of need, and love does not appear to be anything to do with pain or pleasure, but more to do with demand and desire. We will return to this problem.

As the infant gets older the mother feeds him less often, but talks to him more. She is feeding him words. The infant quickly gets the idea, from the mother's power —and his lack of power— that he had better find out what the mother wants, so that he can give it to her, so that she can continue to help him avoid pain, and give him pleasure. In order that the infant can be reassured that he is giving his mother what she wants, as she makes herself increasingly absent, and increases the time between his feeds, he starts learning language, swallowing the words that his mother feeds him. Powerless infants are pressured to speak by their needs, by pain and pleasure, which become identified with the absence and presence of the powerful mother. In this way the baby knots together the management of his suffering with the words of his mother, or the mother tongue. According to Lacan: *'And the discovery of analysis, is that the subject, in the field of the Other, encounters not simply the images of his own fragmentation but, already from the beginning, the objects of the desire of the Other, namely of the mother, not just in their fragmented state but with the privileges that the desire of the mother accords them.'* [58]

Very soon the baby has a whole new set of problems that are far more complicated and difficult than the simple needs he started out with. In addition to managing the old problems —his needs: pains and pleasures— he also has demands, loves and hates, as well as difficulties with ideals, values and ethics. He has problems of conflict with 'the good and the bad', and identifications to make and break. And, crucially, he has to come to terms with the symbolic father. This is traumatic because 'coming to terms with the symbolic father' means coming to recognise that 'my mother desires someone else, someone other than me'. So after the first phase of need there is a kind of movement to demand, and then on to desire.

Demand

'Childhood love is boundless; it demands exclusive possession, it is not content with less than all . . . it is incapable of obtaining complete satisfaction; and principally for that reason, it is doomed to end in disappointment and to give place to a hostile attitude.' [59]

'Demand' is a more difficult idea to explain than need because demand is fundamentally ironic. The subject of demand enlists the cooperation of another so as to prove that the other is not able to satisfy the subject. Put simply the demanding subject sets out to be frustrated. Demand can be formulated as the invitation [60]: *'Will you co-operate with me in order to prove that you are unable to satisfy me?'*

Here is an example of a demanding child who says to his mummy*: 'Can I have some chocolate?'* He is given some chocolate. Within a moment he says: *'Can I have a banana?'* He is given a banana, after which he pleads: *'Can I have a biscuit?'* Whenever the demanding boy is given the physical object he has named, he will ask for something else. What the child is looking for above all is not an actual object, a biscuit or banana, but an object that does not exist. He is looking for something that will not be given. So he will continue testing his mother's resources and patience until he finally succeeds in finding something that she will not give. The subject sets out to prove that the object of demand cannot exist. [61]

---

[59] S Freud, Female Sexuality, Three Essays on Sexuality, *SE 21*, [1931], 1976, p29.
[60] Both mother and child typically make this invitation. If the disappointment is not achieved then the cost will be high, and psychosis may result.
[61] There is a sense in which the object of demand does have a positive existence: the object of demand is the limit of the other's demands and desires. This limit represents

For some children who get spoilt, being refused the object of your demand is something that hardly ever happens. Until demand has been exhausted, the individual will keep on demanding and demanding as he searches for his desire, whatever his age. Freud wrote: *'The undesirable result of "spoiling" a small child is to magnify the importance of the danger of losing the object (the object being a protection against every situation of helplessness) in comparison with every other danger. It therefore encourages the individual to remain in the state of childhood, the period of life which is characterised by motor and psychical helplessness'.*[62]

But there is a popular aspect of demand: love. Demand is the demand for love. What is love? Loving is being in a state of demand, of wanting to give something that you, the lover cannot give, and, at the same time of wanting to receive something that your loved one cannot give you. According to Lacan: *'What is desired, is the desirer in the Other, which cannot happen unless the subject is conversed with as desirable, this is what he demands in the demand for love. But what we should see at this level . . . is that **love . . . is to give what one does not have**. And that one cannot love except by becoming a non-haver, even if one has. That love as response implies the domain of not-having . . .*'[63]

How can you tell if a client is demanding or desiring? Towards answering this important clinical question ask yourself: 'Is this aim, object or ideal of the client's something that is possible for him, or is it something that he is attempting to establish as an impossibility for someone else?' It is possible to act on one's desire: it is not possible for the other —perhaps the lover, mother or analyst— to eliminate the subject's demand. If a five-year-old child insists on being a policeman tomorrow, or on climbing Everest immediately then he is being demanding. A desire is always judged to represent an action and goal from the subject's point of view: if the goal is believed by the subject to be impossible then it is represented as a demand to and for the other.[64]

When someone has worked through his demand he can speak his desire. Such a person might tell you what they desire and how it drives their life. But most

---

the lack or absence of the other's lack. Note that while the object of need —a sensation— can be supplied completely, the object of demand cannot be supplied at all, because it doesn't exist. Need and demand in this sense are opposites.

[62] S Freud, Inhibitions, Symptoms and Anxiety, *SE 20*, [1925], 1976, p167.

[63] J Lacan, Seminar on Transference, unpublished, trans Gallagher, 7 June 1961.

[64] Just what does 'im/possible' mean? This question is given different answers by philosophers and psychoanalysts. Of course it is possible that a particular individual will win the Lottery, but for psychoanalytic purposes it is probable that spending three-quarters of one's income on the Lottery every week does not represent acting on one's desire but acting out one's demand. Such an individual is likely to believe that winning the lottery will be his salvation, representing that object referred to by Freud that will save him from his helplessness.

people live in a sort of trance, half asleep, with hardly any idea what they really want. They are not conscious of their desire and they do not consciously follow it, yet their unconscious desire continues to play a major but compromised role in their life.

But they know best, or at least better than anyone else, what their best course of action should be. Each one of us is The Authority regarding our own resources. If, for example, you live in a homophobic society it may be easier for you not to recognise your homosexual desire, than to risk rejection by your employer, friends and wife and children. It might be best for you to hide your desire from yourself and others rather than suffering the consequences of coming out.

For most of us who do not act on our desire an illicit enjoyment is the compensation we provide for ourselves, through our symptom. The symptom makes an enjoyment, and is a tortured compromise between the demand for love, and the desire to speak the truth of unconscious desire plainly, so that everyone will understand.

A subject's demand for love can never be properly articulated because demand, or love is for an object that does not actually exist. This is why love has always been such a popular theme of songs, poetry and art throughout history. Love is inexhaustible, because its object cannot be grasped; the object of demand cannot be grasped because by its definition it cannot be provided, except as an infinite regress: *'If I frustrate him [the client] it is because he asks me for something. To answer him, in fact. But he knows very well that it would be mere words. And he can get those from whomever he likes . . . It's not these words he's asking for. He is simply asking me, from the very fact that he's speaking: his demand . . . carries no object with it.'* [65]

Desire

Desire is a difficult idea and, Lacan argued, uniquely human, because it is a property of language. Language is communal property, being owned by no one individual, so each individual desire is part of language. An individual's sexual desire, for instance, can often be aroused by a particular form of words, typically those of a potential lover signifying their desire, such as *'I want you'*. The fundamental reason why, for Lacan: *'man's desire finds its meaning in the desire of the other, [is]not so much because the other holds the key to the object desired, as because the first object of desire is to be recognised by the other . . . it is . . . as desire of the other that man's desire finds form.'*

---

[65] J Lacan, *Ecrits*, The Direction of the Treatment and the Principles of its Power, trans Sheridan, Tavistock Routledge, London, [1966], 1980, p254.

Desire dominates our lives and sets us apart from all other animals. Desire is another word for 'lack', for something that is missing, that is the object of desire, whose essence is absence. Desire can change its object, and desire often hides— although it will be revealed in dreams, slips of the tongue and symptoms— but desire always organises the subject's life in a far more comprehensive way than is ordinarily apparent.

Here is a review of some of the terms introduced in this chapter and their relation to each other: there is a movement from need to demand, and then on to desire. During the first phase of need the dependency of the child on the mother is established. In the following phase of demand the child is working in the opposite direction, to separate from the mother, to separate his desire from his mother's by placing on her impossible demands that she cannot supply. Note the similar positions of Freud and Lacan regarding demand. Freud wrote [66]: *'The patient must be left with unfulfilled wishes in abundance. It is expedient to deny him precisely those satisfactions which he desires [that is demands] most intensely and expresses most importunately'*; and *'Analysis must be carried out in a state of frustration'* [67], while Lacan wrote of the *'terrible temptation that must face the analyst to respond, however little, to demand.'* [68]; and of the *'importance of preserving the place of desire in the direction of treatment necessitates that one should orientate this place in relation to the effects of demand, which alone are . . . conceived as a principle of the power of the treatment.'* [69]

When the competent mother fails to meet the child's impossible demands the child's dependence on her has been proved false, and the independence of the child's desire has been proved to exist and properly identified. This proof usually entails the mother being presented with thousands of fatiguing examples and repetitions of demand. The child appears to reason along the following lines: *'If mummy cannot give me everything I ask her for, then I cannot be dependent on her, therefore I must become independent and find out what is possible for me rather than impossible for her'*. Once this proof —that the mother cannot provide all that the child demands— is sufficiently established the child is able to start identifying its own desire; its own desire as separate from its mother's desire. This is why children are so demanding; they are trying to work through their demand in order to give birth to their desire. Desire is the exhaustion of demand, the proof of the existence of their individual desire. Desire emerges from the child's own frustration, from the

---

[66] S Freud, Turnings in the Ways of Psychoanalytic Therapy, *SE 12*, [1919], 1976, p398.
[67] S Freud, Analysis Terminable and Interminable, *SE 23,* [1937], 1976, p231.
[68] Lacan, *Ecrits*, The Direction of the Treatment and the Principles of its Power, trans Sheridan, Tavistock Routledge, London, 1980, p276.
[69] Ibid p269.

demand, addressed to his carers, to which he found an inadequate reply. *'Desire begins to take shape in the margin in which demand become separated from need; this margin being that which is opened up by demand . . . '*[70]

Parents —when they were children— identified their desire out of their frustrated demand with their parents. This is why every generation of parents say: *'I always wanted to give you what my parents didn't give me'*. What the parents are saying is 'my demand —to give you— comes from what is left of my demand, in relation to my parents, and what they gave me'. That is what they failed not to give me. Put another way: *'I give you the leftovers of my demand that I addressed to my parents'*. This explains why there is often a transmission of a specific demand or symptom across generations. Exasperated parents despair of their children's favourite demands and symptoms which they often recognise the irony of, along the lines of *'How and why should this particular problem be visited on me as a parent, since my parents had to suffer something similar with me?* It is not so much the sins of the father that are visited on the children as the demands, desires and secrets of the father and the mother, and their ancestors.[71]

Why is it important for clinicians to distinguish needs, demands and desire?

If the clinician fails to distinguish needs, demands and desire then a central and problematic question arises: What orientates the clinical work? Imagine a 'practical problem' arising in a clinic in which needs, demands and desire are not distinguished, and the client requests a glass of water. What does the clinician do with such a client? At this point there is insufficient material for the clinician to make a confident judgement; the client's thirst could be a need, a demand or even a desire.

If this were the client's first request I would err on the side of caution because the request may well represent their need for water, so I would invite the client to help himself to a glass of water. But if this were the eighth request for a glass of water in as many sessions I might remain silent or perhaps ask if the client generally suffers with thirst. As a clinician I would be asking myself 'Is this client being demanding? Is it possible for the client to gain access to water without my involvement?' The main question in my mind would be: 'Is this an

---

[70] Ibid, p311.

[71] In psychoanalysis demand is regarded a little like sin: the subject is born into demand, just as Christians claim that all are born into sin. One difference is that psychoanalysis offers no guarantees of salvation or happiness once a subject's demand has been worked through, leaving him free to act on his desire. Questions of the relation to Buddhist enlightenment are also relevant.

issue that the client is attempting to make impossible or intolerable for me, or is it a problem that he can solve himself?'

It is only through patiently working through the client's taxing demands, addressed to his clinician —through transference— that the client is able to identify what is possible for him, through the identification of what is impossible for his Other. Because the aim of analysis is for the client to speak on his desire, or act on his desire, it is the policy of the clinician to exhaust the neurotic client's demands. Being presented with another's demand represents the impossible because demands cannot be satisfied. So the Lacanian aims to exhaust the client's demand rather than vainly attempting to satisfy them. According to Lacan, *'desire is always desire for another's desire'*. Here are two different but related ways of understanding it. The first is more abstract:

Desire is expressed symbolically, as a type of language and so is a property of words or signifiers.

Signifiers are public, that is communual property, not belonging to any one individual but to all who use them.

Therefore, an individual's desire is always connected to what other people desire, because it is something that belongs to signifiers, which belong to all language users.

This conclusion may seem absurd because we are used to the idea that our desires are private, not public. Certainly we can hide our desires from others and from our own consciousness. But if I hide my desire from myself then it will find some other way of 'speaking'. Desire always uses signifiers to express itself. Whether or not you are aware of it, or consciously willing, you will be spoken by your signifiers. If you don't speak them, they will speak you, in a slip of the tongue, in a dream or as a symptom or bungled action. [72]

Here is the second: the child's demand is always addressed to an other, or mother, to those who care for him, so the desire becomes established out of the

---

[72] Freud's four formations of the unconscious are: slips of the tongue, bungled actions, dreams and symptoms, taken up in his Psychopathology of Everyday Life (*SE 6,* [1901]), The Interpretation of Dreams (*SE 4-5,* [1900], 1976), Inhibitions, Symptoms and Anxiety (*SE 20,* [1925]).

child's frustrated demand. Demand is always in relation to others, and to the language of others, because it was the other who frustrated the child and fed him words instead of pleasure.

Lacan also observed that *'desire is desire for difference'*. The object of demand is that which the other cannot give. So the child of poor parents might demand money, while the child of liberal parents might well be conservative, like Saffron in the British TV series *Absolutely Fabulous*.

The orientation of the child's demand is in the opposite direction to their parents' demand or desire of them. This is because parents tend to resist some of their child's impossible demands, and so the child's desire is always the efficient establishment of difference, in relation to his parents' demand or desire because, as Lacan put it, *'the neurotic . . . is he who identifies the lack of the Other with his demand'* [73].

This concept of rule breaking or difference is crucial in understanding the transgression presented to clinicians in the form of the symptom. There is an enjoyment in transgression.

Put another way, enjoyment is not innocent; because of the helplessness of the infant at the hands of a powerful helper, typically its mother. Pain, pleasure and enjoyment always refer to one or another version of that helper or 'Other'. One consequence is that 'enjoying myself' —without reference to any other— is not possible. The naive idea that the subject can exist without reference to his other in his every thought, word and deed is false. As soon as an infant seeks pleasure or enjoyment he has started to address his Other, which insists on the subject taking complex positions about who enjoys what and whom, and how

---

[73] J Lacan, *Ecrits*, Subversion of the Subject and Dialectic of Desire, trans Sheridan, Tavistock Routledge, London, 1980, p321.

much. At this point the infant's innocence has disappeared. The subject of enjoyment and suffering always juxtaposes himself with his Other [74].

In the next section we will return to look in more detail at the context in which desire is born and suffered as repression and expression.

Repression and Expression as *'two sides of the same coin'*

'What comes under the effect of repression returns, for repression and the return of the repressed are just the two sides of the same coin. The repressed is always there, expressed in a perfectly articulate manner in symptoms and a host of other phenomena.' [75]

To express yourself —to speak or write— you must have learnt the rules of grammar and word meaning. So repression and expression are essential parts of each other. In order for there to be an expression there must have been repression. For example, it is now common in Europe and America for Jews to assimilate, to become absorbed into the culture of the country in which they live. To do in Rome as the Romans do. Typically such Jews do not practise their religion, and they often marry non-Jews. But if there was to be a strong resurgence of anti-Jewish racism, with Jews being murdered and treated badly, you could be sure that there would be a renewal of Jewish culture, and a failure to assimilate. Many 'Jewish atheists' —those with a Jewish culture but no religious belief— would find God, and there would be a return to the old traditions. So the expression of Jewish culture depends on its repression, on the ways in which it has been learnt.

Sometimes there is too much repression, which is called 'trauma', and sometimes there is too little, which is also a problem. There is probably hardly ever just the right amount of repression, so most of us are neurotic. The rest of us are perverse or psychotic, which variable levels of repression have also caused. Neurotic clients have either too much or too little repression. In both cases there is always some surplus demand nagging to be metamorphosed into desire.

---

[74] In paranoid psychosis this Other is often missing to the extent that a grandiose Other is contrived, sometimes with the identity of the CIA, aliens, or 'the opposite sex'.

[75] J Lacan, *The Psychoses*, ed Miller, trans Grigg, Routledge, London, 1993, p12.

CHAPTER FOUR

Lacan's theory of the real, the symbolic and the imaginary

'I try, because it seems coherent and useful . . . to differentiate . . . between the three orders of the symbolic, the imaginary, and the real . . . Everything that our analytic experience shows us can be satisfactorily classified into these three orders of relationships' [76]

Lacan's theory of the real, symbolic and imaginary is a formalisation arising from Freud's work. When examined in detail it is complicated; however, a cut-down version is fairly easy to explain and understand and of great practical value in the clinic. Put simply, the symbolic is the realm of symbols or language; the imaginary is the realm of images; and the real is the traumatic — that which resists symbolisation. Lacan's theory of the real, symbolic and imaginary is crucial in order to understand and apply his clinical techniques. It is this theory that we turn to next, starting with his theory of the image.

The image and the imaginary

'Man is captivated by the image of his body' [77]

'The sexual relation implies capture by the other's image' [78]

Included within the category of 'the image' are smells, touches and sensations. Images are clearly important; sometimes people fall in love because of the curve of a lip, or an accent, and become captivated and dominated by an image. Most of us have gone to great effort at some point in our lives to produce a particular kind of image that we hope will captivate another because of our sexual interest in them. Anorexia may

---

[76] J Lacan, *The Psychoses*, ed Miller, trans Grigg, Routledge, London, 1993, p148.
[77] J Lacan, Geneva Lecture on the Symptom, *Analysis* No 1, 1989, trans Grigg, p9.
[78] Ibid 1. p77.

qualify in some cases for this category. This idea of 'domination by the image' is tied to the concept of captivation, slavery or bondage. Such a bond can usually be found between a child and mother, between lovers, and between a slave and his master, or between employees and employers. The image —due to its nature— is likely to be used by the ego in making false connections, that is in deception.

The symbolic

'The human subject . . . is prey to the symbol' [79]

The symbolic is a category that includes natural languages such as French and Chinese, as well as all artificial languages such as Morse code, symbolic logic and those languages used to programme computers. There is a very wide range of special properties that are exclusively symbolic, such as truth and falsity, fiction and metaphor, all of which are vital in the clinic.

Clinical work —with minor exceptions— is carried out with language, that is with the symbolic. Exceptions to the practice of working exclusively with language occur in three circumstances. First, when starting work with some children, especially the very young for whom drawings and play are an important way of producing symbols or words. Second, during the preliminary sessions, that is, the first sessions during which the client and clinician spend some time seeing if they can work together. At this time the couch is not used because the clinician is inviting the client to enter into an imaginary relation known as 'transference' (this will be discussed later); possibly in a partial reliance on the clinician's image. At this early stage, then, the imaginary may be more in the foreground than the symbolic. Thirdly, when working with psychotics rather than neurotics, the value of the image is importantly different —and again, though for a very different reason— the imaginary plays a more important role than the symbolic. This is because the psychotic's grasp on language —that is on the symbolic— is fragile no props that help provide reference points and anchors for it should be removed. One such prop are images, in particular those of people who speak, listen and respond to the psychotic. Many psychotics are only able to remain in the ordinary neurotic world of language by investing themselves heavily in such images or bodies of symbolism, by drawing complex diagrams, or maps for instance, and so keeping their eye on their other. For this reason psychotics should never be allowed to use the couch.

---

[79] J Lacan, Transference, 19 April 1961, unpublished, trans Gallagher.

The real

'There is often a passage in even the most thoroughly interpreted dream which has to be left obscure; this is because . . . there is a tangle of dream-thoughts which cannot be unravelled . . . This is the dream's navel, the spot where it reaches down into the unknown.' [80]

'In the subject's relationship to the symbol . . . something is not symbolised and is going to appear in the real. It is essential to introduce the category of the real, it is impossible to neglect it in Freud's texts. I give it this name so as to define a field different from the symbolic' [81]

For Lacan the 'real' does not correspond with 'real' as in the concept of 'reality' [82] but is the vitally important category of 'the mutually exclusive' and the incommensurable. The incommensurable is the impossibility of properly comparing two quite different types of thing, such as an apple with a banana. An apple is not a good banana, nor is a banana a poor apple. The two things cannot be compared as if they were equivalent.

'Mutually exclusive' describes situations in which two or more items are involved, when, if one of the items is selected, then at least one of the other items cannot be selected, because the two items exclude each other. What do the 'mutually exclusive' and 'the incommensurable' mean in clinical terms? That which cannot be spoken, or symbolised.

The 'impossible to say'

Lacan argued that language is a universal trauma, or wound, taking a unique form for every person. People are radically different from all other organisms because we speak, and one word can mean a confusingly indeterminate number of different things. Animals and plants communicate but with a lot less trouble than people: plants and animals use signs of fixed meaning, not confusing signifiers or symbols whose meanings are variable.

---

[80] S Freud, The Interpretation of Dreams, *SE 4*, [1900a], 1976, p525.

[81] J Lacan, *The Psychoses*, ed Miller, trans Grigg, Routledge, London, 1993, p81.

[82] Freud wrote that: *'It will be a long time before [the patient] can take in our proposal that we should equate fantasy and reality and not bother to begin with whether the childhood experiences under examination are one or the other. . . . **in the world of the neuroses it is psychical reality which is the decisive kind.**'* So for the purposes of interpretation Freud equates 'fantasy and reality', but distinguishes them for other purposes, for instance: *'You must not suppose, however that sexual abuse of a child by its nearest male relatives belongs entirely to the realm of fantasy.'*

How do you make an animal neurotic? By introducing variable meanings or indeterminacy. Pavlov, in a variation on his best known experiment conditioned dogs to expect food, after having been shown a circle, and to expect an electric shock after having been shown an oval, ethical issues aside, the dogs seemed content. Then Pavlov increasingly made the circles oval, and the ovals more circular. For the first time the dogs exhibited obvious signs of what we might call 'anxious behaviour'. So a meaning was varied or made indeterminate, and an 'animal neurosis' was simulated.

We will look at two kinds of example of 'the impossible to say': the 'unusual and dramatic impossible to say' experience, that is, traumas, and the 'necessarily everyday impossible to say'. These two examples are at two extremes that describe the ends of a continuum. Every adult has had some of both types of experience.

The rare and dramatic impossible to say experience

The 'unusual and dramatic impossible to say' might well be a trauma, but be careful: it is possible for any type of event to be traumatic in any particular case, including apparently insignificant episodes such as the telling of a joke or the failure to keep a minor promise. Beware of pressing your possibly false assumptions on your client. It is likely but not necessary that a car crash, witnessing the death of a parent, the birth of a sibling and sexual abuse for a child of two are experiences that are likely to leave them unable to sufficiently symbolise —that is, to put into words— and so to constitute traumatic experience.

A clinician can tell in general if a client is traumatised by studying the client's speech. A traumatised child or adult would find a special or indirect way of 'speaking the truth'. This way of 'speaking' will not be understood directly because it would be symptomatic; the symptom 'speaks' that which it has been unable to say.

One young girl, during her therapy sessions would repeatedly throw into the air a handful of small pieces of white paper that she had earlier torn up. It transpired that her repetition of this scene symbolised her trauma in which a man had masturbated and ejaculated over her. By eventually having the trauma symbolised —as words rather than oblique mime —the previously traumatised girl was able to give up her symptoms.

Prior to her therapy the client was not able to symbolise her experience in words, so she was stuck in the repetition of her trauma, her symptom demanding to be heard, preventing her from moving onto other things.

The necessarily everyday impossible to say

'One is never in a position to discover the whole truth' [83]

'I always speak the truth. Not the whole truth, because there is no way to say it' [84]

'The concept of a living being has the same indeterminacy as that of a language' [85]

The necessarily everyday impossible to say does not occur exclusively in the clinic, although it is relied on in the clinic. Whenever anyone speaks what they say is necessarily ambiguous. Any word, phrase or sentence can be understood in a variety of ways. Lacanians make vital use of this universal ambiguity in interpretations, as we will see in Chapter Fifteen.

Lacan argued that there is something uniquely traumatic for each of us that is specially human: language or speech. Why? Language is such that it makes it impossible for us to be completely clear and unambiguous whenever we speak, yet language is the best we can do when it comes to expressing our desire, and to understanding the desires of others: *'[P]sychoanalysis should be the science of language . . . man is the subject captured and tortured by language.'* [86]

Whatever we say we are likely to be misunderstood, at least in part because our words do not have rigidly fixed meanings or uses. The game of Chinese Whispers relies on this principle. Yet we only notice our misunderstandings of each other in a small percentage of such cases, as the following three almost deaf people, who are probably speaking English, suggest:

First person *'Isn't it windy?'*

Second person: *'No it's Thursday'.*

Third person: *'So am I, let's go and have a cup of tea'.*

Which group of nearly deaf conversationalists would you trust better, one that claimed to have arrived at 'an agreement' or one that claimed to have arrived at 'a disagreement?' If I had to bet my money would be on those with the disagreement, that is with those who thought that they had evidence of difference rather than sameness. This principle is relied on clinically, where the aim is to produce and identify difference because difference is an essential ingredient of each subject's desire and subjectivity, originating in their frustrated demands.

---

[83] S Freud, 'Wild' Psychoanalysis', *SE 11*, [1910c], 1976, p226.

[84] J Lacan, Television, trans Mehlman, *October* 40, MIT, Cambridge, USA, 1987, p7.

[85] L Wittgenstein, *Zettel,* 2nd edition, Basil Blackwell, number 326, 1981.

[86] J Lacan, *The Psychoses,* ed Miller, trans Grigg, Routledge, London, 1993, p243.

Apparent agreement may well be the product of the false connections of the ego, glossing over vital differences. However disagreement always incorporates some type of underlying or basic agreement, even if it is only about what terms or signifiers mean. When one disputant says *'I disagree'* he is necessarily claiming to have some meanings in common with the language of the person whose claims he disputes, otherwise he could not even claim to disagree.

Since we all suffer changes in word meanings —and cannot escape them— it is a miracle that we ever manage to communicate at all. The only alternative to dealing with changing word meanings is to give up language, as perhaps some autistics and psychotics have, or to have an 'imaginary language', or one in which meanings are all rigidly fixed. As far as I know there is no one alive who believes that there is or could be such a human language.[87]

Lacan and others, some of whom we will meet, have argued that each and every one of us is burdened with the problem of shifts in meaning, as an *every sentence phenomenon*. This may seem an obscure point, especially when compared to an obvious trauma such as a rape that has apparently been the single cause of a client's search for clinical help, but it is only a difference of degree —not one of kind— between a client's symptom seeking to be heard and anyone's everyday sentence seeking a particular response or recognition. It is the necessary existence of the big Other, with a capital 'O', to whom speech is addressed that makes language a crucial trauma for each one of us, whether it becomes focused on the form of an obvious trauma such as sexual abuse or not.

This unique trauma is always taken up in each subject's speech. Hence *'The Other'* wrote Lacan, with a capital O, *'is not a subject, it is a locus to which one strives . . . to transfer the knowledge of the subject.'*[88] This is why Freud wrote, in a Lacanian moment: *'every man possesses in his unconscious an instrument by which he can interpret the expressions of the unconscious of an other,'*[89] and why Lacan said *'the unconscious is structured like a language'*.

All of us rely on this structure of language when we make our ordinary everyday interpretations of each others' speech, and when as clinicians we listen and speak to clients: yet in every case we are distanced from others' desire by language, whatever the setting.

Because word meaning is not rigidly fixed it is impossible to symbolise your experience perfectly, however poetic or clever you are. We all exist as linguistic beings for whom speech or symbols are necessary, and yet

---

[87] Although two dead philosophers, Carnap and the early Wittgenstein briefly believed in such a language.

[88] J Lacan, Seminar on Identification, unpublished, trans Gallagher, 15 November 1961.

[89] S Freud, The Disposition to Obsessional Neurosis, *SE 12,* [1913], 1976, p320.

necessarily traumatic, because language always misses speaking the exhaustive and comprehensive truth.

Trauma and memory

Trauma is a case of the impossible to say. Sometimes clients —prior to their explicit traumatic episode— managed to go about their everyday lives without too much trouble. Then they were involved in a car accident, or discovered as adults that they had been adopted and everything changed.

Often such clients will explain that the obvious or manifest traumatic experience such as the car accident or rape is what they cannot help recalling. They usually complain and say that they would like to be able to forget it.

No doubt this repeated involuntary recall allows the explicit trauma to be worked through a little further with each repetition, but it probably also works to cover up another —often far more important trauma— that has been unconscious for years prior to the explicit trauma that is being complained about. In these cases the fresh trauma functions as a protective screen, covering the older and greater trauma which has become 'reactivated' by the recent trauma.

So the more important trauma has often occurred many years ago, possibly when the client was a single child: and the arrival of a new baby brother or sister threw the tidy and privileged world of the single child into disorder, when he suddenly had to share his mother —on an unequal basis— with a needy baby. Early and more important traumas are buried in the unconscious and covered up with less important and more recent traumas, just like an archaeological site. This is why many of those diagnosed with 'post traumatic stress disorder' are surprised to find, in their therapeutic work, that they are re-evaluating many experiences that they had taken for granted or long forgotten, that had occurred *prior* to their recent trauma. Such recent traumas are like the punch line of a joke; both retrospectively change the meaning of all that came before in a surprising way.

In 'the talking cure', that is in psychoanalytic work, there is a putting into words, a symbolising of difficulties and traumas. This has the effect of metamorphosing the trauma, of changing the meanings that a particular phrase has for a client. So 'the trauma' is actually changed just by being spoken about. Speaking and acting on one's desire can allow the giving up of clumsy and costly symbolisations that made up the symptom, freeing libido, energy or drive for new or renewed love or work. But it is not possible to remove everything real from the client's speech so that the real becomes an empty category, containing nothing. We all have to live with the real, with the impossible to say. If we manage to find the words to say something that we could not say before, we can only do so at the cost of introducing new items in the real which we then cannot talk about. Language always introduces new indeterminacies, uncertainties and the renewed problems of communication. This is why Lacan argues that language is a universal trauma, or wound, although the form it takes for every person is unique.

How can you tell what is in the real for a subject? Lacan says that the real always returns. 'It' comes back, again and again, while each time 'it' —the object of repetition— may be different in some ways, the pattern or structure is the same. Freud had noticed that when somebody had a particularly difficult experience, a 'trauma' —something important that they had been unable to speak properly about— that some aspect of their experience would always return.

What form does this return take? It takes the form of 'the return of the repressed', an idea from Freud. The trauma always returns in a symbolic form but distorted by the ego and repressed through false connections, so that it is not consciously recognised. In this way the traumatised individual is 'protected' from coping consciously with their difficulty, and also benefits from a compensatory enjoyment. Unless you can consciously remember the relevant trauma, it will return, again and again to haunt you, in symbolic form, as a symptom, slip of the tongue, bungled action or dream.

You might find that your love affairs always last until your partner proposes marriage, or that whenever you speak to your grandmother, you don't know why, but you become depressed. Perhaps you always lose your keys on every birthday or anniversary?

Trauma returns disguised, as for instance as the phobia of a woman who was afraid of falling in public spaces, because she didn't want to be seen as 'a fallen woman', as one who acts on her sexual desire and lives with their conflictual consequences.

What are the differences between 'action and behaviour' and 'will and desire'?

It is possible for two or more people to behave in the same way, for example two alcoholics, or two people eating chips. Yet each person may have totally different reasons for their common behaviour. This fact allows 'behaviour' to be distinguished from 'action'; behaviour is a description of what appears to be taking place, such as drinking or eating: 'action' for Lacan is a very different category because it is also an account of desire, rather than simply of behaviour. So two people may both exhibit 'drinking behaviour', but perhaps only one has the desire to drink: the other may be acting on his demand rather on than his desire.

Both drinkers would no doubt claim 'I wish to drink', that is both have 'the will' to drink, but that is different from having 'the desire'. 'Will' is the conscious thought: desire is usually unconscious. In the case of the alcoholic repressed homosexual man we can see that he had the will to drink but not the desire: his desire was to be homosexual.

The distinction between will and desire is a crucial one to make in the clinic; 'will' is often what Lacanians understand as demand. Clients often claim to suffer their apparently inconvenient symptoms against their will, and present this as a kind of paradox to their clinician: but symptoms speak the truth about desire, not will. When people complain that they have had problems acting in a particular way, because 'I don't have the willpower'; what they probably mean is something like: 'I don't have the desire, I only have the demand for enjoyment and satisfaction.'

For your client to find the words to clearly speak his desire, instead of clumsily relying on his symptom — as a metaphor for the truth of his desire — may take years of difficult clinical work in which the enjoyment of the symptom may be given up, in whole or part, in order that their difficult desire be acted on.

What is sexual enjoyment —or 'jouissance'— and its relation to desire?

'Sensual Pleasure -but I will fence my thoughts round, and my words too: so that swine and hot fanatics shall not break into my garden!' [90]

' . . . I do not want to take leave . . . from that . . . severe sickness whose profits I have not yet exhausted . . . ' [91]

One dictionary defines jouissance like this:

> *'Jouissance [Fr., jouir enjoy]*
>
> *1. The possession and use of something advantageous or pleasing.*
>
> *2. Pleasure, delight; mirth, festivity'.* [92]

But in Lacanian psychoanalysis jouissance has a more technical meaning. Jouissance was theorised by Freud, although he didn't use the same word [93] when he referred to *'the kind of satisfaction which the symptom brings has much that is strange about it. We may disregard the fact that it is unrecognisable to the subject, who, on the contrary, feels the alleged*

---

[90] F Nietzsche, *Thus Spake Zarathustra,* Pelican, trans Hollingdale, [1892], 1961 p207.
[91] F Nietzsche, *The Gay Science*, trans Kaufmann, Vintage Books, [1887], 1974, p35.
[92] *The New Shorter Oxford English Dictionary* on CD-ROM, Oxford University Press, 1996.
[93] One of Freud's equivalents is 'Genuss'.

satisfaction as suffering and complains of it;' [94] and in his comment that '*The passing indications of sexual excitement which accompany the sexual act are employed by the [neuroses] as the most convenient and appropriate material for the construction of symptoms.'* [95]

To understand what Nietzsche, Freud and Lacan are referring to we ought to look at symptoms. In medicine the diagnosis of symptoms is usually in crucial part a visual matter: the trained eye of the doctor inspects the patient. The doctor sees the outward images or signs and then infers the identity of the underlying disease: in psychoanalysis identifying symptoms and diagnosing the underlying structure is very different. So much so that perhaps the word 'symptom' shouldn't be used for both. One big and obvious difference is that the psychoanalyst doesn't look: he listens.

The second big difference is that the psychoanalyst has no diagnostic manual in which he can look up fixed meanings of his client's words. Freud was the first to listen carefully to clients, studying their language rather than their images, and the first to investigate the unique meanings that key words had for each of his clients. He did not make the assumption that he always knew beforehand what his patients' words and associations meant.

This is demonstrated by two clients who had exactly the same outward 'symptom' or behaviour: anorexia, but where each client had completely different underlying problems. One anorexic's symptom was her attempt to symbolise her sexual abuse by her father, while the other anorexic had been traumatised by seeing her mother die painfully of breast cancer and became frightened becoming a woman with breasts, and suffering her mother's fate. So, because of the diversity of human life and language, there never could be a diagnostic dictionary of fixed meanings for psychoanalysis as there is, more or less, for medicine, where meanings are more fixed. The forms of human life are not fixed —except in so far as we all lack something— something unique in each case that is responsible for generating and maintaining our desires and subjectivity. One famous Lacanian, Ira Gershwin, identified the vital importance of this subjective lack: *'I got plenty o'nuttin', An nuttin's plenty for me'* [96]

Psychoanalysis is difficult for clients and analysts because there is no diagnostic dictionary to rely on; it is not always obvious what a client's symptoms are. A symptom might be any behaviour or act. It could be anxiety attacks, a nervous twitch, heterosexual behaviour carried out by a homosexual,

---

[94] S Freud, The Paths to Symptom Formation, Introductory Lectures on Psychoanalysis, *SE 15*, [1915], 1976, p366.

[95] S Freud, The Common Neurotic State, Freud, Introductory Lectures on Psychoanalysis, *SE 15*, (1915), 1976, p391.

[96] Lyrics from Porgy and Bess, 1935.

eating olives, working in a bank, anorexia or voting for a particular political party. The symptom is often something that clients complain about, but it can also be something of whose importance they are unaware.

Analysts when looking out for symptoms listen out for a special kind of sexual satisfaction, excitement or enjoyment; and it is this which Lacan was referring to when he coined the term 'jouissance'. 'Jouissance' is French for 'coming' as in orgasm. Lacan used this word because he thought that people take a sexual enjoyment in their symptoms, usually secretly.

Lacan distinguished human sexual satisfaction or 'jouissance' from 'pleasure', just as Freud had distinguished the categories of 'pleasure' on the one hand from 'satisfaction', 'enjoyment' and 'bliss' on the other. [97]

Jouissance is often an unconscious enjoyment. Lacan argued, along with Freud, that people often take sexual satisfaction or jouissance in all sorts of activities that appear to have nothing to do with sexual intercourse. 'Sexual' for Freud and Lacan is a technical term and covers far more than sexual intercourse. People are radically different from animals in the diversity of things that give them sexual enjoyment or jouissance. People and animals can get sexual satisfaction or enjoyment from smells, images, sensations, but only people can get sexual enjoyment from words, food and from an extraordinarily diverse range of objects including silk, rubber, black leather jackets and lamp posts.

Let's get back to the idea of jouissance as sexual enjoyment, and its connection with suffering. If you ask someone to tell you about their experience of orgasms, usually they will tell you what a wonderful thing an orgasm is. But imagine an experiment: if you were to stop someone having their orgasm just ten seconds before it was due, what do you think they would be experiencing? Extreme discomfort and pain. But people don't talk usually about the discomfort and pain, they only talk about the pleasure that comes afterwards. Now compare this situation with an hysteric, about whom we will find out more in Chapter Nine. Typically the hysteric complains: 'I suffer, the pain is terrible, I have such a terrible life.'

But hysterics won't usually tell you about the satisfaction that they take in complaining. No doubt such hysterics actually suffer, but they also enjoy their symptoms. Their enjoyment is usually unconscious: whereas the subject having an orgasm also suffers pain and discomfort, but it is usually unconscious, while s/he enjoys the orgasm consciously. So orgasms are a kind of hysterical symptom with a change of emphasis.

Come again? The pleasure in sex starts by gradually building, with a linear increase or acceleration of pleasure. Freud called this function the 'Pleasure Principle'. When the increase has been well established, the 'plateau phase'

---

[97] For example in 'Beyond the Pleasure Principle', *SE 18*.

begins, during which the pain and discomfort start setting in. This pain, which is the interruption of the linear increase of pleasure, becomes increasingly unbearable, until, finally, when the pain is at its height, there is a sudden release of jouissance, of sexual satisfaction.

	HYSTERIC'S SYMPTOMS	ORGASM
PAIN / SUFFERING	Conscious	Unconscious
SEXUAL ENJOYMENT/ JOUISSANCE	Unconscious	Conscious

The distinction between will and desire relies on the distinction between conscious and unconscious, and on the functions of forgetting, and of producing jouissance. For more on this topic see 'Jouissance, Pleasure, Pain and Consciousness' in the Appendix.

Forgetting and jouissance

Freud claimed that you will repeat some pattern of speech, behaviour or symptom until you die, or remember the underlying trauma; the repetition of the symptom stands in for the failure of conscious memory. The unconscious is something which comes as a package with language; if you have, or are had by language then you have an unconscious[98]. There is nothing that you can do about it, although you can change some of the items which are within your unconscious. If this were not true then there would be no point being analysed, that is, isolating and purifying your desire through analysing your language. In the course of an analysis some things which were unconscious become conscious, but there will always be things within the unconscious. The unconscious cannot be emptied. The real or impossible to say is always a category that is present in ordinary language and neurosis.

---

[98] This theme is elaborated under the heading of 'the Agency of the Letter' in the Appendix.

One important benefit of having an unconscious is the ability to forget. Imagine how impossible your life would be if you could not forget at least some of your difficulties and traumas? 'Forget' is derived from the old English words 'fore' and 'getan' which translates as 'away to get'.

What happens when there is a trauma? There is a kind of suffering or pain followed by a covering up or putting away. So something is taken out of consciousness; there is a voiding. It is this voiding or hiding suffering and pain that is associated with jouissance. At the point of orgasm the crucially important discomfort and pain that preceded it is voided and replaced with an enjoyment. These issues are developed in the appendix as 'Jouissance and arithmetic: division and multiplication'.

CHAPTER FIVE

What forms do conflict, love, desire and ideas take?

'The ways of what one must do as man or as women are entirely abandoned to the drama, to the scenario, which is placed in this field of the Other which, strictly speaking, is the Oedipus complex . . . The human being has always to learn from scratch from the other what he has to do, as man or as woman / . . . sexuality is established in the field of the subject by a . . . lack.' [99]

'The Oedipus myth means nothing else, if not that, at the origin . . . the desire of the father and the law are one and the same thing, and that the relationship between the law and desire is so close that nothing but the function of the law traces the path of desire, that desire, qua desire of the mother, for the mother, is identical to the function of the law. It is in so far as the law prohibits her that it imposes desiring her . . . a commandment is imposed, is introduced into the very structure of desire, that in a word one desires according to the commandment. What does the whole myth of Oedipus mean, if not that the desire of the father is what has made the law? [100]

How did Freud make sense of conflict, love, desire and ideas? Do they vary at random, or are they ordered in some way, possibly affecting each other?

For psychoanalysis there are two important dramatic, theatrical or mythical scenarios that are different versions of the same story: the 'Primal Horde' and 'Oedipus'. Freud and Lacan rely on these to help explain a surprisingly wide range of human phenomena including problems seen in the clinic such: phobia, hysteria, obsessional neurosis, perversion and psychosis, as well as the origin of laws and rules of all sorts, including the rules of grammar and word meanings. That is the universal stuff of language and ideas, and the popular taboo or rule against incest.[101]

[99] J Lacan, *The Four Fundamental Concepts of Psychoanalysis*, trans Sheridan, ed Miller, Penguin, [1964], 1979, p204.
[100] J Lacan, Seminar on Anxiety, unpublished, trans Gallagher, 16 January 1963.
[101] See J Atkinson, *Primal Law,* Longmans, Green, and Co, London, 1903.

Once Upon A Crime: The Myth of the Primal Horde

Society had to start somewhere: it didn't just arrive, ready-made with culture, families, rules, laws and language. How did humans, as speaking, socialised things come into being? Towards answering this question consider Freud's conjecture of primitive man, that '*it is probable that these human creatures had not advanced far in the development of speech.*' [102]

He speculated that such creatures formed the 'Primal Horde', that is the first group of pre-civilisation primitive women, children, and one man. The Primal Father was the dominant male who enjoyed full and exclusive sexual access to all the women of the horde: his sisters, daughters, aunts and his mother. The law or rule was that the Primal Father had whatever he wanted. It is not easy to imagine what this would have been like. It is clear that Freud was not claiming that this is exactly how things must have been, only that the Primal Horde is a kind of thought experiment, a way of understanding things. In fact he is reported as having said of the myth: '*Oh, don't take that too seriously. That's something I dreamed up on a rainy Sunday afternoon*'. [103]

It is also possible that the Primal Horde myth is a necessary idea for each of us, like the idea that we could not imagine life without the word or idea 'yes', or the number 'one'. The Primal Horde might be a version of a story that we have each imagined ourselves having a crucial imaginary role in. It seems to be necessary for children to imagine vivid stories; if they don't learn them from others they make them up for themselves. For Freud the story of the Primal Horde may have the status of one of these 'necessary stories'.

Life in the Primal Horde must have been uncertain and difficult with just one supposedly all-powerful male in charge. How long could such a situation last? For how many years could one ageing man remain sufficiently powerful to rule the roost? The answer to this question must have depended on the results of the Primal Father's sex with the women; children were born, amongst them sons. Freud thought that many sons would have been killed and eaten by the Primal Father, while a few, hidden by their mothers, survived.

What happened next seems revolutionary, surprising and necessary all at the same time. Some young men managed to grow up, hidden and protected from their murderous father by their mothers. They were in a very difficult situation; on the one hand the sons lived in dread that the Primal Father would discover and kill them, and on the other they were in awe and envy of his uninhibited enjoyment of the women, and, being young men, they were beginning to find

---

[102] S Freud, Moses and Monotheism, *SE 23*, [1939a], 1976, p81.
[103] A Kardiner quoting Freud in *Unorthodox Freud*, ed Crews, Viking, 1998, p36.

the idea that they would never have any sexual enjoyment with any women intolerable.

A short-term solution was found. The horny young men grew in strength and number, killed the Primal Father and ate him. But this raised a question: the Primal Father's desire had been the law. Did any order or structure exist without it? Nietzsche, presumably with this question in mind wrote:

'The will of one man is the command of another. Where there is no will there is anarchy. Anarchy precedes all acts of creation.' [104]

So now there was a dead father, some murderous, lustful and frightened sons and their sisters, daughters, aunts and mothers. What happened next? Each young man understood —as the realisation of his own myth— that he was faced with two alternatives that seemed mutually exclusive:

'If I copy the Primal Father and enjoy all the women, then I'll be eaten and dead, just like the Primal Father';

and:

'If I do not copy the Primal Father, and don't enjoy any women then I will not be eaten and I'll be alive, but I'll burn unbearably with lust'.

So —given these two simple, comprehensive and mutually exclusive formulae— if any son has sex with any woman he faces an intolerable consequence; being eaten: if he does not have sex with the women, again his life will be intolerable.

The murderous sons were each in an intolerable position, only a little different from that of the Jewish beggar who pleaded with the Baron Rothschild that he was starving. The Baron gave him some money. Later that day the Baron saw the beggar in an expensive restaurant, with his plate piled high with smoked salmon. The outraged Baron said: *'This morning I gave you money because you said you were starving: now I find you eating smoked salmon, how do you explain your action?'* The beggar said: *'When I am poor and starving, I can't eat smoked salmon, and when I have money, I can't eat smoked salmon, so tell me Baron, when can I eat smoked salmon?'*

Each murderous son found himself desperately wanting to enjoy women, and desperately wanting to live, without ending up as someone's dinner. We will pass over the very different routes taken through this impossible situation, until we turn to diagnosis, the Oedipus, and the differences between hysteria, obsessional neurosis, perversion and psychosis, each of which are different types of solution to the problems faced by the murderous sons of the Primal Horde.

---

[104] F Nietzsche, *My Sister and I*, Amok Books, Los Angeles 1990, p137.

A collective and revolutionary creation became a solution common to all. The young, men of the horde mutually agreed to create and sustain, God-like, a singular and remarkable entity that would take on a life of its own: the law, a set of laws or prohibitions symbolised by the writing on the Primal Father's gravestone.

The Primal Sons collectively decided that they would all obey and follow an idea, rule or law that would give each man *some* access to *some* of the women, but would not give *any one man* access to *all of* the women.[105] The law would also protect fathers from being murdered by their sons.

There have of course been many different ways of institutionalising these rules. It is probably true to say that every man and woman has their own version. In psychoanalytic work each version becomes detailed, along with an account of the costs and benefits.

The rules allowed each man the hope that he might enjoy some women, with a substantially reduced risk of being eaten, although there was still a risk of some fights over women and cannibalism. In general the conflicts between men over women no longer had to be fatal. Words or symbols, perhaps as legal action, could take the place of murderous deeds.

On a larger scale, rival families and clans kept the peace by trading the produce of the incest taboo. The men would make an exhibition of the fruit of their inhibition: virgin daughters and virgin sisters would be exchanged for other virgins —with someone to whom the incest taboo did not apply— or perhaps in return for goods or other rights, such as for the right to enjoy another clan's territory and hunting grounds. A legal term for such access is the 'enjoyment of rights'. Rape is an example of an 'enjoyment' to which there is no right. One focus for this issue has been the question 'Can a man rape his wife?' which until recently received the answer 'no' in England.

After the murder of the Primal Father the idea of women as a commodity —something with a definable and tradable value— became clearer. A central question for all hysterics, whether they are men or women, may be formulated as: 'what am I worth to the other?' Or 'what is the other's desire for me?'

As part of the law they created and institutionalised the young men of the horde agreed on a series of punishments that each would endure if he broke the law. With their invention of the law the horde ceased being a horde; they had teachers to teach the law, scribes to write the law, teachers, judges, police, lawyers and traffic wardens. Just as the helpless infant learns language to

---

[105] This idea of 'some' or 'not all' is also a reference to Lacan's theory of the different ways in which men and women enjoy. See Lacan's seminar 20 known as *'Encore'* or 'En corp', published by Norton as *On Feminine Sexuality, the limits of love and knowledge, Book 20, Encore 1972-1973*, trans Fink, 1998.

comprehend and survive his torturous mother, and in so doing ceases to be a helpless infant.

They had language, or were had by it. The fatherless horde progressed from a lawless chaos in which, as Freud had put it: *'human creatures had not advanced far in the development of speech'* to one where their lives appeared to be comprehensively structured by rules: the rules of grammar and word meaning, the rules against incest, as well as the rules about where you could not hunt, graze, grow your crops, drive your car, smoke, speak, eat, sleep . . .

The death of the Primal Father caused an explosive growth of the law and language, that is of symbolism or representation, or the phenomenon of one thing standing for another. There had to be such representation in order to discuss and legislate the taboos against incest and murder, and to police, judge and punish offenders. Any subject seeking the services of a lawyer is seeking representation, much as a symptom does.

The idea of 'one thing standing for another', that is the idea of 'representation' is central in understanding and applying Lacanian techniques. We will return to this theme later and to the question 'What represents whom for what?'[106]

The dead father and his tomb, with its inscriptions, represented the liberation and repression of the murderous first generation of lawmaker through the creation of the law. His death had given birth to the law, with all its costs and benefits. So a consequence of the death of the Primal Father was that every man benefited from protection by the law. Each man could enjoy some women in the knowledge that he need not die for it. Part of the price that each man must pay his enjoyment, for his rights under the law, is his guilt or debt for his part in the murder of the Primal Father. Kafka and Lacan explore the theme of 'Desire, guilt and The Law' in the appendix.

This is one reason why some men and women work so hard, investing so much when it comes to establishing their enjoyment, and the ways that their enjoyment is governed by unique 'rules'. Some people specialise in having affairs with people who are already in supposedly exclusive relationships with another. For every one of us there is a unique solution to the problematic question *'Where is my place in the economy of enjoyment?' How do I enjoy?*

The idea of debt may explain two phenomena: the guilt experienced by many young men whenever they are in the proximity of the police —the guardians of the law— and the popular fantasies of young boys who imagine that they have been responsible for saving the world from some terrible menace or disaster. Such a deed would presumably repay in full the debt they are looking to take

---

[106] We will explore Lacan's formulation: *'the signifier represents the subject for another signifier' (Ecrits*, trans Sheridan, Tavistock publications, London, Subversion of the Subject and Dialectic of Desire, 1977, p316) in Chapter Fourteen.

on, for their imagined reward of manhood and access to sexual enjoyment. But being an ordinary neurotic man requires the servicing of one's debt for a lifetime: a single early repayment with full redemption never happens in neurosis, but always in psychosis.[107]

Freud's understanding of the myth of the murder of the Primal Father also explains some religious doctrines. The idea for instance that every man throughout history is each individually guilty for the death of 'Jesus, our Father', 'who died for our us'. The eating and drinking of bread and wine, which many Christians believe are the authentic blood and body of Jesus, not just metaphors, recalls the sons of the Primal Father cannibalising their father's body.

These speculations about prehistoric anthropology may seem a long way from clinical practice but with the closely related myth of Oedipus, they allow us to start making sense of the diverse range of problems presented by clients.

Once Upon A Crime: the Myth of Oedipus

The story of Oedipus comes from an Ancient Greek play by Sophocles. There are three versions, so here is a summary: a young boy was cruelly raped by a king. The Gods decided to punish the king, so they arranged for him to learn of a prophecy: *the king would have a son who would grow up to kill him and marry his wife, the queen.*

The king was horrified and instructed a servant to kill his newborn son. But the servant disobeyed: instead, the little boy had his feet pierced with a chain, and was adopted by a couple who knew nothing of the boy's background. They removed the chain and called him 'Oedipus' which means 'swollen foot'. Oedipus grew up, knowing nothing of his father's crime or the prophecy. One day, in a classic case of road rage, he had an argument with a man in a chariot who im*ped*ed him. Oedipus killed him.[108]

Years later Oedipus became a great hero because he rescued a city threatened and besieged by a monster, by cleverly answering a riddle about feet. The monster asked Oedipus: *what is on four in the morning, two at midday, and three in the afternoon?*

---

[107] This heroic position was been taken up by Oedipus in his solving of the monster's riddle —which we will come to— and by Superman's and James Bond's world saving exploits. Another way to understand this idea of debt is as a kind of universal taxation on the ordinary neurotic use of language.

[108] This footnote is a note on a foot: the root of 'impediment' is a problem with a foot, and it was an impediment to patricide and incest that was absent in the case of Oedipus.

Perhaps due to the trauma his feet had endured, and because of his name, 'Swollen Foot', Oedipus was able to answer the monstrous riddle: *'A baby crawls on all fours, an adult stands on two, and an old man or woman get about with the help of a stick, making three.'*

Having saved the besieged city, thanks to the insight gained from his own wound or trauma, Oedipus did the obvious thing and married the queen, who happened to be a widow. Her widowhood was not surprising, given that Oedipus had years earlier killed his own father who had been her husband, the king. Oedipus and his wife-queen-mother had some children together and a series of plagues and disasters then struck the city, which were eventually revealed to be a punishment, sent by the Gods for incest and parricide, the crimes of Oedipus, who, in turn, was being punished for the sin of his father. When Oedipus discovered what he had done he was filled with shame, guilt and remorse and plucked out his own eyes.

So a father committed a crime that was partially paid for by his son, who having been symbolically marked or injured, killed his father, married his mother and blinded himself, symbolising his ignorance of his incestuous desire. This grisly end is just one example of the 'life sentence' that all those passing through the tragedy of the Oedipus complex must endure.

The foot trouble of Oedipus turned out to be both a blessing and a curse, just as language is for each of us. It caused him pain, and to struggle and cleverly solve the monster's play with words and so save the city. And it caused him to have a forbidden enjoyment with his mother: incest. In short, Oedipus's ignorance led him to pay a high price. Oedipus was his parents' symptom. His whole existence was focused on giving meaning to an act of his father's, his rape of a boy, and the transmission of this ancestral guilt. Transmission and transference always occur together and are difficult to disentangle without the help of psychoanalysis and other sciences.

If we choose ignorance, that is, not to have knowledge of our unique passage through the Oedipus, then we are likely to end up putting our foot in it. This 'out of sight-out of mind' approach that most of us take with the history of our separation led Oedipus to so much suffering that he choose to blind himself; a blind man could never fall in love because of what he saw, or become road enraged, causing him to murder his own father.

Freud's use of the Oedipus Myth

Freud did not claim that young boys or girls consciously wish to have sexual intercourse with their father or mother. Such a claim is obviously nonsense to anyone who has listened to children's wonderfully inventive theories of reproduction or sex. It has been repeatedly proven that humans do not intuitively understand or instinctively know what the biological facts of life are, and do not know what sexual intercourse is, or its consequences, without having been told. Many adolescents and even some adults are confused, or believe totally false theories about human reproduction, such as 'kissing can make you pregnant', or that 'sex only makes you pregnant if you are in love.' But ignorance of the biological facts of sexual life does not stop every child from having their own fantasy version of a kind of privileged enjoyment or special access that they alone have, with the parent they love the most. It is this special access to a kind of enjoyment with one of their parents that is primordial and taken up in the myth of Oedipus much more than the caricatured idea of genital intercourse.

Of course young children usually enjoy a profound intimacy with their mothers. But nearly always, as they grow up, particularly if a sibling is then born, their privileged place is threatened or vanishes. Someone else is judged to have taken his or her place. Someone or something separates them from their mother. It may be that the mother leaves her child to go to work or to care for another child. Lacan calls the agency that is identified with this separation 'the symbolic father'.

So these are stories of separation: of the child from the mother, of the sons of the Primal Horde from some of the women, and of Oedipus from his mother. But there is more to understanding the myths of the Primal Horde and Oedipus than 'simple separation', or loss; much follows from loss and separation; they are the cause of our suffering, desire, identifications, our ideas, language and culture.

Before we consider this we should try and compare humanity with other organisms, under the heading of instinct. Understanding the radically different role of instinct for people and animals explains why discontinuity (belief four) and variable meanings (belief one) are so essential in describing the human condition.

Not only is it unclear exactly what it means to be 'man' or 'woman', but even for monkeys it has been shown that when reared in isolation, they totally lack the know-how or instinct for sexual intercourse. One ethologist notes that in such circumstances : *'Sex behaviour was, for all practical purposes, destroyed; sexual posturing was commonly stereotyped and infantile. Frequently when an isolate [surrogate-raised] female was approached by a normal male, she would sit unmoved, squatting upon the floor — a posture in which only her heart was in the right place. Contrariwise, an isolate male might approach an in oestrus female, but he might clasp the head instead of the hind legs, and then engage in pelvic thrusts. Other isolate males grasped the female's body laterally, whereby all sexual efforts left them working at cross purposes with reality.*' [109]

With people, sexual know-how is still more indeterminate than it is for monkeys. One manifestation of this ignorance is the multitude of manuals offering to instruct people how to have sex. If there is a sexual know-how for people it is highly indeterminate and diverse, as can be seen in the enormous variety of human sexual practices relative to all other organisms.

An instinct is simply a piece of behaviour that is genetically programmed. This means that for any one species, all of the animals of similar age will behave in exactly the same way, when they are in the same circumstances. For a male stickleback fish 'seeing red' is not a metaphor; at the right time of year red reliably produces the identical instinctive mating behaviour. It could be another stickleback marked red, it could be a stick painted red or a red stamp. It makes no difference, all these red things produce the same instinctive behaviour in all male sticklebacks.

You have probably noticed that when given a particular stimulus —say something red— different people often do very different things, so it is not possible given our ignorance about our genes to claim that 'people have instincts for this or that behaviour'. In fact people appear to possess so little instinct, that they may as well be without. If your clients did have instincts, that is genetically programmed behaviours, then the meanings in your client's life would also be fixed, and you would probably have little effect working with their speech. [110]

What is extremely clear to any adult is that what it means to be a man, or a woman is not instinctive. That is we do not appear to have been genetically programmed to behave in specific sexual ways. This is easy to prove. If we were genetically programmed to behave sexually then most or almost all women would behave sexually in just one way or with one of a small set of behaviours, assuming that there were a few different genes for a few different behaviours, and so would men. But we know that neither men's nor women's sexual behaviour is uniform. There are professional celibates such nuns and monks, there are male and female paedophiles, the promiscuous, prostitutes of both genders, people who have sex with shoes, animals, only with blondes, with those with Cockney accents or moustaches. The idea that there are genes for these types of behaviour is simply ridiculous.

---

[109] H Harlow, reported in *Principles of General Psychology*, John Wiley and Sons, 1980.
[110] To date no genes have been discovered for adult behaviour. It is though widely thought that very young babies have a few instincts, which quickly fade, such as the 'rooting reflex', which instruct them to suckle.

Another problem for those who believe that genes direct our behaviour is the rate of change of human behaviours: the gene for telephone sex must have evolved very recently. So if people do not have genes for sexual behaviour, or at least a comprehensive set, what is it that determines their sexual behaviour? Freud and Lacan are very clear in their answer to this crucial question, about what it is that determines, uniquely for each one of us, the meaning of being a man or a woman. The object that is lost. Which object? They say that each of us has discovered an object that is uniquely absent in our own individual myth. This is the 'lost object', a topic we will return to in Chapter Fourteen. For an individual to be a man or a woman is a unique trauma. The empty place left in us, by the genes that lower animals have for their fixed sexual behaviours is taken by another structure: the structure of language. If the words or signifiers that make up language had fixed meanings then sexual identity —being male or female or something else— would also have fixed meanings, but the meanings of words changes, and so does sexual identity.

Now we can return to the question: how is it that desire, ideas and language have come to be so important for people? Because, according to Freud and Lacan[111] we have so little instinct that each human baby insists on a far longer period of dependency than any other organism.

A consequence of our lack of instinct is our prolonged dependency. Our separation from those we depend on to help us is uniquely drawn out. Human babies have the lengthiest and most torturous separation in the whole of the known animal kingdom. It is this period that allows the Oedipus complex to provide the many variations that take place that result in the variety of solutions and problems that we see in the clinic, and the exclusively human phenomenon of language and the universe of human culture. Freud's and Lacan's similar positions on the relative absence of man's instinct, and the consequent and unique presence of the '*loss of the object*' for each individual subject are clear in the following quotes where '*instinct*' has the standard biological sense of a 'fixed and standard predetermined behaviour'. Freud claimed that:

'*Man seems not to have been endowed, or to have been endowed to only a very small degree with an instinctive recognition of the danger that threatens him from without. Small children are constantly doing things which endanger their lives, and that is precisely why they cannot afford to be without a protecting object. In relation to the traumatic situation, in which the subject is helpless, external and internal dangers, real dangers and demands of the drive converge. Whether the ego is suffering from a pain which will not stop, or experiencing an accumulation of needs of the drive which cannot obtain satisfaction, the economic situation is the same, and the motor helplessness of the ego finds expression in psychical helplessness . . . In man, only that part of*

---

[111]   J Lacan, *The Psychoses*, ed Miller, trans Grigg, Routledge, London, 1993, p12.

this archaic heritage is appropriate which has reference to the loss of the object.' [112]

And Lacan said that:

'This is the basis of the distinction between the human world and the animal world: Human objects are characterized by their . . . indefinite proliferation. They are not dependent on the preparation of any instinct . . . What makes the human world a world covered with objects derives from the fact that the object of human interest is the object of the other's desire.' [113]

and:

'If psychoanalysis teaches us anything, if psychoanalysis constitutes a novelty, it's precisely because the human being's development is in no way directly deducible from . . . instincts.' [114]

Nietzsche, a philosopher who influenced Freud, claimed that:

'To stop an animal from moving forward in the course laid out for it by its natural instincts you have at least to hit it on the head with something hard. To obtain the same results with a man you only have to talk to him.' [115]

Lacan's similar position is that:

'Man is the subject captured and tortured by language.' [116]

In recognition of their subjectivity, children chant the playground lie 'Sticks and stones will break my bones but words will never hurt me'. One crucial difference between humans and animals is their innate defences and means of attack: people have soft skin, unprotected by fur, sharp teeth or poison:

According to the *Art of Warfare*: *'That animals have fangs in their mouths and carry horns on their heads, have claws in front and spurs on their heels, that they come together when happy and fight when angry —this is the natural condition— and there is no putting a stop to it. Thus, animals not equipped with natural weapons have to make their own defences.'* [117]

Man is one of the few animals without natural weapons and defences. We even lack the means for a speedy escape. Man's condition is that of being forcibly occupied by the unnatural defences and weapons of language. Just as some organisms are burdened by their weapons, as reindeer are by enormous antlers

---

[112] S Freud, Inhibitions Symptoms and Anxiety, *SE 20*, [1926d], 1973, p168.

[113] J Lacan, *The Psychoses*, ed Miller, trans Grigg, Routledge, London, 1993, p39.

[114] Ibid p189.

[115] F Nietzsche, *My Sister and I*, Amok Books, Los Angeles 1990, p41.

[116] J Lacan, *The Psychoses*, ed Miller, trans Grigg, Routledge, London, 1993, p243.

[117] Sun Pin, *The Art of Warfare*, trans Lau and Ames, Ballantine Books, New York, 1996, p29.

or the chilli by its fiery taste, so man is burdened by his defining characteristic, language, and the cost of the burden is far greater than that which any other animal bears. Language structures neuroses, psychoses, families, wars and all human culture.

In the Primal horde ideas and language were only articulated clearly when the sons symbolised their separation —with rules of the incest taboo— that denied each son the right to sexually enjoy his mother, sisters or aunts. It is this combination of our lack of instincts and natural weapons —that constitute our prolonged helplessness— and our potential for incest that constitute the conditions in which language dominates the human condition.

In the next 15 or 20 years sophisticated robots will produce and consume something like ordinary language. As such a robot's use of language approaches that of an ordinary person, we can expect these robots to fall over with neurosis and psychosis just like people.

Freud's theory of the Oedipus Complex again

'A neurosis without Oedipus doesn't exist.' [118]

Put simply Freud claims that there are two kinds of love: the love of 'objects' and the love of ideas or 'identifications'. The narcissistic love of oneself qualifies as love for an object: the love of ideas or ideals arises out of the interruptions and problems we have with our loss and love for objects. Ideas are born as a consequence of the existence of objects lost and disappointed love relations.

Sexual difference, gender and sexuality are subjected to the vagaries and vicissitudes of language. What does it mean to be a man? What does it mean to be a woman? Every subject has a unique answer to each of these questions because we are not pre-programmed with specific instincts for sexual behaviour but are pre-programmed instead with a lack or absence of sexual knowledge or instinct. This lack of a given or prior sexual knowledge or know-how has clinical consequences, and can be understood as a loss, to which each of us finds a unique solution. The clinician cannot justify taking a position of knowledge from which he can safely redirect 'the client's misguided conduct and beliefs' such as are focused on by 'cognitive analytic therapy' and 'rational emotive therapy'. One illustration of the radical absence of sexual knowledge is the idea of 'sexual abuse'. 'Sexual abuse' has a wide variety of legal and clinical definitions. Invariably these definitions rely on the idea of power being used by one individual in order to gain sexual satisfaction from an other who has less power.

---

[118] J Lacan, *The Psychoses*, ed Miller, trans Grigg, Routledge, London, 1993, p201.

Power and Abuse

'Power' —who has it and how they exercise it— often turns out to be a highly problematic issue for clients. For this reason it is important for the psychoanalyst to abstain from power relations with clients. The psychoanalyst's duty is to provide interpretations, including the ending of sessions. This may appear obvious but it is certainly not a universally held belief. For instance, one guide to counselling advises that *'it is important to reject the pursuit of authority or control over others and to seek to share power.'* [119]

How might a clinician 'share power'? Is power like a cake over which the clinician has exclusive control and possession, and which he can hand out according to his will? If the clinician uses any power beyond the minimum of suggestion required for clinical practice, such as directing the client to say whatever comes into their mind and ending sessions then the client's work is likely to be obstructed.

There is no question of the clinician 'sharing his power': the clinician must not use 'his power' beyond this minimal set; the position and work of the clinician can only take place because he has not used the power that clients often wildly attribute to him. Being a psychoanalyst requires that the one's power remains a kind of reserve that —if ever used— would prevent clinical work from proceeding: keeping it in reserve allows psychoanalysis to take place. It is solely by virtue of the analyst not using any power —in the ordinary sense of the word— that the treatment is able to take place.

Just how widespread are discrepancies of power? If Freud and Lacan are correct then the family and society, gender and each of our lives are constructed on the premise that power is unequally distributed. The inaugural discrepancy is between the powerlessness of the infant who does not speak and the power of the speaking parent. This profoundly discrepant power relation is the foundation of all that is human. The powerless child first enters the slave master relation with the powerful mother, as the slave to her demands and desires.

One of the most remarkable facts about people is that we derive a sexual satisfaction from such an extraordinarily wide variety of acts. Freud observed that one popular source of sexual satisfaction for good mothers are their children:

'A child's intercourse with anyone responsible for his care affords him an unending source of sexual excitement and satisfaction from his erotogenic zones. This is especially so since the person in charge of him, who after all is,

---

[119] D Mearns and B Thorne, *Person Centred Counselling In Action*, Sage, London, 1988, p54.

as a rule, his mother, herself regards him with feelings that are derived from her own sexual life: she strokes him, kisses him, rocks him, and quite clearly treats him as a substitute for a complete sexual object.' [120]

The conclusion here then is that to be male or female is to have been powerless and to have been enjoyed sexually by an other who possessed power. To speak as 'a man' or as 'a woman' is to establish beyond doubt that you have already been sexually abused. There is not one single neurotic who has not been sexually abused, who has not come to their own version of sexual identity through their unequal struggle for pleasure, love, identification and power, and through subjection to their Other's power. The Other is in a special power relation to the subject because the Other has determined their subjectivity.

Without the necessary reliance that mothers and fathers have on their power, in relation to their powerless infants, humanity and language would not exist. Human existence is necessarily conflict-ridden because of the necessity of conflicts of interest and power relations. If there were no power relations we could give up all of our conflicts. Would all then be well? No! Humanity would rapidly become extinct because we even lack the instinct for mating, and, without being instructed we would fail to copulate. The indeterminacy of gender, sexual identity and sexual knowledge plague and torture humanity, while at the same time being one of the essential ingredients that press us to speak and enjoy.

The idea that we should renounce all hatred and conflict and comprehensively love everyone ignores the fact that the human condition is fundamentally premised on loss. It is this loss, which leads to the necessary conflict that always comes as a package with love[121]. This conclusion is mostly a cocktail of the ideas introduced as beliefs two and five.

The concept of 'abuse' insists on a comparable reference as a contrast: on the idea of 'use' as correct or proper. But there is no single example of the 'proper use of sexual enjoyment'. Even the popular example of heterosexuality between consenting adults is problematic. Every single example of sexual enjoyment takes place in the context of pain and power. This is even true of solitary masturbation. During the plateau phase, prior to orgasm, the subject experiences an accelerating and ultimately high level of discomfort and pain. Without this suffering there would be no enjoyment. An essential part of the fundamental fantasy of a neurotic is a power relation: he who suffers and enjoys orgasm always does so with reference to the power of the Other. *'You*

---

[120] S Freud, Three Essays on Sexuality, *SE 7*, [1905], 1973, p223.
[121] Love is a consequence of loss, yet the necessity of loss is usually associated with 'evil'!   See footnote 529 on page 350 for a development of this idea.

make me feel . . . ' describes how the Other is attributed with a power to cause sensations in the subject, and recalls the mother infant relation.[122]

I am not claiming that those who have experienced what falls into the category of sexual abuse for legal purposes have not often suffered an extra, specific and damaging trauma. I am claiming that sexual identity for all people could not exist without cruel and vital discrepancies in the amounts of power that people exercise over each other in love and other relations. Those who have been 'sexually abused' in the legal sense have typically had their eyes forced open to some of the discrepancies of power that all neurotics have suffered but often choose to remain unconscious of.

Girls and the Oedipus complex

The part taken by girls and boys in respect of the Oedipus complex is not the same.[123] The passage of the girl through the Oedipus is not the same as the boy's. Freud claimed that the girl *'slips along a symbolic equation'* from the phallus. Unfortunately Freud sometimes confused the 'penis' with the 'phallus'—whatever form it may take— with a baby[124] although it is perfectly clear that he often intended 'phallus' by his use of 'penis', as in, for instance:

'Yes, in . . . [the fetishist's] mind the woman has got a penis, in spite of everything; but this penis is no longer the same as it was before. Something else has taken its place, has been appointed its substitute, as it were, and now inherits the interest which was formerly directed to its predecessor. But this interest suffers an extraordinary increase as well, because the horror of castration has set up a memorial to itself in the creation of this substitute . . . It remains a token of triumph over the threat of castration and a protection against it. It also saves the fetishist from becoming a homosexual, by endowing women with the characteristic which makes them tolerable as sexual objects.'
[125]

Rather than facing the dramatic life and death oppositions of the boy's Oedipus, which we shall come to in more detail in Chapter Ten on obsessional neurosis, the girl often imagines that she is to receive the value of a gift. So a

---

[122] For an elaboration of this theme see Freud's 1919e paper 'A Child is being Beaten', *SE 17.*

[123] Freud's key papers on this topic are: On Transformations of Drive as Exemplified in Anal Eroticism, 1924, *SE 7*, and: The Downfall of the Oedipus Complex,' [1924d)], *SE 19*, Female Sexuality, [1931], *SE 7*, Three Essays on the Theory of Sexuality [1905] and: Some Psychical Consequences of the Anatomical Distinction between the Sexes, *SE 19,* [1925j].

[124] S Freud, The Downfall of the Oedipus Complex, , *SE 19* [1924d].

[125] S Freud, Fetishism, *SE 21*, [1927], 1973, p154.

boy typically represents a debt: a girl a gift. Debts get repaid *with interest*, while gifts are exchanged or 'given away', as women are in marriage. What is her value exactly? 'Her dowry' is one answer, the ability to produce others who will then produce valuable debt with interest payments, in the form of sons, is another. The question of value cannot be determined privately, without reference to any others because 'value' is a necessarily social concept. This is one reason why women tend to be hysterics; they understand the fundamental truth that value is defined by the Other, that is by exchange, trade or shopping. Note the common theme of the little girl's identification with an object identified with the father. For Freud:

'The girl's Oedipus complex is much simpler than that of the small bearer of the penis; . . . it seldom goes beyond the taking of her mother's place and the adopting of a feminine attitude towards the father. Renunciation of the penis [Lacan would substitute 'phallus' for 'penis'] is not tolerated by the girl without some attempt at compensation. She slips —along the line of a symbolic equation . . . from the penis to a baby. Her Oedipus complex culminates in a desire, which is long retained, to receive a baby from her father as a gift— to bear him a child . . . It must be admitted, however, that in general our insight into these developmental processes in girls is unsatisfactory, incomplete and vague.' [126]

Whereas in Lacan: *'For the woman, the realisation of a sex is not accomplished in the Oedipus complex in any way symmetrical to that of the man's, not by identification with the mother, but on the contrary by identification with the paternal object, which assigns her an extra detour . . . But the disadvantage the woman finds herself in with respect to access to her own sexual identity, with respect to her sexualisation as a woman, is turned to her advantage in hysteria owing to her imaginary identification with the father, who is perfectly accessible to her, particularly by virtue of his position in the composition of the Oedipus complex. For the man, on the other hand, the path is more complex.* [127]

We will return to women, questions of the nature of the phallus, to 'objects' and their relation to the myths of Oedipus and the Primal horde later. Before we can explain diagnosis in terms of the Primal Horde and Oedipus there is one more crucial concept, without which psychoanalysis cannot take place: 'transference'.

---

[126] S Freud, The Downfall of the Oedipus Complex, [1924d], 1973, *SE 19*, p178-9.
[127] J Lacan, *The Psychoses*, ed Miller, trans Grigg, Routledge, London, 1993, p172.

What is 'transference' and what does it have to do with conflict, love, desire and ideas?

'We mean a transference of feelings on to the person of the doctor, since we do not believe that the situation in the treatment could justify the development of such feelings. We suspect, on the contrary, that the whole readiness for these feelings is derived from elsewhere, that they were already prepared in the patient and, upon the opportunity offered by the analytic treatment, are transferred on to the person of the doctor. Transference can appear as a passionate demand for love . . . transference is present in the patient from the beginning of the treatment and for a while is the most powerful motive in its advance. **We see no trace of it and need not bother about it so long as it operates in favour of the joint work of analysis.** *'* [128]

' . . . the patient is frightened that she is transferring onto the figure of the [clinician] the distressing ideas which arise from the content of the analysis. This is a . . . regular occurrence. ***Transference onto the physician takes place through a false connection*** *[that is through the ego].* *'* [129]	*'What distinguishes this . . . animal [my dog] from . . . the . . . man [who] speaks . . . is that . . . she never takes me for another . . . by taking you for another, the subject puts you at the level of the Other with a big O. It is precisely this which is lacking to my dog'/// 'One must start from the fact that transference, in the final analysis, is the automatism of repetition. And moreover we arrive here at the point where transference appears as . . . a source of fiction. The subject in transference pretends, fabricates, constructs something and it then seems that it is not possible not to integrate immediately into the function of transference this term which is first of all: what is the nature of this fiction, what on the one hand is its source, and on the other hand its object?' /// 'In order to situate what the place of the analyst should be in the transference . . . this relationship or this situation can only be engaged on the basis of a misunderstanding. It is clear that there is no coincidence between what the analyst is for the analysand at the beginning of analysis and what precisely the analysis of the transference is going to allow us to unveil as regards what is implied, not immediately, but what is truly implied, by the fact that a subject engages in this adventure, which he does not know about, which is analysis.'* [130]

---

[128] S Freud, General Theory of the Neuroses, Transference, *SE 16,* [1917], 1976, p442-443. This idea is repeated in 'On Beginning the Treatment', *SE 12,* [1913a], 1976, p139.

[129] S Freud, Psychotherapy of Hysteria, *SE 2,* [1893], 1976, p302.

[130] J Lacan, Seminar on Identification, unpublished, trans Gallagher, 29.11.61.

Freud's and Lacan's theories of transference explain that *whenever* a symbol or letter is heard, moves, or is written, there is transference. We will explore this idea of symbolism or letters moving under the heading 'the agency of the letter' in the appendix. Freud's German word for 'transference' is *'ubertragung'*, but importantly this word also means 'translation'. Transference is a kind of translation, and every translation insists on some transference. Translation or transference are a kind of carrying over or moving of something to another place, perhaps an image, a demand or love or some words or letters.[131]

Transference is not a rare and isolated phenomena, to be found exclusively in psychoanalytic consulting rooms. Transference is everywhere. You are reading this book because of your transference, to the bookshop you bought it in perhaps, to the publisher, to the author or perhaps an image or phrase on the cover? You supposed this book to contain something that will be of value to you. It's not certain that this supposition is justified. Your guessing or prejudging which book is for you now is a task that insists on transference, on a supposition of knowledge. There is always transference attached to every word we speak, write, read or hear. Your choice of a film will be due perhaps to your transference to an actress, director, or genre of film. You phone a friend, visit a country or a restaurant because of your transference, although there may be other reasons, causes and explanations.

In the clinic the effects of transference can be observed in a specially purified environment. Because nothing of any direct practical value goes on in the psychoanalytic clinic, and because the clinician should not disclose his transference or have much to say about his desire, a special focus is allowed on his client's transference. The only desire the psychoanalyst can safely and consistently express is his desire for his client's desire. This is one reason why psychoanalysis is unique; psychoanalysis provides a privileged playground for the client's transference, with a universe of imaginary and symbolic playmates.

Transference is like friction. Imagine trying to walk on a surface with which you have zero friction, like an extreme version of an ice skating rink. However much you try it will be impossible. Now imagine the opposite, trying to walk on a surface where extremely high levels of friction exist because your shoes are glued or nailed down. Again walking will be impossible because the forces against you will be too high. Without the friction and resistance of transference psychoanalysis would be impossible. Whenever letters are spoken, written or heard transference occurs. But psychoanalysis requires a particular kind of transference, and a particular quantity of transference. Without it no important work will take place. And if the transference is of too great a quantity, that is,

---

[131] This theme is elaborated in the appendix under: 'A note on the *"Ubertragung"* of Freud' —German for both 'translating' and 'transference'.

with too high a level of friction, then no movement or clinical work will be able to take place.

In transference an image or idea of the other is carried over or projected on to someone else, or something other, where that someone else is not the original love object. There may also be a transfer of love or hate and supposed knowledge to a new person. If a man's mother had a big nose, he may marry a woman with a big nose because he 'mistakes' his wife for his mother; he transfers or translates his love for his mother to his wife.

What does fantasy do?

'Fantasy . . . at the level of interpretation, plays the function of an axiom in it, namely, is distinguished from the variable laws of deduction which specify in each structure the reduction of symptoms, by figuring there in a constant mode.' [132]

'The neurotic it can be seen . . . only approaches the fantasy through opera-glasses, so busy is he sustaining the desire of the Other by keeping it in suspense in different ways. The psychoanalyst would do well not to make himself its servant.' [133]

The most important function of fantasy is to help keep desire going. Desire is the stuff of life, the most important fact of human existence, but it is at the mercy of something variable, word meanings, manifest as the desire of others. So how does fantasy help maintain desire given the flux of word meanings? By fixing so as to reduce the variable effects of word meanings:

'We know, something analysis has shown us, has found, that what the subject has to deal with, is the object of the fantasy in so far as it presents itself as alone being capable of fixing a privileged point . . .' [134]

Usually an individual's fantasies are variations on a single theme. Lacan called the single underlying fantasy that generates these variations the 'fundamental fantasy'. Because the subject's fantasies are all similar they have the effect of minimising the variations in meaning, which might otherwise cause a problem for desire. Here is one example: if you desire your lover, but your lover is on the other side of the planet, what do you do? Why does your desire not disappear, in the absence of its object? How do you prevent your desire from flagging? You wheel in fantasy which functions to keep desire roughly constant, within tolerable limits.

---

[132] Lacan's summary of the seminar of 1966-1967. (Year book of the Ecole Pratique des Hautes Etudes) trans Gallagher, *The Letter*, Spring 1999, p92-4.
[133] Ibid, p95.
[134] J Lacan, Transference Seminar, unpublished, trans Gallagher 19 April 1961.

Fantasy not only functions to maintain desire but also has a determining role in the construction and maintenance of the symptom, because of the relation that desire has to the symptom. Perhaps it is because fantasies of making love in public spaces are popular with women that most of those with phobias of public spaces are women?

Further Reading

Zizek, S The Seven Veils of Fantasy, Rebus Press, in *Key Concepts of Lacanian Psychoanalysis*, edited by Nobus, London 1998.

CHAPTER SIX

Diagnosis

A diagnosis or structure cannot be 'read off' from a person's behaviour or appearance in any simple way, as it often is in medicine. Freud and Lacan focussed on the apparently few underlying structures that generate the bewildering variety of symptoms. Given that symptoms can take any form, such as drinking alcohol, eating olives, heterosexuality or gardening, and that any symptom can have any meaning or meanings, what is the psychoanalytic idea of health or a cure? This is a difficult question. In Freud's and Lacan's theory life itself is pathological, conflictual or 'dis-ease'. What does disease mean in general? Disease is not something that may happen to living things; disease is a necessary condition of life, for all living things. Everything that lives is necessarily diseased, for as long as it lives. Death is the only absolute cure: there is no 'healthy state', free of disease.

The problems that get so much attention from psychoanalysis are not suffered exclusively by just a few diseased people but by all of us. There is no human being who is not either psychotic, perverse or neurotic. This way of thinking is radically different from most American therapies and from the school of Ego Psychology where the clinicians claim that after completing their treatment you will end up 'healthy, in part or whole, with a part of your ego telling you the truth about reality. For Lacan and Freud, the different pathologies exhaustively describe humanity: there is no special extra category of 'health' that allows one to avoid the truth distortions of the ego. We will explore the possibilities that this leaves for a cure in the last chapter.

What are the clinical structures and why is diagnosis crucial?

In accordance with Freud's ideas Lacan identified a set of diagnostic categories or 'psychic structures' that are thought to be comprehensive, although more detailed research is called for. Both claimed that there are four different structures in three groups: psychosis, perversion, and the three main neuroses: phobia, hysteria and obsessional neurosis. To understand this diagnostic universe we will have to look more closely at some of the five basic beliefs introduced in Chapter One.

Some regard Freud's and Lacan's diagnostic universe with scepticism, distrusting diagnostic systems and categories as arbitrary, or intruding unnecessarily on clinical work. But remember that if you want to work psychoanalytically, ordinary ideas or common sense just don't do the job.

Presumably that is why you are reading this. You cannot make much sense of a client's suffering or symptoms with common sense, or help enable him to change his position. For effective clinical work you must have a workable theory, just as a mechanic has his tools and his theory of how engines work. You might change your theories over time for better ones, but —for as long as you work— you will always find a use for theory, and the best use will be made of the best theory. One of the best ways to improve a theory is to test or use it, noting its shortcomings, which will inform the construction of the next theory.

Until recently atoms of carbon always took only one of three very different forms or structures: soft black charcoal, graphite —the black silvery, slippery stuff of pencils— and diamond, one of the hardest substances, and usually transparent! These three categories completely exhausted the forms of carbon. There was no known example of a carbon atom that had not taken one of these forms. However each collection of carbon atoms is unique; no one diamond is the same as any other, yet all diamonds share the same underlying molecular underlying molecular structure. No one piece of charcoal is the same as any other, yet all bits of charcoal share the same structure. Every person is structured as psychotic, perverse or neurotic, yet every person is different. All hysterics have certain things in common, just as every obsessional is also unique but again share structural aspects of his psyche with every other obsessional. There are different subcategories within these main types but they are not considered here. Fairly recently a new fourth form of carbon molecule was created, called 'Buckminsterfullerene'. In the same way it is possible that Freud's and Lacan's diagnostic categories will come to be detailed.

If you don't have a diagnostic system then how will know what to do with different clients? They are clearly not 'all the same', and there are also clearly profound similarities between certain clients. It is crucial to have a hypothesis as to whether any particular client you are working with is either neurotic or psychotic. Why? There are two reasons: your variable diagnoses ought to closely inform your variable techniques, and you may find that there are some clients you would rather not work with. So you will need a tool for separating those you want to work with from the rest.

The methods and techniques that are used to treat clients with different diagnoses are often very different, and sometimes exactly the opposite of each other. If you do not diagnose you will sooner or later use the wrong technique and risk being responsible for sparking off a psychotic breakdown and causing much unnecessary suffering. Some clinicians have been very surprised when they accidentally caused their client to have a psychotic breakdown for the first time, because they were unaware that their client was psychotic. This can only happen if a client's structure had not been correctly diagnosed. A correct diagnosis is sometimes difficult to achieve. Careful and experienced clinicians are occasionally startled to discover that their client has a psychotic structure, rather than a neurotic one as they had earlier diagnosed. A more common error of diagnosis is not a psychoanalytic one but psychiatric: psychiatrists often diagnose psychosis in their reliance on the Diagnostic Statistical Manual, when the client would have been diagnosed as hysterical from a Freudian or Lacanian perspective.

Working with psychotics is very different from working with neurotics. A psychotic will always have a psychotic structure. It cannot change its type whatever clinical work you do, or however long you do it for. Neurotics can change their specific neurotic structure, from obsessional neurosis to hysteria, or from hysteria to obsessional neurosis: but no neurotic ever became psychotic, and no psychotic ever became a neurotic.

Some clinicians have no interest in working with psychotics and regard such work as similar to housekeeping: the work goes on indefinitely. But others report that very careful work with some psychotics appears to produce permanent and helpful changes allowing them to love and work, outside hospitals and sometimes without debilitating medication.

One interesting technique used with psychotics with some success involves carrying out the clinical work with a different language from their mother tongue, insisting that the client speaks in a language with which he is not initially at home. This method perhaps functions to impose a more explicitly detailed and effective imposition of the Other of language, and may work to de-emphasise the imaginary narcissistic image that psychotics are plagued by, that arose in their relation with their mother's tongue and their self image reflected in her eyes.

The experience of working with psychotics is importantly different from working with neurotics. Work with psychotics is focused on the policy of strengthening their fragile egos, on supporting the often weak neurotic facade that psychotics rely on to hold their delicate world together. Working with psychotics is often challenging and draining, and is commonly complicated by involvement with external agencies such as the police, psychiatric hospitals and lawyers.

Another non-existent diagnostic category for Freud and Lacan, in addition to 'borderline psychosis' is the currently popular 'personality disorder'. This is something of a dustbin category into which those clients who do not obviously fit into the other psychiatric categories are placed.

It is not possible to make a neurotic psychotic, and that it is not possible to make a psychotic neurotic. So while clinical technique is important, and in most or all cases it is possible for harm to be caused, there is a sense in which you will not be able to drive neurotic clients 'crazy'.

There are some problems of diagnosis that arise for both clinical and theoretical reasons that we will return to: from the subject's point of view, finding your way around Lacanian structures is not difficult; there is a single diagnostic road down which everyone travels. At a very early point there is a left turning, a one-way road to psychosis. Once an individual has started down this road there is no return. If you continue past the turning to 'psychosis' you will come to a roundabout called 'anxiety hysteria' or 'phobia'. These are two names for what is structurally the same thing. You can go around this roundabout many times, and it seems that this is exactly what most children do, sometimes exhibiting extreme and dramatic behaviours which —if adults carried them out— would probably lead to their admission to a psychiatric hospital. But this roundabout appears to remain open to neurotic adults. There are cases of adult hysterics becoming obsessional, and vice versa.

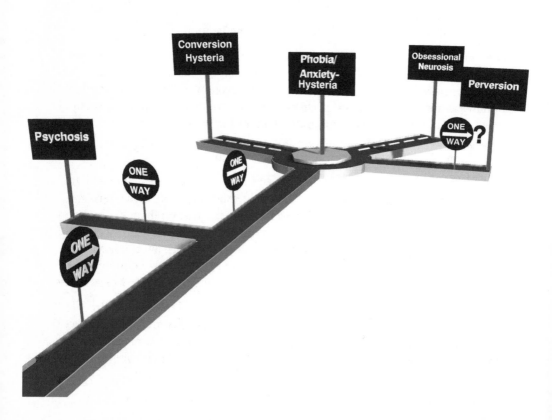

Here is a summary of the different clinical structures and how they can change
—or fail to change— in the course of clinical work:

STRUCTURE AT THE END OF CLINICAL WORK

STRUCTURE AT THE START OF CLINICAL WORK	Hysteria (anxiety, conversion or phobia)	Obsessional Neurosis	Perversion	Psychosis
Hysteria (anxiety, conversion or phobia)	possible	possible	possible	impossible
Obsessional Neurosis	possible	possible	possible	impossible
Perversion	uncertain	uncertain	uncertain	impossible
Psychosis	impossible	impossible	impossible	necessary

The most important diagnostic group for most clinicians is the neuroses, that is
hysteria and obsessional neurosis, unless you are working with a special
population, perhaps in a psychiatric hospital or with the long term homeless
where psychosis is more common.

Note that a client may present as someone who has been sexually abused,
another as someone with confusion regarding his sexual orientation, and a third

as 'depressed' but it is certainly possible that all three clients, whatever their presenting problems are within the same Freudian and Lacanian diagnostic category, for instance hysteria.

Chronology, logic and pathology or 'pathologic'—diseased logic

The five following chapters are concerned with the five different structures found in the clinic, introduced in the order in which the underlying structures are formed rather than in the order in which the surface symptoms appear.

Psychosis is the first possible structure, although its symptoms often first emerge in late adolescence or middle age. A few cases of childhood psychosis have been observed but they all appear to be within a specific sub-category of psychosis and may be some variety of autism. After the possibility of a psychotic structure forming has passed, the next structure to be formed is phobia, a highly elastic kind of hysteria that can be staging post for all the other structures: conversion or anxiety hysteria, obsessional neurosis and perversion.

CHAPTER SEVEN

The first diagnostic structure: Psychosis

Psychosis is in some ways the most dramatic and extraordinary of the clinical structures. Psychotics caricature the popular idea of 'the mad person' and are often unable to follow a career or intimate long-term relationships for some or for all of their lives. Psychotics may have hallucinations of voices, and be uncomfortably conscious of being looked at. Remember these phenomena of 'the gaze' and 'the voice' when we return to question the nature of objects in Chapter Fourteen. These hallucinations are often accompanied by grandiose and persecutory erotomaniacal ideas. Some psychotics are paranoid and believe that television newscasters are personally addressing them, that aliens are monitoring and controlling their thoughts, or that they alone are responsible for the welfare of the nation. Beliefs such as 'I am Jesus Christ', or that 'Aliens are following me' are not unusual. These symptoms can be understood as a grandiose emphasis on their absent Other.

Subcategories of Psychosis

Freud and Lacan used the following subcategories within psychosis: 'paraphrenia', 'schizophrenia', 'paranoia' and 'manic depression'. Elaborating these diagnostic categories, and their relation to autism, and all of these to Lacan's theory of psychosis responsibly calls for a lengthy essay on the history and practice of psychiatry, which you won't find here.

Autism is a complex category that is often regarded as a kind of psychosis. Because 'autism' covers a particularly divergent range of presenting symptoms each case of autism should be considered on an individual basis. In some cases where a great deal of clinical work has been done with autistic children over many years a psychotic structure has become far more obvious.[135]

'Asperger's syndrome' is regarded as within the category of autism yet it is certain that many of those with Asperger's are not psychotic: some are clearly obsessional neurotics while others are hysterics. Whatever the diagnosis from the psychiatric, medical or psychological point of view it is crucial that

---

[135] Lacanian work in this field includes Autism and Topology, *Drawing the Soul*, Rebus Press, Burgoyne B, 2000. See also *The Birth of the Other*, Rosine Lefort, & Robert Lefort, Urbana and Chicago, Illinois University Press, and From Autism to Psychosis, L Guimaraes, *The Clinical Florilegium of the year 2000*, World Association of Psychoanalysis, 1994, and L Rodriguez, At the Limits of the Transference: Psychoanalysis and Autism, p73.

psychoanalytic diagnosis be made independently for each subject, relying on a study of each subject's language.

Autism viewed from a psychoanalytic perspective challenges the current popular theory proposed by Barron-Cohen [136] and others who argue that autistics are without an account or theory of others' minds. The aversion and intolerance that many autistics clearly demonstrate to manifestations of others' minds, such as the other's gaze, surely suggests the opposite, that autistics do possess a theory of others' minds, and a response and sensitivity to their Other that is more dramatic than that of most neurotics?

Diagnosing psychosis: can a subject be just 'a bit psychotic' or 'a borderline case'?

Freud and Lacan argued that you can't be a bit psychotic. Psychosis is like pregnancy: you can't be 'a bit pregnant'. You either are, or are not psychotic. This position is importantly different from Melanie Klein's: she thought that we are all a bit psychotic, but that some of us are more psychotic than others. Some other schools use the idea of 'borderline psychotic'. This, for Lacanians is a clear case of professional fence sitting; 'borderline' refers to a clinician who is on the border of being able to make a diagnosis.

Assessing this important difference between the approaches of Klein and Lacan is complicated by two facts that often make it difficult to diagnose psychosis. We have already met the first problem of the same outward behaviour often having different underlying psychic structures. For example three alcoholics can have three totally different psychic structures. That is to say, although they have the same manifest symptom, drinking, it may have three quite different functions. This clinical fact is also a consequence of the variation in word meaning: in this case the meaning of the word *'alcoholic'*. 'Alcoholic' does not refer to any underlying psychic structure, but to behaviour. The same variation in meaning applies to all or almost all psychiatric categories and diagnoses because psychiatric diseases are generally diagnosed with an emphasis on observable behaviour rather than the underlying structures that generate the client's language and behaviour.

There are some important consequences of not being able to 'read off' a clinical structure from a behaviour: a psychoanalyst cannot legitimately claim to be an expert or specialist in alcoholism or anorexia or any other type of behavioural category, whatever their experience in working with that variety of behaviour. There is nothing to suggest that the speech of anorexics is uniform, any more

---

[136] S Baron-Cohen, *Mindblindness An Essay on Autism and Theory of Mind*, Cambridge, MA, MIT Press, 1997.

than the speech of alcoholics is. In order to diagnoses a client's structure we have to study their individual speech: not their behaviour. So, for example, some of those who are often diagnosed by psychiatrists as 'manic depressive', are psychotic, while others are hysterics. There are examples of symptoms that seem to mimic psychosis —for psychiatric purposes— such as hysterics who also hear voices and sometimes believe that they are being persecuted; so the diagnosis of psychosis is not always straightforward.

The second problem in diagnosing psychosis is that some people will lead their lives, apparently as ordinary neurotics, and then suddenly have a psychotic episode. For some psychotics, symptoms are not continuous but may appear every few months, or few years or only once or twice in their lifetime, or even never at all. They have a neurotic layer or facade that lies over their psychotic structure. So it is possible, if nothing disturbs and triggers the underlying psychotic structure, for there to never be any obvious psychotic symptoms throughout their life. But Lacan argued that it is possible to detect the presence of the underlying psychotic structure in such cases.

This situation regarding diagnosis is a bit like someone who would be allergic to penicillin if they took it, although they never have. We would probably still want to say —assuming we knew— that such a person 'is allergic to penicillin', or would be, because they are capable, with their structure, of generating an allergic response to penicillin.

The principal difference between a neurotic and a psychotic is their language. Psychotics use language —or to be more Lacanian— are used by language in a different way from neurotics. Note Freud's and Lacan's stress on identifying special language functions in psychosis. Freud wrote:

'In schizophrenics we observe —especially in the initial stages, which are so instructive — a number of changes in speech, some of which deserve to be regarded from a particular point of view. The patient often devotes peculiar care to his way of expressing himself, which becomes 'stilted' and 'precious'. The construction of sentences undergoes a peculiar organization . . .' [137]

And Lacan:

'I refused to diagnose [a female patient] as psychotic for one decisive reason, which was that there were none of those disturbances . . . , which are disorders at the level of language. We must insist upon the presence of these disorders before making a diagnosis of psychosis.' [138]

To consider in more detail Lacan's development of Freud's idea that special language functions are central in psychosis, we need some more theoretical

---

[137] S Freud, The Unconscious, *SE 15*, [1915], 1976, p197.
[138] J Lacan, *The Psychoses,* ed Miller, trans Grigg, Routledge, London, 1993, p92.

ideas: these include the distinction between the Names of the father and symbolic father, to which we will turn next.

The symbolic father distinguished from the Names of the father

'The Oedipus complex means that the imaginary, in itself an incestuous and conflictual relation, is doomed to conflict and ruin. In order for the human being to be able to establish the . . . relations . . . between male and female, a third party has to intervene, one that is the image of something successful, the model of some harmony. This does not go far enough — there has to be a law, a chain, a symbolic order, the intervention of the order of speech, that is, of the father. Not the natural father, but what is called 'The Father'. The order that prevents the collision and explosion of the situation as a whole is founded on the existence of this Name of The Father. I emphasise this. The symbolic order has to be conceived as something superimposed, without which no animal life would be possible for this misshapen subject which man is.' [139]

A pregnant adolescent says to her mother *'I am pregnant'*. The mother replies: *'Are you sure it's yours?'* The basis of this joke is the fact that while there is nearly always a question of paternity —as to who the father is— there is hardly ever a question of maternity. So your knowledge of your mother's identity is relatively certain or fixed, while your knowledge of your father's identity is far less certain and, as a consequence is more likely to change. Can you claim, for yourself —with the same degree of certainty as you can for your mother— what the name of your biological father is?

With this mixture of paternity and identity in mind Lacan conceived 'the Names of the father', which, he argued, has the special function of distinguishing psychotic structure radically from neurotic structure.

Unfortunately, there is more than the usual amount of guesswork required here because Lacan never gave a course of seminars on the Names of the father as he did with many of his other ideas. To explain the Names of the father we will need a brief detour around proper names and the symbolic father. We will also need to consider the extraordinary work of the logician Kurt Gödel.

Lacan thought that to speak —to use language— you have to be separated from your mother. If you are not properly separated from your mother —by the 'mother tongue'— then it will show in your language. Expression relies on repression, and separation is repression. What counts as proper separation? What is it in the separation from the mother that allows the subject to speak? Lacan's answer is 'proper names'.

---

[139] Ibid p96.

Lacan argued that proper names mark a separation from the mother, which in turn allows language. Without the special function of names we would not be able to speak and understand language. Because psychotics have not been properly separated by proper names —from their mother— they have a different relation to language, and a different way of speaking from neurotics.

To make sense of this we should review Lacan's concept of 'the symbolic father'. The symbolic father carries out a kind of separation of the child from the mother. This symbolic father could be the child's siblings, or the mother's work or lover. But the symbolic father is not enough for the proper and permanent separation that would prevent psychosis, because the identity of the symbolic father often changes. So the separation of the child from the mother would also vary as the identity of the separator —of the symbolic father— varied. What is required to prevent psychosis is a permanent separation that is fixed and unchanging. This permanence is a property of proper names, of the Names of the father. So, for example, while the symbolic father may be mother's work, the mother's lover, or the child's siblings: for the same child the names of the father may be 'Mr Jones', 'Safeway' or 'George'.

The symbolic father is any agency separating the child from the mother. To find out how this Names of the father idea is different from the 'symbolic father' we should first look at some differences between proper nouns like 'Fred', 'Smith' and other types of word such as 'table', 'house', 'white' and 'gay'.

Take the adjective or noun 'gay': it used to mean 'jolly, happy', but today it usually means 'homosexual'. Or the adjective 'blue' which at one time meant a specific colour but now also refers to a melancholy mood. But a proper name like 'Fred Smith' doesn't change its meaning in the same way as a word like 'blue' or 'gay': 'Fred Smith' will always refer to the particular person or persons called 'Fred Smith', whatever happens to the English language over time. Proper names are forever glued to whatever they originally referred to. So Lacan argues that there is a fixity about proper names that is absent in other words whose meanings shift far more.

In neurosis, the Names of the father are properly repressed and lie forever in the unconscious. In psychosis the Names of the father have not been properly repressed. To compensate for this lack of repression psychotics often attempt to introduce new identities into their lives that provide some new repressive force. These new repressions —if they can be produced— prop up their psychic structure and allow them to continue using language. The problem is that a subject cannot properly repress itself, leading to the question: What form do these new repressions take? Paranoid psychotics for example will often speak in a very marked way about their 'being persecuted' or 'controlled by aliens', of 'seeking asylum in a foreign country', or of 'changing gender'. In these cases there is the introduction of a new and conspicuous repressive identity that has the function of holding language together for them. These new and conscious entities contrive —inefficiently— the repressive function for psychotics that the Names of the father have in the unconscious of neurotics. How does this 'holding together' of language by the proper name work? To answer this we will look further at the distinction between proper names and other words, which is where Gödel comes in; and the distinction between the symbolic father and the Names of the father.

Kurt Gödel's Incompleteness Theorem

We need to start with some background, and consider what one might call 'the nearly completed jigsaw picture of science'. In the popular imagination science has been the inexorable accumulation of knowledge. In this picture of science as completing a finite jigsaw puzzle, the progress of science is the gradual elimination of all legitimate questions, until eventually no questions remain, science having exhaustively answered them all. This jigsaw picture of science is certainly false: while science continually answers questions, in so doing it elaborates specific impossibilities or indeterminacies and so always gives birth to new unanswered questions. These indeterminacies are questions with necessarily unclear answers. [140] As science has progressed the number of impossible-to-answer-questions has increased. Some of these are not about some tiny detail that has no relevance or interest for our everyday lives, but concern certain central and uniquely human activities such as using language and counting.

Until Gödel, mathematicians and logicians believed that their job was to prove things, that is, to demonstrate that particular truths were true by logical necessity rather than by true by accident. Of course there are a great many 'accidental' truths, for instance the proposition that 'Fred's hair is black', when it could be blond or blue. Proving that any particular truth or set of truths are necessary rather than accidental is a special and often difficult job.

Before Gödel's revolutionary work it was taken for granted by all logicians and mathematicians that what was true could always be proved, and that everything that was true would eventually become proven, in the same way that it was taken for granted after Newton's discoveries that we would comprehensively understand all the workings of the world. But, as with Heisenberg's work — which overthrew Newton's tidy scheme— Gödel discovered a very surprising impossibility, a logically necessary impossibility, something that cannot be avoided. He destroyed the naive and ideal conception of mathematics as 'the true and provable'. Gödel proved that there are rules that are *true yet unprovable.*

---

[140]   Such as Heisenberg's Uncertainty Principle and Russell's Set Paradox.

Put simply, Gödel proved that if you want to make a complete list of every rule for making numbers, like a kind of grammar of numbers, then there are only two possibilities:

Either the list of rules will be incomplete, that is there will be some rules missing —which is a serious problem if you want a complete list— or there will be some inconsistency, that is there will be contradictions between some of the rules. Obviously if two rules contradict each other it follows that they can't both be true; at least one of them must be false. This is a problem because inconsistency is something that mathematicians and logicians avoid like the plague. Inconsistency guarantees that there is something fatally wrong. Here another great mathematician, John Von Neumann summarises Gödel's Incompleteness Proof:

'*Gödel was the first man to demonstrate that certain mathematical theorems can neither be proved nor disproved with the accepted, rigorous methods of mathematics . . . [Gödel] proved that . . . it will never be possible to acquire with mathematical means, the certainty that mathematics does not contain contradictions . . . this is not a philosophical principle or a plausible intellectual attitude, but the result of a rigorous mathematical proof.*' [141]

It is also worth quoting another professor of mathematics, Morris Kline —who wrote of an overvaluation in a surprisingly Freudian style— in his book *Mathematics, The Loss of Certainty*:

'*We know today that mathematics does not possess the qualities that in the past earned for it universal respect and admiration. Mathematics was regarded as the acme of exact reasoning, a body of truths in itself, and the truth about the design of nature . . . These values are false . . . Many mathematicians would perhaps prefer to limit the disclosure of the present status of mathematics to members of the family. To air these troubles in public may appear to be in bad taste, as bad as airing one's marital difficulties. But intellectually oriented people must be fully aware of the powers of the tools at their disposal. Recognition of the limitations, as well as the capabilities, of reason is far more beneficial than blind trust, which can lead to false ideologies and even to destruction.*' [142]

So for Morris Kline an important ideal —that was held in high esteem— has become devalued, just as love and sex relations are idealised, and later come to be revalued by the disappointments of each individual in the course of their life

---

[141] J Von Neumann, On the Presentation of the Albert Einstein Award to Gödel, 1951; Tribute to Gödel, Foundations of Mathematics, *Symposium Papers Commemorating the Sixtieth Birthday of Kurt Gödel*, ed Bullof et al, Springer Verlag, Berlin, 1969.
[142] Morris Kline, *Mathematics —The Loss of Certainty*, OUP, New York, 1980, from the Preface.

in their Oedipal journey through loss, love, idealisation or identification and separation.

To summarise the above: the history of mathematics and the history of science have been the increasingly detailed specification and growth of indeterminacy —of things that are necessarily missing— or of what Lacan called 'the real': the jigsaw picture of science, with its promise of comprehensive certainty and complete knowledge can never be realised. The ideas of science as the means of eliminating all ignorance and so perfecting our knowledge of the world, each other and all our communications has been shattered. We are systematically incapable of comprehensively describing anything as complicated or more complicated than arithmetic, without becoming plagued by contradictions or absent rules.

The missing jigsaw pieces, such as the impossibility of providing consistent and complete rules even for systems as simple as arithmetic, and the impossibility of measuring certain things ensure that the human condition will always be constituted by unanswerable questions and indeterminacy. What form does this uncertainty take? The existence of our symbols or language. Language constitutes both a key part of science and of human sexuality. The philosopher Ludwig Wittgenstein made a similar point: *'The concept of a living being has the same indeterminacy as that of a language.'* [143]

This view of science as a jigsaw —with parts necessarily missing— is a version of the story of Babel: men in search of all the answers to all questions were unified, working hard together on a singular project, the building of a tower that would reach God. Progress was made until the builders suffered a terrible affliction, making it impossible for them to finish the tower. The efficient communications essential to their work became impossible because the workers involuntary started to speak different languages.

Problems with communications also became necessary when Plato's eight-limbed asexual creature was split, producing two four limbed sexed people, each afflicted with languages of variable meanings.

One impossibility we all suffer from is the ideal of perfect communication, and with it perfect sexual rapport; that is, the elimination of our problems and suffering through the right love or sexual relationship and practice. We all have to continually endure being misunderstood, misheard and misquoted. We are condemned to use language and to be misunderstood, whatever precautions we take, even by people who do their best to understand us. Language is terrible way of communicating yet it is the best we have.

Specific ambiguities and indeterminacies can sometimes be eliminated, but only at the cost of introducing new ones. It seems that there is a minimum of

---

[143] L Wittgenstein, *Zettel*, 2nd edition, Basil Blackwell, number 326, 1981.

indeterminacy that we must endure. Word meaning is something that seems to be in flux. Word meaning shifts about beyond our control. If you want to know exactly, and without any doubt, what a word means you might try looking up the word in a dictionary. What do you find? More words, and each of those words has a meaning, but only as more words, and each of these words has a meaning offered by still more words with their potentially infinite connections to more words. This sea of signifiers or words constitutes our beliefs and knowledge.

Gödel proved that any system that is more complicated than counting must be either inconsistent (contradicts itself) or incomplete. People can count and much more besides —we are much more complex than simple counting machines— so people must be 'either incomplete or inconsistent'. How does this forced choice between inconsistency and incompleteness relate to Lacan's theory of psychosis?

Lacan, Gödel, incompleteness, inconsistency, neurosis and psychosis

For all those who have passed through some kind of resolution of their Oedipus —typically between the ages of four and six— their generative base, that is, the set of rules that produce language, has become partially fixed. This presumably explains why five-year-old children possess ninety per cent of language skills of an adult. The generative base is like a grammar or fundamental fantasy that generates the diversity of language and symptoms that each of us possess. When we can use a language properly we can make a potentially infinite number of sentences, with every one of them grammatically correct, if we are not drunk or tired.

The underlying rules for generating all this extraordinary variety gradually become more fixed as children learn language. But it is probably true to say that there is a partially different set of rules for every single adult who speaks the same language. This would explain why we sometimes argue about the meanings of words, and why grammar and word meanings change over time.

When the fixed rules are laid down, as if written irrevocably in stone, some rules can be fixed that are not consistent with others, so that the rules contradict each other. For most people —for neurotics and perverts— the rules are not generally inconsistent but incomplete, that is, there are rules missing.

But for psychotics some of the fundamental rules are contradictory; at least one fixed rule conflicts with other fixed rules. So every pervert and neurotic lives his life with his own unique incompleteness, but the psychotic endures a complete set of rules that contradict one another[144].

---

[144] The following, from Gregory Chaitin's Information-Theoretic Computational Complexity and Gödel's Theorem and Information, *New Directions in the Philosophy of*

Where do the contradictory rules of psychotics come from? From the symbolic father, and from the Names of the father. The fixity of proper names and the flux of adjectives and nouns are mutually supportive and mutually dependent. They feed off one another. So it is with the symbolic father and with the Names of the father. The symbolic father is a thing in flux. It changes because what separates the child from its mother can change, but the Names of the father are fixed and once written they can never be erased. The fixity of proper names and the flux of common nouns and adjectives seem to be properties that rely mutually on one another. So proper names depend on the other bits of language, and the other bits of language depend on proper names.

Consider the jobs of weaving and being a blacksmith. The meaning of 'weaving' is not precisely fixed; it might refer to weaving baskets, cloth or magic spells. In times when people were called after their occupations such as 'Simon Blacksmith' or 'Helen Weaver'. Nouns became proper names. In their passage to proper namehood nouns with variable meaning have come to have at least part of their meaning fixed; 'Simon Blacksmith' will always refer to a particular individual whatever 'Blacksmith' comes to mean as a noun, even thousands of years after he has died.

How does this help explain Lacan's claim that in psychosis: *'there has been a foreclosure of the Names of the father'*? What does 'foreclosure' mean? Foreclosure is a kind of exclusion that occurs following the breaking of a contract. For instance when a lender forecloses on your mortgage, he excludes you from your home because you have failed to keep to the rules on your side of the contract you made with him.

Everyone, psychotics and neurotics, has had a contract with the Names of the father. Each individual takes as permanently fixed certain items that mark his or her separations from their mother or carer. The terms of the contract are that as long as you do not speak the Names of the father you will be permitted to live in the house of ordinary neurotic language. Neurotics maintain their contracts with the Names of the father while psychotics often cannot. How does the psychotic break his contract? His Names of the father are not properly repressed and so do not remain unspoken.[145]

Mathematics, ed Tymoczko, Princeton University Press, 1998 is broadly concordant with this view: *'From the point of view of information theory . . . [Gödel's theorem] seems simply to suggest that in order to progress, mathematicians, like investigators in other sciences, must search for new axioms.'* (p287); and *'Information theory suggests that the Gödel phenomenon is natural and widespread, not pathological and unusual.'* (p308).

[145] This perhaps is the explanation why Jews are forbidden on pain of death to properly pronounce God's proper name.

A psychotic fails to maintain his contract with the Names of the father because he has not been rigidly and properly separated from his mother, so the rules of language and meaning have not been 'properly' fixed for psychotics, because of the contradictions within the rules. So when psychotics speak they always have some meanings that are far too fixed and some that are far too fluid: the rules which do not accord with the contract that bind a neurotic's language. So for example, when a psychotic heard that a messy room looked like a bomb had gone off in it, he jumped in fright, as if a bomb had literally gone off.

From a clinical point of view many psychotics are preoccupied in an extraordinary way with identity and with names. They may insist that they have been reincarnated and demand to be called by a different name, or wish to change their nationality, specie, their sex or gender, or claim that a spell has been put on them that is changing their gender, identity or sexual orientation.

There is a clinical history often seen in cases of psychosis that involves either an absent and hence inconsistent symbolic father, or a very harsh or powerful symbolic father. We will see that these two sorts of symbolic fathers can amount to the same thing in terms of producing an inconsistent repressive function.

The Role of an Absent Symbolic Father in Psychosis

In the case of an absent symbolic father the child first establishes that the symbolic mother must have had a desire for someone other than himself, when he learns that someone was necessary for his conception, in addition to his mother. That is, the mother had desired someone who was not the child.

When the child finds that the symbolic father is not present he establishes his belief that the mother does not desire anyone else. She does not desire the symbolic father, so the symbolic father was present and then absent; hence the inconsistency, or contradiction, and the accord with Gödel's work.

It is not unusual for psychotics to have a history like that of a young man whose father left the family home when the son was two. From that time until he was ten he slept in his mother's bed, and did not know of any interest his mother had in any lover who might have taken his absent father's place. When he was seventeen he was persecuted by voices telling him that he was gay, and imagined that UFOs were communicating with him. These complaints completely dominated his life, preventing him from loving and working.

The inconsistency in this case is the presence and absence of the symbolic father, who also happened to be the biological father. Not the physical absence but the symbolic absence; for the son had taken his father's place in the matrimonial bed. This psychotic man presumably had a pair of inconsistent rules along the following lines:

1. Up to age two, while there was someone —the symbolic father— separating him from his mother, we could speculate that his belief was formulated: *'There is someone my mother desires who is not me'.*

2. After his second birthday, when he started sleeping with his mother, when there was no symbolic father separating him from his mother, suggesting that: *'There is no one my mother desires who is not me; I am the only person she desires, because there is no one to separate us.'*

With neurotics and perverts, there is a triangular relation between a child, its mother and the symbolic father. Put simplistically, this triangular relation has three rather than two people, and refers to 'The Oedipus' that ensures that the child is separated from its mother, preventing the inconsistency described above from arising.

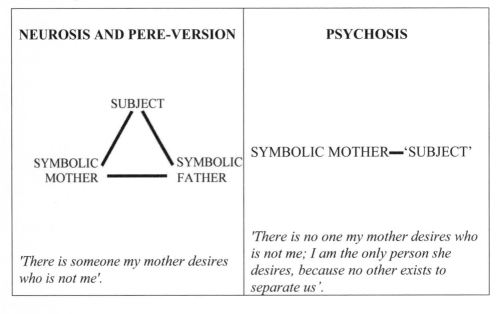

NEUROSIS AND PERE-VERSION	PSYCHOSIS
SUBJECT SYMBOLIC MOTHER — SYMBOLIC FATHER	SYMBOLIC MOTHER—'SUBJECT'
'There is someone my mother desires who is not me'.	*'There is no one my mother desires who is not me; I am the only person she desires, because no other exists to separate us'.*

Narcissism, the image and psychosis

Nietzsche wrote:

'"Better a debtor than pay with a coin that does not bear our image!" says our sovereignty.' [146]

So the one from whom payment is accepted pays with the image of an ideal, the image of an Other. This formula describes the position of ordinary neurotics. What image does the psychotic pay with? If we can't pay with an image of the

---

[146] F Nietzsche, *The Gay Science*, trans Kaufmann, Vintage Books, New York, p216.

Other then, according to the ruling authority, we ought not pay at all. The psychotic doesn't pay because he both suffers and enjoys a profound narcissism, a relation to his own image mirrored in his mother's eyes. Their mutual gaze remains undisturbed by a third, by the symbolic father. So the psychotic fails to have an image of an Other, the ideal for instance of a sovereign: the psychotic's image is principally his own of himself. This is why some paranoid psychotics contrive fictional sovereigns who are supposed to have authority over the psychotic, such as the CIA, aliens, or those of one gender or race; for psychotics there is a problem identifying anything other than an image of self. This is why their symptoms often include beliefs in a variety of 'non self' objects that act to persecute 'the self'. This is why Freud wrote of a narcissistic function operating in a variety of psychoses:

'Megalomania may perhaps be a more effective way of keeping the distressing idea away from the ego . . . The delusional idea is maintained with the same energy with which another intolerably distressing idea is warded off from the ego. Thus [psychotics] love their delusion as they love themselves.' [147]

Psychotics have a profoundly narcissistic relation to themselves that is only held at bay by their delusions. They have failed to find anyone else whom their mother desires, besides themselves. Imagine, if you have someone who is enormously important in your life —your mother— and you fail to find her desire for anyone except yourself? Another way of understanding this narcissistic relation is as a profound enjoyment or jouissance. In paranoia this jouissance is located in the Biggest Other, who will hopefully have a regulatory role, like a policeman of enjoyment, preventing the psychotic from being overcome by his enjoyment of himself.

In order to escape this vision of your life as totally dominated by this one person's exclusive desire for you, psychotics have a solution: persecution, the supposedly intrusive presence of the Other!

'Chronic paranoia is a . . . defence . . . People have become paranoid over things that they cannot put up with, provided that they have the peculiar psychic disposition for it.' [148]

The idea of persecution introduces an Other who separates the subject from the mother. In the case of the young man who had slept in his mother's bed since he was two, we can see his thorough identification with his mother, that is, his lack of separation from her. He complained that he was persecuted by images of sex with men, but protested *'I am not homosexual'*.

---

[147] *The Complete Letters of Sigmund Freud to Wilhelm Fliess*, ed Masson, Belknap, Harvard, Draft H, 1985, p111.
[148] Ibid, p108.

If the psychotic young man was to have become a practising homosexual then an important difference would have been established: a distinction would have been drawn between the young man and his mother, for they then would then have become separate, because there would be a third person between them. In fantasy the homosexual lover would be someone who both desired the young man, and, because he was a man he could also be desired by the mother, so breaking the child-mother dyad with a kind of quasi-Oedipal triangulation.

His feared object of love is the same as his mother's object of love, a man. The imagined mutual object of love contrives the third element of a simplistic triangular or Oedipal relation. This masquerade may allow a psychotic to function, some of the time, as if he were a neurotic, despite his underlying psychotic structure.

In this case, the psychotic fantasies of sex with a third person, a man, caused torment, but seemed also to have the function of preventing a more devastating breakdown. The fantasy of the third person had the effect of preventing the inconsistency in the rules becoming apparent, by insisting —through his paranoia— that there exists someone who separates him from the mother. The symptom is not the primary problem but a solution to a prior problem.

In Chapter Fourteen we will look at Lacan's slogan: *'the signifier represents the subject for another signifier'*. This formula does not apply properly to psychotics; the psychotic is not properly speaking a subject. Psychotic speech is very different from neurotic speech. Psychotics cannot usually free associate in the same way that neurotics do: psychotics will often suddenly stop talking, or repeat themselves, because the signifier with which they have stopped does not 'represent the psychotic for another signifier' because the psychotic is not a subject. Some psychotics fail and become mute, others speak exclusively with perfectly formed paragraphs that resist interruption.

Many psychotics are painfully aware of this discrepancy between themselves and neurotics and desperately try to maintain a grip on language by writing for hours or talking endlessly, trying to put off the point at which the signifier fails to represent. Paranoia is one such attempt in which the one with paranoia contrives a grand Other who might function as a signifier, for another subject. Some psychotics contrive fabulously elaborate symbolic systems in which they have a clearly limited mastery such as technical drawing or computer programming that stand in, in a weak sense, for the incomplete symbolic functions of everyday neurotic language. The neurotic's relation to language is incomplete: the psychotic's is inconsistent.

The Role of an Overbearing Symbolic Father in Psychosis

'The father is not simply the generator. He's also the one who has rightful possession of the mother —and in peace, in principle. His function is central to the realisation of the Oedipus complex and conditions the son's accession — which is also a function, correlative to the first —to the model of virility. What happens if a certain lack occurs in the formative function of the father?

The father may well have had a certain mode of relation such that the son does indeed adopt a feminine position, but it's not through fear of castration. We are all familiar with cases of these delinquent or psychotic sons who proliferate in the shadow of a paternal personality of exceptional character, one of these social monsters referred to as 'venerable'. They are often characters strongly marked by a style of radiance and success, but in a unilateral manner, in the register of unbridled ambition or authoritarianism, sometimes of talent, of genius. They don't necessarily have to be a genius, have merit, or be mediocre or nasty, it's sufficient that this be unilateral and monstrous.'

Here Lacan explains another familiar history seen in psychosis, besides the absent or overly weak symbolic father, or the absence of another figure of the mother's desire: the opposite, a *'venerable father'*:

Let's suppose that this situation entails for the subject the impossibility of assuming the realisation of the signifier father at the symbolic level. What's he left with? He's left with the image the paternal function is reduced to. It's an image which isn't inscribed in any triangular dialectic . . . The image, on its own, initially adopts the sexualised function, without any need of an intermediary, an identification with the mother, or with anything else. The subject then adopts this intimidated position that we can observe in the fish or lizard. The imaginary relation alone is installed on a plane that has nothing typical about it, that is dehumanising, because it doesn't leave any place for the relation of reciprocal exclusion that enables the ego's image to be founded on the orbit given by the model of the more complete Other.

The alienation here is radical, it isn't bound to a nihilating signified, as in a certain type of rivalarous relation with the father, but to a nihilation of the signifier. The subject will have to bear the weight of this real, primitive dispossession of the signifier and adopt compensation for it, at length, over the course of his life, through a series of purely conformist identifications with characters who will give him the feeling for what one has to do to be a man.' [149]

The situation Lacan is describing is not a case of the wanting it both ways, but of marking out two extremes, and excluding the larger part of the continuum in the middle.

---

[149] J Lacan, *The Psychoses*, ed Miller, trans Grigg, Routledge, London, 1993, p204.

How can an overbearing, powerful and highly repressive symbolic father, a leader of the sort studied by Freud in the case of Schreber's father [150] be equivalent to an absent symbolic father? Such a man is likely to be 'too much' for some or all of his children. He may, by being 'too strong' and highly repressive, increase the chance of having children who grow up to become psychotic. How can we explain this? By the fact that the father cannot possibly be present all the time. So that when he is absent, his absence is felt far more traumatically, and so is impossible to adequately symbolise. The early failure to symbolise another whom the mother desires is the condition that Lacan theorises as leading to psychosis.

Another way to understand psychosis suggests three constitutional or genetic categories: the first group, any member of which would hardly ever become psychotic, even if they were never physically separated from their mothers, a second group whose members would almost always become psychotic, however well they were physically separated from their mothers, and a third group whose members would all be highly responsive to the amount of separation provided by their symbolic father, so that all the members of this group who did not experience attempts to separate them by their symbolic father would become psychotic, and all the members of this group who were separated from their mother by their symbolic father would be neurotic or perverse.

I suspect that most psychotics fall into this last category; that is, they would have been neurotics if only they had been separated from their mother. So, given my speculations here there is a minimum of separation required for some individuals, in order for neurosis to result, while no ordinary amount of separation will prevent psychosis in other cases. Freud was clear on this question of value of innate, constitutional or genetic factors; he wrote: *'The manifestation of the innate disposition is indeed not open to any critical doubts'* [151]; and:

'I take this opportunity of defending myself against the mistaken charge of having denied the importance of innate (constitutional) factors because I have stressed that of infantile impressions . . . Psychoanalysis has talked a lot about the accidental factors in aetiology and little about the constitutional ones; but that is only because it was able to contribute something fresh to the former, while, to begin with it knew no more than most commonly known about the latter . . . Rarely or never one of these powers alone. The amount of etiological effectiveness to be attributed to each of them can only be arrived at in every individual case separately.' [152]

---

[150] S Freud, Psychoanalytic Notes on an Autobiographical Account of a Case of Paranoia, *SE 12*, [1910], 1976, p59.

[151] S Freud, The Paths to Symptom Formation, Introductory Lectures on Psychoanalysis, *SE 16*, [1915], 1976, p361.

[152] S Freud, The Dynamics of Transference, *SE 12*, [1912b], 1976, p99.

Future studies of both the psychoanalytic study of the paternal function and immunogenetics may clarify this issue. However suggestive studies report a high incidence of psychosis in cultures where the paternal function has been badly damaged, such as amongst Africans whose ancestors were enslaved and exiled.[153]

Africans had possessed powerful paternal structures until they were enslaved, uprooted and dumped in the West Indies and other foreign cultures, and given other men's names, with which they had to struggle to identify their paternal function. African exiles had their fathers' names eradicated and other names substituted in their place. These ex-Africans have made great efforts to properly identify effective paternal functions. Among these are the numerous changes of identity and leadership that the black liberation and black religious movements have undergone in North America. One consequence —and a probable cause of psychosis— for those denied a clear paternal function has been the high rate of single mothers rearing children in the absence of a clear paternal function or symbolic father.

Another race of slaves has had a different history. The Jews were Egyptian slaves. Their exodus was very different from the passage of African slaves: the Jewish exodus from Egypt was 'voluntary' and forced a number of powerful paternal functions upon the exiles: Moses was one such paternal figure who was to die —that is take the position of the dead father— before seeing his children enjoy the benefits of his suffering, preceding Jesus in this respect. Another paternal function was provided to the Jews through a God who made himself present shortly before the Jews gave up Pharaoh as their Other. The Jews' invisible God came to represent himself and the Jews through writing: through the Ten Commandments, written on the tablets of stone. They —and writing— became the foundation through which Jews perpetuated their paternal function, the names of the father and their being 'chosen', that is *separated* from all others, from other Egyptians and non-Jews. The Commandment of the invisible God forbade the creation of any image that represented him. The Jews took this rather seriously as a taboo on all representational art. All pictures were

---

[153] *'Several studies in the UK have observed that the inception rates of schizophrenia among the African-Caribbeans are well elevated when compared with White populations. However, on the basis of available data on biological factors it appears that social factors play a more important role in the aetiology of schizophrenia in this group.'* Schizophrenia and African-Caribbeans: a conceptual model of aetiology (D Bhugra et al, *International Review of Psychiatry*, 1999, 11, p145—152).] This is a complicated topic. One explanation put forward for the phenomenon of increased psychosis amongst Afro-Caribbeans has been the alleged racism and cultural ignorance on the part of those psychiatrists who diagnose. Unfortunately I know of no reliable, culture independent method of testing this possibility. The unreliability of diagnosis and the systematic psychiatric misdiagnosis of psychosis has been confirmed by Rosenhan for instance in 'On Being Sane in Insane Places' D L Rosenhan, *Science*, vol 179, 1973, p250-159.

forbidden! Such a prohibition of images functions to underline the symbolic function, that is the effects of language, and is an inverted version of the analyst's discretionary invitation to the client to lie on the couch and to speak of the laws and gods to whom he has been subjected, whilst the analyst is removed from the client's field of vision.

Writing is an essential part of the transmission of paternity in Jewish culture. Jews relied on their religious writings to preserve their difference and separation from non-Jews: the African slaves in exile possessed no such collective form of transmission, no doubt because many did not share a language. Tragically it is both the children of the Africans, stolen from their paternal function, and the 'host societies' or colonies in which they now live who pay a high price for the slaver's profit and jouissance. Perhaps this goes some way towards explaining the transgressive behaviour of some of the children of the dispossessed slaves and their unusually high levels of psychosis?

Globalisation and psychosis

One attack on the paternal function that Lacan called foreclosure of 'the Names of the father' is 'globalisation'. Globalisation is a term used to describe the extraordinary acceleration that technology has produced, increasing the amount of signification or 'communication' and accelerating the speed of travel. Increasingly over the last five hundred years our ability to transfer, to move people, goods, services and above all signifiers have become magnified, and in proportion the world has shrunk to become the global village. What consequences has this had? To answer this question we should consider the structures that existed at some arbitrary and imaginary point 'prior to globalisation'.

Who, or, put another way —where— was the paternal function? When feminism was relatively absent, and the principal methods of travel were foot and horse, questions about the identity and location of the paternal function were more limited and relatively easy to answer; biological fathers would have been more closely identified with their children, although the paternal function does not reduce down to producing children. Now that biological fathers can now travel large distances rapidly, it is possible for a would-be father to instruct that his semen be used to inseminate in his absence, from the other side of the planet, or even after his death. Today's paternity is extremely mobile relative to that of our ancestors, and as a consequence is more fragile.

In terms of the Primal horde, in which women were equated with the land[154], the paternal function becomes questioned because the variable 'land' is no longer

---

[154] When in 1992 raped and often pregnant Bosnian Moslem women were released into the territory that they and their families had occupied before the Serbian invasion their

tied or identified tightly with the paternal function, to a father's name. A man, or woman for that matter can be wealthy by virtue of their intellectual property. This category may include writings that cannot be identified within three-dimensional space. One example of intellectual property that does not occupy three-dimensional space are all those entities within the Internet, such as web sites. Web sites do not occupy three-dimensional space but have a symbolic topological existence, rather than a geometric one. Many lives are lived out in crucial part on the Internet. For example there are those who have sex on the Internet, and there are businesses that trade exclusively on the Internet. Without the Internet they would not exist. So where exactly are these businesses assets? A very similar question is: 'Where is language?' Would English disappear if every English speaker were to go to sleep? Such questions are best approached topologically, with reference to a kind of rubbery or elastic space and time that is not bound by either angle or distance or the simple passage of clock time.

Just because there are assets that are not located as straightforwardly as a house made of bricks and mortar does not make them any the less worthwhile as assets, but, at least temporarily, while our search for new techniques that will better identify or fix paternal functions goes on, the identification of the paternal function is made far harder by globalisation. One consequence of this problematic identification of the symbolic father is the apparent increase in psychosis that we are presently suffering.

'The house of the father' is a popular signifier of paternity, perhaps because the address or name is often the bonding together of paternal and maternal significations as a piece of land or territory and the record or registry of who has rights to enjoy that property or 'that woman' who is identified with the father's name. The same function can be seen on a national scale: *'The White House'*, *'Number 10, Downing Street'*, and *'Pharaoh'* which translates as *'big house'*.

---

family structures became damaged. The raped women's exchange value exhausted, as marked by a baby or pregnancy of enemy paternity. The traumatic exhibition of their fathers' and brothers' broken taboo was clear as the mark of Cain. With the Moslem women's impossibility of being positively valued by their paternity, the inevitable break up of their families and the expansion —phallic concept— of the Serbs into the previously Bosnian territory became less hindered. The idea of 'going where no man has gone before' confuses vagina with territory in the formulation: 'going where no Bosnian man has gone before'. Globally there are many square kilometres of unconquered vagina. Since the standardisation of English spelling this passes as 'country'. 'All is fair in love and war' is an appeal to an equation of love and war, with respect to equity. It is this equation that is operative in the confusion of 'vagina and territory' and women as 'the fair sex'. See the appendix on 'Relations of women and their bodies' for an elaboration of this theme.

Repression and expression, foreclosure and indebtedness

Psychotics have a kind of freedom, despite and because of their terrible symptoms. Some can question in a more radical way than the rest of us, taking issue with things that most of us do not even realise we take for granted. Neurotics and perverts have more that is rigidly fixed and cannot be questioned. Perhaps this is one reason why psychosis is associated with creativity and genius, and some of the greatest talents, including Van Gogh, Cantor, Gödel and Joyce, all of whom seem to have been psychotic.

How can psychosis be understood as 'foreclosure of the Names of the father'? By viewing life as a debt rather than a gift. It is usually only self-serving parents and priests who pronounce *'life is a gift'*: life is not simply or straightforwardly a positive and rewarding experience: life insists on suffering and repression. Without repression there is no expression. Without the rules of language, grammar, word meaning and pronunciation nobody would ever be able to value anything. To be a subject of language is to be subjected to rules of language, that is to pay a price. Part of the price paid by neurotics is not optional but comes as a package with language. As soon as you are burdened with language your debt exists. The way you live your life is the technique that you use to service your debt, the method use to pay the interest due. The way a parent services his debt will form an essential part of his child's debt. The concept of debt is crucial in all 'honourable practices': in some cultures fathers are dishonoured or markedly indebted by their daughter's sexual activities.

A singular way to repay your debt is to die anonymously, without having had any children, friends, writings, legacy or a gravestone, burying your nameless debt in an infinitely small or unidentifiable hole. Perhaps this is why debtors used to be buried at crossroads in unmarked graves, and why many poor people will not hesitate to spend beyond their means on their own funerals? Insurance policies taken out to pay for funeral expenses guaranteeing that their death does not perpetuate a debt exclusively identified with the last rite.

Just as the only way for vampires to survive is to recreate in others exactly the method of survival on which their life has depended —drinking the blood of human victims and perpetuating the chain— so one of the most popular ways of coping with the guilt and indebtedness of neurotic life is to set about recreating one's debt and guilt by having children.[155] By the time that innocent infants have been infected with language they are no longer innocents, or infants, and are

---

[155] Lacan said that *'love is the need to be loved by whoever might make you guilty. And . . . if one is loved by her or by him, it feels much better.'* (Transference Seminar, unpublished, trans Gallagher, 31 May 1961) While Nietzsche wrote: *'Love forgives the lover even his lust.'*, *The Gay Science*, Vintage Books, trans Kaufmann, 1974, p124.

likely to be seeking victims of their own, on whom they can inflict their unique linguistic curse, dressed up no doubt as 'a blessing' or 'gift'.

How does a psychotic's condition differ from that of the ordinarily indebted neurotic? In psychosis there has been a foreclosure: that, is a debt was arranged, but the debtor repaid his debt, and yet he continued to 'live'. But this is not life as we know it! In neurosis, this debt is properly repaid only by dying, or, as a token, by leaving little debtors to take on debt, imposing language on others. In some cultures, the sons and brothers of a debtor are regarded as equally liable as the debtor himself; the debt is always repaid. The psychotic is not properly burdened by the rules and regulations of language that afflict neurotics. Language may be a curse but it carries benefits too. If you are neurotic then you live in the ordinary neurotic house of language. You have a life tenancy. The cost is a mortgage, a deathly arrangement; a neurotic's debt to language is only repaid on death, when his relation to language is finalised: in psychosis the occupation of the neurotic house of language is at best partial, incomplete and uncertain, his tenancy unsure. The psychotic's debt or mortgage has been foreclosed, so he is sometimes evicted from house of language.

Because the psychotic has repaid his debt he 'enjoys' a strange kind of freedom. A crucial type of repression is relatively absent in psychosis. Another consequence is that psychotic symbolic functions or language are often radically altered, as can be seen in Joyce's writing, and the extraordinary mathematics of Cantor and Gödel. As a result, the jouissance of psychotics is sometimes extreme and overwhelming, perhaps equivalent to the debilitating effect of an intense orgasm of twenty-four hours duration.

All neurotics face and endure an impossible task: determining their Other's desire. What does the Other want? In place of the neurotic's necessarily incomplete task of determining the Other's desire is the psychotic's completed task of determining the Other's desire. He is it, the short circuit. He is both the comprehensive cause and object of the Other's desire. The 'mother and psychotic child' are a unit from the psychotic child's point of view. The task of determining the Other's desire has been completed, but the rules, although complete, are inconsistent. That is, some of the rules contradict each other.

The mother used language to insist that she would not be separated from her psychotic child and nothing else separated her from her child; so the psychotic is the sole object of the mother's desire, yet this fact is above all symbolic! It is symbolic because the psychotic has failed to discover the mother's desire —her words— for someone other than him; that is, the mother's desire for the symbolic father. It is the mother's words that have spoken of the crucial lack of separation between her and the child.

The mother's words symbolise the lack of separation, which led to the conclusion: there is no Other, no one besides me, whom my mother desires. So the mother's words demonstrated the unique and singular object of the mother's desire, and words also, inconsistently, demonstrated that it is not possible with language to determine any other object of desire for the mother.

Language is the casualty of this inconsistency, so the subject of language in psychosis does not exist. One consequence of psychotic structure, of this foreclosure of generative naming is that psychotics have a different relation to language from neurotics and perverts. Another way of expressing this inconsistency is in terms of the Oedipus: the structure of ordinary neurotic language is supported by the third term, the symbolic father allowing the Oedipal triangle, due to the fact that language and people are generated sexually. That is the fabric of society, of families and language rely on desiring the Other's desire, where the Other is not the subject. That is they rely on the mother's desire for someone other than the child. Language, families and society cannot be consistently created or sustained by mothers who have not been separated from their psychotic children. The existence of society and language insists on the existence of a symbolic father, for some subjects at least. Society cannot exist without neurotics, without their investment and service in the discourse of the slave and master; so psychotics are martyrs with heroically completed but tragically inconsistent rules. This inconsistent completion has a high cost for them and sometimes for society.

One cause of psychosis that leads to the phenomenon of 'unity with the mother' is the mother's jouissance. Some mothers who insisted on not being separated from their child —on keeping others away— have ended up with psychotic children. The problem in these cases is that the mother enjoys the child too much, no one can say 'no' to her; the symbolic father is absent, with the consequence that the psychotic child will also enjoy, without limit, because there will have been insufficient rules of repression, that limited either the mother's or her child's indistinguishable enjoyment.

Psychosis and the Primal horde

How might psychosis be theorised within the Primal horde? Because the death of the Primal Father failed to create a sustainable debt or guilt for a particular psychotic son, that son was unable to repress his wishes to kill or have sex, or any other wishes. Because he was unable to repress, he was equally unable to express himself clearly. The psychotic son of the Primal horde suffered no lasting indebtedness when the Primal Father was killed and eaten, so it's not surprising that he underwent no dramatic changes, unlike the rest of the horde when they created the law; the psychotic son failed to suffer from the primal guilt and the fear of punishment that the neurotic sons suffered.

The debt and the gift

One solution attempted by many women to the problem of their debt is to 'write it off', in exchange for access to their sexual and or child bearing services as payment. A similar writing off is practiced in accountancy and insurance where the risk of an event occurring is discounted —prematurely— against other values. In this fantasy a woman has a value determined typically by 'the promise' of a man, perhaps an engagement ring. The man gives the woman a gift. This gift will be in proportion to her value, and may take the form of a child or a home. If the man is wealthy or titled he can give the woman status for which she has traded sexual services and perhaps child rearing.

One important question for many women who have entered some variety of this fantastic yet popular arrangement is *'What is left of me now that the exchange has been completed and my value determined and or exhausted?'* This type of fantasy is typically neurotic, not psychotic: in psychosis the support for neurotic language is missing. The question of gender is always, at least in part, a questioning of the Other's desire. Perhaps this explains why many psychotics seek surgical and hormonal treatment that will change their bodies' gender, allowing them to better perpetuate the façade of an ordinary neurotic gender, and why some women become profoundly depressed as soon as they have given birth.

While many women put themselves in the place of a 'gift', men often put themselves in the place of a debt. Perhaps these phenomena go some way towards explaining dowry practices? One reason why the idea of a 'gift' is so problematic is because the gift is always presented in relation to a debt![156] Look at the rituals around the presentation of gifts where it is common for givers to apologise along the lines that *'I'm sorry it is such a small thing'*, and for receivers to reciprocate along the lines *'you didn't have to give me such a wonderful present; it is far too generous'*. These popular apologies and objections refer to the size of the debt created by the gift and the resultant problem for the recipient along the lines: *'How am I going to repay this debt?'* A woman is more likely than a man to regard a gift as valuation of her person: a man will tend to treat a gift as the creation of his debt. Because gifts ritualise the repayment of debt, there is a well-defined repayment schedule, a structure according to which the representation will be made, perhaps on a birthday, or next Christmas. In this way the economy and circulation of debts and gifts is perpetuated, but they never manage to cancel each other out without a remainder.

---

[156] The idea that the value of gifts can only be analysed in terms of the more fundamental notion of debt is concordant with Lacan's claim that *'The Woman does not exist'*, that is the definitive woman does not exist, nor, despite millions of examples of women, does a positive psychoanalytic definition of 'The Woman' exist.

The creation of debts and gifts has much in common with sexualised behaviour, with attempts to be 'a man' or 'a woman'. If, in the attempt to produce a 'sexual relation', a man and a woman are 'united' in marriage or sexually, there is always some suffering and subjectivity, that is the absence of unity. Men and women are fundamentally incompatible, so are men and men, and women and women. So in the attempt to eliminate or balance 'a sexual economy', a debt and a gift are 'united', there is always some difficulty, problem or frustration. At least one of the partners nearly always believes that they've been short changed, or compromised, regrets their choice of lover, or believes that they could do better.

Another fundamental short-changing, or unequal exchange routinely occurs in the mother-infant relation: the baby is often fantasised by the mother as something that has been given to her as a gift. What does the mother do with her gift? Following one ideal she recreates a primal debt by creating an ordinary neurotic: a psychotic child's debt is prematurely repaid, putting the value of the mother's gift very much in question, because the relation of the psychotic child to its father —as gift— is in question because a fundamental debt has been repaid; the Names of the father have been foreclosed.

When a mother has a neurotic child what happens to the value of her gift? Does it gain in value or fall? What is the value of the subject's lack for the Other? How does a child set about managing their lack? By presenting herself as a gift, or as the means of repaying a debt? In one version of this question some mothers regard their grandchildren as a grand return on the value of their gift, while others take into account alternative techniques for the creation of new debt, such as the building of a business or a career. The recognised repayment of a debt always entails the creation of a new one, except in cases of psychosis.

Whenever there is a value for others, it is always in relation to debt because the signifier represents the (neurotic) subject for another signifier, and, as Lacan puts it, the neurotic *'never finds anything but a distinct object since he must by definition refind something that he has on loan'.* [157] Freud, describing the ordinary neurotic Oedipal relation explained that: *'[The superego] . . . borrowed strength to do this, so to speak, from the father, and this loan was an extraordinarily momentous act.'* [158]

What is the purpose of this loan referred to by Freud and Lacan? The enjoyment of the mother, by the child, in the Name of the father. In the eyes of the child the father has the means to deny the child access to the mother, so the enjoyment of the mother by the child is achieved by way of a foundational loan

---

[157] *The Psychoses*, ed Miller, trans Grigg, Routledge, London, 1993, p85.
[158] S Freud, The Ego and the Id, *SE 18*, [1923b], 1976, p34.

granted by the father.   What are the items on loan, that mark the child's enjoyment? Signifiers, the Names of the father [159].

Psychosis and clinical technique: tactics, strategy and policy

This book sets out primarily to address the clinical problems of working with neurotics: working with psychotics requires a very different set of techniques from those used with neurotics. Not only are the tactics and strategy of the clinician quite different when working with psychotics, but even the policies and ethics are, in part, different. Many techniques used with neurotics and psychotics are the inverse of each other.

Freud preferred not to work with psychotics: *'It would be entirely legitimate to guard against failures by carefully excluding such cases [of narcissistic and psychotic conditions].'*[160]

Because Lacan developed Freud's theory of psychosis, along with a set of techniques for working with psychotics there are many Lacanians who work successfully with psychotics, but Lacan also warns clinicians to be wary:

'It sometimes happens that we take prepsychotics [that is psychotics who have not had a conspicuous 'psychotic episode'] into analysis, and we know what the result of that is —the result is psychotics. The question of the contraindications of analysis would not arise if we didn't all recall some particular case in our practice, or in the practice of our colleagues, [of] a full-blown psychosis — a hallucinatory psychosis.' [161]

For ethical reasons the psychoanalyst must possess an identified desire: the desire for the Other's desire. But there is a clinical and logical problem applying this formula in psychosis; psychotics do not have the same relation to either desire, to the little other or little object, to the big Other or the unconscious, or to the Names of the father that neurotics have. If the clinician pursues the policy of attempting to identify the psychotic's absent desire then the psychotic's fragile ego is very likely to crash and burn.

The differences of technique revolve in part around the fragility of the psychotic's ego, and the strength of the neurotic's ego, and the very different relations that psychotics and neurotics have to 'objects'. The neurotic is a

---

[159] Branded goods —names— are often sought after as if they were the key to a prized enjoyment, often at the price of a loan or debt.

[160] S Freud, New Introductory Lectures in Psychoanalysis, Explanations and Applications, *SE 22*, [1933], 1973, p155.

[161] J Lacan, *The Psychoses*, ed Miller, trans Grigg, Routledge, London, 1993, p251.

subject: the psychotic is not properly speaking a subject[162]. Clinical work with psychotics aims at maintaining or producing a stable façade of neurosis. For this reason it is important not to invite psychotics to lie on your couch, outside your visual field. You should be within their visual field, providing an accessible image: underlining the variable symbolic value of your exchange —by placing the client on the couch— brings into question the relation of the image and the symbol, that is of the imaginary, the symbolic and the real. The psychotic already has to struggle hard to keep language —the symbolic— in its quasi-neurotic place, and should not be challenged in this already difficult and sometimes vain labour. The clinician remaining within the field of view should help prevent the fragile pseudo pseudo-object a of the psychotic client from disappearing:

'An analysis can, right from its first stages, trigger a psychosis . . . but no one has ever explained why. It's obviously a function of the subject's disposition, but also of an imprudent handling of the object relation.' [163]

When working with neurotics it is important to point out the contradictions and inconsistencies in their speech, especially in the first phase of analysis. Lacan's jargon for this technique is *'rectification to the real'*. Using this technique with psychotics is likely to precipitate a florid episode or breakdown. With neurotics it is important to end a session on a question, ambiguity or revaluation: with psychotics a session should generally be ended on an answer or solution.

Put crudely, there is a flow of meanings and words, and their connections with one another in all cases of neurosis and perversion: in many cases of psychosis speech will halt without pointing the way or even hinting at any connections. In neurosis and perversion the ego functions to camouflage unconscious desires, and always leaves traces or gaps: in psychosis, some or all of these traces are absent. It's not as though there are a few details or matters of fact which the psychotic is ignorant of, or one or two straightforward questions that he cannot answer: the psychotic's relationship to the whole of language is totally different from the relationship that neurotics have to language. Listening to a neurotic's

---

[162] What does it mean to be a subject? One way to answer this question is to ask: 'To what is one subjected?' In neurosis a relatively straightforward and universal answer is ordinary language functions: in psychosis there is not the same subjection to language, because the names of the father have been foreclosed. So any subjectivity in psychosis is akin to the security of tenure that squatters possess. Squatters can be evicted on little or no notice. A psychotic's expulsion from the ordinary neurotic house of language can be triggered by a single episode or event: neurotics have a secure lifetime tenancy in the ordinary house of language from which they cannot be evicted. This Freudian and Lacanian idea is has been taken up in a restricted form by T Crow in 'Schizophrenia as the price that homo sapiens pays for language . . .' *Brain Res Res Rev,*. 2000 Mar 31 (2-3) 118-29.

[163] J Lacan, *The Psychoses*, ed Miller, trans Grigg, Routledge, London, 1993, p15.

speech nearly always leaves one with the impression that there is something unsaid, something profoundly absent —not unconscious— but missing altogether. The speech of psychotics sometimes comes to a full but jerky stop without further associations [164]. Psychotic speech tends to either associate wildly, producing multiple neologisms or word salads, or fails to make ordinary neurotic slips. Some psychotics speak seamlessly as if they had prepared the whole paragraph beforehand, and insist on not being interrupted. This kind of speech is very different from ordinary neurotic speech which typically has far more slips of the tongue. Here is what Lacan had to say on this topic:

'A minimum of the sensitivity that our trade gives us clearly demonstrates something that can always be seen in what is known as 'prepsychosis', namely the feeling that the subject has come to the edge of a hole. This is to be taken literally. It's not a matter of understanding what is going on when we aren't present . . . It's a matter of understanding, not imagining, what happens for a subject when the question comes to him from where there is no signifier, when it's a hole, a lack, that makes itself felt as such . . . In psychosis it's the signifier that is in question, and as the signifier is never solitary, as it invariably forms something coherent — this is the very significance of the signifier — the lack of one signifier necessarily brings the subject to the point of calling the [whole] set of signifiers into question.' [165]

And: *'There is another form of defence that a forbidden tendency or meaning will provoke. It's the defence that consists in not approaching the place where there is no answer to the question. One is more at ease this way and, after all, this is the characteristic of normal people. Don't ask us questions, we've been taught, and this is why we're here. But as psychoanalysts it's nevertheless our business to try to enlighten these poor unfortunates who have asked themselves questions. We're certain that neurotics have asked themselves a question. Psychotics, it's not so sure.'* [166]

Further reading

F Kaltenbeck, Case of Schizophrenia, *Journal of the Centre for Freudian Analysis and Research* (JCFAR), Issue 10 & 11, 1998, p172.

V Palomera, The Fragmentation of Identity in the Psychotic Experience, *Analysis*, No 7, 1996, p5.

J Lacan, *Ecrits*, On a question preliminary to any possible treatment of psychosis, trans Sheridan, Tavistock, 1977.

---

[164] For psychotics the signifier fails to represent the subject for another signifier.
[165] J Lacan, *The Psychoses*, ed Miller, trans Grigg, Routledge, London, 1993, p202-3.
[166] Ibid, p202.

CHAPTER EIGHT

Phobia as a roundabout

Phobia is a kind of hysteria and the common starting point of a roundabout for conversion hysteria, obsessional neurosis and perversion.

In ordinary language terms an obsession is the opposite of a phobia. Phobics avoid an object or situation: obsessionals insist on being close to an object, situation or ritual. But these ordinary language, behavioural or medical-style diagnoses fail to take any account of the underlying language structures that generate behaviours. To illustrate how clinically impractical these surface descriptions are it is easy enough to reclassify every obsessional as a phobic, simply by placing the opposite of their ritual within a phobia. Here is an example: an obsessional who had to check that every window and door was locked, five consecutive times before he went to sleep, could just as well be construed as someone who had a phobia of breaking in.

Phobia is the structure with which almost all children play or experiment at some time. But if we were to judge the behaviour of children with the same standards we use for adults then most children would be psychiatric patients at some point. Children, often briefly, and almost universally struggle with phobia, trying to find some path through the entanglements and knots of their Oedipus complex. The phobic object appears to stand for a paternal function, for the symbolic father, as the child's failed attempt to make good its separation from its mother, due to the inadequate paternal function.

The inadequacy of the paternal function that structures phobia comes at a later stage, after the question of a different but related paternal function has been answered in relation to psychosis. For both Lacan and Freud phobia is the second structure, becoming available only after the question of psychosis has been given the answer 'no'. According to Freud:

'The first neuroses of childhood are phobias, states in which we see so clearly how an initial generation of anxiety is replaced by the later formation of a symptom . . .' [167] And: *'The series [of anxiety hysteria, conversion hysteria, obsessional neurosis, dementia praecox, paranoia, melancholia, mania] seems to repeat phylogenetically an historical origin. What are now neuroses were once phases in human conditions'* [168]

---

[167] S Freud, New Introductory Lectures, mistranslated as 'Anxiety and Instinctual Life': it ought to be 'Anxiety and the Life of the Drive', *SE 22*, p84.
[168] S Freud, *A Phylogenetic Fantasy —Overview of the Transference Neuroses*, The Belknap Press of Harvard University Press, 1987.

Phobia and hysteria

Freud struggled with the terminology of phobia, although he was clear that it was a sort of hysteria:

In the classificatory system of the neuroses no definite position has hitherto been assigned to 'phobias' . . . For phobias . . . which are in fact the most common, the name of 'anxiety hysteria' seems to me not inappropriate . . . It finds its justification in the similarity between the . . . structure of these phobias and that of hysteria — a similarity which is complete except upon a single point . . . For in anxiety hysteria the libido which has been liberated from the pathogenic material by repression is not converted (that is, diverted from the mental sphere into a somatic [bodily] innervation), but is set free in the shape of anxiety. In the clinical cases that we meet with, this 'anxiety hysteria' may be combined with 'conversion hysteria' in any proportion. There exist cases of pure conversion hysteria without any trace of anxiety, just as there are cases of simple anxiety hysteria, which exhibit feelings of anxiety and phobias, but have no admixture of conversion . . . Anxiety hysterias are the most common of all . . . neurotic disorders. But, above all, they are those which make their appearance earliest in life; they are par excellence the neuroses of childhood . . . An anxiety hysteria tends to develop more and more into a 'phobia'. In the end the patient may have got rid of all his anxiety, but only at the price of subjecting himself to all kinds of inhibitions and restrictions.' [169]

What is the relation of phobia to hysteria? Phobia is a kind of hysteria. There are two forms of hysteria: 'phobia' also known as 'anxiety hysteria', and 'conversion hysteria'. In cases of conversion hysteria the client has 'converted' some of the psychic material into a bodily form of suffering, for example, headaches, paralysis or insomnia. Anxiety hysteria is one and the same as phobia. In some cases where a client suffers panic attacks —high levels of anxiety— there is no obvious object as there usually is with a phobia. This apparent absence or lack is dealt with in Chapter Fourteen when we look at the question: What is an object?

'My kingdom for a horse', or 'the fall of my mother's captivating kingdom for the fall of my father's horse'

'Does it really matter what these affectionate people do so long as they don't do it in the street and frighten the horses?" [170]

---

[169] S Freud, A Phobia in a 5 year old boy, *SE 10*, [1909b], 1976, p115.
[170] Mrs Patrick Campbell, an English actress of the 19th-20th centuries referring to homosexuality.

Freud was consulted in the case of 'Little Hans', a five-year-old boy, by the father of Little Hans.[171] Hans was a mummy's boy, and his mother was the one who wore the trousers. The father was hen-pecked, yet showed no signs of suffering. How was Little Hans he going to separate himself from his mother?

Such a separation would constitute something of a dramatic passage from little boyhood to manhood. This separation would require giving something up, something which presumably the father —as such a man— had already given up in his coming to manhood, in his separation from his mother and his proximity to his wife?

As a baby, Little Hans had been spoilt by his mother, when he almost had her to himself: later he struggled to find a position in the family that would allow him to share his mother with his father and his new sister. This new position insisted on Little Hans finding some way of being apart from his mother, but even Hans' father was dominated by his wife, and his mother, Hans' grandmother! What way out could Little Hans find?

Perhaps Little Hans reasoned along the following lines: *'Daddy is somebody who mummy loves, and like me, he is male. If I identify with Daddy, then I will be able to have Mummy's love, just as Daddy has mummy's love'*. But in this family it was Little Hans' mother who wore the trousers. Daddy was given a hard time by Little Hans' mother, and even by his own mother, Little Hans' grandmother. Little Hans saw his father as a man dominated by women, yet the father showed no signs of suffering. What had Daddy given up in order to be a Daddy? What was his qualification, his castration?

To be separated from his mother would mean giving something up, and Little Hans supposed, would allow him the freedom to have a privileged enjoyment with a woman of the sort his father had with his mother. What would Little Hans have to give up in order to be a man? It's not a simple matter for a child to change its relation to his mother, from one of extreme dependency to one of independence. Much must be given up in order for this Oedipal drama to be overturned because whenever a love relation is given up there is always the formation of an idea or ideals, whose intensity or strength is in proportion to the love lost.

For Little Hans what his father had given up in becoming a man —in relation to women— was totally obscure. So it appeared to Little Hans that being a man —for Daddy— entailed a profound contradiction, getting something of value for nothing. Little Hans was searching hard for some method of paying his debt to be, the price of manhood, which would be incurred through his being allowed some access to some women, along the lines of the Primal Horde.

---

[171] See S Freud's Analysis of a Phobia in a 5 year old boy, *SE 10*, [1909b], 1976.

What price should be paid for this? Towards answering this question here are two columns of text. In the right column are my comments; in the left column Daddy Hans reports his observations and conversations with Little Hans who can be observed trying to answer the above question:

'Hans suddenly ran indoors as a carriage with two horses came along. I could see nothing unusual about it, and asked him what was wrong.	Daddy sees nothing wrong.
'The horses are so proud,'** he said, **'that I'm afraid they'll fall down.' *(The coachmen was reining the horses in tight, so that they were trotting with short steps and holding their heads high. In fact their action was 'proud'.)*	Little Hans responds: what is wrong is connected with falling and pride. Falling can be understood as the loss of a privileged position, of a castration, a loss of power.
'I asked him who it really was that was so proud.	
*'He: **'You are, when I come into bed with Mummy.'***	Little Hans then explains that the pride and the falling is with Daddy, in relation to Mummy.
'I: 'So you want me to fall down?'	
*'Hans:. **'Yes. You've got to be naked and knock up against a stone and bleed, and then I'll be able to be alone with Mummy for a little bit at all events. When you come up into our flat I'll be able to run away quick so that you don't see.'** [172]*	Little Hans details the benefits for himself of the fall he would like his father to take. If the father suffers some demonstrable castration then little Hans will be able to tolerate his mother's desire *'for a little bit'*, without being overwhelmed.

Lacan explains Little Hans' anxiety and phobia as the failure of the father to properly interrupt and punctuate the mother's desire. It is a symptom of the mother's desire, her matronising Little Hans —that is the presentation of her lack— as continuous and uninterrupted that Little Hans finds intolerable:

---

[172] Ibid p82.

"OH, MUM, I WISH YOU'D NEGLECT ME SOMETIMES!"

'What provokes anxiety? It is not, contrary to what is said, either the rhythm . . . nor the alternation of the presence-absence of the mother. And what proves it, is that the infant takes pleasure in repeating this game of presence and absence: **this possibility of absence, is what gives presence its security***. What is most anxiety provoking for the child, is that precisely this relation of lack on which he establishes himself, which makes him desire, this relation is all the more disturbed when there is no possibility of lack, when the mother is always on his back, and especially by wiping his bottom, the model of the demand, of the demand which cannot fail.'* [173]

Little Hans' urgent requirement to find some way of separating himself from his mother's demands and desires found no solution in the figure of his father. Little Hans had to make his own solution; he found a paternal metaphor that represented the 'something missing' that represented a price to be paid for his manhood. This new solution would have to be something that Little Hans could rely on in his experiments to forge a separation between himself and his

---

[173] J Lacan, Seminar on Anxiety, unpublished, trans Gallagher, 5th November, 1962.

mother. His solution was to become phobic with horses. How might a phobia of horses solve his problem? Little Hans took horses as a paternal metaphor: the fallen horses stood for something that his father lacked: a crucial castration or fall. Little Hans relied on this paternal metaphor as grounds for not leaving the flat, and in particular for not leaving his mummy. What did Little Hans fear would happen to the horse that stopped him separating from his mother? A fall.

The father's lack in this case is his absent castration. What is missing is something missing! What Daddy has not given up prevented Little Hans from giving up his bondage and attachment to Mummy. Little Hans was overwhelmed by her desire. So on the one hand he wished to be spared from his mother's desire, and on the other hand he could not see what price to pay for this separation to be. This explains why Little Hans created an object with his phobia that simultaneously prevented him from leaving his mother, as well as the possible means by which he might escape her: the horse. The phobia as an object or variable with two values: the horse that is proud and the horse that falls. The horse that is proud is relied on by Little Hans to keep him close to his mother, yet the same horse is presented and maintained as a serious problem for the parents because its fall would symbolise the escape and liberation of Little Hans from the overwhelming clutches of his mother on his manhood.

The 'fallen horse' that Little Hans feared represented the lack: the 'proud horse' represents the lack of a lack: the first lack was his father's castration, the second its problematic absence. The two-valued horse made a space for Little Hans in which he could explore his separation and identification with his mother and father. According to Freud:

'The formation of his phobia had the effect of abolishing his affectionate object investment of his mother . . . though the actual content of his phobia betrayed no signs of this. The process of repression had attacked almost all of the components of his Oedipus complex . . . **His phobia disposed of the two main impulses of the Oedipus complex —the aggressive impulses towards his father and his over fondness for his mother.'** [174]

According to Lacan:

'What constitutes anxiety*, is* **when something . . . corresponds to . . . the object of desire** *. . . It is the imaginary phallus, the something which reminds us that what everything starts from is imaginary castration, that there is no —and for good reason — image of lack. When something appears there, it is because . . .* **the lack is lacking** *. . . [M]any things can disappear which are anomalous, this is not what makes us anxious. But if all of a sudden* **all norms are lacking***, namely what constitutes the lack — because the norm is correlative to the idea*

---

[174] Inhibitions, Symptoms and Anxiety, *SE 20*, [1925], 1976, p106.

of lack — if all of a sudden it is not lacking . . . it is at that moment that anxiety begins.' [175]

What does Lacan mean when he claims that that *'there is no . . . image of lack'*? The image is within the domain of the imaginary, while the idea of something lacking or missing is always symbolic, that is, is judged lacking with reference to the truth. So for example the image of a special version of a playing card such as the nine of hearts —with one heart missing— will only come to have its lack identified through reference to the concept or number nine, or some such procedure that invokes the truth. Images themselves are neither true nor false. 'The true and the false' are entirely and exclusively properties of the symbolic, of language. 'The real' emerges from the ongoing and impossible to eliminate leftovers and mismatches between the world of images and the world of symbols: *'Lack is graspable only by means of the symbolic'* [176] Lacan identifies the emergence of anxiety at the point when this lack —the real— disappears because the symbolic has become unstable or fragile:

'Here . . . with little Hans, the universal signifier that the phobic object realises is that, and nothing else. Here it is at an advance post . . . well before one approaches the hole, the gap realised in the interval where the real presence threatens that a unique sign prevents the subject from approaching. This is why the role, the mainspring and the reason for the phobia is not, as people who have nothing but the word 'fear' on their lips believe, 'a vital danger' or even 'a narcissistic one'. It is very precisely, according to certain privileged developments of the position of the subject with respect to the big Other (in the case of little Hans, to his mother) this point where **what the subject dreads meeting is a . . . return into the previous nothingness the whole . . . signifying system.** *'* [177]

In another case a two-year-old boy produced a phobia of all flying insects, no doubt in response to the common absence of his father who would leave his son alone in his mother's hands, in order to fly as an airline pilot. Here *'the imaginary phallus . . . namely what constitutes the lack . . . is not lacking . . . it is at that moment that anxiety begins.'* [178] The child's phobia was designed to interrupt the mother's excessive enjoyment of the child in the absence of the father. 'Flying object' or 'flying insect', the signifier of the father's absence

[175] J Lacan, *Ecrits*, On the Possible Treatment of Psychosis, trans Sheridan, Tavistock Routledge, London, [1966], 1980, p198.

[176] J Lacan, Seminar 10, 1963, quoted in B Fink, *A Clinical Introduction to Lacanian Psychoanalysis,* Harvard, 1997.

[177] J Lacan, Transference Seminar, unpublished, 26th April, 1961, trans Gallagher.

[178] J Lacan, *Ecrits*, On the Possible Treatment of Psychosis, trans Sheridan, Tavistock Routledge, London, [1966], 1980, p198.

was relied on by the child's phobia as a stand in for the symbolic father's lack, that is for the absent desire of the father: had the father's desire or lack been sufficiently present the child would have been saved from the excessive enjoyment his mother took in her relation with the overwhelmed boy. For an elaboration of this theme see Shylock's Phobia in the Appendix.

Phobia and the Primal Horde

The phobic member of the primal horde may have had insufficient exposure to the Primal Father to be properly separated from his mother. His fear of the phobic object would have stood in for the absent fear of the absent Primal Father. The repressive power of the phobic object would be an attempt to compensate for the absent repressive power of the absent father. Another way of understanding the same phenomenon is to think of the phobic's libido or drive as having been insufficiently or unevenly repressed, so that it sought and found a phobic object to which the drive attached and so became represented.

Phobia, globalisation and aliens

The increasingly popular fascination with discovering alien life can be understood as the post-globalisation demand for the Other by the phobic subject. Phobics are running out of candidates for their Other. Before globalisation, the dreaded Other of the phobic might have lived in the next village or valley. Now Other nationalities and even Other races no longer suffice. Globalisation has eradicated many of our differences. Universal culture of the McDonald's variety is taking over the world so it is becoming increasingly urgent that a conspicuously distinct proud/fallen Other be identified by the phobic, and in particular by the xenophobe.

Because it appears that man is the organism that endures the most profound conflicts of interest —those necessary for the acquisition of language— it seems that there are consequences for the possibilities for 'a species of alien more advanced than ourselves'. The price that people pay for their relation to language is very high; for many, at different points in their lives, the price is too high. The division of the subject comes as a package with language, and it is almost inconceivable that any organism could endure greater division than that which man suffers in relation to language. If, as is probably the case, aliens do exist, then, if they have a similar relation to language, and they too will also suffer with neurosis and psychosis. Aliens may well be more advanced than us technologically but it is unlikely that they will have advanced significantly further in the structures of their language, mind and society because it seems that man —burdened so heavily due to his capacity for language— is already at breaking point and sometimes beyond it.

An essential part of the explanation offered by bin Laden for his part in the destruction of the Twin Towers in America, and of thousands of lives on the 11th September, is the presence of American soldiers in Saudi Arabia, where he was born.   His argument is that this 'invasion' by non-Islamic foreigners —although at the invitation of the ruling Saudi Royal family— must be punished. He argued that his actions are to be regarded as the justified response of one who has been violated and aggrieved. One consequence of his actions has been an increase in American nationalism. America has become better distinguished from other nations in the global community; the attacks can be understood as a variety of xenophobia and an attack on globalisation.

Tactics, strategy and policy

Freud had some advice for differential technique in cases of conversion hysteria and anxiety hysteria:

'Our therapy was, in fact, first designed for conversion hysteria; in anxiety hysteria (phobias) we must alter our procedure to some extent. The fact is that these patients cannot bring out the material necessary for resolving the phobia so long as they feel protected by retaining their phobic condition. One cannot, of course, induce them to give up their protective measures and work under the influence of anxiety from the beginning of the treatment. One must therefore help them by interpreting . . . until they can . . . do without the protection of their phobia and expose themselves to a now comparatively moderate degree of anxiety. Only when they have done so does the material necessary for achieving solution of the phobia become accessible.' [179]

We will consider tactics, strategy and policy for phobia, which are the same as those for hysteria, at the end of the next chapter.

---

[179] S Freud, The Future Prospects of Psychoanalytic Therapy, *SE 11*, [1910], 1976, p145.

CHAPTER NINE

Hysteria — the simplest neurosis

Putting phobia on one side there are two forms of hysteria: 'anxiety hysteria' and 'conversion hysteria'. In conversion hysteria the client has 'converted' some of the psychic material —the words or signifiers— into a bodily form of suffering such as headaches, paralysis, insomnia or irritable bowel syndrome. An elegant young woman had been preoccupied with her problematic relation with her father, and complained of her inability to cease savagely biting her fingernails down to the quick. Eventually she interpreted the near elimination of her own nails as a protective measure; she was defending herself from the consequences of '*scratching his eyes out*'.

In hysteria there is at least one desire that the hysteric does not properly recognise as his or her own. Typically they achieve this by over-emphasising the importance of other people's desires, and by under-emphasising their own. So a hysteric might complain: *'Without you I am nothing'*, *'He wants this from me, and she wants that . . . They are all placing their demands on me. Why does everyone want so much from me when I want nothing from them'*. A hysterical car driver might imagine that every single horn she heard was a critical response to her driving. Hysterics will prefer to talk about what other people in their life want —especially of them— while they play down what they desire.

One of the main functions of psychosomatic symptoms is to be an address to the Other, like a letter. The symptom speaks the hysteric's desire and demands, addressed to her Other. It calls out for a response and for interpretation from her Other; the fallen woman's phobia demonstrated her hysterical symptom as her demand for the Other's desire: she was afraid of the consequences of her sexual desire, and of the shame that would follow from acting on her desire. Her fantasy was that she would be seen lying in the street. It is the 'being seen' that is important in this case, her little other, the gaze of her Other that saw her and occupied a crucial place in her conflict with her desire, as her symptom.

The policy, strategy and tactics of the hysteric are to camouflage her own desire by focusing on and exaggerating her Other's desire. One consequence in the clinic is that hysterics are often very perceptive about their clinician's tastes, desires and moods. Such an exquisite sensitivity can be disconcerting for the clinician.

Hysterics typically believe that suffering is a beautiful honour! Many hysterics won't be quiet about their discomfort or pain, sometimes limping about making their suffering obvious, or complaining to complete strangers. Hysterics with psychosomatic symptoms almost certainly suffer genuine discomfort and pain. 'Psychosomatic' simply means that there is a mental or psychic component in someone's medical condition. So a heart attack could be psychosomatic, if a psychic factor of the sufferer played an important role in causing the heart attack. They may be 'making up' their symptom in some sense but that does not mean that they are not suffering or that there are not physiological effects. Important questions here are: what value does the suffering have for the client? And: What does the suffering represent for whom?

Of all the clinical types hysterics are closest to the terrible and profound truth that *'desire is desire for the Other's desire'*, in their emphasis on the Other's desire. Hysterics are —in a sense— telling the truth when they complain that the Other's desire is the problem, whereas obsessionals complicate matters, hiding away both their Others, offsetting one against the Other. Perverts don't complain as a rule —they are having too much fun— and psychotics struggle to keep hold of any solid reference, or truth, as it threatens to slip away, along with their grasp of ordinary neurotic language.

Because hysteria recognises —in dramatic form— the importance of the Other of language, that is the Other's desire, hysteria is regarded by Freud and Lacan as the privileged pathology to aim for in the clinic. There is nothing simpler. Hysteria represents the fundamental truth that all humanity, language, meaning and the problematic desires that come with it, have been completely dependent, in their origin and support, on the Other's desire. In a hysterical denial schoolchildren sometimes boast that: *'Sticks and stones may break my bones, but words will never hurt me.'* A popular adult version is *'I don't care what other people say or want'*.

Complaining about the Other's desire is a kind of knowing return to the position of the infant: the infant is the one to whom all good parents address their demands, and on whom they cruelly thrust their desires. Once a neurotic has come to terms with this major trauma in his life —the lack of the Other which can also be understood as the demands and desires of the Other— then he has gone as far as is possible in understanding his symptom as his solution to his suffering, and come to terms with the ways in which his life, desire and fantasy have been addressed and constructed around the Other's desire: *'In psychoanalysis, the hysteric is cured of everything except her hysteria.'* [180] We will return to these issues when we look at The End of Analysis.

---

[180] J Lacan, The Psychoanalytic Act, unpublished, 21 February 1968, trans Gallagher.

Gender and Hysteria

'I am an ass, I am a woman's man and besides myself.' [181]

'The hysteric's question: What is a woman?' [182]

'What characterizes the hysterical position is a question that refers precisely to the two signifying poles of male and female. The hysteric addresses it with all his being —how can one be either male or female? This does indeed imply that the hysteric nevertheless possesses its reference. The question is this —what is it that the entire structure of the hysteric, with his fundamental identification with the individual of the sex opposite to his own, by which his own sex is questioned, is introduced into, suspended from, and preserved in?' [183]

Most hysterics are women and most obsessionals are men, but beware. Many meanings are in flux for people, including the meaning of gender; 'a man' is not necessarily someone with a penis, nor is 'a woman' necessarily a person with a uterus, as pre-operative transsexuals complain. Queen Elizabeth I for example claimed to *'know I have the body of a weak and feeble woman, but I have the mind and stomach of a king.'*

Lacan made a distinction between the type of genitals a person has, and their psychic structure; a person with a penis may have a woman's psychic structure, and a person with a womb can be a man. Lacan, following a case of Freud's[184], theorised that some of those with the appearance of men —who live their lives as Don Juans— having sex with large numbers of women, have the psychic structure of a woman.[185]

One common fantasy for men —for those who typically have penises— is *'of having sex with men'*: a common fantasy for many women —I mean mostly for those with a uterus— is: 'I am a man'. Fantasies are important in any attempt to understand gender and sexuality because desire arises out of difference, often sexual difference. So important questions for the hysteric identifying his desire —from within the confusing field of sexual difference— are: *'How is it that I am desired by the Other? Actively or passively? As a man or as a woman?'* *'Am I a man or a woman?'*

---

[181] Dromio in Shakespeare's *The Comedy of Errors.*

[182] J Lacan, *The Psychoses,* ed Miller, trans Grigg, Routledge, London, 1993, p173.

[183] Ibid p248-9.

[184] S Freud, Introductory Lectures on Psychoanalysis, Lecture Six, The Technique of Interpretation, *SE 15*, [1916], 1976, p107-8.

[185] This theory is outlined in Lacan's unpublished seminar 'Logic of Fantasy text, and his difficult Encore, Lacan's seminar 20 known as 'Encore' or 'En corp', published by Norton as *On Feminine Sexuality, the limits of love and knowledge, Book 20, Encore 1972-1973*, trans Fink, 1998.

It is also common for daughters to identify with their fathers, and to become in some ways like their fathers. The questions: 'What is male' and 'What is female?' do not have obvious or straightforward answers, nor do they simply focus on a subject's genitals. Human sexuality is not 'a given value'; a thing of fixed meaning but something that is a part of the infinite diversity of culture and language. Sexuality therefore has a symbolic value, and is more determined by a person's language and fantasy than their genital type. In the following quotation, Lacan explains how Freud's concept of polymorphous perversity relates to hysteria and questions of gender:

'The initial opening of identification with the other, that is, with an object, starts from here. An object is isolated, neutralised, and as such particularly eroticised. This is what makes an infinitely greater number of objects enter the field of human desire than enter animal experience.

In this interweaving of the imaginary and the symbolic lies the source of the essential function that the ego plays in the structuring of neurosis. When Freud's famous hysterical female, Dora [186]*, finds herself wondering, What is a woman?, she is attempting to symbolise the female organ as such. Her identification with the man, bearer of the penis, is for her on this occasion a means of approaching this definition that escapes her. She literally uses the penis as an imaginary instrument for apprehending what she hasn't succeeded in symbolising.*

'There are many more women hysterics than men hysterics —this is a fact of clinical experience— because the path to the woman's symbolic realisation is more complicated. Becoming a woman and wondering what a woman is, are two essentially different things. I would go even further: it's because one doesn't become one that one wonders and, up to a point, to wonder is the contrary of becoming one. The metaphysics of the woman's position is the detour imposed on her subjective realisation. Her position is essentially problematic, and up to a certain point it's inassimilable. But once the woman is locked into hysteria, it must also be said that her position presents an unusual stability by virtue of its structural simplicity: the more simple a structure is, the fewer the points of rupture it displays. When her question takes shape in the form of hysteria, it's very easy for the woman to raise it by taking the shortest path, namely identification with the father.

In masculine hysteria the situation is certainly much more complex. To the extent that in man the Oedipal realisation is better structured, the hysteric's question has less chance of arising. But if it's raised, what is it? Here there is the same asymmetry as in the Oedipus complex —hysterics, whether men or

---

[186] S Freud, Fragment of an Analysis of a Case of Hysteria ('Dora'), *SE 7*, [1901], 1976.

women, ask themselves the same question. The question of the male hysteric also concerns the feminine position.' [187]

Hysteria and the Primal Horde

In the Primal Horde the desire of the father is the law. In order for any individual in the horde to get clear about his own desire he will have to first find a way of locating his place relative to the desire of the Primal Father. How might this be done? Desire is a property of language. Language operates according to rules or laws and the origin of the whole universe of rules and laws in the Primal Horde is the desire of the Primal Father. So in order to even get a bearing on one's own desire in the Primal Horde it must be necessary to first ask: *'What does the Primal Father desire?'* The hysterical subject of the Primal Horde claims: *'I do not have any desire. But the Primal Father plagues me with his desires. I don't know what he wants. Sometimes he wants this, sometimes that, I don't know where I am. I can't work out what his desire is, but it remains the most important thing in my life.'*

Hysteria and clinical technique: tactics, strategy and policy

Hysterics rely on the strategy and tactics of over-emphasising the other's desire, and under-emphasising their own. It is also common for hysterics to believe and act as if there was dignity and honour in suffering, which the hysteric can proudly wear like a medal. This often allows the clinician to deduce contradictions within the hysteric's speech [188]. This technique is known as 'rectification to the real', and should be used generously with all hysterics, especially in the first phase of clinical work. Some of these contradictions will hint at or implicate the client's desire in a way that they have not been able to previously acknowledge without the disguise of a symptom. For example one client repeatedly complained: *'I hate my father'*, yet she devoted much energy to the project of impressing her father and gaining his approval. The clinician asked: *'Is what your father thinks of you important?'*. This question prompted a series of contradictions, including: *'I think of my father boasting of my achievements to his friends'*, allowing the clinician to deduce the interpretation: *'You devote much energy towards gaining your father's approval and you hate him'*. This technique —if used with caution— will probably provoke new material from hysterics and obsessionals.

---

[187] J Lacan, *The Psychoses*, ed Miller, trans Grigg, Routledge, London, 1993, p178.
[188] This Freudian and Lacanian technique has something in common with Rational Emotive Therapy. See A Ellis & W Dryden, *The Practice of Rational-emotive Therapy*. New York: Springer, 1987.

Because hysterics have their eye, ear and nose on the other, and are generally on surveillance, sniffing out the other's desire in order to better hide their own, a little personal information about the clinician goes a very long way. Generally the clinician should be secretive about his life without giving the impression that he is a robot. But in the first stage of the clinical work hysterics may find it impossible to stay unless they believe they have the measure of their clinician. Obviously this is upside-down; the client's psychoanalytic work is to make discoveries about themselves. Sometimes, with very anxious or demanding clients I give away some abbreviated answers to one or two of many personal questions during the preliminary sessions. But I rarely answer questions straightforwardly. I may ask: *'Why is that an interesting question for you?'* Or: *'Some questions I will answer, and some I won't'*, or *'What difference would it make to you if my answer was "yes"'?* This approach may engage a flighty hysteric more efficiently then the blanket refusal to give any personal information. Not only does this technique allow one to work with clients who may not otherwise be regarded as 'therapeutically orientated', but if carefully done does not endanger later work.

One hysteric, in the second session, repeatedly pressed me for information about my qualifications, training, experience, age, race, religion and whether I had children or not. Failing to answer any of these questions would probably have allowed this client to become too anxious to proceed any further. He demanded some measure of my desire. I asked him about the value of his questions, and asked what his response might be if a particular question was not answered. This opened the way for the client to provide more material. When he pressed ahead, demanding answers, I provided a small part of the information asked for.

Working with hysterics is generally efficient and lively because it is usually easy for them to produce new material. Hysterics will often vary their tactics and strategy quickly with the aim of manipulating the clinician's desire, so it is important for the clinician to be responsive and to be able to vary his tactics and strategy.

It is important not to assume or bolster the position that the client invites you to take of being 'the subject supposed to know'. If a client demands 'to know' wholesale, *' What is the meaning of my symptoms?'* or *'What does the future hold?'* you should not answer, except perhaps with silence, a declaration of your ignorance or a question. Hysterics will often persist in trying to identify you with a precious knowledge. Another tactic used by hysterics is name-dropping, and the making of references to books, films and people supposedly known to both of you. If a client asks if you have read a particular book, or seen a film it is helpful to sidestep this question, perhaps by asking: *'what did the film mean to you?'*, or *'assume I haven't, and tell me what it meant to you'*.

You may well have seen the film, but you will have little information about its meaning for your client unless they speak about its value for them.

Some clients try to get away with saying little, perhaps waving their hands about, making obvious exaggerations, or relying heavily on phrases such as *'you know what I mean', 'all that sort of thing'*. Ask for clarification, and take the part of an interested but ignorant person. If you assume that you are ignorant —which is probably justified— you'll be in a much better position to learn of the client's issues, and to help them to a conscious knowledge or to acting on their desire. If a client uses a word or phrase that you are not familiar with you should ask its meaning, but perhaps not straightaway: it may be a slip of the tongue or be just about to be clarified. If you fall into the trap of assuming a knowledge that the client has not articulated then the client is likely to use your supposed knowledge against you, and as an excuse for leaving the clinical work. Towards the end phase of a hysteric's analysis: *'A calculated vacillation of the analyst's 'neutrality' may be more valuable for a hysteric than any amount of interpretation —though there is always a danger of frightening the patient.'* [189]

Beware: many psychotics produce a fake hysteria that also over-emphasises the importance of the Other's desire and under-emphasises their own. This strategy or policy is important to bear in mind in making a diagnosis because psychosis is sometimes diagnosed when the client is hysterical. It is certainly possible for hysterics to become difficult to 'manage', highly disturbed, violent, and to experience hallucinations without being in the least bit psychotic. Logically it would seem that there is a risk of paranoid psychotics being diagnosed as hysterics, but as far as I know it does not happen, perhaps because hysteria is an unfashionable diagnosis in psychiatry.

Further Reading

P Verhaeghe, *Does the Woman Exist?* London, Rebus Press, 1996,

T Hughes, Exchange Value and Use in Psychoanalysis, *The Letter*, Spring, 1999.

---

[189] J Lacan, *Ecrits*, Subversion of the Subject and Dialectic of Desire, translated Sheridan, Tavistock Routledge, London, 1980, p321-322.

CHAPTER TEN

Obsessional Neurosis —a complicated 'dialect of hysteria'

While hysterics often ask: *'what does it mean to be a woman?' 'Am I a man, or am I a woman?'*, obsessional neurotics often have a different fundamental question: the obsessional asks *'Am I alive or dead?'* The obsessional 'plays dead' so as to cheat his Other, and so save paying the cost of following his desire.

'Whenever I have succeeded in penetrating the mystery [of obsessive acts], I have found that the expected disaster was death.' [190]

Paradoxically they usually achieve this kind of death or passivity through an extraordinarily uniform activity of the type seen in the film *Groundhog Day*. An obsessional complaint might sound like this:

'On the one hand . . . but on the other . . . Nothing changes in my life. I do this very long and complicated task, but it's impossible, it doesn't get me anywhere, so I try and do this other impossible task, and then I go back to the first, and then . . . I have trouble choosing because I doubt everything.'

Children usually go through obsessional games, rituals and phases. These might include touching everything made out of wood, or insisting that they must not step on the lines of pavements. Adult obsessionals often exhaust themselves with similar activities as well as compiling endless lists, being plagued by doubt, having a lot of trouble finishing anything, and amassing huge collections, which are typically incomplete. Obsessionals get horribly tangled in labyrinthine impossibilities and become unable to decide, one way or another, on a course of action that would lead them out of their mess. According to Freud:

'The symptoms belonging to [obsessional neurosis] fall, in general, into two groups, each having an opposite trend. They are either prohibitions, precautions and expiations —that is, negative in character— or all they are, on the contrary, substituted satisfactions which often appear in symbolic disguise.' [191]

---

[190] S Freud, Totem and Taboo, *SE 13*, [1912],1976, p87.
[191] S Freud, Inhibitions, Symptoms and Anxiety, *SE 20*, [1926], 1976, p112.

At the heart of an obsessional's symptoms —his fundamental fantasy— is not one hidden desire (which the hysteric has) but two. These two desires are believed by the obsessional to be mutually exclusive, that is, they are 'in the real'; they are desires whose individual goals are believed to rule each other out.

There is a famous clinical case of Freud's known as 'The Rat Man'[192]. This young man was a daddy's boy. He wanted his father's approval for whatever he did. He wanted to marry his girlfriend, but his father had disapproved of women like his girlfriend, so either the young man was to follow his love for his girlfriend, or his love for his father. This obsessional's two mutually exclusive desires were:

1. To have the love and approval of his father, who disapproved of the girlfriend.

2. To have the love of his girlfriend.

He had a compulsive idea that tied and knotted his love for his girlfriend to his love for his father. So that any sexual enjoyment or jouissance would automatically be equated with an attack on his father. This formulation can be seen in two of the Ratman's beliefs:

'If I marry the lady some misfortune will befall my father'.

and

'If I have a wish to see a woman naked, my father will be bound to die' [193]

Because the obsessional believes that his two desires are mutually exclusive, that for him to act on the one desire would be to rule out his acting on the other, he reasons:

'Either I do X, which is impossible because I want Y, or I do Y, which is also impossible, because I want X. I can't give up X because I desire X, and I can't give up Y because I desire Y.'

In a naive sense it might have been possible for the Ratman to reconcile his love for his father with his love for his girlfriend, but in the young man's mind it was impossible, because he saw his two desires as incompatible. His whole life became centred on this impossibility; he found himself endlessly repeating tasks, backwards and forwards, to and fro, and he repeatedly moved, from one mutually exclusive desire, to the other, and then back again, without understanding why, as he wrestled with his impossibility or the real.

---

[192] S Freud, Notes Upon a Case of Obsessional Neurosis, *SE 10*, [1909], 1976.
[193] Ibid p226.

The obsessional is a bit like an accountant who is desperately trying to balance the books of a company that trades very rapidly. The oscillating income and expenditure —the two desires are offset against one another— push and pull, dominating the obsessional's life. This is why an obsessional asks *'Am I alive or dead?'* His frenetic activities are designed to make little or no difference to either of his desires overall, because he always sets one against the other, in order to make them both null. The obsessional often imagines that he is living a kind of death because he fails to complete anything, or to act so as to produce consequences from either of his desires.

What has obsessional neurosis to do with hysteria?

Obsessional neurosis is a more complex structure, dependent on the simpler structure of hysteria. Freud's idea was that:

'The language of an obsessional neurosis . . . is, as it were, only a dialect of the language of hysteria' [194]

And: *'Obsessional neurosis is not so popular as the universally familiar hysteria. It is not . . . so objectively noisy, it behaves more like a private affair of the patient's, it dispenses almost entirely with somatic phenomena, and creates all its symptoms in the mental sphere.'* [195]

'Obsessional neurosis originates, no doubt, in the same situation as hysteria, namely, the necessity of fending off the libidinal demands [the drive for love] of the Oedipus complex. Indeed, every obsessional neurosis seems to have a substratum of hysterical symptoms that had been formed at a very early stage.' [196]

Lacan claimed that obsession is *'a jargon of hysteria'.*[197] There is also —more importantly— an argument based on clinical experience with the same conclusion. We will look at an example of Freud's shortly. First a question: Why do Lacanian clinicians set about hystericising their obsessional clients? There are two related reasons for this policy: hysteria is far simpler, and hysterics are much closer to facing and acting on their desire than obsessionals. This is because hysterics understand and are traumatised by the fundamental truth that *'their desire is for the other's desire'.* Hysterics have one or more inefficiently repressed desire contra the desire or demand of another person —

---

[194] Ibid p157.

[195] S Freud, The Sense of Symptoms, Introductory Lectures on Psychoanalysis, *SE 16*, [1915], 1976, p258. I believe that this point is exaggerated: it is my experience that some obsessional neurotics suffer with somatic symptoms.

[196] S Freud, Inhibitions, Symptoms and Anxiety, *SE 20*, [1926d], 1976, p113.

[197] Quoted in Ellie Ragland-Sullivan, The Limits of Discourse Structure: Obsession and Hysteria, *Papers of the Freudian School of Melbourne*, 1988, p69.

who stands in for their Other— while obsessional neurotics juggle two inefficiently repressed desires, at a speed that allows the obsessional to fail to grasp either. On this theme Freud wrote:

'The conflicts of feeling in our patient which we have here enumerated separately were not independent of each other, but were bound together in pairs . . . the contradiction between his love and his hatred within each of these relations'. [198]

And: *'True obsessional acts . . . are only made possible because they constitute a kind of reconciliation, in the shape of a compromise, between the* **two antagonistic impulses'.**[199]

Lacan related the structure of hysteria to obsessional neurosis via the logical function of negation:

*'The hysterical manner of questioning, 'either . . . or . . .', contrasts with the obsessional's response, negation, '**n**either . . . **n**or . . .', neither male nor female. This negation is made on the basis of . . . hiding his being from the question, which is a way of remaining suspended from it. The obsessional is precisely neither one nor the other — one may also say that he is both at once.'* [200]

Here is a case of Freud's in which the relation of hysteria to obsessional neurosis is explored with a once hysterical woman who became an obsessional:

'The case was at first one of pure anxiety hysteria [manifest by panic attacks], following on a traumatic experience, and it preserved that character for some years. One day, however, it suddenly changed into an exceedingly severe obsessional neurosis . . . The obsessional neurosis was not a further reaction to the same trauma which had originally called forth the anxiety hysteria; it was a reaction to a second experience which had entirely eclipsed the first . . . Before she fell ill the patient had been a happy and almost entirely contented married woman. She wished to have children, a wish itself determined by infantile fixation, and fell ill when she realised that her husband, to whom she was entirely devoted, could not satisfy this longing. The anxiety hysteria with which she reacted to this frustration corresponded to a rejection of seduction fantasies in which she achieved her enduring wish for a child . . . The husband . . . began to react . . . by becoming . . . impotent during sexual intercourse. Immediately after he went on a journey . . . his wife, believing him to be permanently impotent produced her first obsessional symptom on the day before his expected return.

---

[198] S Freud, Notes Upon a Case of Obsessional Neurosis, *SE 10*, [1909], 1976, p238.
[199] Ibid, p244.
[200] J Lacan, *The Psychoses*, ed Miller, trans Grigg, Routledge, London, 1993, p 248-9.

The content of the obsessional neurosis consisted in a tormenting obsession about washing and cleanliness and in exceedingly vigorous protective measures against wicked injuries which others might have to fear from her . . . In such forms her sexual need was driven to find expression, as a result of the entire bankruptcy of a genital life brought about by the impotence of the husband, who was the only man to whom she could look for satisfaction.' [201]

Note that this woman possessed two desires: the desire for children and the desire for sex. Her being unable to follow her desire for children suited her hysterical structure: being additionally unable to enjoy sex led, along with other things, to her obsessional structure. Generally , when the subject has problems expressing one desire hysteria results: when there are problems expressing two desires —which are taken to be mutually exclusive— then obsessional neurosis is structured. We can speculate that Freud's obsessional neurotic above constructed mutual exclusivity regarding her desires along the following lines:

If my husband continues to have sex with me I will not have the children I desire, but I will continue to enjoy having sex with a man I love: if I have sex with another man —whom I do not love— and as a consequence have children, I will have to discontinue having sex with the man I love, therefore having sex with the man I love and having children are mutually exclusive.

The woman's childlessness was tolerable —within her hysterical structure— as long as her husband was making love to her. When he stopped she was no longer sufficiently compensated for the lack of children in her life. At this point the lack or desire for children and the sexual desire, or lack of sexual gratification became paired as mutually exclusive desires and an obsessional structure was born.

Obsessional neurosis and the Other

One way of analysing this idea of Freud's that there are *'two antagonistic impulses',* or two repressed desires in obsessional neurosis is to analyse the Other in hysteria and obsessional neurosis. This technique allows hysteria to be distinguished from obsessional neurosis: the Other for the hysteric always seems to be a far simpler entity than the Other of an obsessional.[202] This theme is developed in the next chapter when the concept of the big Other is reviewed, under the heading: Obsessional neurosis, the big Other and jouissance.

---

[201] S Freud, The Disposition To Obsessional Neurosis, *SE 12*, [1913], 1976, p320.
[202] Compare Freud's cases of the Ratman with Little Hans: I would suggest that the Other of Little Hans was his mother, while the Ratman's Other appear to have been both his father and his mother/girlfriend.

Because hysteria is simpler than obsessional neurosis, and complexity takes time to be produced or evolve, hysteria is prior. So every obsessional neurotic was first —before they became obsessional— an hysteric. This fact informs the tactics and strategy of clinical technique with obsessional neurotics, and explains why Lacanians hystericise their obsessional clients.

The Sick Logic of Obsessional Neurosis

'All beings are born in delusion, the delusion of division which comes from desire and hate' [203]

'If we consider a number of analyses of obsessional neurotics we shall find it impossible to escape the impression that a relation between love and hatred such as we have found . . . is among the most frequent, the most marked, and probably, therefore, the most important characteristics of obsessional neurosis.' [204]

Reintroducing logic

As a preliminary to exploring obsessional neurosis further we should look at a little logic. Logic is a package in which truth is guaranteed to be: truth comes in many other packages, but never with guarantees!

Whatever the truth may be, it is the exclusive property of language or signifiers: the world itself, or 'reality' is neither 'true' nor 'false', it just is. Only words or signifiers as propositions can be 'false' or 'true'. Only the proposition that desire is the exclusive property of language, based on the idea that *'the unconscious is* structured *like a language'*, explains the Freudian and Lacanian project of inviting the client to discover *the truth* of his own desire through analysing the structures of language that it produces.

Another reason for discussing logic is interpretation; this section will be relied on heavily in Chapter Thirteen on Interpretation because it is the analysis of the logical structures in the client's speech that reveal the client's truths.

A third and more specific reason for discussing logic here is that the structure of obsessional neurosis is a structure also found in logic called 'reduction to absurdity', which is a kind of formal or logical argument. This approach is part of the Lacanian tradition of *'studying the functions of speech'*, because logic is the exclusive function of language or symbols. Reduction to absurdity arguments are not esoteric but are used informally by ordinary people in everyday language.

---

[203] *Bhagavad-Gita*, Penguin, 1962, p76.
[204] S Freud, Notes Upon a Case of Obsessional Neurosis, *SE 10*, [1909], 1979, p239.

The summaries of some rules of logic below have been inspired by Lemmon's 'Beginning Logic' [205]. It is almost certain that most or all these rules will be familiar to every reader in one or another form. In the examples below I have been very sloppy or informal by logicians' standards. The formalisation that there is has the benefit of making the rules easier to understand and hopefully easier to apply in the clinic, hopefully allowing more truths to be identified more easily in the client's speech.

Why is it compulsory for the clinician to assume the truth of everything the client says?

Logic is concerned simply with the transmission or passage of truth: not with how you actually find out whether a particular claim —in isolation from others— is true or false. Only the client's speech is admissible as evidence. As a clinician all you have reliable access to are your client's words; it is not possible in general to check up on the truth or falsity of any specific claim, except by referring to words spoken by your client. For this reason it is necessary initially to assume the truth of everything said by a client. Why?

Because a project within each analysis is to question the truth of some of the client's beliefs, often sexual ones about the meaning of being male or female. There are only two ways to test the truth of an idea: to first assume that the client's every statement is false, and then test the results. This method often works well in science, but could never work in psychoanalysis because clients would very soon stop revealing their beliefs if it was clear that everything they said was systematically assumed to be false: the only remaining technique for testing the truth of a belief is the opposite, to start by assuming that the words spoken are true, and then exploring the consequences. It is compulsory then, for the sake of the analysis that the truth of all that the client says is assumed. Only then can the client's truth be questioned and explored, and then, perhaps, discovered to be false. Below is an example of a logical argument, that is of the transmission of truth from the assumed truth of two premises, to the proven truth of the conclusion:

[205] E Lemmon, *Beginning Logic*, Thomas Nelson and Sons, 1969, London.

1. 'If there is a cat then it sits on a mat'.	This is an assumption and relies on no other assumptions or arguments.
2. 'There is a cat'.	This is another assumption and relies on no other assumptions.

3. There is a cat sitting on a mat.	This is a deduction, and relies only on the assuming the truth of the two assumptions above, and an argument or logical principle.

Logic has absolutely no interest in whether cats actually sit on mats, or even in what a cat is. In the same way clinicians should not preoccupy themselves with the truth or falsity of the statements produced by the client, *except* in so far as they relate to the other things that the client has said or hinted at. Remember *that 'the signifier (or word) represents the subject for another signifier'*. It is the relations between signifiers —the representations— that psychoanalysis explores through the logic of interpretations. Everything else is bracketed out. Whether the client was actually sexually abused, or just reporting a dream or a fantasy are not distinctions that the psychoanalyst should be called upon to make or share.

In the examples below I have —for simplicity's sake— taken the unjustified liberty of putting all the assumptions in the mouth of the client, and all the deductions in the mouth of the clinician, but often, with good clinical practice, clients make most deductions or interpretations of this sort themselves. Bear in mind that the clinical material available for deductions or for any interpretation will often have been produced over a number of sessions, rather than being contained within a single session. Deductions are no less valid if their assumptions come from different sessions. Such deductions are likely to be more valuable since the ego is less able to cover its deceptive tracks over a larger area. Perhaps this is why detectives use the technique of repeating the same question in a number of different sessions, and why generals prefer to attack on more than one front.

Interpretation is not simply the robotic production of random deductions by the clinician: the timing and delivery of deductions or interpretations is a difficult, complex and sensitive issue and is considered later. So logic is required or necessary for interpretations, but logic alone is not sufficient.

'Should I use logic or not?' is not a question for a clinician, or for any language user; all clinicians use logic whenever they interpret, and rely on grammar and word meanings. The relevant question here is whether the clinician makes a good use of logic or not. The only way for a clinician to set about answering this question is by making a study of logic, and using it to help the client discover their truths, within their own speech. But psychoanalysis is not the robotic production of truths, nor is it the wild and speculative assertion of supposed truths by the clinician. To illustrate this point imagine that you guess that your apparently straight client is a repressed homosexual during the second session. It would be entirely inappropriate to share your speculation with your client, whether it is the truth or not. The truth that you rely on in your interpretations should generally be present in your client's speech but:

'What truth, when it emerges, has [the property] that is soothing can from time to time be fortunate, and then, in other cases, disastrous. One fails to see why truth would always necessarily be beneficial. One has to have the devil in you to imagine such a thing . . . everything demonstrates the contrary.' [206]

There is no choice for the clinician as to whether he relies on logic or not; if the clinician ever says anything about the client's speech then the question of truth automatically arises since one structure the clinician's interpretations— are taken to refer to truths in another— the client's speech. So what is the relation of the clinician's speech to the client's speech? Some clinicians try and sidestep this issue by substituting 'metaphor' for truth, but unless there is some truth at stake then the clinician will necessarily be producing a metaphor for another metaphor, for yet another metaphor . . . This infinite regress is absurd, because if metaphor is itself a metaphor, for metaphor, then we may as well all give up now, because in this case there is no truth of any kind, anywhere, including this sentence. This proof is a reduction to absurdity argument, not a metaphor.

It is certain that some crucially important items in language are not metaphors, for example proper names, which in the case of the father's name, in most cultures, are essential in marking out the functioning of the taboo against incest and concordantly, the Oedipus complex. Fathers, for instance are forbidden from having sex with their children.

If there were no non-metaphors, that is, via an argument of double negation, if all of language were metaphors, then we could not even disagree.
Disagreement insists primarily on some common ground of meaning, that is on

---

[206] J Lacan, The Inverse of Psychoanalysis, unpublished seminar, trans Gallagher.

something that is the same. If *'something is the same as something else'* then it is true to say that *'one thing is the same as the other'*, rather than 'a metaphor' for it. If you and I disagree then there is some one thing in common about which we disagree. So in this case a truth has been established through difference.[207]

'Free association' means any thing the client speaks about, including philosophy, football or fashion. Whatever a client speaks about is a way of speaking the truth —a way that the client often cannot yet recognise— of his unconscious desire. So true interpretations can be made whatever the topic. There is no such thing as a topic chosen by client that has no bearing on his suffering and desire. Whenever anyone speaks their desire is always functioning, however well hidden it may be. For this reason the client should not be dissuaded from speaking about his chosen topic, except in exceptional circumstances.

If a prospective lover, or a work of fiction or mystery has caught your interest you will no doubt be ready to admit any apparently miscellaneous fact as a crucial clue, which you may use later in order to explain the enigma: the clinician should not discard anything said by the client as being without value or irrelevant. The client's mysteries include those of the meaning of his symptom, the constitution of his fundamental fantasy, the meanings of his dreams and slips of the tongue. Everything the client says should be carefully listened to as if the whole truth was somehow contained in each part.

Reduction to absurdity arguments and their reliance on: To P or not to P[208], that is the obsessional question

This argument or rule appears complicated but it is widely used, not only in the clinic but also in courts of law, science and everyday life. The idea is to use assumptions or deductions in order to produce an interim contradiction, that is an inconsistent set of statements. In logic such inconsistent statements or contradictions always take a particular form: 'P is not true and P is true', or 'P and not P', with reference to the same time and place: These contradictions tell us something; they conclusively demonstrate that at least one of the assumptions that were used to produce the contradiction is false, and therefore should be negated, so as to point the way to another truth. Negating assumptions is, more or less, putting a 'not' in front of it. So negating:

'If my boyfriend loved me, then he would hit me'

produces:

---

[207] There are at least three non-metaphor candidates: proper names, the fundamental fantasy and 'standard meanings', explored in the Chapter Fifteen on interpretation.
[208] See Freud's 'On the Acquisition and Control of Fire', *SE 22,* [1932a], 1976.

'It is not true to say that if my boyfriend loved me, then he would hit me'.

Below are descriptions of some rules of logic that will help explain the clinic of obsessional neurosis with reduction to absurdity arguments.

Logic rules

The rule of assumption (A)

This rule allows us to introduce any assumption or premise into the structure of truth, or the 'argument of the client'. This sounds presumptuous but in Lacanian practice rarely is because any assumptions made by the clinician should have be supported by evidence that can easily be found in the client's speech. That is the clinician generally has a policy of assuming the truth of what the client says.

In general the clinician's assumptions should not be controversial —with reference to the client's speech— but assumptions with which the client would almost certainly agree, if the appropriate question were to have been asked.

To avoid taking unnecessary risks it is usually helpful for the clinician to form the assumption that he wishes to rely on as a question, so obtaining the client's response before completing the deduction or interpretation. The clinician must always assume the truth of everything said by the client. If the clinician has compelling doubts, these should either be ignored or relevant questions put to the client. For instance early on in the work clients sometimes exaggerate, much as they might in an ordinary conversation. Simply asking a naïve question about the item will usually lead the client to the conclusion that what they say is being taken seriously, and that the truth is being privileged over their demand to have an effect on their listener.

Relying on the rule of assumption universally, for everything that the client says is crucial and follows Freud's formula of working with the *'logical thread'* [209] within the client's free associations. Of course it is not necessary for the clinician to *believe for all purposes* what his client says but it is necessary for the clinician to *assume the truth* of all that the client says in his interpretations. In the same way someone learning a foreign language often does not understand much of what they hear and say in the first stage of learning the language. Taking this analogy further we can see that at best there will always be a necessary ignorance of some ambiguities and multiple meanings in every language, including the mother tongue. The one who interprets never has a 'full command' —that is without ambiguity— of the meanings at stake because language is public property, not the private property of an individual.

---

[209] S Freud, The Psychotherapy of Hysteria, *SE 2,* [1893], 1976, p289.

1. *X is true.* Assumption (A)

or:

1. *X is the case.* Assumption (A)

This rule allows us to assume the truth of anything at all that the client has said, however absurd it may seem. Obviously assuming the truth of a proposition is not the same as establishing, testing or proving the truth of that proposition: assuming truth is what you have to do first in order to prove the truth or falsity, at least in psychoanalysis[210].

Deducing the consequent from the antecedent (abbreviated to MP)

This rule allows us, if we are given two particular kinds of assumption or truth, to deduce —that is, to prove— a third truth. In the simple example below one of the assumptions is of the form 'if A then B'. These 'if . . . then . . .' statements are called 'conditionals'. The other assumption required here is that 'A actually exists', or 'A is the case'. Together these two assumptions allow us to deduce that the 'B' in the conditional assumption is true. Here is an example of a wife who had reliably produced violent behaviour in her husband, John, on a number of occasions by disclosing her infidelity. The client was surprised, given the report of her latest infidelity, that John's violence was absent:

1. *'If John loved me, then he would hit me'.* (If A then B). Assumption produced by client.

2. *'John loved me'.* (A is true). Assumption produced by client.

3. *'So John will hit you'* (B is true). Deduction produced by clinician.

Here is the same structure of argument in more abstract form:

1. If A then B. Assumption

2. A is true. Assumption

3. B is true. Deduction (of the consequent (B) from the antecedent (A))

---

[210] In some other fields such as science it is possible to assume the falsity of a proposition in order to later prove its truth.

Deducing the negation of the antecedent from the negation of the consequent (abbreviated as MT)

This useful rule allows the negation of the first part of a conditional, known as the 'antecedent', if the second part of the conditional, called the 'consequent', has been negated:

1. *'If John had loved me, then he would have hit me'*. (If A then B). Assumption produced by client.

2. *'John did not hit me'*. (B is not true). Assumption produced by client.

3. *'John does not love you'*. (B is not true). Deduction produced by clinician.

Here is the same structure of argument in more abstract form:

1. If A then B. Assumption

2. B is not true. Assumption

3. A is not true. Deduction (by negation of the antecedent from the negation of the consequent)

Double negation (DN)

With this rule we can add up negations, and whenever there are multiples of two we cancel them out:

1. *'It is **not** true, that my father was **not** gentle'*. (Not not A). Assumption produced by client.

2. *'So your father was gentle'*. (A). Deduction produced by clinician.

Here is the same structure of argument in more abstract form:

1. Not not A. Assumption

2. A. Deduction (by double negation)

And introduction (&I)

This simple rule means that we can introduce any two assumptions or deductions that have been produced earlier, without restriction:

1. *'If a boyfriend loved me, then he would hit me'*. (If A then B). Assumption produced by client.

2. *'My father was violent'*. Assumption produced by client.

3. *'So your father was violent **and** if a boyfriend loved you he would hit you'*. Deduction produced by clinician. (C, and: If A then B).

Here is the same structure of argument in more abstract form:

1. If A then B.   Assumption

2. C.   Assumption

3. C and if A then B.   Deduction (by and introduction)

And elimination (&E) [211]

This rule is, in a way, the opposite of the 'and introduction rule'. If two or more assumptions or truths happen to be conjoined, then it follows that each assumption on its own is true. This may sound banal, but in the right circumstances this type of truth will surprise a client. In this case the client had complained of her relations with men, and equated this complaint with her relations with her difficult brother. The first assumption was produced some months before the clinician's deduction:

1. *'I love and hate my brother'*. Assumption produced by client.

2. *'You love your brother'*. Deduction produced by clinician.

Some deductions by the clinician are best posed as questions. This topic is considered at greater length under the heading 'over and under generalisation' in Chapter Fifteen on interpretation. Here is the same structure of argument in more abstract form:

1. A and B. (Assumption)

2. B.   (Deduction, by and elimination)

Reduction to Absurdity (RAA)

This rule appears complicated but it is useful, not only in the clinic but in courts of law, science and everyday life. The intermediate goal is to use the client's assumptions or deductions in order to produce a contradiction, that is an inconsistent set of statements. In logic all contradictions take the form: *'It is true to say P and it is not true to say P'*, that is both *'P and not P'*. Contradictions demonstrate that *at least one* of the assumptions that were used to produce the contradiction must be false and therefore should be negated, that is identified as false. Contradictions within the neurotic client's speech ought to be identified, not to make the client look stupid, but to help him discover the truth of his desire. Discovering the truth of one's desire is easier once some of the fog of false connections have been identified. This technique of identifying

---

[211] For an illustration of this technique see Charraud N, A Calculus of Convergence, *Drawing the Soul*, Rebus Press, 2000.

absurd premises or consequences by inviting their negation should not be used with clients who are or may be diagnosed psychotic.

Reduction to Absurdity arguments and choice

There are always a number of premises relied on in reduction to absurdity arguments which means that there is a choice, once the contradiction has been deduced, as to which assumption you select for negation.   For example a detective interviewing a murder suspect may argue: *'When I asked you three days ago you said that on the night of the murder, at 7pm GMT you were in London: I asked you the same question a moment ago and you said that on the night of the murder at 7pm GMT you were in Manchester. It is not possible to be in both these different places at exactly the same time, to believe otherwise would be to believe in a contradiction, therefore it is clear that not all of your statements are true. At least one of the two statements is false and should be negated, which is it?'*

A reduction to absurdity argument often has four assumptions or premises. This means that you can carry out any four different reductions to absurdity arguments with the same four assumptions, but only one at a time, selecting a different premise each time to negate. Below, a special reduction to absurdity argument has been reconstructed with material from Freud's case known as 'the Ratman'. Unusually each of the four choices is completed: usually only one is completed:

COMMON SET OF ASSUMPTIONS

1	*If X is the case then P is the case.*	Assumption resting on line 1
	***If** I my father exists **then** I am loved by my father.*	
2	If Z is the case then P is not the case.	Assumption resting on line 2
	***If** my lady exists **then** I am not loved by my father.*	
3	X is the case.	Assumption resting on line 3
	My father exists.	
4	Z is the case.	Assumption resting on line 4
	My lady exists.	

COMMON SET OF DEDUCTIONS

5	P is the case.	Deduction resting on lines 1 and 3, MP
	I am loved by my father.	
6	P is not the case.	Deduction resting on lines 2 and 4, MP
	I am not loved by my father.	
7	P is the case and P is not the case.	Deduction resting on lines 5 and 6, &I
	I am loved by my father and I am not loved by my father.	

CHOICE OF FOUR DEDUCTIONS

REDUCTION TO ABSURDITY ONE

8a	P is the case and P is not the case, and if X is the case then P is the case. *I am loved by my father and I am not loved by my father, and if my father exists then I am loved by my father.*	Deduction resting on lines 7 and 1, &I
9a	IT IS NOT THE CASE THAT IF X IS THE CASE THEN P IS THE CASE. *It is not the case that if my father exists then I am loved by my father.*	Deduction resting on lines 8a and 1, RAA. Negation of assumption 1

REDUCTION TO ABSURDITY TWO

8b	P is the case and P is not the case, and if Z is the case then P is not the case. *I am loved by my father and I am not loved by my father, and if my lady exists then I am not loved by my father.*	Deduction resting on lines 2 & 7, &I
9b	IT IS NOT THE CASE THAT IF Z IS THE CASE THEN P IS NOT THE CASE. *It is not the case that if my lady exists then I am not loved by my father.*	Deduction resting on lines 8b and 2, RAA. Negation of assumption 2

REDUCTION TO ABSURDITY THREE

8c	X is the case and P is the case and P is not the case. *My father exists and I am loved by my father and I am not loved by my father.*	Deduction resting on lines 4 & 7, &I
9c	X IS NOT THE CASE. *My father does not exist.*	Deduction resting on lines 3 and 8c, RAA. Negation of assumption 3

REDUCTION TO ABSURDITY FOUR

8d	Z exists and P exists and P does not exist. *My lady exists and I am loved by my father and I am not loved by my father.*	Deduction resting on lines 5 & 7, &I
9d	Z IS NOT THE CASE. *My lady does not exist.*	Deduction resting on lines 4 and 8d, RAA. Negation of assumption 4

Because of the wide choice of premises to be negated in reduction to absurdity arguments clients often decide that one contradiction is less absurd or difficult than another. In the middle phase of work with obsessional clients it is often useful to use the technique of 'and elimination', so as to try and isolate the separate conditionals that the obsessional has tied together. In the case of the Ratman, Freud appears to be describing these contradictions:

'The conflicts of feeling in our patient which we have here enumerated separately were not independent of each other, but were bound together in pairs . . . the contradiction between his love and his hatred within each of these relations'. [212]

And: *'[The Ratman's] hatred within each of these relations — had no connection whatever with each other, either in their content or in their origin. The first of these two conflicts corresponds to the normal vacillation between male and female which characterises every one's choice of a love-object. It is first brought to the child's notice by the time-honoured question: 'Which do you love most, Daddy or Mummy?' and it accompanies him through his whole life, whatever may be the relative intensity of his feelings to the two sexes or whatever may be the sexual aim upon which he finally becomes fixed. But normally this soon loses the character of a hard-and-fast contradiction, of an inexorable 'either-or' ['either P or not P']. Room is found for satisfying the unequal demands of both sides, although even in a normal person the higher estimation of one sex is always thrown into relief by a depreciation of the other.'* [213]

I understand Freud to be alluding to the richness of reduction to absurdity arguments, and in particular to the usual minimum of *four assumptions* within reduction to absurdity arguments and when he wrote:

'[O]ne gets the impression that the simple Oedipus complex is by no means its commonest form, but rather represents a simplification or schematisation which, to be sure, is often enough justified for practical purposes. Closer study

---

[212] S Freud, Notes Upon a Case of Obsessional Neurosis, *SE 10*, [1909], 1976, p238.
[213] Ibid p238.

usually discloses the more complete Oedipus complex, which is two fold, positive and negative, and is due to the bisexuality originally present in children: that is to say, a boy has not merely an ambivalent object choice towards his mother, but at the same time he also behaves like a girl and displays an affectionate feminine attitude to his father and a corresponding jealousy and hostility towards his mother . . . It may even be that the ambivalence displayed in the relations to the parents should be attributed entirely to bisexuality . . . **At the downfall of the Oedipus complex the four trends** [214] *of which it consists will group themselves in such a way as to produce a father identification and a mother identification.'* [215]

One year later, writing on the same theme Freud explained that:

'The Oedipus complex would go to its destruction from its lack of success, from the effects of its internal impossibility. Another view is that the Oedipus complex must collapse because the time has come for its disintegration . . . The Oedipus complex offered the child two possibilities of satisfaction, an active and a passive one. He could put himself in his father's place in a masculine fashion and have intercourse with his mother as his father did, in which case he would soon have felt the latter as a hindrance; or he might want to take the place of his mother and be loved by his father, in which case his mother would become superfluous . . . In this conflict the . . . child's ego turns away from the Oedipus complex . . . The object-investments [objects] are given up and replaced by identifications [signifiers].' [216]

Note that this sophisticated approach of Freud's is very different from the crude and simplistic version that critics such as Cioffi have fabricated, presumably in order that they can more easily criticise it:

'To be a good classical Freudian is to hold, first, that all children entertain highly explicit sexual designs on at least one parent and murderous designs on the other . . .' [217]

Of course Freud's notion of 'the sexual' is very different from the ordinary language notion of 'sexual as in 'sexual intercourse', and it is usually far from explicit:

'[W]hat psychoanalysis called 'sexuality' was **by no means identical** *with the drive towards a union of the two sexes or towards producing a pleasurable*

[214] For a cinematic version of Freud's four Oedipal positions see *Multiplicity* (Ramis, 1996).

[215] S Freud, The Ego and the Id, [1923b], 1976, *SE 19*, p34.

[216] S Freud, The Downfall of the Oedipus Complex, *SE 19*, [1924], 1976, p173-176.

[217] F Cioffi, Was Freud a Liar?, *Unauthorised Freud*, ed Crews, Viking, 1998, p34.

sensation in the genitals; it had far more resemblance to the all inclusive and all preserving Eros of Plato's Symposium.' [218]

Moreover Freud's theory of the Oedipus complex entails *'four trends'*, rather than the *'two'* referred to Cioffi. It is clear from almost any clinical vignette that children's — and for that matter adults' *'sexual designs'* both as fantasies and actions— are often hidden rather than being explicit.

Freud's description of the Oedipus accords with the reduction to absurdity structure, and its choice of contradictions, and the choice of neurotic positions taken up when the Oedipus is not wholly resolved or dissolved. Obsessional neurosis, described by Freud as having *'four trends'* operates within the structure of reduction to absurdity, with its four premises. So each obsessional neurosis represents the failure of a particular subject to work thoroughly through his Oedipal impossibilities and contradictions, and to negate any of the four premises in the reconstruction above. It also suggests that obsessionals do not respond to reductions to absurdity arguments as a temporary tool or vehicle used to arrive at a destination, but as a technique for ensuring that their desire goes nowhere perpetually. Obsessional neurotics are usually very busy with activities that efficiently prevent them from following their desire.

Now it is time to return to our earlier question of the relation of hysteria to obsessional neurosis: How does reduction to absurdity relate hysteria, as 'a dialect', to obsessional neurosis? One reading of the boy's Oedipus has two conditional premises:

1. *If I love mother exclusively than I will possess mother's love, but I will **not** possess father's love.*

2. *If I love father exclusively then I will **not** possess mother's love, but I will possess father's love.*

The last phrases or consequents of these two conditionals above are the negation of one another, that is when taken together they have the structure of 'P or not P'. In isolation the formulations in each of 1 and 2 are hysterical formulations focusing primarily on the Other's desire, not on the subject's desire; hysterics typically overvalue their Other's desire, and undervalue their own. So two hysterical questions, typically taken up in Freud's *'A Child is being Beaten Fantasy'* [219] arising from the above two conditionals are: *'Will Mummy love me?'* and: *'Will Daddy love me?'*

In obsessional neurosis there is a pairing of two conditional propositions that individually would form the basis of hysteria. Only when appropriately paired can an obsessional neurosis be structured. This seems to be Freud's idea:

---

[218] S Freud, Resistances to Psychoanalysis, *SE 19*, [1925], page 218.
[219] S Freud, A Child is being Beaten, *SE 17*, [1919e], 1979.

'The conflicts of feeling in our patient which we have here enumerated separately were not independent of each other, but were bound together in pairs'. [220]

Lacan developed along logical lines the obsessional neurotic's compulsive series of negations:

'The hysterical manner of questioning, 'either . . . or . . .', contrasts with the obsessional's response, negation, 'neither. . . nor. . .', neither male nor female.

This negation is made on the basis of . . . hiding his being from the question, which is a way of remaining suspended from it. The obsessional is precisely neither one nor the other — one may also say that he is both at once.' [221]

The Primal Horde and reduction to absurdity

We can imagine the sons of the Primal Father being faced with two conditionals, or *'if . . . then'* propositions, arranged here as *'antecedent-consequent'* or *'before-after'* sentences, which can be substituted into the reduction to absurdity structure:

1. *'If I enjoy the women, then I'll be eaten and dead'.*

2. *'If I do not enjoy the women then I will not be eaten and I'll be alive'.*

If a son has sex with the women he faces the intolerable consequence of being eaten: if he does not have sex with the women, again his life will be intolerable. So the murderous obsessional son of the Primal Horde imagines that if he has sex he will be eaten, and if he doesn't have sex, life will be unendurable. This is the absurdity of the obsessional's fundamental fantasy.

The formal contradiction takes the form: *'If I enjoy the women I won't live a long life, and if I live a long life I won't enjoy women.'* So life and its enjoyment —from which it cannot be separated [222]— appear to be mutually exclusive.

Some clinical evidence

For Freud's Ratman there are many pairs of negated propositions that operate reduction to absurdity arguments. Each pair, with their negations make four propositions suggestive of Freud's *'complete Oedipus'*. For example the

---

[220] S Freud, Notes Upon a Case of Obsessional Neurosis, *SE 10*, [1909], 1979. p238.

[221] J Lacan, *The Psychoses*, ed Miller, trans Grigg, Routledge, London, 1993, p248-9.

[222] Life, and the enjoyment of life cannot be separated because of the compulsory nature of jouissance.

Ratman was *'extremely fond'* of children, yet his girlfriend had her ovaries removed, making it impossible for her to have children.

Here is another pair of such propositions:

'If I marry the lady some misfortune will befall my father'. [223]

And:

'If my father dies, I will have enough money to marry.' [224]

The Ratman's two desires —to love his lady, and to be loved by his father— are met in part through his corresponding fears of harming his father and his lady. By perpetuating his impossibility, by building a shrine, a monument of inaction with his symptom, the obsessive symbolises his impossibility. Obsessional acts, thoughts and deeds symbolise mortification with the fixedness of gravestone inscriptions.

The 'spielratte' —German slang for gambler— superstition, money and jouissance.

Animal psychologists sometimes experiment with pigeons or rats in a box of about two cubic feet. There is an internal lever which when pressed, releases a pellet of food inside the box. These experimenters have observed, from their own slightly larger boxes, that if a rat happens to do a 360 degree turn just before pressing the lever for the first time, he will thereafter continue to do a turn, every time, before pressing the lever. These psychologists call this style of behaviour 'superstitious'. Freud wrote of the Ratman that *'our patient was to a high degree superstitious.'* [225] There are traces, even in the 'superstitious behaviour' of pigeons, of obsessional neurosis, of attempts to revalue, to attribute 'the good' and 'the bad'. According to Freud the theme of money is the distillation of enjoyment or jouissance in the Ratman's *'whole complex of money interest centred round his father's legacy to him.'* [226]

One rationale for operating the incest taboo was to keep the peace with rival clans; virgins could be exchanged as a commodity, thus inhibiting murderous and cannibalistic raids amongst competing hordes. The incest taboo is the basis of the social contract, the glue that holds us together, and apart. So money, for the Ratman, is symbolic of: women as a commodity, of jouissance quantified, acquired and inherited, of the law against incest. One Ratman expression of this relation is 'spielratte', game rat, the German slang for 'gambler', picking out his father as he who gambled with his honour as a man and won a rich woman.

---

[223] S Freud, Notes Upon a Case of Obsessional Neurosis, *SE 10*, [1909], 1976, p226.
[224] Ibid.
[225] Ibid, p229.
[226] Ibid, p213.

Daddy Ratman had been without money, and almost without honour, because he gambled with his regiment's money. The so-called 'law of gambling' or 'gambler's fallacy' is that the gambler is more sure to win after a loss, because 'a win is sure to follow a loss'. This formulation of gambling lore is a specification of obsessional neurosis, that one must lose, in order to win, to lose, to win to . . .

Those addicted to gambling are notorious for repeating obsessively, a practice that provides money to the gaming house. The gambler takes an enjoyment or jouissance in his recurrent play with loss, which he pays for with cash, which he could otherwise use in exchange, perhaps to enjoy women and honour his father, and make little Ratpeople. The gambler slaves to master loss.

Obsessional Neurosis and clinical technique: tactics, strategy and policy

It is not unusual to find women who present as obsessional neurotics, but —in some of these cases— the obsessional neurosis is fragile and responds within six months or so to reveal a more stable underlying hysteria. Such 'fragile obsessional neurotics' have always been women in my experience: male obsessionals appear to be possessed by a more resilient obsessional neurosis that takes far longer to shift.

In some cases of obsessional neurosis diagnosis is difficult, usually for one of two reasons: either the client has an underlying structure of psychosis, overlaid with a facade of obsessional neurosis, or the client is a genuine obsessional neurotic but he does not present the classic 'obsessional compulsive signs' such as ritualised behaviour or compulsive thoughts. Such obsessionals may appear to invite a diagnosis of hysteria! Obsessional structures sometimes manifest themselves in subtle ways. But in either cases of hysteria or obsessional neurosis clients should be hystericised because the strategy of the obsessional is to avoid acting efficiently on one of his desires by offsetting it against another desire. In this way he manages to avoid the consequences of any one of his desires. If an obsessional is successfully hystericised then his strategy will have changed, from offsetting one desire against the other to having becoming preoccupied with a single problematic desire. The obsessional will have shifted his complicated strategy of hiding two problematic desires, to dealing with one problematic desire. The early Freud claimed that there is no difference in the technique of analysis for obsessional neurosis and hysteria:

'The psychical mechanism of obsessions has a very great deal of internal kinship with hysterical symptoms and . . . the technique of analysis is the same for both of them.' [227]

---

[227] S Freud, The Psychotherapy of Hysteria, *SE 2*, [1893], 1976, p275.

While Lacan agreed with Freud on the question of '*internal kinship*' there is a different emphasis on some techniques for each diagnosis. In general the tactics and strategy of the clinician should be closely informed by the tactics and strategy of the client, just as they are in war and judo. Obsessionals, despite and because of their suffering, attempt to imprison their two sets of unconscious desires, demands and the problems they produce, as if they were on an island, in a self perpetuating quarantine. What is it that prevents any one desire from escaping? The other desire, whose identity is quickly shuffled before any decision can be made or acted on.

Because this technique of defence, of protecting themselves from their own desire is so efficient, working with obsessionals can be frustrating for the clinician. It's not unusual for clinicians to fail to see any important change in obsessional clients for years, as they appear to return to explore different positions or deductions within the one reduction to absurdity structure. But this lack of apparent movement outside their main argument does not usually correspond to a lack of clinical progress but to an almost invisible preparation for change. Following the 'logical threads', as Freud prescribed, of the obsessional's arguments often, especially early on in the work, leads one back to revalue an earlier and important part of the same argument. Perhaps for this reason a more mature Freud also privileged hysteria, in anticipation of Lacan's strategy of hystericising obsessionals:

'*The change from obsessional to hysterical symptoms seems to point to an inner progress in sexual organisation, and is favourable . . .*' [228]

Because obsessionals do not properly follow either of their desires, so leaving their fantasised acts of desire incomplete, they are often painfully sensitive to tasks being left incomplete. Lacanians have a policy of ending a neurotic's sessions on something incomplete, typically on a question or ambiguity. It is just loose ends such as these that obsessionals find so difficult to bear because they often symbolise the obsessional's incomplete action with reference to his desires. Of course this does not mean that sessions should not be ended on a question, but only that such endings should be used with caution at the start of the work.

Between the middle and end phases of analysis there should be enough information to reconstruct an obsessional's incomplete reduction to absurdity argument, inviting completion or abandonment. Because of the wide choice of premises to be negated in reduction to absurdity arguments it may sometimes be fruitful to deduce a contradiction, inviting the client to select which premise to negate. One technique is to offer for comparison the results of two or more reduction to absurdity arguments. Clients often conclude that one contradiction

---

[228] S Freud, *Sigmund Freud and Lou Andreas-Salome Letters*, ed Pfeiffer, Hogarth Press, [1919] 1972, p3.

is less absurd than another, or that two or more are absurd, or even that the whole argument is absurd. In the middle phase of work it is often useful to use the technique of 'and elimination' so as to try and isolate the separate conditionals that the obsessional has tied together.

So the clinician should be active in producing a range of alternative deductions or intermediate pathways to truths from the obsessional client's material: with hysterics it is often possible, after the first phase of analysis, to make very few interpretations. Hysterics, because their structures are simpler, are often able to work more efficiently and quickly than obsessionals. Some useful sessions with hysterics will require no interpretation from the clinician except to end the session. Of course it is ideal for the client to do most or all of the work, but with obsessionals this, at least in the early and middle phase of the work, is far less likely. The clinician working with an obsessional should actively focus on emphasizing the underlying fantasy of paired and mutually exclusive desires:

'It is not enough to go round in circles in some well explored area of obsessional neurosis in order to bring him [the obsessional neurotic] to this roundabout, or to know this roundabout in order to bring him to it by a route that will never be the shortest. What is needed is not only the plan of a reconstructed labyrinth, or even a batch of plans already drawn up. What is needed above all is to possess the general combinatory that governs their variety certainly, but which also, even more usefully, accounts for the illusions, or rather shifts of perspective to be found in the labyrinth.' [229]

The superego often has a marked function for obsessional neurotics, so that certain forms of enjoyment are compulsory while others are forbidden to the same degree. Typically the superego of obsessional neurotics is harsh, producing much guilt and 'self criticism'. This symptom is usually presented to the clinician in order that he or she contradict the self-accusation of moral worthlessness. Obsessional neurotics often demand that the clinician reassure them and identify their worth. Lacan was clear on the clinician's tactics when dealing with this popular symptom: *'But the demand to be a turd . . . makes it preferable to move . . . [a] little to one side when the subject becomes aware of it.'* [230]

Why? Because*: 'What you all know, at least those of you who have done a little bit of therapeutic work, namely that with obsessionals you must not give them the least bit of encouragement, of deculpabilisation, indeed even of interpretative commentary which goes a little bit too far, because then you have to go much further and that, what you would find yourself coming to and conceding to your own great disadvantage, is precisely to this mechanism*

[229] J Lacan, *Ecrits*, The Direction of the Treatment and the Principles of its Power, trans Sheridan, Tavistock Publications, London, 1977, p266.

[230] J Lacan, *Ecrits,* trans Sheridan, Tavistock Publications, London, 1977, p270.

through which he wants to make you eat, as I might say, his own being as a shit. You are well taught by experience that this is not a process in which you will be of any use to him, quite the contrary.' [231]

And, '*. . . what is more he [the obsessional] is demand, he is shit which only demands to be eliminated. This is the true foundation of a whole radical structure that you will find, especially in the fantasies, in the fundamental fantasy of the obsessional in so far as he devalues himself, in so far as he puts outside himself the whole game of the erotic dialectic, that he pretends, as someone has said, to be its organiser. It is on the foundation of his own elimination that he grounds the whole of this fantasy.*' [232]

---

[231] J Lacan, Transference Seminar, unpublished, trans Gallagher, 15th March 1961.
[232] Ibid.

CHAPTER ELEVEN

Perversion

What is perversion and how is it different from hysteria, obsessional neurosis and psychosis? There are two senses of 'perversion'. Perversion in the ordinary language sense is any non-standard or deviant behaviour identified in the vague field of 'sexual life' but as Freud and Lacan argued, perversion cannot be understood or diagnosed simply by reference to behaviour or set of behaviours, but only by identifying an underlying structure:

'What is perversion? It is not simply an aberration in relation to social criteria, an anomaly contrary to good morals, although this register is not absent, nor is it an atypicality according to natural criteria, namely that it more or less derogates from the reproductive finality of sexual union. It is something else in its very structure.' [233]

Infants are what Freud called 'polymorphously perverse'; they are able to enjoy an infinite variety of objects and get a sexual enjoyment from them. Yet most men and most women end up enjoying each other sexually. This fact is surprising given the wide range of choice of objects we might enjoy. So the fact that most of us enjoy either men or women makes us perverse, to a

degree; we have selected one type of thing or object to love from the whole universe of possible objects of love. Any restriction of love object, including the restriction called 'heterosexuality' is a kind of perversion. Heterosexuality in this sense is no more or less a restriction of love object than loving just shoes

---

[233] J Lacan, *The Seminar of Jacques Lacan, Book One, Freud's Papers on Technique 1953-1954,* ed Miller, trans Forrester, Cambridge University Press, England, 1988, p221.

or only donkeys. It is a commonly observed and curious clinical fact that the sexual practices of perverts correspond to the sexual fantasies of neurotics. Freud noted that: *'All . . . neurotics are persons with strongly marked perverse tendencies, which have been repressed in the course of their development and have become unconscious. Consequently their unconscious fantasies show precisely the same content as the documentary recorded actions of perverts . . . Neuroses are, so to speak, the negative of perversions.'* [234]

And Lacan wrote: *'The pervert imagines himself to be the Other in order to ensure his jouissance, and that is what the neurotic reveals when he imagines himself to be a pervert — in his case, to assure himself of the existence of the other. It is this that gives the meaning of the perversion that is supposed to lie in a very principle of neurosis. The perversion is in the unconscious of the neurotic as fantasy of the Other.'* [235]

These observations led Lacan to ask: *'Of what use the perverse fantasy is to the neurotic?'* He claimed that the neurotic imagines his Other to be a pervert. Perhaps this is demonstrated by the protest of incredulity commonly made by women —most of whom are hysterics— with the question: *'But how can he be attracted to me?'* Perhaps the question at stake here is: *'What does his perversion make me?'* Towards explaining this phenomenon Lacan relies on the different functions of an item that he discovered, the little object a, the cause and object of desire for neurotics and perverts:

'It is that this fantasy that the neurotic makes use of, that he organises at the moment that he makes use of it — there is . . . something of the order of the little object a which appears at the moment . . . of anxiety . . . is what serves him best to defend himself against anxiety, to cover up the anxiety . . .this little object a which the neurotic puts into his fantasy, suits him . . . the way gaiters suit a rabbit. This indeed is why the neurotic [unlike the pervert] never makes very much of his fantasy. It succeeds in protecting him against anxiety precisely in the measure that it is a false little object a.' [236]

Lacan provides an example of such a false little object a in a famous dream retold by Freud, dreamed by a butcher's beautiful wife, a neurotic. Here is the hysteric's dream, reported by her to Freud:

'I wanted to give a dinner party, but I had nothing in the house but a little smoked salmon. I thought I would go out and buy something, but remembered then that it was Sunday afternoon and all the shops would be shut. Next I tried

---

[234] Fragment of an Analysis of a Case of Hysteria, [1905], 1976, *SE* 7, p50.

[235] J Lacan, *Ecrits*, trans Sheridan, Tavistock publications, London, Subversion of the Subject and Dialectic of Desire, 1977, p322.

[236] J Lacan, Seminar on Anxiety, unpublished, trans Gallagher, 15th December 1962.

to ring up some caterers, but the telephone was out of order. So I had to abandon my wish to give a dinner party.'

I answered [said Freud] . . . : 'But what material did the dream arise from?

. . . My patient's husband, an honest and capable wholesale butcher, had remarked to her the day before that he was getting too stout and therefore intended to start on a course of weight reduction. He proposed to rise early, do physical exercises, keep to a strict diet, and above all accept no more invitations to supper. She laughingly added that her husband, at the place where he regularly lunched, had made the acquaintance of a painter, who had pressed him to be allowed to paint his portrait, as he had never seen such expressive features. Her husband however had replied in his blunt manner that he was much obliged, but he was sure the painter would prefer a piece of a pretty young girl's behind to the whole of his face. She was very much in love with her husband now and teased him a lot. She had begged him, too, not to give her any caviar. I asked her what that meant; and she explained that she had wished for a long time that she could have a caviar sandwich every morning but had grudged the expense. Of course her husband would have let her have it at once if she had asked him. But, on the contrary, she had asked him not to give her any caviar, so that she could go on teasing him about it. This explanation struck me as unconvincing. Inadequate reasons like this usually conceal unconfessed motives. They remind one of . . . a post-hypnotic suggestion and if asked why he is acting in this way, instead of saying that he has no idea, he feels compelled to invent some obviously unsatisfactory reason . . . I saw that she was obliged to create an unfulfilled wish for herself in her actual life; and the dream represented this renunciation as having been put into effect. But why was it that she stood in need of an unfulfilled wish?

The associations which she had so far produced had not been sufficient to interpret the dream. I pressed her for some more . . . she went on to tell me that the day before she had visited a woman friend of whom she confessed she felt jealous because her (my patient's) husband was constantly singing her praises. Fortunately this friend of hers is very skinny and thin and her husband admires a plumper figure. I asked her what she had talked about to her thin friend. Naturally, she replied, of that lady's wish to grow a little stouter. Her friend had enquired, too: 'When are you going to ask us to another meal? You always feed one so well.'

The meaning of the dream was now clear, and I was able to say to my patient: 'It is just as though when she made this suggestion you said to yourself: "A likely thing! I'm to ask you to come and eat in my house so that you may get stout and attract my husband still more! I'd rather never give another dinner party." What the dream was saying to you was that you were unable to give any dinner parties, and it was thus fulfilling your wish not to help your friend to grow plumper. The fact that what people eat at parties makes them stout had been brought home to you by your husband's decision not to accept any more invitations to dinner in the interests of his plan to reduce his weight.' All that was now lacking was some coincidence to confirm the solution. The smoked salmon in the dream had not yet been accounted for. 'How,' I asked, 'did you arrive at the salmon that came into your dream?' 'Oh,' she replied, 'smoked salmon is my friend's favourite dish . . .'

The same dream admits of another and subtler interpretation, which in fact becomes unavoidable if we take a subsidiary detail into account . . . My patient, it will be remembered, at the same time as she was occupied with her dream of the renunciation of a wish, was also trying to bring about a renounced wish (for the caviar sandwich) in real life. Her friend had also given expression to a wish —to become stouter— and it would not have been surprising if my patient had dreamt that her friend's wish was unfulfilled; for my patient's own wish was that her friend's wish (to put on weight) should not be fulfilled. But instead of this she dreamt that one of her own wishes was not fulfilled. Thus the dream will acquire a new interpretation if we suppose that the person indicated in the dream was not herself but her friend, that she had put herself in her friend's place, or, as we might say, that she had 'identified' herself with her friend. I believe she had in fact done this; and the circumstance of her having brought about a renounced wish in real life was evidence of this identification.' [237]

Now we can return to Lacan's description of the false little object a in relation to the fantasy of Freud's patient:

'The butcher's beautiful wife loves caviar; only she does not want it because this might give too much pleasure to her big brute of a husband who is capable of swallowing that with the rest, even that would not stop him. Now what interests the butcher's beautiful wife, is not at all of course to feed her husband with caviar, because, as I told you, he would add a whole menu to it, because he has a huge appetite. The only thing that interests the butcher's beautiful wife is that her husband should want the little nothing that she holds in reserve. This formula . . . applies to all neurotics. This little object a functioning in their fantasy, and which serves as a defence for them against their anxiety, is also, despite all appearances, the bait with which they hold onto the Other.' [238]

From the original text of the dream it is clear that the butcher's wife is anxious. How does she manage her anxiety? By focusing on something, some supposed object of her Other's desire according to Lacan's formula: 'Desire is the desire for the Other's desire'. What is the Other's desire here? Her husband's wish to give her caviar. This is *'the little nothing that she holds in reserve.'*

---

[237] S Freud, The Interpretation of Dreams, *SE 4*, [1900a], 1976, p147.

[238] J Lacan, Seminar on Anxiety, unpublished, trans Gallagher, 15th December 1962.

Why in perverse acts does the subject makes himself *'the instrument of the Other's jouissance'* [239] while in neurotic fantasy the subject makes himself *'the instrument of the Other's jouissance'* [240] ? There is another related question: do the differences between fantasy and action explain the differences between neurosis and perversion?

One difference between neurosis and perversion is the difference between the phallus, with its focus on jouissance, and desire with its focus on the Other's desire. The pervert's transgressive actions are consistent, focusing on himself as the means of providing the Other's jouissance: the neurotic's acts focus inconsistently on the Other's demands and desires. The pervert and neurotic distinguish in their acts between the jouissance of the Other, on the side of the pervert, and the desire of the Other, on the side of the neurotic. Put crudely, the pervert aims to be the Other's jouissance: the neurotic the Other's desire.

The pervert aims his symptom at the castration of his Other. He attempts a consistent disavowal of his castration and transgression of some key rule or law of sexual difference: the neurotic uses symptoms inconsistently, as a patch, a sporadic but repeated demand to return to a mythical time when the subject was not yet castrated. The pervert consistently remains committed to the structure in which he is the phallus of the mother.

Perversion can be distinguished from psychosis in the same way that hysteria and obsessional neurosis can be distinguished from psychosis. It is only in psychosis that the Names of the father are foreclosed. This leaves the question: how can perversion be distinguished from hysteria and obsessional neurosis? To answer this we will have to investigate the phallus and castration.

What is the phallus?

'Something thick and strong' [241]

*'In Freudian doctrine, the phallus is not a fantasm, if by that we mean an imaginary effect. Nor is it such 'an object' (part, internal, good, bad, etcetera) in the sense that this term tends to accentuate the reality pertaining in a relation. It is even less the organ, penis or clitoris, that it symbolises . . . **the phallus is a signifier . . .**'* [242]

---

[239] J Lacan, *Ecrits*, trans Sheridan, Tavistock publications, London, Subversion of the Subject and Dialectic of Desire, 1977, p320.

[240] Ibid.

[241] The description an analysand gave to the principle of her mother's power.

[242] J Lacan, The Signification of the Phallus [1958], *Ecrits*, trans Sheridan, Tavistock, London, 1977, p285.

'The lack of being that constitutes alienation . . . takes up its place through this incarnation of the subject called 'castration', and through the organ of failure that the phallus becomes in it. Such is the void that is so uncomfortable to approach.' [243]

The phallus is not defined as 'the penis', although the penis is one example of the phallus, a privileged one. Why is the penis privileged? Because it is a popular signifier of sexual difference.

There are rude and phallic caricatures, that *'a man thinks with his penis'*, and its counterpart, that *'a woman thinks with her womb'*. Both these ways of understanding sexuality are phallic because the penis and the womb expand and contract, and are attributed with power. Power is represented by the phallic function and loss of power is represented by the technical term 'castration'. Wherever the phallus functions there is also 'castration'. Castration in this sense is not the removal of testicles or ovaries but a loss of power, that is a diminution or narrowing of the phallic function, with the identification of limits. The phallus and castration are counterparts, like 'black and white', 'good and bad', 'repression and expression'. So a psychoanalyst might say of an athlete, suffering with a heavy dose of flu and due to run an important race, that *'she is castrated'*. A woman might be 'castrated' if her business fails, if her car breaks down, or if she discovers that she is not able to have the children she wanted. So the idea of a limit or boundary, as demonstrated by the interruption of a rise or fall is the phallic function. Women often regard a man or baby as the phallus, which they might possess: a man typically believes that a woman has the phallus. The phallus is often regarded —whatever it may be— as *'my pride and joy'*. Castration for Freud was clearly not a straightforward biological issue that referred simply to the gonads: *'Castration can be pictured on the basis of the daily experience of the faeces being separated from the body or on the basis of losing the mother's breast and weaning.'* [244]

It is unfortunate that Freud did little to prevent the confusion of *'the phallus'* with *'the penis'*. Lacan [245] is critical of Freud's use of *'penis envy',* which would be far better termed: *'phallus envy'*. Generally it is only Kleinians and young children who confuse the penis with the phallus. The young child is typically the phallus of the mother, but never the penis of the mother! Freud explained how the mother uses the child to produce enjoyment or jouissance for herself:

'A child's intercourse with anyone responsible for his care affords him an unending source of sexual excitement and satisfaction from his erotogenic

---

[243] J Lacan, Summary of the Seminar of 1966-1967, *The Letter*, Spring, 1999, trans Gallagher, p92.

[244] S Freud, Inhibitions Symptoms and Anxiety, *SE 20*, [1925], 1976, p129-130.

[245] J Lacan, The Inverse of Psychoanalysis, unpublished, trans Gallagher, p71.

zones. This is especially so since the person in charge of him, who after all, is as a rule, his mother, herself regarding him with feelings that are derived from her own sexual life: she strokes him, kisses him, rocks him, and quite clearly treats him as a substitute for a complete sexual object.' [246]

Lacan explained perversion as the child's equation of itself with the phallus of the mother, unchallenged by the symbolic father:

'The whole problem of the perversions, consists in conceiving how the child, in his relation to the mother . . . identifies himself with the imaginary object of this desire in so far as the mother herself symbolises it in the phallus.' [247]

This jouissance that the mother typically has from her child should be borne in mind by those who regard paedophiles as exclusively male. The mother's enjoyment of the child as the phallus is often profound. Some mothers orgasm while breastfeeding. In this important sense the vast majority of practising paedophiles are mothers. Children are not ignorant of the fact that they represent their mother's enjoyment, and often aim to produce the opposite effect so as to wrestle with the impossibility of their mother's frustration, towards identifying their own desire as different. The role that this eroticism plays in the young child's life is crucial in its future love and sex relations.

It is the enjoyment or jouissance of the phallus by the mother that is aimed at by the pervert's symptom. He does not aim an arrow like Eros or Cupid: he always aims himself as the arrow at the one object, the phallic mother and her representatives. For one French pervert sexual satisfaction took the form of masturbating while a prostitute defecated on him, saying, as the shit emerged: *'M E R D E'*. There are two translations or interpretations of this utterance: one is 'shit': another is 'mere de' which translates as 'mother of'. The shit appears in this fantasy as 'the phallus of the mother'. Lacan explained that it was:

'Through the fact of his disavowal, the subject is divided between his recognition of the reality that the mother has no penis and the fact that he attributes a phallus to her.' [248]

So the jouissance of the pervert is taken up by his symptom that distinguishes the penis from the phallus. This is an attempt by the child to return to being treated as *'a complete sexual object'* by the mother, without interruption or castration. Lacan spoke of 'pere-version', where 'pere' is French for 'father', because he understood jouissance to be at the heart of perversion, and jouissance is always transgressive, as an illicit variation, suggesting an activity

---

[246] S Freud, Three Essays on Sexuality, *SE 7*, [1905], 1976, p223.

[247] J Lacan, *Ecrits*, On the Possible Treatment of Psychosis, trans Sheridan, Tavistock, London, [1958], 1977, p198.

[248] Ibid, p237.

that occurs only because it has not been interrupted by the symbolic father as 'The Law'.

Paradoxically, to take jouissance is against rules, and also, in accordance with (another set of) rules; there are always rules and taboos about how we must and must not enjoy ourselves. Pere-version refers to the symbolic father because it is the symbolic father who separates the child from the mother and so is identified with the rules of taboo and enjoyment. The rules against incest forbid the son from enjoying the mother in the same ways as the father, and forbid the daughter from enjoying the father as the mother has. The symbolic father should also prevent the mother from enjoying her child too much. So 'pere-version' invokes the issues of the Primal Horde and the question of the late separation of the child from mother's enjoyment. We can imagine a young child of the Primal Horde who has been hidden by his mother, where the mother's enjoyment of the child is uninhibited because it has not been effectively prohibited or interrupted by the Primal Father. The mother's uninhibited enjoyment of the child has some parallels with the Primal Father's uninhibited enjoyment of the women. This maternally phallic version of the Primal Father is 'pere-version'.

The failure of separation in perversion of mother and child is of a different order from the failure of separation that takes place between mother and child in psychosis. The failure of separation in perversion occurs far later in the child's psychic development than the failure that is essential in the creation of psychotic structure. With psychosis an important question is: *'Does the mother's desire exist for someone other than me?'* Or: *'Is there any object of my mother's desire that is not me?'* With perversion we can speculate that there is a different question: *'Is there any method by which my mother can enjoy that does not rely on me?'* The perverse answer is: *'I am the mother's sole means of enjoyment or jouissance; I am The Phallus of the mother'.*

The phallus is perhaps the most complex of Lacan's objects. We will look at some aspects of it rather than attempting a comprehensive review. A simple approach is to regard the phallus as representing 'one', a single undivided whole, in contrast with the divided subject. How does the phallus acquire this status as 'the whole'? Through being contrasted with that which is not whole.

What falls into this category of the 'not whole'? There are two candidates of the not whole category. The castrated, where castration is simply with reference to the phallus as a unique psychoanalytic object that exists due to a particular lack or absence in one case, rather than the positive presence of a physical or biological object such as 'testicles' or 'ovaries'. The other candidate of the not whole is the presence of one who is believed to 'have the phallus', rather than the one who 'is the phallus'. Why should this be so? Because of the structure that exists around the birth of the subject. What is this structure? One in which the baby discovers that he or she is the phallus of the mother:

'The child . . . identifies himself with the imaginary object of . . . the mother . . . symbolise[d] in the phallus.' [249]

And: *'What the child wants is to become the desire of desire, to be able to satisfy the mother's desire, that is, "to be or not be" the object of the mother's desire . . . To please the mother . . . It is necessary and sufficient to be the phallus.'* [250]

'The mother's role is the mother's desire. That's fundamental. The mother's desire is not something that can be supported like that, that you are indifferent to. That always wreaks havoc. A huge crocodile in whose teeth you are—that's the mother. One does not know what may suddenly come over her, making her shut her trap. That's what the mother's desire is. *Thus, I have tried to explain that there was something that was reassuring . . . There is a roller, in stone . . , which is there, potentially, at the level of her trap, and it is a restraint, it is a wedge. It's what is called the phallus. It's the roller that shelters you, if, all of a sudden, that closes up.'* [251]	**Dare you play with The Biting Shark?**  The ferocious shark has 13 teeth, one of which is unlucky for someone. The idea of this nerve-wracking game is to take turns to press the teeth down until you hit on the one that makes the sharks jaw snap shut. Only super-quick reactions stop you getting a gentle bite. You can never tell which tooth it will be (its selected randomly each time) and to make matters more exciting, he shakes and growls menacingly. 20 cm (8') long. Uses 2 X AA batteries, not included. Age 5+ [252]

---

[249] J Lacan, *Ecrits*, On the Possible Treatment of Psychosis, trans Sheridan, Tavistock, London, [1958], 1977, p198.

[250] J Lacan, 1957 to 1958, seminar of January 22nd, 1958, unpublished, trans Gallagher.

[251] J Lacan, The Inverse of Psychoanalysis, 1969-70, unpublished, trans Grigg.

One way to understand the phallus is with an image of the child in a crocodile's mouth. It is not clear to the child whether the teeth exist for the protection of the child or for its digestion.

Hence the mother has the phallus because she has the baby, but the mother is not the phallus. Lacan developed this aspect of Freud's theory and claimed that: *'One may, simply by reference to the function of the phallus, indicate the structures that will govern the relations between the sexes . . . these relations will turn around a 'to be the phallus' and, on a 'to have the phallus . . .'* [253]

Being or having the phallus

The phallus is something that by definition circulates rather than having a fixed position. This is why, along the lines of 'you can't have your cake and eat it', you can't both have the phallus and be it.

Why is it not possible to both be the phallus and have the phallus? Why is it not possible to simply be the phallus? A comprehensive answer to this difficult question would be complicated. A simple answer is that the phallus is a polar concept, that is, taking a form such as 'black and white', 'tall and short' and 'wet and dry': *'[the phallus] belongs to being, and man, whether male or female, must accept having it and not having it, on the basis of the discovery that he isn't it.'* [254]

Because the phallus is, amongst other things, the *'ratio of the Other's desire'* [255], it is possible for any particular subject to present or represent their Other's desire, and in principle to be their phallus. How can a subject have the phallus? By their Other being the phallus! So, the question of either 'having the phallus', or 'being the phallus' revolves around the question: 'which of us is without, divided, and which of us is whole, undivided? One popular answer to this question and its consequences is sexuation, the masculine and feminine positions, being and having the phallus. A woman typically masks her castration with love[256]: men mask their castration with women.

---

[252] Biting Shark Game £10.95 MC5383, *Brainwaves*, GUS Home Shopping Ltd, Universal House, Devonshire St, Manchester, M60 6EL, 1998.

[253] J Lacan, *Ecrits*, trans Sheridan, Tavistock Publications, London, The Signification of the Phallus, 1977, p289.

[254] J Lacan, Direction of the Treatment and Principles of its Power, *Ecrits*, trans Sheridan, Tavistock, London, p277.

[255] *'The . . . phallus is . . . veiled, as ratio of the Other's desire, it is this desire of the Other as such that the subject must recognise, that is to say the Other in so far as he is himself a subject divided . . .'* J Lacan, *Ecrits*, trans Sheridan, Tavistock, London, The Signification of the Phallus, 1977, p288.

[256] The phallic power of love is perhaps at its height in maternity.

Lacan's development of Freud's theory of the phallus appears to explain much of the conflict between men and women, which is often expressed in terms of 'justice' and 'power'; men and women who are unhappy or unsatisfied with their sexual and love relations typically complain that their difficult position is unfair, and due to their 'not having x' or 'not being y'. The other as the sexual object or object of love is attributed with a power —being or having— that the subject lacks. Surely there is a conceptual problem here? If the subject is the phallus then what problem remains? The subject can only be the phallus in so far as the Other is not the phallus or does not have the phallus. And a subject can only have the phallus insofar as the Other is the phallus.

Having and being the phallus may be at play in the children's game 'it' where one child —it— chases the others, and perhaps in games of hide and seek too. When an other child has been touched by it then the other becomes it, and does the chasing. The game has 'active' and 'passive' positions as chaser and chaste.

'Being it' is a polar concept that only makes sense if there is an other with a

I don't **chase men who can't run away.**

4·3% ABV.
Not to be taken lightly.

different status of lack who is not it, who has provoked the desire of it, of the one with the phallus.?

Having and being, being and coming: how the pervert becomes the phallus and the phallus becomes the pervert, and the pervert comes

There are two questions to which perverts find different answers, when compared to hysterics and obsessionals: Who enjoys whom? How do they enjoy? Some perverts, perhaps exhibitionists, insist —through their symptom— on trying to castrate their imaginary other or mother. They might frighten a woman by pressing on her the fact that she has no penis. But the fact that a pervert wants a woman to recognise that she does not have a penis demonstrates that he actually attributes to the woman special power: he imagines that she has the pervert as phallus. He believes that she has the phallus: while he only has a penis —but with her— becomes the phallus.

'Such is the woman concealed behind her veil: it is the absence of the penis that turns her into the phallus, the object of desire.' [257]

All neurotics have some perverse traits. Some women demonstrate their awareness and manipulation of men's perversion in the detailed attention they give to the images and objects associated with their phallic power and sexuality, such as shoes, while simultaneously complaining that men treat them as objects. A common question for someone choosing clothes is: *'Which article of clothing will excite and interest wo/men the most?* Sometimes women ridicule a man's interest in a particular perversion or fetish, resenting their own best efforts to appeal to such perversions, especially when they fail. A shoe fetishist and a woman in high heels make a fine pair.

The emphasis of the pervert is not so much on the desire of the Other —as it is for the hysteric and obsessional— but on the jouissance of the Other, with the pervert as its vehicle, with himself as phallus. What distinguishes neurotics from perverts is not castration, but what they do with their castration:

'What the neurotic retreats from, is not castration: it is from making of his own castration what is lacking to the big Other, it is from making of his castration something positive which is the guarantee of this function of the Other . . . Dedicating his castration to this guarantee of the Other is what the neurotic comes to a halt before.' [258]

And: *'This [theory of fantasy] would help to distinguish [the neurotic] from . . . the pervert, much more closely confronted with the impasse of the sexual act. Just as much subject as he of course, but one who makes . . . the fantasy the*

---

[257] J Lacan, Subversion of the Subject and Dialectic of Desire, *Ecrits*, trans Sheridan, Tavistock, London, 1977, p322.

[258] J Lacan, Seminar on Anxiety, unpublished, trans Gallagher, 15th December 1962.

conducting system through which he steals by a short-circuit an enjoyment
from which the locus of the other separates him no less.' [259]

Phobia and perversion

Phobia and perversion can be understood as opposites in a limited ordinary
language sense. In phobia 'an ordinary object' is avoided, such as the horse in
the case of Little Hans: in perversion or more obviously in fetishism 'an object'
is sought out. Phobia can be understood as the distance, weakness or failure of
the paternal function, that is as caused by the lack of the father's lack, while
perversion can be understood as caused by the excessive lack of the mother.

In the perverse child's imagination the mother lacks any effective interruption
of her enjoyment of the child by a third party, that is, by the symbolic father: in
the phobic's imagination the child is not the exclusive object of his mother's
enjoyment, but that other who his mother desires —the symbolic father— is
not a sufficiently credible figure for him to properly identify with. The
castration of the phobic's symbolic father is not apparent or visible, so the
symbolic father's castration, that is his relation to the phallus, to the mother's
means of enjoyment, cannot be clearly identified by the phobic. So in phobia it
is not possible for the child to successfully identify with the symbolic father
because he is like a mythical or fairy tale figure who —unlike the child— is not
castrated: in perversion it is the mother who is not castrated because of the
child's fantastic and singular identification with the phallus of the mother. In
phobia the father is present but weak: in perversion he is symbolically absent.
The phobic object is a negative identification with the symbolic father; the
perverse object or fetish is a positive identification with the symbolic mother.

This neurotic position —of being identified with the Other's lack— is reversed
in perversion where the pervert instead dedicates himself to preventing the lack
in the Other becoming manifest. The pervert disavows castration wholesale; the
neurotic avoids identifying his own castration with his Other's castration. The
phobic insists that there exists a symbolic function that castrates, interrupting
and regulating his enjoyment and that of his Other. For Little Hans it was a
horse that —through the structure of a phobia— provided the interruption and
regulation of his enjoyment of his mother. His fear of horses took the place of
his lack of 'fear' of his father.

---

[259] J Lacan, Summary of the Seminar of 1966-1967, trans Gallagher, *The Letter*,
Spring, 1999.

Tactics and strategy with perverts

I have the impression that it is often too difficult for perverts to continue clinical work beyond six months or a year. It may be helpful to treat perverts as if they were hysterics with whom one should use the technique of 'rectifying to the real' very sparingly. Perversion is in some ways the joker in the pack of psychopathology; it is rarely seen in the clinic because perverts enjoy their symptoms so much that they rarely want to make any changes. It is common for perverts to turn up at a clinic only when they are in trouble with the law. This background —the wish to avoid punishment for transgression— makes clinical work difficult, not least because the symptom of perverts is always markedly transgressive, at least in the pervert's imagination. Hence a popular tactic in the pervert's transference is to locate the clinician in the position of supporting his alibi of conformity. Nevertheless Lacan claimed that:

'Perversion is indeed something articulate, interpretable, analysable, and on precisely the same level as neurosis. In the fantasy . . . [of the neurotic] an essential relationship of the subject to his being is localised and fixed. Well, whereas in the perversion, the accent is on the object a, the neurosis can be situated as having the accent on the other term of the fantasy, the divided subject.' [260]

Because there is little clinical material on perverts it is difficult to make generalisations about the possibilities that psychoanalysis can open up for those with perverse structures. Perhaps the most import aspect of perversion is the function that 'the pervert' has for the hysteric, in the hysteric's construction of their symptom and fantasy in juxtaposition with 'the pervert's'.

The next section discusses the different techniques used by each diagnostic category for making jouissance in relation to the big Other. It is important to understand that the big Other is not to be simply identified with a particular person but is typically a composite, made up of various aspects taken from different people:

'We depend on the field of the Other, which was there long before we came into the world, and whose circulating structures determine us as subjects.' [261]

' . . . our subjectivity is something we entirely construct in plurality . . .' [262]

---

[260] J Lacan, *Desire and Interpretation of Desire in Hamlet, Literature and Psychoanalysis,* ed Felman, Baltimore and London, Johns Hopkins University Press, 1982, p16.

[261] J Lacan, *The Four Fundamental Concepts of Psychoanalysis*, trans Sheridan, ed Miller, Penguin, [1964], 1979, p244-246.

[262] J Lacan, Transference Seminar, unpublished, trans Gallagher.

Paranoid psychosis, the big Other and jouissance

In paranoid psychosis a 'Biggest Other' is contrived, and is usually on a grand scale, perhaps taking the form of God, aliens or the FBI. The psychotic's Other is perceived to be particularly greedy for jouissance, and effective at getting it, allowing a kind of pseudo-subjectivity. The Biggest Other of psychosis is a construction, a symptom, improvised in order to masquerade a pseudo-subjective division of the psychotic. Why does the psychotic masquerade such a division? Because there is an important sense in which a psychotic is not a subject, at least while their fragile grasp on ordinary neurotic language is at risk of slipping away. Constructing such an Other who produces some effects of subjective division helps the paranoid psychotic to keep the facade of ordinary neurotic language functioning. Another way to understand the same phenomenon is in terms of stability or complexity; a neurotic structure —whether pseudo or genuine— is vital in supporting ordinary human language functions. Because this Other of the paranoid psychotic is so grandiose, fragile and inflated that he deserves the title 'Biggest Other'.

Hysteria, the big Other and jouissance

The hysteric typically complains that the cause of their suffering is the Other and the Other's desire. This is the truth in a profound sense: the hysteric recognises that desire is a property of language, and that language is public property, and that as a consequence their desire relies on the Other. But this truth is also used as a lie or camouflage for another truth, the specific identity of the subject's desire. That is the truth of desire and its expected consequences. Put another way this other truth is also the complicated and impossible to articulate clearly truth of the little other, as the cause and object of the hysterical subject's desire.

How do hysterics make jouissance? Answering this question returns us to the division of hysteria into the categories of phobia, anxiety hysteria, and conversion hysteria.

The conversion hysteric enjoys their bodily symptom. For example, the faces of those who have just finished self-mutilating[263] usually look as though they have just had an orgasm. These clients often report 'a sexual release' on cutting. Orgasm itself is the paradigm of a hysterical structure, and usually insists on a kind of repeated action or beating that is imagined by the hysteric to be carried out by their Other. This theme is elaborated in Freud's paper *'A Child is Being Beaten'* [264], in which the ordinary sexual activity of the adult variety is understood as a special kind of beating, followed by a forgetting or

---

[263] Those who self mutilate are not necessarily hysterics.
[264] S Freud, A Child is being Beaten, *SE 17,* [1919e], 1979.

loss of consciousness. The experience of the series of sensations of pleasure and pain, and jouissance in orgasm are the somatic or bodily conversions of anxiety hysteria of phobia.[265]

The phobic or one who experiences anxiety attacks is a hysteric. Their jouissance —which can also be understood as 'their forgetting'— is generally at its height at the point when the anxiety or panic attack are at their height. Anxiety is the original precursor or antecedent of all other symptoms. In some cases the only obvious symptom is anxiety, for instance in panic attacks. In phobia the anxiety has been transferred or invested in an object or set of objects. The phobic object always has two opposing or contrasting properties, such as the 'proud' and the 'fallen horse' of Little Hans whose opposition allowed him to explore a new position. When the subject experiences high levels of anxiety he is able to forget the underlying cause of his suffering; it is usually at this point, ironically and usually unconsciously that the subject enjoys their symptom the most; in this sense the enjoyment of the symptom is a compensation for the suffering.

Obsessional neurosis, the big Other and jouissance

The obsessional neurotic appears to have two big Others: Freud's Ratman for instance had his father, and his mother or girlfriend. These two Others are offset against each other. Obsessional symptoms are the attempt to perpetuate a vital but fake feud or rivalry between two big Others. They are paired off, and function to prevent the obsessional's desire from being acted on through a balancing act carried out by opposing one desire, in relation to one of the big Others, with the other desire that refers to the other big Other. Obsessional neurotics find acting on their desire particularly difficult because they are always being pulled by an Other, in an apparently incompatible direction.

Because the Lacanian clinician works to hystericise obsessional neurotics, and sometimes succeeds, a question is raised as to the relative status of the 'two big Others' of the obsessional. Were they both really big Others, or was there really only one?

Here is a similar question: Konigsberg is a town that has, at various points in its history been within Germany, and at others part of Russia. The question: 'Is

---

[265] This does not imply that everyone who experiences orgasm has a hysterical structure, but rather one of three possibilities: either the individual is straightforwardly hysterical, or there was once a simpler hysterical structure, as in the case of obsessional neurosis, and this simpler structure now functions within a more complicated structure. The third category includes psychotics who experience orgasm, where their enjoyment is with reference not to the big Other of the hysteric, but to the pseudo and fragile 'Biggest Other' that they have contrived.

Konigsberg a Russian or German town?' can only be answered by referring to the other structures that existed at a particular time. So, for any particular neurotic subject the relevant question is: What is the Other at that point? Does his mother or lady on one hand, or his father on the Other represent the Other of the Ratman? If there is a concerted attempt at dual nationality —that is at maintaining the two Others— then the subject maintains his obsessional neurosis: if he has become hysterical then he is the subject of one state, and there he lives.

Perversion and the big Other and jouissance

Perverts achieve a kind of revolutionary jouissance. How? The answer to this question relies on some additional concepts that we will look at first, returning to this question in Chapter Eleven.

Jouissance as the con-fusion of repression with castration

What is a difference between repression and castration? This question is not straightforward to answer because the functions of castration and repression overlap to some degree, especially for 'the subject' of jouissance and the subject of desire. The subject of jouissance confuses castration and repression, and typically complains of too much repression, and of too little jouissance:

Lacanians tend to understand this in reverse: that such a client is likely to have suffered uneven or too little repression which explains why they make so much jouissance. The difference between repression and castration that allows psychosis, neurosis and psychoanalysis. Castration is with respect to the phallus, while repression is with respect to the law.[266]

---

[266] The phallus is not the same as the law but the two are related. The phallus is, in the first instance, the law of the mother's desire. The law proper only comes to exist for the child through the interruption of the mother's demands and desires. That is through the symbolic father. The law is symbolic, while the phallus is more complex, having two categories in three registers: the little phallus and the big phallus, in the registers of the imaginary, the symbolic and the real. So any particular neurotic subject can *imagine* his or another's castration, but this is quite different from *symbolising* his or another's castration. For example the Ratman imagined that: *'If I have a wish to see a woman naked, my father will be bound to die'.* Because the Ratman wanted the love of his father, and the love of women, and in his obsessional neurosis the two were mutually exclusive, he imagined that he would lose his father —and his father's love— if he enjoyed women. So the Ratman's enjoyment is conditional on the death of his father. His obsessional imperative to enjoy is something like: *'Either: enjoy the woman and suffer the loss of your father, or: enjoy your father and suffer your celibacy.'* Either way the loss or castration is imaginary, standing for a lack in the laws regulating the

But distinguishing repression and castration is not always easy. There are different types of repression, and there are different types of castration. For example in cases of psychosis a fundamental repression has become established as absent. How has this come to be? There is a window of opportunity that lasts, possibly until the child is 18 months old, during which this fundamental type of repression may become established. If this repression is not properly established and functioning during this period then a psychotic structure will always result.

At a later stage, if another kind of repression has been absent phobia, hysteria or obsessional neurosis results; and again, if another kind of repression has been absent then perversion becomes the stable structure. The pattern of repression is specific to the pathology.

Considerations of repression must take into account both the quantity of repression and its quality. The quality is determined in crucial part by the time at which the repression took place or is absent, or put another way, the relevant structure to which the repression is applied.

At The End of analysis the neurotic subject is able to symbolise, to talk of repressions that have been too little and too much. He has only arrived at this point through an analysis of his speech, by metamorphosing much of his imaginary castration into three components: a new symbolic castration, a revised real castration, and a revised imaginary castration.

Castration that has become symbolised is the closest to the law because it is only through castration that transgression —as the breaking of rules and laws— is achieved. The symptomatic symbolisation of castration in neurosis is always carried out with failed, inefficient or excessive repressions.

'What the neurotic does not want, and what he strenuously refuses to do, until The End of the analysis, is to sacrifice his castration to the jouissance of the Other by allowing it to serve that jouissance. . . . why should he sacrifice his difference to the jouissance of an Other? . . . [The neurotic] imagines that the Other demands his castration. What analytic experience shows is that . . . castration . . . governs desire . . . ' [267]

The Other of the neurotic is identified as the source of the subject's repression; therefore, in a weak paradox, as the source of his expression too.

---

economy of enjoyment, representing an absent repression, something that has not been properly symbolised. The imaginary castration is easy to demonstrate in this case because the Ratman's father had already been dead for many years prior to his analysis by Freud!

[267] J Lacan, *Ecrits*, trans Sheridan, Tavistock publications, London, Subversion of the Subject and Dialectic of Desire, 1977, p323.

The mother infant relation as torture

In the simplistic story that follows, of the infant as the phallus of the mother, that is the infant as the means of satisfaction and enjoyment for the mother, and in the evolution of hot pepper or the chilli, signifiers are equated with genes.[268]

In the beginning the mother is the sensation manager of her young baby. The infant's primary concerns are sensations of pain and pleasure. These sensations are causally regulated according to the pleasure principle, a physiological version of the laws of thermodynamics. Pleasure is provided to the baby, or it is relieved from unpleasure, from pain, by its mother, and simultaneously the baby becomes the means, the measure of jouissance or the phallus for the mother.

The helpless infant requires insurance, a guarantee, some tool of negotiation over which he possesses control. The event he needs to insure against is that of his mummy no longer managing his sensations: she should continue to be the gratifier of his needs, the provider of pleasure and remover of unpleasure, that is his pain. Ironically the baby is best able to establish the guarantee and discover what mother demands and desires by becoming a language user. Not least because when baby presents a sensation need, mother increasingly delays gratification and instead feeds him a morsel of language. The baby eats language because he has a requirement for pleasure, or for pain to be removed, and the mother has her requirement for jouissance, to have her child say *'I love you'*. So the good mother systematically tortures her baby, delaying his pleasure, increasing his pain, depriving and frustrating, until her symbols are swallowed. Torture invariably has the aim of producing speech from the suffering victim. If torture victims speak it is primarily to plead *'What do you want?* [269]*'* of their torturer, of the one who has power over their sensations. The victim may say whatever she believes her torturer wants to hear. So it is with mother's and their infants. Sometimes children deny their mother's wishes: sometimes victims of torture are defiant. The price initially set for helping the helpless infant is the insistence that the infant comes to have knowledge of the mother's demands and desires, and above all that he speaks.

The infant identifies the gratification of his needs —his pleasure and pain— with his mother's demands and desires. This crucially drawn out juxtaposition of pleasure-pain and words is uniquely human because it is a description of erotica in general, not simply of the mother infant relation; it is not only sadomasochists for whom the fantasy *'you make me feel x'* is the essence of erotic.

---

[268] As '*the signifier represents the subject for another signifier*', so the gene represents the organism for another gene.

[269] See Lacan's graph of desire for an elaboration of this theme on p312-3 of the *Ecrits*.

Just as the experience around orgasm is generally reported as positive or 'good'
so mothers are deemed 'good'. Just as the experience around orgasm
necessitates suffering and pain, so does being mothered.

The structure around orgasm and the mother infant relation as torture

	Who has the power to regulate pain?	Who suffers pain?	Who is speech demanded of?	Who demands speech?	Who loses consciousness?
Mother infant relation	*mother*	infant	infant	Mother	infant and sometimes mother
Torture	*torturer*	victim	victim	Torturer	victim and sometimes torturer
Structure around orgasm	big Other (of fantasy) *'you make me feel…'*	subject	the one who is the phallus	the one who has the phallus	subject of orgasm

The relation to the mother is necessarily problematic for the infant because the
mother's desire is symbolic, that is expressed in language. So for the infant to
ensure that his sensation needs are met and managed by the mother there is a
compelling pressure for him to understand the mother's desire, that is her
language. But the child, even in the worst cases of psychosis never manages to
identify himself comprehensively with his mother's desire. As the infantile
subject is entered by language, he is also formulated —to radically different
levels in neurosis and psychosis— by the symbolic father, that is by he who

marks the infant's separation from the mother. The symbolic father limits the possible identification of the child's desire with the mother's desire by representing the mother's desire for a desire other than the child's desire. The young baby is like the tasteless chilli of old. Many thousands of years ago the bland ancestor of the chilli changed so that it would no longer be eaten. It evolved to become burning hot in the mouths of those who ate it, its predators. This step towards recognising the desire of the Other and unwittingly into the discourse of gastronomy was originally designed to prevent it from being consumed, and for a while it worked because in general animals aren't crazy enough to eat something that burns. But now millions of chillies are specially cultivated in huge fields where any competitive species is eradicated and weeded out. Juicy chillies are now plucked at their prime and pulverised into tasty sauces and curries. No organism cannot deny its organisation, its structural dependence on the Other. [270]

The technique used to prevent the fragmentation and destruction of the chilli has caused not only its enormous success, but also its wholesale destruction. The chilli is subjected to the letter of genetic desire, to burn in the mouth of its Other. So it is with the symbolic, entered into by baby so that he can be mummy's phallus, so that he won't have to suffer. The very medium he enters will ensure both his continued suffering and that any success he might have, will, in addition to his world of sensations, be in the overwhelming realm of language, including the imaginary and the real. The infant entered language only to solve his problem of sensations, but finds himself taking on a whole new set of problems that come as an integral package with language. This lack of rapport or absence of reciprocation between the mother's requirements, and her infant's requirements is the prototype for the infamous lack of sexual rapport between adult lovers. This is the fact that broadly, women want from men what men cannot give, and men want from women what women cannot give. This same lack of rapport is also found in homosexual relations.

The life and death of the chilli are largely determined by our gastronomic and economic structures. Its being is defined by the appetites of its Other, by the Other's desire, so too with the infant, who, in his attempt to evade displeasure, enters the structure of language, causing his mind to become constituted by the discourse of the Other, initially at least by his mother's desire, becoming institutionalised as his unconscious.

---

[270] As the title of a biological paper puts it: *There is no such thing as a one celled animal or plant* (L Margulis, D Mehos, and Kaveski S, *Science Teacher* 50:34-36, p41-43) that is there is always an other in relation to the organism. So, for instance every cell contains 'mitochondria'. These are crucial to the life of the cell and are now widely believed to have once been external and independent organisms that became mutually dependent on the cells in which they are now found.

Any pity for the chilli might be tempered by reflecting on the fact that the chilli has proliferated and succeeded in a way that would have been inconceivable without our suffering, without the jouissance of our burning mouths and the profits of chilli farmers and hot pepper sauce manufacturers. A similar conclusion could be reached for the poor, tortured infant.

The reaction that most people have to the idea of torture is not simply explained by pain; many or most people suffer physical pain through ordinary illness, starvation, and rituals such as circumcision, foot binding and other fashions. Many accept pain and often go some way towards making sure that they are 'getting enough', or banish their pain to an unconscious or preconscious level. So what is different about torture? What explains the strong emotional or ethical objections that most people produce on hearing reports of torture? Is torture a slander on maternity, or is maternity is a slander on torture? Are licences that permit the pain to be experienced held exclusively by those with a supposedly professional knowledge of 'The Sovereign Good', by mothers, doctors and prostitutes? [271]

The incomparable primal power of the mother in relation to the infant, and the set of necessarily broken deals between the mother and her hopefully ordinary neurotic child form the prototype and institutionalisation of the lack of sexual rapport as the basis of language, as the words the mother tortures her infant with. It may also explain the popularity of misogyny and male violence against women as a kind of revenge and recognition of an archaic maternal power over her subject.

Further Reading

L Rodriguez, Fantasy, Neurosis and Perversion, *Analysis*, Melbourne Centre for Psychoanalytic Research, Number Two, 1990.

S Freud, Three Essays on the Theory of Sexuality, *Standard Edition 7*, [1905], 1976.

---

[271] In England it is illegal for consenting adults to perform sadomasochistic practices on one another. English law insists that the right to inflict pain, or to have pain inflicted is not a voluntary matter, but one of compulsion or legal duty open principally to either licensed professional carers such as doctors and mothers. The state takes a sharp interest in the administration of pain.

CHAPTER TWELVE

What have space and time to do with clinical practice?

Many Lacanians who regard themselves and each other as psychoanalysts see their clients only once or twice a week, while some other psychoanalysts insist that *'anything less than four or five sessions a week is not proper psychoanalysis'*.

Some Lacanian clients —who live a long way from their clinician— have their sessions over a weekend, once a month, having four or five sessions over one or two days. It may be unusual but it is certainly possible to do effective work this way. Other clients are only able to see a clinician once every two weeks, perhaps due to their anxiety, because they cannot afford to pay for more, or because they do shift work. It is possible that the client who sees his clinician once every two weeks makes changes on a bigger scale than some clients who see their clinician five times a week. The rate at which clients do therapeutic work is not simply determined by the number of hours per week that the client is with the clinician; the client does most of the work, and in the main it is done between sessions, not during them.

From the client's position it is often ideal if the clinical work is not time-limited; the client can finish when he is ready, but this does not mean of course that some limited psychoanalytic work cannot be done in a time limited context. Psychoanalytic work always involves doing something unique: helping the client to ask questions in ways that have not been posed before, so allowing the possibility of the client taking a new position in relation to their suffering. Ideally this means that the work done is not dictated arbitrarily by a clock or calendar, but by the issues that turn out to be important for the individual client.

Because of the uniqueness of the questions and issues that each of us have, our individual circumstances and the idiosyncratic uses we make of language, it is not possible to know in advance how long clinical work would take, if the client were allowed to complete the work, and to go to 'The End of Analysis'. This fact is usually in conflict with institutional demands on clinicians to provide time-limited therapy and quick results. Sometimes clients demand these things too, often as a distraction in order to avoid coming to terms with bigger underlying difficulties.

Sometimes objections are raised along the lines that clinical work in the Freudian or Lacanian tradition is *'self indulgent'* because it often takes many years to properly finish, even though many benefits are often enjoyed long before 'The End'. The most important question surely is not *'How long someone chooses to spend seeing a clinician?'* but, how long he or she choose to spend hiding from their truth, from the truth of their desire? Life itself usually takes many years to complete, is expensive and often follows an unpredictable course, yet most people do not object to it on these grounds.

If you take five to fifteen years of difficult work to discover what really makes you tick —in a fundamental sense— can anyone justifiably criticise you? All they can do is compare how they would have spent their time and money. Usually the bitterest criticisms of psychoanalytic work come from those who, if they had the courage to do the work themselves, would have much to gain, from having faced their demons and made changes in their own lives. Will they ever do it? As long as the critic can identify with a client who is actually going through the struggle of learning about themselves, they may be able to justify keeping away from therapy themselves.

The very idea of 'self indulgence' begs two questions: 'What exactly is a self?'— a question to which Lacan had an interesting answer[272], and 'What is indulgence?' Most clients spend most of their clinical time talking about other people rather than themselves. Surely this is not what is meant by 'self-indulgence'? When a neurotic client can finally speak clearly about himself — without using others as some kind of alibi or excuse for his life— then his clinical work has come to The End.

To explain why Lacanians use variable length sessions we first have to reflect more broadly on the nature of time and space. We know that the perception of space and time is not a constant and perhaps varies with each subject and their circumstances. So a reasonable question to ask here is 'What theory of time and space is being assumed and relied on in clinical practice?' and 'What possible reasons might exist for clinical sessions lasting for a fixed period?'

Freud had discovered that if you want to understand the mind then ordinary three-dimensional space is not sufficient:

'Now let us, by a flight of imagination, suppose that Rome is not a human habitation but a psychical entity with a similarly long and copious past . . . There is no point in spinning our fantasy any further, for it leads to things that are unimaginable and even absurd . . . The same space cannot have two different contents. Our attempt seems to be an idle game. It has only one justification. It shows us how far we are from mastering the characteristics of mental life by representing them in pictorial terms.'

---

[272] *'"[S]elf". . . can be adapted to nothing in analytic theory, nothing corresponds to it.* J Lacan, The Psychoanalytic Act, unpublished seminar, trans Gallagher, 10 January 1968.

And: *'Our psychical topography has for the present nothing to do with anatomy; it has reference not to anatomical localities, but to regions in the mental apparatus, wherever they may be situated in the body . . . With the . . . topographical hypothesis is bound up that of a topographical separation of the unconscious system and conscious and also the possibility that an idea may exist simultaneously in two places in the mental apparatus.'* [273]

Lacan, writing on the same topic elaborated Freud's idea, claimed that:

'In order to grasp its [the little object's] extent, one must abstract oneself from three dimensional space, since it is a question here only of a topological reality that is limited to the function of a surface.' [274]

'Time and space' come together as a package; as time is the measure of change, so space is the place of change. 'Topology' is concerned with time and space and is also known as 'rubber sheet geometry', because angle and distance are not variables in topology; they do not exist. So, for example, a car tyre and a needle are identical topologically because within topology you could deform a needle —as if it were elastic— so that it took the form of a tyre, or vice versa, because both objects have a hole in them. Topology assumes all objects and space to be rubbery or distortable rather than fixed by angle and distance.

To make sense of a train or underground network from the point of view of a traveller means ignoring the angles and distances between the stations. The map of the London Underground system is set out just like an electrical circuit, that is topologically. If all the additional assumptions regarding angle and distance were represented on diagrams of electrical circuits or maps of train systems then they would become difficult or impossible to understand and use.

Topology deals with a kind of space that is more fundamental than our ordinary everyday three-dimensional space. Of course we ordinarily see the world as three dimensional: but many processes in psychoanalysis, physics, mathematics, genetics, immunology and linguistics can only be understood with a far more general topological scheme of time and space, a scheme that each of us has a version of in our minds. One illustration of this is the fact that time and distance are famously elastic from the position of the subject's desire. Typically, if you want something, it takes a long time to happen: and if you don't want it, it happens much too soon. Topology sometimes breaks fleetingly through the façade of our everyday three-dimensional geometry, twisting and distorting in dreams, hallucinations and fantasies.

---

[273] S Freud, Civilisation and its Discontents, *SE 21*, [1929], 1976, p70-2.
[274] J Lacan, *The Four Fundamental Concepts of Psychoanalysis*, trans Sheridan, ed Miller, Penguin, [1964], 1979, p271.

Topology is especially important in understanding language and its role in psychoanalysis because it doesn't make any sense to speak of 'the distance between words'. Words are connected to each other, but the connections do not seem to have any length. This topological view, with the disappearance of the ordinary understanding of distance, is what is meant by *'the shrinking world'* or the *'global village'*, in the flow of signifiers in telecommunications. In a telephone conversation between someone in England and someone in Australia there is no distance at all between their signifiers.

Why do Lacanians use variable length sessions?

The question: *'Why have fixed length sessions?'* is no more obvious or important than: *'Why have variable length sessions?'* If 'all things were equal', then fixed length sessions would probably suit everyone very well, clients and clinicians could plan their day with precision: but all things are certainly not equal; one of the aims of the Lacanian clinician is not to establish some kind of thorough uniformity or equality, but rather to achieve difference. That is the absence of equality.

Put another way, everything said by the client should be carefully listened to, and the clinician's interpretations should address the client's speech. Because every client speaks differently the ending of a session should take account — uniquely— of the individual client's words. It follows then that ending the session automatically, at or around the totally arbitrary point of '50 minutes' means that the client's speech is systematically ignored. The system here is the 'fifty minute system'.

If the time you spent with a friend, lover, doctor, dentist or lawyer always lasted a fixed length of time then you would no doubt find those relationships very contrived and difficult to maintain. What you want in each relationship would be obstructed by the arbitrary duration of the time available to achieve it in.

Imagine the absurdity having an argument for precisely five minutes, in the style of Monty Python, or making love, or cooking a meal for a rigidly predetermined time! The only things that last exactly fifty minutes today are school lessons, with their prior and rigidly fixed curriculum, and the clinical work of some schools. Unfortunately clinical work in many of non-Lacanian traditions also has a rigidly fixed curriculum that is supposed to be part of the knowledge of the clinician. Just as children at school are saved by the bell from an adversarial interrogation that might expose their ignorance, so many clients who have fifty-minute sessions thrust upon the varied presentations of their unique problems will often be saved from talking about a difficult truth. When the fifty minutes are up the client makes good his escape, maintaining his rivalry and struggle with the clinician.

With fixed length sessions it is usual for clients to try and leave their clinician with a question: with variable length sessions clinicians try and leave their clients with a question. With fixed length sessions the clinician unavoidably asserts his supposition of knowledge: with variable length sessions the clinician knows that he is ignorant of the truth of his client's desire, which resides, not primarily in the consciousness of the clinician, but in the unconscious of the client.

Some Lacanians argue that arbitrarily fixing the length of sessions —regardless of what is said— promotes obsessional neurosis:

'Obsessional ideas, as is well known, have an appearance of being either without motive, or without meaning' [275]

The arbitrary is the meaningless, that which attempts, vainly, to disregard language and the symbolic. Fixed length sessions impose an effect of meaninglessness on the client's speech. In contrast Lacanians seek to hystericise their clients so as to discover what individual meanings are functioning uniquely for each client.

Other reasons for using variable length sessions were given in Chapter One in the justification for 'Belief Four'. People both perceive and remember interruptions or discontinuity in time far better than continuity or the lack of change. In brief there are three sorts of the evidence for Freud's and Lacan's claim that people remember interruptions or discontinuity in time far better than continuity:

1. Formal scientific studies of large numbers of people by psychologists, most famously by Zeigarnik .

2. Studies carried out by psychoanalysts on individual clients.

3. Investigations that each of us can carry out on ourselves, by self-observation and introspection.

Many researchers have produced much empirical evidence supporting this view, for example Bigge and Hunt [276] have claimed:

'. . . allowing students to leave each class with some unanswered questions . . . is much more effective than passive reception . . .'

This technique is very similar to ending a clinical session on a question or ambiguity. The student is encouraged to actively pursue their own answers rather than the teacher's.

---

[275] S Freud, Notes Upon a Case of Obsessional Neurosis, *SE 10*, [1909], 1976, p186.
[276] *Psychological Foundations of Education*. 2nd ed., New York, Harper & Row, 1968, p244.

On two occasions clients have said that there is still something they want to say after I ended a session. In these cases I have invited the client to speak and the client has then taken more two or three minutes to finish. An alternative would be to suggest that 'we could discuss that next time?'

The ending of a session should not be used sadistically. Sessions should not be ended at points of convenience from some practical point of view: the end of a session should always underline an important point or question that the client has reached, an ambiguity, joke, the change of position or the clear identification of a position. Sessions should generally be ended on the client's words, laughter or pregnant silence, not on some sermon of the clinician's. One of the most important functions of ending a session is to recognize the importance of a client's interpretation.

Early on in the work I never use a sharp ending which might be startling for the client and frighten them, before either the transference has been established, or I have a firm idea of my diagnosis. Only when you are confident of both the responsiveness of your client's transference and your diagnosis should you consider using a surprising end to a session.

What might indicate the responsiveness of the client's transference? It is certain that the client has a transference to his clinician by virtue of the fact that he has made an appointment and attended a session. Such a clinician has a place in his client's imagination, but this is not sufficient. Only when the client is able to signify their transference in some other way, besides their attendance, might the clinician properly judge that the client's transference is 'responsive'. Examples include the client reporting a dream that stars the clinician, slips of the tongue and bungled actions such as missing sessions and turning up at the wrong time.

CHAPTER THIRTEEN

The clinic and the institution

Some clinical aspects of Lacan's theory of the four discourses

'Psychoanalysis is not a game of questions and answers, now is it?' [277]

L acan, following Freud, theorised the human condition as uniquely dominated by language. Given this approach it is not surprising that Lacan developed a novel theory of discourse. For Lacan there are four fundamentally different ways of speaking and being: the discourse of the master and slave, the university discourse, the hysteric's discourse, and the analyst's discourse.

The discourse of the master and slave

'[I]t's by what the truth of the discourse of the master is masked that analysis derives its importance.' [278]

The discourse of the master and slave is a good starting point because each of us starts with it, more or less as a slave, ignorant of our master's or mother's desire yet devoted to it. The helpless and speechless infant is helped by a powerful speaker. The one with the power, usually the mother, with the mother tongue is in the position of master. The infant —the one who doesn't speak— can survive only with the help of the one who speaks, with her words and power.

The helpless infant comes to believe that his life depends on finding meaning in the mysterious words spoken to him by his helper. Words represent the overwhelmingly important and enigmatic desires and demands of his mother. The mother's speech at this early stage, has the value of a guarantee or insurance that the helpless infant will continue to be helped, if only the

---

[277] J Dorsey, *An American Psychiatrist in Vienna, 1935 to 1937, and His Sigmund Freud*, Centre for Health Education, ed Lohser, 1976, p16.

[278] J Lacan, The Inverse of Psychoanalysis, unpublished, trans Gallagher, 18 February 1970.

mother's enigmatic will be done. The place of the mother is at least in part that of a terrifying omnipotent god whose desire is unknown.[279]

So a question is formulated for the child along the lines: how can I understand my mother's desires and demands, how can I become what she wants, that is, her phallus? It is this position of serving the Other's desire or demands that describe the position of the slave, with the mother as master.

The discourse of the master and slave is important, not only because it is the first for each of us, and starts the ball rolling for the other types of discourse, but because on the larger scale of sociology and history the master slave discourse is also inaugural; it easy to imagine a society without psychoanalysts, such as a feudal one, or one without universities, because in history they have been many examples, but it seems that there have always and will always be masters and slaves, however families and societies are structured.

Lacan argued that slavery and mastery operate universally. Democracy is one popular solution to political injustice but democracy does not eliminate slavery and mastery, it merely disguises it. Hierarchies offering promotion invite slaves to master within a system of licensed bullying. Those who regard themselves as slaves suppose 'their masters' to possess knowledge and to have special access to jouissance. Many of those deemed to be 'masters' also promote the propaganda that they possess a special knowledge and power that would constitute a solution to the slave's problems. The resulting slave-master relation is collusion, a drama of compounded fictions. Each master is a slave to his own mastery. So the warders in a prison are a kind of prisoner too, confined in almost exactly the same way as the convicted prisoners. A prison officer with 40 years service has done about as much time inside jail as the average prisoner with a life sentence.

The idea and practice of being a slave are always entangled with the idea of being a master: the idea and practice of being a master is always entangled with the idea of being a slave, In the slave-master discourse jouissance or enjoyment is a central issue because infants and mothers both play at being the slave and the master, in a complex exchange. This is vital because the mother-infant relation, with its power and jouissance, is the prototype for future adult sexual

---

[279] The unknown desire of the omnipotent Other describes the curse or blessing of the Jews as God's 'chosen ones'. God's desire is mysterious; why should he have chosen the Jews, a helpless band of Egyptian slaves? What exactly is God's desire, it's object and expression? The persistence of Jews and their culture can be explained by the joint existence of two properties: the indestructibility of an invisible and typically silent God, and his compelling invitation to transfer, effected by the demonstrable agency of the Ten Commandments.

relations and economic relations. Slavery in the mother-child relation arises
from the suffering of the powerless child at what it understands to be the

powerful hands of the masterful mother. Who is really in control of absence and
presence in peek-a-boo games? Is it the baby as he gazes at the mother, or is it
the mother who has far more power to leave and reappear? For the baby, the
mother has the masterful position because she plays with her presence and
absence by allowing her child a pretend mastery. At the same time the mother
may believe that her baby has made a slave of her, and wish her virginity or
single pre-maternal status to be returned to her.

In a slight caricature those who identify themselves as slaves, including
prisoners, children, husbands, wives, employees, and those in any service
industry usually believe that their master has an unfair share of fun, of
jouissance; while paradoxically those who identify themselves as masters
usually believe that the slaves have a privileged access to jouissance. Sometimes
slaves say that they are getting a fair deal, but will usually complain at the
earliest opportunity and try to better their deal with their master.

One demonstration of the importance of jouissance in the slave-master
relationship can be seen in submissive-domination sex enjoyed by so many, and
in the popular erotic literature on 'slaves and masters'. This literature details
who takes jouissance from whom, and how much, detailing an economics of
enjoyment.

In our racist society it is no coincidence that black people are sometimes thought
to take more enjoyment from sex than non-blacks. The extra enjoyment
supposedly enjoyed by blacks is imagined to be a kind of compensation for the
racism, lack of education, employment and opportunities that so many blacks
have endured.

Plays like *Oleanna* by Mamet and *Miss Julie* by Strindberg dramatically switch
around the roles of slave and master, like the TV series *Upstairs Downstairs*.
Each of these works illustrate the slave-master discourse: when the class or race
barrier that holds the distribution of jouissance safely in place is threatened by
love, by an interclass or interracial marriage, all hell breaks loose as the assuring
structure of mastery and slavery is in danger.

Slaves and masters have so much invested in the system that expresses and
represses their desire, which both allows and forbids their enjoyment, or
symptoms, that it is common for both to show extreme loyalty or bondage to
their slave-master culture. So much are the two entwined that it is often difficult
distinguishing the slaves from the masters. This is one reason why revolution is
so difficult to achieve: the oppressed are usually unconsciously invested in their
own repression! The class system in England has as much life in it as the
monarchy.

The main variables in the discourse of the slave and master are recognition, desire and enjoyment. The slave, because of his subjectivity and loss, has some chance of reflecting and recognising his own desire: the master has far less chance of recognising his desire because he instead pressures the slave to recognise his demand for enjoyment at the expense of his desire. As slaves we can enjoy the comforts of having a master, much as a domestic dog does. As masters we can deceive ourselves about our desire by distracting ourselves with slaves whose purpose is to provide us with enjoyment. This, to some extent, is the relation of parents to their child. Parents often complain of the price of parenthood: 'the time, the money . . .', so an interesting question to ask is: What value do children have for their parents? Why did the parents have the child? How does the child provide satisfaction to the parents? Often the answer is a secret because the child is the symptom of the parents, that is a secret jouissance that is a fantastic solution to the parent's trauma(s).

One adolescent anorexic was her parents' symptom. The anorexia —of many years duration— was her family's way of speaking the terrible truth about the father's frequent beatings of the mother, which no one in the family ever spoke about. The anorexic was simultaneously protesting her position in the family, by (b)eating her own body, and colluding in the silence regarding her mother's suffering and father's enjoyment. The adolescent was sacrificing her body to the truth of the mother's suffering, and to both her parents' demands for silence. Her body slaved to master the truth of her desire as she identified with her mother's suffering, and what it might mean for her to become a woman, one who is masterfully beaten by a silent man. For an analysis of this hysterical structure see Freud's paper 'A Child is Being Beaten'.

The university discourse

'If knowledge about the unconscious were as important for the patient as people inexperienced in psychoanalysis imagined, listening to lectures or reading books would be enough to cure him. Such measures, however, have as much influence on the symptoms of nervous illness as a distribution of menu cards in a time of famine has upon hunger.' [280]

'This technique [of psychoanalysis] cannot . . . be learnt from books, and it certainly cannot be discovered independently without great sacrifices of time, labour and success.' [281]

'The psychoanalyst has a position which happens to be able ultimately to be that of a discourse. He doesn't transmit a body of knowledge with it, not that there isn't anything to be known.' [282]

---

[280] S Freud, Wild psychoanalysis, *SE 11*, [1910c], 1976, p225.
[281] Ibid p226.

Just as a certain structure describes the speech of the master and slave, so another describes academic talk. The most important aspect of university discourse —from the clinical point of view— is negative. The clinical practice of Freud's and Lacan's work are not primarily a university discourse; you cannot learn how to be a psychoanalyst simply from a book or a university course. Clinical work in the psychoanalytic tradition requires the clinician to have undergone analysis himself. Another negative point about the discourse of university is that it is *not* the same as the discourse of science: Lacan argued that the discourse of science was very close to the discourse of the hysteric.

The discourse of the analyst

Psychoanalytic work is special. There is nothing else like it. Lacan theorised the discourse of the analyst as distinctive because the analyst invites his client to identify his little object a, or the little other with the analyst. The discourse of the analyst is specially marked by the ethics of psychoanalysis to which we will turn in the last chapter.

Why are there necessarily special problems in all clinical trainings?

'It almost looks as if analysis were the third of those 'impossible' professions in which one can be sure beforehand of achieving unsatisfying results. The other two, which have been known much longer, are education and government.' [283]

There are necessarily special problems in all clinical trainings, and there are necessary conflicts of interest found in each of Lacan's four discourses. The four discourses are: 'hysteria', 'mastery and slavery', 'the university discourse' and 'the discourse of the analyst'. Psychoanalytic trainings take place with all four! So the problems of all four discourses affect clinical trainings. In order to train as an analyst it is necessary —but not sufficient— to:

1. Be in analysis oneself, where the Lacanian clinician's speech ought to converge towards the discourse of the analyst.

2. Attend seminars and study groups where the speech probably approximates the discourse of university, or that of the master. Lacan's special format of psychoanalytic study group known as the 'cartel' goes some way towards solving some of the problems of working in groups.

---

[282] J Lacan, Television, trans Mehlman et al, *October*, 40, MIT, Cambridge, USA, 1987, p117.
[283] S Freud, Analysis Terminable and Interminable, *SE 23*, [1937], 1976, p248.
Education is principally the discourse of the slave and master, and the discourse of the university: government is the discourse of the slave and master.

What is the relation of the psychoanalyst in training to these kinds of speech, to the institution that trains him? The trainee will always have a transference to his training organisation. He will suppose that those who train him possess some kind of knowledge that is of value to him.

If his training institution is in the business of providing recognition, of handing out titles or badges such as membership of an institution he will always be in the position of a slave demanding recognition from his master, to some extent. Yet it is just this sort of discourse, that of the slave and master, in which we are all more or less invested, that the discourse of analysis aims to offer recognition of!

Another way of framing the problem is to focus on the two functions of language: 'transmission and transference'. In medicine 'transmission' is used to describe the spread of agents of disease: in psychoanalysis it refers to the spreading of letters, words or ideas. Freud's and Lacan's theories of transference, and Lacan's theory of the four discourses, suggest that there is transference wherever letters are transmitted. So psychoanalytic training insists on discourse. There is no other way around the problem because it appears that there are no other ways of speaking and being besides Lacan's four discourses. Suggesting a question: What is the relation of the four discourses to Lacan's diagnostic categories?

Discourse and Psychosis

Psychosis does not represent a discourse but the absence or failure to establish a discourse. Speech or language typically brings the infant into subjectivity and ordinary neurotic being: most psychotics speak but their relation to their speech is always frail, in contrast to the extreme resilience of neurotic speech. A neurotic will maintain an unconscious relation to language for as long as he lives, whether he likes it or not: psychotics are without an unconscious and so are always at risk of losing their fragile grip on language.

Discourse, Neurosis and Perversion

Hysterics privilege the discourse of the hysteric, whether they are phobics, anxiety hysterics or conversion hysterics, but typically have a soft spot for one or another master, and, at the same time a profound resentment of another master or certain authority figure. Because the hysteric has an important investment in slaving to master it is often difficult to distinguish the discourse of the master from the discourse of the hysteric.

What is the definition of capitalism?

The exploitation of man by man

What then is the definition of communism?

That is the other way around

Obsessional neurosis is a *'dialect of the language of hysteria'* [284]. Perhaps Freud's observation that *'neuroses are . . . the negative of perversions'* [285] suggests that the pervert's discourse is a slavish attempt to pervert the slave-master discourse and its reliance of on the foundation of the jouissance of the Other.

---

[284] S Freud, Notes Upon a Case of Obsessional Neurosis, *SE 10*, [1909], 1976, p157.
[285] S Freud, Three Essays on Sexuality, [1905], 1976, *SE 7*, p165.

The Clinic and the Institution: working in hospitals, schools, GPs practices and within multidisciplinary teams.

Working with doctors and psychiatrists

'Co-operation in medical practice between an analyst and a psychotherapist who restricts himself to other techniques would serve quite a useful purpose.' [286]

'There is nothing in the nature of psychiatric work which could be opposed to psychoanalytic research. What is opposed to psychoanalysis is not psychiatry but psychiatrists.' [287]

An important conceptual and practical problem for counsellors, psychotherapists and psychoanalysts working in a multidisciplinary team with medical staff arises because it is common for clients to be segregated and treated according to their medical diagnoses. All anorexics together, all those who are depressed in another category, alcoholics . . .

From a medical point of view this may be a fine or even a compulsory arrangement but psychoanalysts don't work from a medical point of view. Four different anorexics can have four different psychic structures: one could be a hysteric, another an obsessional neurotic, a third perverse and the fourth psychotic. Only their surface symptoms are similar, not their speech or underlying psychic structures. The Lacanian treatment of four such anorexics would be quite different in each case. For example some of the techniques used with a hysteric and a psychotic are precisely the opposite of each other.

When anyone proclaims that *'all anorexics are like this'*, or *'everyone with symptoms x should be treated like y'* you should be sceptical. Someone who has made a speciality out of treating a medically defined set of problems such as anorexia is likely to have more to teach us about how to make a career in a medically mastered establishment than about the clinical practice of psychoanalysis. Psychoanalysts rely on studying the client's words not their medical status. Medical approaches can reduce or sometimes even appear to eliminate symptoms efficiently. Questions that we return to in the final chapter are: What is a symptom? And what is a cure?

While eliminating symptoms is not a psychoanalytic goal clinicians are sometimes pressured to compromise by colleagues and clients. Towards minimising the effects of such compromises on your psychoanalytic work it can be useful to develop some awareness of medical approaches, diagnoses and symptoms.

---

[286] S Freud, New Introductory Lectures in Psychoanalysis, Explanations and Applications, *SE 22*, [1933], 1973, p153.
[287] S Freud, Introductory Lectures on Psychoanalysis, Psychoanalysis and Psychiatry, *SE 16*, [1915], 1976, p254-5.

Of course there need not be competition between two or more members of a multidisciplinary team with different skills who are working with the same client in different ways. The client may, through his demands, try and play one off each the other, but there is no need to collude with the client and become part of his symptom.

Psychiatry and Psychoanalysis

'[Common sense is] the collection of prejudices acquired by age 18.' [288]

It is the exceptional psychiatrist that has trained to be a psychoanalyst: generally psychiatrists are medical specialists. Psychiatry has many forms and is a confused mixture often made up of the following parts: medicine, sociology, statistics, law, a smattering of general psychology and most problematic of all, a large dose of 'common sense'. Typically psychiatry devotes much energy and emphasis to a surface description of symptoms rather than the underlying structures and issues that have caused the surface symptoms. It is also usual for psychiatry to emphasise important management issues such as self-harming, suicidal behaviour, aggression to others, legal aspects of sexual abuse, the effects of psychotropic drugs, delinquency and other broad social issues.

Psychiatry can be extremely useful to society and even, sometimes, to disturbed individuals. Psychiatrists have two important roles: they are society's policemen, locking up and medicating some of those who self harm or harm others, and they prescribe drugs for people who are extremely disturbed, anxious or upset. Many patients in the long term prefer their symptoms to the effects of the drugs.

Prescribed drugs are often helpful in dealing with a severe short-term problem such as acute anxiety or a florid psychotic state. Once the client has calmed, which may be days or weeks later, it is sometimes easier to engage with an approach that focuses on his language instead of his 'psychiatric symptoms'. Sometimes psychotic symptoms are held at bay for as long as drugs are taken, though such drugs usually inhibit and suppress many important aspects of the client's activities and speech.

Of course some psychiatrists do listen carefully to their clients' language, and a few even use some psychoanalytic techniques. But the extent to which a psychiatrist uses psychoanalytic techniques is the extent to which that clinician is not a psychiatrist, but a psychoanalyst! No knowledge of medicine is required to practise psychoanalysis: no knowledge of psychoanalysis is required to practise medicine. Whatever the difficulties and benefits of psychoanalysis, it seems like a waste of a lengthy and expensive medical training not to use

---

[288] A Einstein, quoted in *The Sickening Mind, Brain, Behaviour, Immunity and Disease*, P Martin, HarperCollins, 1997, p165.

medicine when it comes to helping people who have medical problems. Medicine is clearly impotent when it comes to helping many who seek the help of those who instead offer to study their speech.

Confusing cause and affect; and 'organic' versus 'psychic or linguistic'?

'[The physician] will either endeavour to remove the organic basis [of the patient's complaint], without bothering about its noisy neurotic elaboration; or he will attack the neurosis which has taken this favourable opportunity for arising and will pay little attention to its organic precipitating cause. The outcome will prove the one or the other line of approach rights or wrong; it is impossible to make general recommendations to meet such mixed cases.' [289]

What is meant by the term 'organic' here? Simply that the client's suffering can be understood in physiological or biochemical terms, that is, in the language of conventional Western medicine. Note that a diagnosis of 'organic' does not imply that a medical solution would be ideal or even helpful. Nor does the diagnosis of 'organic' suggest that psychoanalytic work would be without value. My leg may be broken, and 'the best' short term treatment may be to have it set in plaster, but I may have broken it by acting on my unconscious desire or demand, suggesting a potentially interesting psychoanalytic question: Why?

There are examples of medical diagnoses that could be relevant to a cautious psychoanalytic approach, for instance problems with the thyroid gland. Some people's thyroid makes too much thyroxin, and some too little. In both cases there are symptoms that sometimes lead to medical solutions. In cases of hypothyroidism, when the thyroid gland makes too little thyroxin the client often puts on weight, becomes lethargic, sleeping more and losing motivation: in hyperthyroidism too much thyroxin is made, often leading to a loss of weight, mania, anxiety, and sometimes to bulging eyes. In either of these cases a simple blood test will make the thyroxin level known. What is a psychoanalytic position prior to diagnosis, and post diagnosis, if you are working with a client who has some or all of these symptoms?

It is important to keep an open mind. If a client has somatic (that is, bodily) symptoms of any kind, and wants to discuss them you, it is often useful to ask 'Why?' If —in the first session— a client tells me that he has backaches for instance, I might ask him why he has chosen a psychoanalyst to consult, rather than an osteopath or doctor. In this way I am not taking for granted things that I do not know, and I am taking steps to eliminate future objections that the client might produce as soon as some progress is made, along the line: *'I've been*

---

[289] S Freud, The Common Neurotic State, Introductory Lectures on Psychoanalysis, [1915], 1976, *SE 15-16*, p391.

rethinking my problem(s), I've decided to take some pills/more exercise/consult a different kind of specialist instead of coming here.'

I want to attack the simplistic idea that there is only one basic question of importance here: *'Is the problem medical or not?'* Presenting problems do not exhaustively divide up into two sorts, the medical and the non-medical.

Take a client who has the symptoms of hyperthyroidism, who then has a blood test that confirms that he has high levels of thyroxin, allowing the confident diagnosis of 'hyperthyroidism'. Surely this is a clear case of a client that any psychoanalyst should steer clear of? Not necessarily! It is far from clear that hyperthyroidism has simply been visited upon this person in some random statistical sense, like a lottery win: it is possible that psychoanalytic work could cast light on the causes and consequences of this client's hyperthyroidism, and their meaning for the client, although it would not aim to do so from a medical angle.

In a similar way anorexia or obesity can be regarded as 'medical conditions', which no doubt they are, but the interesting questions for us are: 'What are the client's words and associations?' 'What —in a psychoanalytic sense— might have determined or caused the anorexia or obesity?' And, 'What does the client's body and symptom mean to the client?'

Take the example of a raised level of adrenaline in the blood, which on the face of it appears to be a straightforward physiological or medical issue. How has the level of adrenaline come to be raised? Like most other people I can increase the concentration of adrenaline in my blood by thinking about something exciting. To date medical science has had little or nothing to say about fantasies and desire. Just because medical science can describe some aspects of the client's problem does not mean that a medical approach will be the most important for the client [290]. Which discourse should be used to explain this phenomenon of increased adrenaline? Is the cause 'organic', or is it caused by my exciting thoughts? Many libraries have been filled with competing philosophical answers to these questions. Your job as a clinician working in the Lacanian tradition is not to place yourself in a position of knowledge. There is no good reason why

---

[290] In the *New Scientist* (12th January, 2002) it was reported that: *'Placebos cause measurable changes in the electrical activity of the brain, but only in patients who get some benefit from them. Psychiatrist Andrew Leuchter from the University of California, Los Angeles, and his team gave 51 patients with depression either antidepressants or capsules containing an inert powder. Within eight weeks, 52 per cent of the medicated patients recovered, as did 38 per cent of the placebo group (American Journal of Psychiatry, vol 159, p122). Patients helped by the placebo showed increased electrical activity in their prefrontal cortices —a brain area influenced by depression and by antidepressants. "The placebo effect is not just 'in their head'," says Leuchter, "it's in their brain."*

you should know the causes of your client's suffering, especially early on in the work. But it is your job to keep an open mind, and to help your client generate questions and explore the different meanings that they attach to their suffering through an analysis of their speech.

This questioning approach is also likely to be of value in some cases of broken bones! Why for example might a particular individual be accident-prone? What difference does it make to this person's life that they now need to be cared for, or are unable to carry out certain actions? The client's answers to such questions —that is their speech— will be uniquely informative in answering these non-medical questions.

So the existence of an organic cause does not rule out the existence of either psychoanalytic causes or of psychoanalytic consequences. It is often the case that a person will find the onset or diagnosis of an 'organic' or physiological condition traumatic. Such phenomena could include the first experience of menstruation, ejaculation or being informed that you will inherit a disease. Being 'a man' or 'a woman' is a perhaps an example of just such a trauma in which a man or woman may believe that they have inherited their gender from their parents, along with a fixed set of costs and benefits.

Just because medical science can describe some aspects of the client's problem does not mean that a medical approach will be the most important for the client, nor does it mean that a medical approach will not be of value. Clinicians need not side for or against any medical diagnosis or masterly discourse. It has been suggested that a psychoanalyst is someone who knows when *not* to psychoanalyse! It takes some time before a psychoanalyst can become confident that a client is ready to be analysed. A psychoanalyst should not 'wildly analyse', that is prematurely or inappropriately apply psychoanalytic technique, say by providing a dream analysis at a dinner party, or analyse a client whom he has not yet diagnosed, or analyse clients who have only just been traumatised, by a very recent rape for example.

If a client tries to ask for advice as to the benefits of other approaches it is probably safest to be neutral; the more the clinician takes any other position, the more it is likely that the client will use it as ammunition against the clinical work as soon as it becomes difficult.

The placebo effect revisited

'Depression' is a popular complaint and a good example of a controversial diagnosis for psychoanalysis and psychiatry. Many tons of identical antidepressants are prescribed for this supposedly uniform problem each year. Recent research suggests that pills made of sugar or salt —fakes— or 'placebos' have about the same effect as chemical antidepressants, and that the small differences that occur in some cases can be explained by the accidental side effects of the antidepressant drugs, as this quotation argues:

'The benefits of antidepressant drugs could be almost entirely due to the psychological boost derived from taking a pill rather than their effects on brain chemistry. Every patient in this study had been given either an active drug or a chemically inactive placebo, and their psychological conditions had been evaluated at the beginning and end.

*Pharmaceuticals companies claim that antidepressants are 40 per cent more effective than placebos . . . The drugs were only 25 per cent more effective. In addition, 25 per cent could be due to an additional placebo effect derived from the side effects caused by the anti-depressants, which alerted patients to the fact that they were receiving an active drug rather than a placebo . . . Studies could have wrongly ascribed this additional effect to a chemical change induced by the drugs . . . Simon Wessely, Professor of Psychiatry at King's College London, agrees: "There's tremendous uncertainty about how they work . . . **The public thinks the doctors know, but they don't. Any decent psychopharmacologist will tell you this.** If patients know they're getting treatment, their expectation will be raised and with it their optimism that they will get better. It's a self-fulfilling prophecy."'* [291]

There are two suppositions of knowledge: the public thinks the doctors know, and those patients in the drug trials who experienced side effects then suppose that the drugs 'are working'. So there is an issue here about who has the knowledge, and how it is spoken of. It is often useful to ask if the discourse, the way of speaking is that of a master or slave, of someone in a university, that of a hysteric or an analyst. Freud claimed that a medical approach —from a position of knowledge, as a master or from the university— to problems of the sort presented by phobics, hysterics and obsessional neurotics is completely inappropriate for psychoanalysis:

'In his medical school a doctor receives a training which is more or less the opposite of what he would need as a preparation for psychoanalysis.'

And:

'It would be tolerable if medical education merely failed to give doctors any orientation in the field of the neuroses. But it does more: it gives them a false and detrimental attitude . . . The less such doctors understand about the matter, the more venturesome they become. Only a man who really knows is modest, for he knows how insufficient his knowledge is.' [292]

---

[291] M Day, *New Scientist* 11.7.98, p13.
[292] S Freud, On the Question of Lay Analysis, *SE 20*, p230-1.

Legal issues and confidentiality

It is because confidentiality is such an important topic with implications for the ethics of psychoanalysis that I have given some space to discussing some current clinical practice and legal aspects so as to provide a perspective for a Lacanian approach. A Lacanian approach —by happy coincidence— is in almost perfect accordance with the English law on this point. Unfortunately very few clinicians in England are aware of either their legal obligations or the Lacanian orientation. I will argue that there are compelling therapeutic, legal and ethical reasons why a client's confidentiality should be maintained as far as possible, which in almost every case would be absolute.

For legal reasons it is not possible to fully guarantee clients confidentiality in England because it is possible —although very unlikely— that a clinician will be called to court and ordered by the judge to give evidence about his client, in exceptional circumstances. The only professionals who are able to promise their clients unconditional confidentiality are priests and lawyers. A court may even order a clinician to produce his file on a client. You may wish to hold more than one file on the same client, keep only sketchy notes, or none at all, or to always add a note to each file to the effect that you do not find it possible to distinguish your client's reports of his actions from those he imagines or fantasises.

I have been horrified by the number of clinicians and agencies in England who are vague or ignorant about confidentiality. Many clients who learn that they have been betrayed in this way will never again trust a professional and talk openly, never mind free associating. What exactly are your client's legal rights to confidentiality? The answer to this important question depends on your client's 'competence' but not usually on their age. This topic is explored in the next section.

When working in an institution or agency a special set of the rules is always imposed on clinical work. Nearly always these include directions for breaking or modifying the rule that the clinician should always keeps the client's material confidential. In many organisations it is common for a client's material to be discussed during group supervision with colleagues, where it is often said that the client's material is 'kept confidential within the agency'. The nature and implementation of these rules vary, but it is usual to find a policy of reporting to the police certain violent and illegal acts.

Freud was very clear on the topic of confidentiality. He argued that if clinicians expect clients to perform the difficult task of free associating —of saying whatever comes to their mind— then it is necessary to reassure clients that they will be protected because everything they say will be in confidence.

If there are *any* circumstances in which you would not be able to offer a client confidentiality —for any reason— then you owe it to the client to say so *at the start of the work*. This responsibility is the clinician's. If there are limits to confidentiality it does not mean that no psychoanalytic work will take place, but that any work is likely to be limited by the obstacles you present —in the client's imagination— to his free associations.

Clinicians are not policemen, judges or forensic scientists. The truth psychoanalysts search for is the unconscious truth of desire: this is very different from the question as to whether a client has actually broken a law of the land: Lacanians study the making and breaking of the laws of language within the unique dialect that is established between every clinician and client. Most people have fantasies of either breaking the law, or of carrying out acts that would cause offence of some sort. Clinicians who play the part of policemen are likely to make clinical work impossible.

What do Lacan's ideas have to offer to those working with children and adolescents?

'There is only one kind of psychoanalysis' [293]

'From the Lacanian perspective, therefore, there is no 'psychoanalysis of children', but simply psychoanalysis with children. There is only one psychoanalysis that is applied to the clinical experience as its conceptual framework, although there are as many possible variations in its applications as there are analysands. ***There is no other good than that which may serve to pay the price for access to desire'*** [294]

From the point of view of psychoanalysis are children different from adults? No, children are like adults but more so. The range of pathology —psychosis, phobia, hysteria, obsessional neurosis and perversion— are found in both children and adults, but because young children are often still shopping for their favourite pathological category they will often demonstrate symptoms that are more extreme than those seen in average or typical adult cases [295]. 'Child' is not a clinical structure, but this does not mean that clients who are children should be treated in exactly the same ways as adults. It is often necessary to be especially flexible when working with children. Some children will only become therapeutically orientated, taking up speech for analysing and identifying their desire, if they have first been able to play with toys or draw.

---

[293] J Lacan, *The Four Fundamental Concepts of Psychoanalysis*, trans Sheridan, Pelican, London, 1979, p273.

[294] L Rodriguez, The Position of the Analyst with Children in Psychoanalysis: the Lacanian contribution compared with other perspectives, *Analysis*, Number Three, 1991, Centre for Psychoanalytic Research, p104.

[295] Although childhood psychosis does appear to be different —and more severe— than psychoses that have their onset in adolescence or adulthood.

The crucial ethical principle of not assuming 'the good of the client' applies equally when working with children or adults, but is worth stressing in the case of children because children's demands are often taken more seriously because they are commonly imagined to be without desire, or even without valuations of 'the good and bad'. Perhaps this is part of a picture of children as 'innocent angels' that some adults rely on in their view of themselves as fallen, corrupted and guilty.

Just because some children are less competent than some adults at certain practical tasks does not justify ignoring the fact that the child is a wholly autonomous subject with regard to its desire and symptoms. Of course this does not mean that children are fully responsible for any suffering they may endure at the hands of others. Unfortunately some clinicians attempt to take responsibility for the suffering and symptoms of the child they are working with. This is a serious ethical problem, but no less of an ethical problem than clinicians attempting to take responsibility for the suffering of an adult client. The child's speech should be regarded as the material to be analysed with the same respect as the adult's.

I recommend readers who are interested in working with children to read *Lacanian Psychotherapy with Children —the broken piano* by Catherine Mathelin (Other Press, New York, 1999). This book is a highly accessible collection of clinical vignettes of work carried out with younger children. Whilst I don't agree with everything in it she clearly demonstrates the practical value of Lacanian theory in working with a wide variety of difficult children, and the ways in which their symptoms took on meanings and values in the context of the family.

Most adolescents are disturbed by some of their emotions and anxiety, and at times find them overwhelming. If such clients are to do effective clinical work then anxiety is bound to surface. It should not be inhibited or dismissed, but worked with. Unfortunately many clinicians try and take responsibility for the client's anxiety. As with any client who is new to psychoanalytic work, it is sometimes very helpful to explain a little about the work that may lie ahead. It is important to remember that for many children and adolescents their experience of the psychoanalytic clinic will be their first. I always explain that 'you will be in charge of what we talk about, and when we talk about it.' I have found it necessary to explain the principal of confidentiality to children. I say that I'm not a teacher or social worker and that I will not discuss any of the private things that they might want talk about with anyone else, including their teachers, the police or their parents.

Some clients or settings make psychoanalysis proper impossible, but group and family therapy can be practised in a way that is informed by Lacan's ideas. For instance the use of variable length sessions, ending on questions and difficulties, working closely with the words spoken by the clients and not supposing a knowledge that the clinician has a duty to give to the family or group. Clinicians who work with children and those with learning difficulties sometimes suppose that they know the best course of action for their client. On this topic Freud wrote:

'We [have] refused most emphatically to turn a patient who puts himself into our hands in search of help into our private property, to decide his fate for him, to force our own ideals upon him, and with the pride of a Creator to form him in our own image.' [296]

And: *'I have been able to help people with whom I had nothing in common neither race, education, social position not outlook on life in general — without affecting their individuality . . .We cannot avoid taking some patients for treatment who are so helpless and incapable of ordinary life that for them one has to combine analytic with educative influence; and even with the majority, occasions now and then arise in which the position is bound to take up the position of teacher and mentor but it must always be done with great caution, and the patient should be educated to liberate and fulfil his image, not to resemble ourselves.'* [297]

Beware of the appearance of helplessness. Helplessness or its appearance in the clinic is nearly always a ruse or excuse that is used symptomatically by the client as a demand, to camouflage their problematic desire with the supposition that the Other has their power or knowledge. In these cases:

'Nothing can be done but to leave the patient to look for protection wherever he thinks he may find it; and he is merely regarded with a not very helpful contempt for his "incomprehensible cowardice".' [298]

How might the client's helplessness operate as a demand: to whom is the demand addressed? Is the helplessness necessary or a sophisticated choice? Often it is not possible for the clinician to answer this question, at least until some preliminary work has been carried out. Perhaps as a clinician you are anxiously demanding to take the position of helper or professor of knowledge? Hopefully supervision will pick up serious problems of this sort. Equally, it is worth remembering that just because an adult client has an apparently successful life as a particular kind of slave, master, hysteric or academic does not mean that he will not try to address you as if you are a powerful helper. 'Success' according to one or another socio-economic or professional measure, and acting on one's desire are not the same. Psychoanalytic work is carried out in reliance on the discourse of the analyst. One consequence of this discourse is that the analyst should not adopt a position of knowledge or power, but analyse the

---

[296] S Freud, Lines of Advance in Psychoanalytic Therapy, *SE 17*, [1918], 1976, p164.

[297] S Freud, Lines of Advance in Psychoanalytic Therapy, *SE 17*, [1918], 1976, p165.

[298] S Freud, A Phobia in a 5 year old boy, *SE 10,* [1909b], 1976, p117.

client's positions in the discourses of the slave and master, the university and hysteric.

The Child's Right to Confidentiality

What exactly are your client's rights to confidentiality when he is a child? The answer to this important question depends on your client and the law of the land. In England, in 1983 there was an important case in which a Mrs Gillick challenged her daughter's doctor, who had prescribed the contraceptive pill to the daughter while she was under 16. This case [299] was taken to the House of Lords where Lord Scarman decided that the key issue was 'understanding' or 'competence'.

'[T]he parental right to determine whether or not their minor child below the age of 16 will have medical treatment terminates if and when the child achieves a sufficient understanding and intelligence to enable him or her to understand fully what is proposed' [300]

A piece of legal jargon resulting from this ruling: *'Gillick competence'* is attributed to a client under 16 who —in the judgement of the professionals working with him— has demonstrated his or her understanding and competence on the issues in question. Scarman's ruling allowed important rights to children and also clarifies the role of the parent or guardian:

'The common law has never treated (parental) rights as sovereign or beyond review and control. Nor has our law ever treated the child as other than a person with capacities and rights recognised by law. Parental rights are derived from parental duty and exist only so long as they are needed for the protection of the person and property of the child.' [301]

What were perceived as 'parental rights' have, since this ruling, become 'parental responsibilities. The Children Act (1989) took this theme further:

'Before making any decision with respect to a child whom they are looking after, or proposing to look after, a local authority shall, so far as is reasonably practicable, ascertain the wishes and feelings of . . . the child'. [302]

So the *Gillick* ruling establishes the role of the child's 'understanding' and recognises their right to make their own informed decisions on key issues concerning their own welfare, if they are considered to be Gillick competent. Importantly for psychoanalysts the *Gillick* ruling has broad implications that

---

[299] Gillick v. Norfolk & Wisbech Area Health Authority, 1985.
[300] Lord Scarman. House of Lords. 1986 House of Lords, *Hansard*, vol. 502, No.7, Col.488.
[301] Ibid.
[302] Children Act, 89, s.22.

cover more ground than contraception. Another lawyer, and a social worker have written:

'The implications of the Gillick judgement are far greater than the specific issue of a child's right to confidentiality when seeking advice on contraception when under the age of 16, 'sufficient understanding' means that all children should be as involved as possible in decisions which affect their health or welfare. Not only should the child be consulted but his views must be taken into account'. [303]

The above statement should also be applied to matters concerning the child's right to confidential access to therapeutic treatment, and any parent opposing such treatment for their child could be overruled. It is sadly common in my experience for parents to try to deny their children 'permission' to see a clinician, even though they have no legal or moral rights to do so. Why should this happen? Because the child is the symptom, the one who both represents and conceals the truth of the parents.

'The child's symptom is found to be in a position of answering to what is symptomatic in the family structure . . . as the representative of truth. The child too realises the presence of . . . the object little a in fantasy . . . In it he alienates all possible access by the mother to her own truth, through giving it body, existence and, even, the requirement of protection.' [304]

So the parent often has something at stake and stands to lose something if the child tells the truth about the family. Often the child's symptoms tell the truth about what is going on in the family; the parents unconsciously recognise this fact and don't want the truth to take any other form, especially a clearly spoken one that would cause them to change their position. As Freud noted:

'No one who has any experience of the rifts which so often divide a family will, if he is an analyst, be surprised to find that the patient's closest relatives sometimes betray less interest in his recovering, than in his remaining as he is. When, as so often, the neurosis is related to conflicts between members of a family, the healthy party will not hesitate long in choosing between his own interest and the sick party's recovery. It is not to be wondered at, indeed, if a husband looks with this favour on a treatment in which, as he may rightly suspect, the whole catalogue of his sins will be brought to light.' [305]

Parents do not have the right to prevent the child seeing a clinician. Indeed there is often no good legal, moral or clinical reason for parents to be informed by the

---

[303] Mitchels and Prince, 1992, p83.
[304] J Lacan, Note to Jenny Aubrey, Note on the Child, *Analysis*, Number Two, 1990, p7.
[305] S Freud, Introductory Lectures on Psychoanalysis, Analytic Therapy, *SE 16*, [1917], 1976, p459.

clinician of the child's attendance: there are though very good reasons why such client confidences should be kept.

Every client I have worked with has been able to speak, write or type, and has been capable of understanding the likely consequences of the different courses of action open to them, including those with learning difficulties. I have yet to meet a client whose confidence I could justifiably betray.

The ability to speak suggests Gillick competence. If the client has a secret to tell then they are bound to understand the concept of consequentiality, since they judged that it is not in their interests to speak the truth directly.

Children who have been sexually or physically abused often find it very difficult to disclose their traumatic experience, and when they do, it is often retracted, and revised, repeatedly. These revisions can be seen as the child's working through of his demand, and the simultaneous testing of the trustworthiness of his clinician.

In the case of one adolescent girl who had been sexually abused by her father, her disclosure to her clinician had disastrous effects: because her clinician reported this confidential material without the client's permission her father was jailed and the mother blamed her daughter for causing her husband to be taken away. In this tragic story the reason that the clinician abused her client's confidentiality was the clinician's own anxiety. The broken confidentiality caused the client to suffer as many as five traumas rather than one original sexual abuse by the father. There was the subsequent loss of her father who she continued to love, her mother's attacks on her for depriving her of her husband, the break-up of her family and her betrayal by her clinician. Social services, the police and the justice system intervened at a point when this client was unprepared. All too often carers and professionals find sophisticated excuses for betraying the client's interests because of their own issues and problems.

The clinician should have discussed many options and their possible consequences with the client, in confidence. When the client was ready she would have chosen the course of action that best suited her resources, expressed as her desire. Every child and adult I have worked with has been or become fully competent to make such difficult decisions for themselves, including those with 'learning difficulties'. Such decisions make take six months or longer to make, and further abuse may continue during this time, but the client is always or nearly always remains the one who is in the best position to act: not the clinician. If the clinician finds his position impossibly anxiety provoking or overwhelmed by tragedy he should work in a different field. A good clinician should not betray a client's confidence because of his own anxiety or identifications; the clinician's anxiety ought to be his own problem: not his client's.

A crucial principle of Lacanian practice is that the clinician is not in a position of knowledge in relation to his client, but one of ignorance. The clinician does not know what is best for his client. This principle is true for adults and children so generally there are compelling legal, ethical and therapeutic reasons why client material should always be kept confidential.

Further Reading

A useful reference for the section on Lacan's theory of the four discourses is 'The Master Signifier and the Four Discourses', B Fink, Rebus Press, in *Key Concepts of Lacanian Psychoanalysis*, ed Nobus, London, 1998.

D Daniels & P Jenkins, *Therapy with Children: Children's Rights, Confidentiality and the Law*, Sage Publications, 2000.

CHAPTER FOURTEEN

Interpretation — the background

'What is a person?' is a grand and difficult question to which hundreds of philosophers over thousands of years have contributed millions of words. Towards answering this question Freud and Lacan, inspired by ancient Greek philosophy, formulated their own method. Psychoanalysis is not the same as philosophy, yet there are common issues and questions. Psychoanalysis can discover what it means for each individual to be a particular person. That is, to be a man, woman, child, black, white, heterosexual and so on. Psychoanalysis is the means by which it is possible to demonstrate that every one of us is a philosopher with their own —often unconscious and— unique theory of what it is to exist.

The importance for all clinicians of the question 'what is a person?' will also be emphasised in the next chapter where the different answers to this question, from different clinical orientations, have important consequences for interpretation; 'person', 'subject', 'object', 'self', 'ego' and 'unconscious' are used in different ways by the various clinical theories

'Person' is of course an ordinary language term. We may have some intuitive idea or hidden theory about what it means to be a person but that isn't enough here: we require a theory that will inform our clinical practice and help us to work with difficult clients. Intuitive or ordinary language ideas just don't do the job. Many ordinary language ideas and intuitions —once clarified— can be seen to be wrong or useless.

Some of the alternative theories to Lacan's are formal, whilst others are informal, inconsistent or have vital parts missing. In trying to understand Lacan's work it is helpful to look at some of the alternative theories which inspired him to develop his own.

Because psychoanalysis sets out to answer the question: 'What is a person?', 'person' must not have its meaning taken for granted; the meaning of person is just what we want to explain. In contrast some clinical approaches have at their core a vague appeal to the concept of 'the whole person' without ever explaining clearly just what a person or what 'being whole' really means. For example:

'The person centred counsellor's creed . . . That individuals should be related to as whole persons.' [306]

If psychoanalysis is going to have any success in explaining the human condition it must introduce some special technical terms and theory that go deeper than our ordinary language terms such as 'person'. By analogy, most people would probably be sceptical if chemists were only able to speak informally, in ordinary language terms without using a carefully worked out vocabulary of technical terms, formulae and concepts. Such explicit and systematic approaches can be taught and criticised, providing an important advantage: a theory that is clear enough to be criticised is a theory that can be improved. Yet in many popular clinical approaches there is a clearly stated rejection and abhorrence of technical and theoretical terms:

'In some academic quarters the person centred approach to counselling currently receives scant attention . . . The [Person Centred] approach . . . travels light as far as theoretical concepts are concerned. Rather than be seduced by theories it is more productive to empathise with our client . . .' [307]

The widespread Anglo-Saxon clinician's phobia of theory has had a terrible effect on practice because there is nothing as practical as a good theory. In any case every practice is theoretical, whether it admits knowledge of its underlying theory or not. Theory should not be regarded as a continental disease to be avoided, but as an unavoidable and useful part of psychoanalytic clinical work.

Freud and Lacan not only go beyond ordinary language descriptions of people by providing a coherent theoretical framework and vocabulary, but they also contradict some popular beliefs. It would it be surprising if psychoanalysis simply came up with evidence that supported popular beliefs or so called 'common sense', without contradicting them in any way. Two such popular beliefs or ideals are that a person should have 'high or good self esteem', and that a person can or ought to be 'whole' or 'complete'.

What is the clinical value of 'self esteem?'

'The person centred counsellor's creed: 'Self regard is a basic human need . . .' [308]

Many clinicians such as Kernberg have stressed the role of positive self-esteem or of *'good self image'* versus *'bad self image'* [309] but Lacan analysis is

---

[306] D Mearns and B Thorne, *Person Centred Counselling in Action*, Sage, London, 1988, p18.

[307] Ibid p5 and p54.

[308] Ibid p18.

primarily of unconscious desire, not of 'self esteem' which is often a conscious function, and always a function of the ego. In any case, if clinical work with a neurotic goes well they will become demanding of the clinician by putting themselves down, finding some way to deprecate themselves in order to make a demand of their clinician. Lacan's advice in this situation is straightforward:

'But the demand to be a turd, that something that makes it preferable to move a little to one side when the subject becomes aware of it.' [310]

Why step to one side? What are the alternatives? If you pronounce a negative judgement on your client's worth —in anything other than a quotation— he is likely to enjoy it masochistically, or to take offence and use it as a reason for leaving. If you assume a position of superior knowledge and contradict a client, praising him, attempting to encourage a 'high self esteem' then you will again be working in reverse: satisfying your client's demand and frustrating his desire. If, following Lacan's advice, you allow your client to work through his demand at his own pace, regardless of his 'self esteem', he will come closer to his desire sooner. If you block his path by getting between him and his image of himself you will be setting yourself up in a position of superior knowledge and moral guardianship. One certainty for all neurotic clients is that they have problems with certain kinds of belief or knowledge and conduct and authority, typically the knowledge or know-how of what it means to live as a man, or as a woman and of how such beings exist together.

Whatever the problems of sexual knowledge that appear as a universal epidemic there is no shortage of greedy and malevolent parasites who appear to have a high regard for themselves, while some of those who make the most important contributions to society have low self esteem. Self esteem is governed by the ego, by the part of psyche that deceives; if you rely on what is effectively a professional liar to orient your clinical work then you will be colluding with your client's symptoms, and working with his ego against his unconscious. Because the ego is committed to producing false connections, and 'self' seems to correspond to part of the ego, Lacan's view is that: *'"[S]elf". . . can be adapted to nothing in analytic theory, nothing corresponds to it.'* [311]

Work outside the Freudian and Lacanian tradition is often orientated by the deceptive and seductive images of the ego and self esteem. Searles for instance has, in his appropriately entitled 'Oedipal Love in the Counter transference' confessed to falling in love with every one of his clients, and then telling them

---

[309] O Kernberg, Further Contributions to the treatment of narcissistic personalities, *International Jrnl of Psychoanalysis 55*: 216-240, 1974..

[310] J Lacan, *Ecrits*, Direction of the Treatment and Principles of its Power, trans Sheridan, Tavistock, London, 1977, p270.

[311] J Lacan, The Psychoanalytic Act, unpublished seminar, trans Gallagher, 10 January 1968.

so, believing that: *'The patient's self esteem benefits greatly from his sensing that he (or she) is capable of arousing such responses in his analyst . . .'* [312]

No doubt this is true but this potentially injurious technique is founded on a number of false assumptions. Analysis is primarily of unconscious desire, not of 'self esteem'. Secondly the client is driven to carry out their difficult clinical work because of their historical problems: placing new complications before the client, such as the clinician declaring his love for the client discounts the value of analysing earlier problematic relations, and tragically attempts to synthesise a new relation that at best will cover up and perpetuate the difficulties of the old ones. It is far from clear why Searles believes that his 'Oedipal love' and his 'transference' have anything to do with his clients' problems. I suspect that the policy of declaring your love for your client would be deemed unethical by most prostitutes.

Besides moving a little to one side when the client identifies himself with shit, how can the clinician usefully work with the image the client has of himself, without becoming hopelessly entangled in the ego's labyrinthine defences? To approach Lacan's answer we have to turn briefly to Lacan's grand formulation: *'the signifier represents the subject for another signifier'*. This idea is explored in more detail in the next section.

The interesting question is not whether a particular client suffers or enjoys low self-esteem or high self esteem, but what this particular image or description means to the client, assuming such material can be found in their speech. Asking: *'Who is it that the client imagines viewing him in this position of low or high self esteem?'* is often useful because the images or signifiers that an individual associates or identifies with him or her 'self' refer to their Other, to the image that they believe their Other has of them. Because 'the signifier represents the subject for another signifier' it will be of far greater value to a client complaining of *'being a worthless failure'* to carefully identify *who* it is that the client imagines that he is being a failure for. Who is this other? What value does 'failing' have for your client's Other?

---

[312] H Searles, Oedipal Love in the Countertransference, *Int J Psychoanalysis*, 40, 1959, p180-90. Freud's advice to Searles was written in 1915, long before Searles wrote the above: *'It has come to my knowledge that certain physicians who practise analysis frequently prepare their patients for the advent of a love-transference or even instruct them to 'go ahead and fall in love with the analyst so that the treatment may make progress'. I can hardly imagine a more nonsensical proceeding. It robs the phenomenon itself of the element of spontaneity which is so convincing and it lays up obstacles ahead which are extremely difficult to overcome.' SE 12,* Observations on transference-love, [1915], 1976, p213.

One client was conspicuously less successful than his older brother. In the economy of family love the older brother was the favourite of the father, while the client was the favourite of the mother. The client had failed over many years to achieve any success in numerous types of work, despite his apparent talents. Why? He had a profound fear of success; the success of his love relation with his mother was —in his imagination— dependent on his continuing failure in his father's eyes. Establishing these crucial points in the family history and dynamics relied on working with Lacan's formulation: 'the signifier represents the subject for another signifier', and not being content with resting on the premature conclusion of the client's *'low self esteem'*. A central question in this case was: What does *'failing'* represent to this client for his Other? 'Failing' represented the client for whom? The client's answer was *'father'*, suggesting the question: What does failure in Father's eyes signify? *'My Mother's love'* was the client's own interpretation. The price that this client had been paying, for the privilege of his mother's love was his wholesale failure in all his other ventures.

On being *'a whole person'*

'The heart of the object relations approach is a mutual involvement of both patient and therapist as complete human beings' [313]

'The whole is only the ghost of the part' [314]

'The couple is no more a whole than the child is a part of the mother.' [315]

'Man cannot aim at being whole; the 'total personality' is another of the deviant premises of modern psychotherapy.' [316]

'The true structure of the subject —which as such is not complete, but divided, and lets fall an irreducible residue— the logical analysis of which is in process.' [317]

How might a person be 'whole'? Freud's and Lacan's work explain this popular goal. Both thought that people are hardly ever whole; they devote a lot of time and energy into trying to cover up the fact that they are not whole. Mostly people suffer because they cannot be whole. For the brief moment that 'a person is whole' there is only the illusion of being one through the loss of

---

[313] D E Scharff, *Refinding The Object and Reclaiming The Self*, Jason Aronson Inc, London, 1992, p.

[314] J Lacan, The Psychoanalytic Act, unpublished, trans Gallagher.

[315] Ibid.

[316] J Lacan, The Signification of the Phallus, 1958, *Ecrits*, trans Sheridan, Tavistock, London, 1977, p287.

[317] J Lacan, Presentation of the Memoirs of President Schreber, trans Lewis, *Analysis,* Number 7, 1996, p3.

consciousness of their underlying subjective division, as in the case of orgasm. Orgasm and other forms of jouissance such as being high on drugs temporarily eliminate subjectivity or division. This mathematical problem of wholes and parts, or division and multiplication is considered under the topics of 'jouissance' and 'subjectivity' in the Appendix.[318] The necessarily important illusion of wholeness, the making of one that is sought in sexual union or jouissance is imagined to eliminate the suffering and conflict of division. Sexual enjoyment or jouissance does eliminate suffering, but only for an all too brief moment. Before and after jouissance the subject suffers division. So being alive is mostly division, with brief interruptions of illusory wholeness.

One way of understanding the popular response of the subject to division — making jouissance— is multiplication. If a number is divided, it can be made whole again by multiplication. Just as the lack of sexual rapport was first introduced to the subject by the mother tongue, so the attempt at multiplying away the lack of sexual rapport often aims at a return, reproducing some imagined and unified aspect of the mother infant relation, because it was the mother who was responsible for introducing the lack of rapport. The lack of rapport in the mother infant relation appears as the impossibility of perfectly co-ordinating the separate requirements of mother and infant. This problem, in successful cases, produces the symptom of the child's speech.

One popular way of eliminating division is multiplication: multiply two divided people to produce zero, the infinite or one, depending on your mathematics. Usually the division of the subject produces a remainder, something left over that Lacan called 'the real'. At the points of jouissance there is a temporary multiplication or division of the subject without a remainder, and with a loss of consciousness or bliss.

Freud and Lacan took on the distinction between 'subject and object', inspired by an Ancient Greek approach to the question 'what is a person. 'Subject and object' are a pairing, a bit like 'up' and 'down', 'good' and 'bad', 'true' and 'false'. 'Object' in this psychoanalytic sense does not refer to physical items such as bricks and chairs which are of course objects but in quite a different sense: 'object' in psychoanalysis is an abstract term that covers a range of very different items. For Lacan:

'The object of psychoanalysis is not man; it is what he lacks —not an absolute lack — but the lack of an object. Even then agreement must be reached as to the

---

[318] This theme is also explored in Ancient Greek philosophy as the relation of 'the one to the many'.

lack in question —it is that which excludes the possibility of naming its object.'
319

So for Lacan the identity of a subject's non-relations, or his unique lack cannot be known prior to his analysis. Here is an incomplete Lacanian catalogue of objects, each of which has a different status and form of life, although they sometimes overlap each other:

- Words or *signifiers*

- *The 'little other' or 'little object'* (also abbreviated as 'a' from the French for autre and is sometimes as 'o' in English).

- *The 'big Other' or 'big object'* (also abbreviated as 'A', French for autre and as 'O' in English).

- *The 'Names of the father'.* These are the never expressed names of the symbolic father for neurotics, which are expressed in psychosis.

- *The 'phallus'* This complex idea was explored briefly in Chapter Eleven on perversion

- The fantasy.

Even though this list is not comprehensive it covers a wide range of theoretical ideas. We will look at each object, and relate them to each of the different diagnostic categories. Each object has a special and often different value for each of the diagnostic categories: neurosis, perversion and psychosis. We will also selectively compare Lacan's distinctive approach with those of Melanie Klein's school, the object relations school and those who follow the work of Carl Rogers.

'In the beginning was the word'

The first object in this section is the word or signifier. Parents often name their child before it is even conceived, give it a religion and sometimes even a job! We are all born into the demands and desires of others. These take the form of language. Language is an infinite sea of objects that Lacan called 'signifiers'.

What do words or signifiers have to do with being a person or subject?

Kafka suddenly stood still and stretched out his hand. 'Look! There, there! Can you see it?'

---

[319] J Lacan, February 19, 1966, Responses to Students of Philosophy, Television, trans Mehlman et al, *October,* Volume 42, MIT, 1987, p133.

Out of a house . . . ran a small dog looking like a ball of wool, which crossed our path and disappeared round the corner . . . 'A pretty little dog,' I said.

'A dog?' asked Kafka suspiciously . . .

'A small, young dog. Didn't you see it?'

'I saw. But was it a dog?'

'It was a little poodle.'

'A poodle? It could be a dog, but it could also be a sign. We . . . often make tragic mistakes.'

'It was only a dog,' I said.

'It would be a good thing if it was.' Kafka nodded. 'But the "only" is true only for him who uses it. What one person takes to be a bundle of rags, or a dog, is for another a sign.' [320]

'A sign . . . is something for something else in some respect or capacity. '[The sign] addresses somebody, that is, creates in the mind of that person [a] . . . sign.' '[T]he object as the sign itself represents it, and whose being is thus dependent upon the representation of it in the sign.' [321]

'The signifier represents the subject for another signifier' [322]

Theories of language are crucially important for psychoanalysis because psychoanalysis is carried out exclusively with words: the client speaks, and the analyst speaks: in psychoanalysis there is no artwork, dance, massage or focus on the image[323]. It is for this reason that Lacan said that: *'Psychoanalysis should be the science of language, inhabited by the subject . . . man is the subject captured and tortured by language.'* [324]

For Freud meaning is also variable: *'My procedure is not so convenient as the popular decoding method which translates the given piece of a dream's content by a fixed key. I, on the contrary, am prepared to find that the same piece of*

---

[320] G Janouch, *Conversations With Kafka,* Encounter, Quartet Books 1971, p116.

[321] 2.228 & 4.536, Collected Works of Charles Sanders Peirce, Hartshorne et al, Harvard University Press, 1930-1958. See *Pierce and Pragmatism*, (W B Gallie, Penguin, 1952, p118) for the question: *'Why does Peirce maintain that every sign requires another sign to interpret it?'* which is very similar to: Why does the signifier represent the subject for another signifier?

[322] J Lacan, Subversion of the Subject and Dialectic of Desire, *Ecrits*, trans Sheridan, Tavistock, London, 1977, p316.

[323] Although this is not of course to claim that art, dance, massage are without therapeutic effects.

[324] J Lacan, *The Psychoses*, ed Miller, trans Grigg, Routledge, London, 1993, p243.

content may conceal different meaning when it occurs in various people or in various contexts' [325]

Following Freud, Lacan argued that each word's meaning comes from its being contrasted with other words, for example: *'black with white', 'hard with soft'* . . . This is why a word's meaning changes over time; it comes to be contrasted in new and different pairings. For example *'gay'* used to be simply contrasted with *'melancholy'* or *'sad'*: since gay liberation the term is contrasted with *'straight'*. The contrasts of each word change over time because word meanings are not fixed.

'Subject' and 'signifier' are an important pair of binary opposites in Lacan's theory of the subject, recalling the ancient Greek binary pair 'subject and object'. His theory of the subject is —put very simply— a theory of what it means to be a person. He argued that each subject is represented by language, or set of special objects called 'words'. Lacan's technical term for 'word' is 'signifier'. Whenever anyone speaks or writes, they represent themselves with language. No surprise here. What might it mean in practice for words to represent a person? If we are being analytical we can say that each sound or word represents the person who speaks or writes it. That is, in Lacan's terms, *'the signifier represents the subject'*.

But how is the representation actually achieved? How is it that a person or subject gets to be represented by their words?

Because word meaning is not fixed but varies with use, there are no rigidly fixed meanings or universal dictionaries that will tell us what associations or attachments any one subject will have with any one signifier, although a dictionary may approximate some of the more popular associations in a given culture. The same signifier will often have a different set of associations for every single subject. You might associate *'dog'* with *'cuddly friend'*, while my association with *'dog'* is *'rabid animal that killed my sister'*. Whenever I speak, hear or write the signifier *'dog'* it represents dead sister to me. How is this representation achieved?

*'Re*presentation' is a second, or further presentation. Any representation is an old presentation that has come round again. How can we set about establishing that something has come round again or repeated? Only through the use of a symbolic process such as counting or using some other kind of language to check. It is only through such signifiers that 'presentation' becomes 're-presentation'. In the above case: *'Dog'* represents me for my dead sister. 'Dog' —as a signifier— represents a subject for another signifier.

---

[325] S Freud, The Interpretation of Dreams, *SE 4*, [1900], 1976, p105.

The only way to establish such representation is through establishing further associations with the first signifier. Other signifiers necessarily constitute the associations. In this case of 'dog' the other signifiers are 'rabid' and 'dead sister'. This is why Lacan said that: *'The signifier represents the subject for another signifier'.* [326]

There are many applications and consequences of this general formula.[327] The very concept and practice of representation relies on repetition and on some means for detecting it. What are the clinical means for detecting repetition? A study of the client's speech informed by Freud's theory of the return of the repressed.

The **lawyer** represents the **client** for another **lawyer**

I represent my client...

The **signifier** represents the **subject** for another **signifier**

If you have a legal case against me your lawyer will establish a legal discourse with my lawyer. For the purposes of the legal dispute the most important exchange of signifiers will not be directly between you and me, but between our lawyers. Even if there is much discussion about what we —the clients— said or did to each other, it will always come to be reformulated or represented within the lawyers' language or discourse.

As legal clients we will be *both* separated by the legal discourse of the lawyers, *and* our legal relationships will become defined by it, in ways that we are

---

[326] J Lacan, Subversion of the Subject and Dialectic of Desire, *Ecrits,* trans Sheridan, Tavistock, London, 1977, p316.

[327] These include: 'the gene represents the organism for another gene', 'the antigen represents the antibody for another antigen', 'the number represents the set or function for another number'. Dawkin's theory of the meme in his *The Selfish Gene* (1976) is a confused version of Peirce's sign and Lacan's signifier. Blackmore's recent elaboration of Dawkin's theory, *The Meme Machine* (Oxford University Press, 1999) is no clearer because of the failure to treat memes formally with respect to the sent, the present and the represented.

unlikely to fully understand. In a similar mode we are sometimes surprised to hear our own words such as slips of the tongue, which embarrass us, and cause difficulties. It is common for lawyers to confuse their clients, and to fail to get the best deal for them. So lawyers are separated from their clients by language, but it is only language, including the language of money, that keeps the whole discourse of clients and lawyers together.

Signifiers or words both constitute and divide us. Representation is *only* achieved through signifiers or language, rather than through some other more direct and supposedly less troublesome route, such as 'through people', or 'through emotions'.

The idea that there is 'another technique' of representation besides language or symbols has never been properly demonstrated, and is not even coherent or plausible. It has even been suggested that telepathy and extra sensory perception are only achieved through representation too, that is that there exists some kind of symbolic exchange at work in telepathy and extra sensory perception. In any case, whatever the truth of such mysteries, the modesty of psychoanalysis insists on the exclusive use of the spoken word. Here is another illustration of Lacan's idea that the signifier represents the subject for another signifier:

'The Prime Minister represents the nation for another Prime Minister'.

In international politics, it is what the Prime Minister says that represents me in the international community, whether I agree with him or not. When nations are represented by Prime Ministers the views or interests of that nation are often confused, twisted or reformulated. But this, says Lacan, is the relation of the subject to language. We are all alienated by language. Language is the best we can do when it comes to communicating; our forced reliance on language guarantees that we will often be misunderstood, however well intentioned our audience might be.

Lacanian theory explains the necessary entanglement of individual and collective meanings; you cannot properly separate and isolate subjects from language or signifiers: signifiers are connected to each other. No word is an island: all signifiers are endlessly interconnected. A demonstration of this is provided whenever an individual tries to exhaust the meaning of any particular term by looking it up in a dictionary; he only finds more words, followed by more words, ad infinitum as the following experience demonstrates:

'They don't know I'm a man . . . I want to be a man . . . I have to look in the dictionary to find out what a virgin is.   I know the Mother of God is the Virgin Mary and they call her that because she didn't have a proper husband, only poor old St. Joseph. In the Lives of the Saints the virgins are always getting into trouble and I don't know why. The dictionary says, 'Virgin, woman (usually a young woman) who is and remains in a state of inviolate chastity'. Now I have to look up inviolate and chastity and all I can find here is that inviolate means 'not

violated' and chastity means 'chaste' and that means 'pure from unlawful sexual intercourse'. Now I have to look up intercourse and that leads to 'intromission', which leads to 'intromittent, the copulatory organ of any male animal'. 'Copulatory' leads to 'copulation, the union of the sexes in the art of generation' and I don't know what that means and I'm too weary going from one word to another in this heavy dictionary which leads me on a wild goose chase from this word to that word . . . All I want to know is where I came from but if you ask anyone they tell you ask someone else or send you from word to word.' [328]

So the author has a problem with his gender or sexuality, and towards finding the meaning of being a man, of being represented by the signifier 'man' he finds himself on a chase from signifier to signifier.

So for Lacan the signifier is at the heart of human existence and being. There is a parallel or example of this fundamentalism of the signifier: a bee will ordinarily sting a hungry bear that threatens to destroy the hive in his search for honey, but in stinging the bear the bee dies. However the rest of the hive is promoted through the sacrifice, and that gene —or signifier— which causes bees to sting those who threaten the hive, represents that bee for all other genes. Only in its death has that bee's representation been clearly identified and established. So the gene for sacrifice is both responsible for destroying and promoting that individual's beeing. The signifier represents the subject, that is constitutes subjectivity, but at a terrible price. People commonly die for signifiers, sacrificing their lives in war for the signifier of their nation.

A popular alternative to Lacan's formulation

Towards understanding Lacan's formulation it is worth considering an alternative and popular formulation that many non-Lacanian clinicians such as Klein rely on in making interpretations: 'the signifier represents the subject *for an object'*. Signification for such Kleinians is subjected to the object: for Lacan it is the subject that is subjected to the signifier. What is given for Lacan are signifiers, what people speak: what is given for Kleinians are the set of metaphysical objects. What is 'object' here?

These are the fixed objects of objects relation theory and Kleinian theory such as *'the good breast'*, and are always given beforehand. For this reason interpretations in the Kleinian tradition are very different from Lacanian interpretations in which meaning is forced open.

Lacan had a vocabulary of technical terms and notations. His abbreviation for the 'subject' is an 'S', but it is not usually written this way, because an essential part of subjectivity is our division and constitution by language. Because we are

---

[328] F McCourt, *Angela's Ashes,* Flamingo, 1997, p302 and 333.

represented by language, often against our own interests, so Lacan wrote an S with a bar through it, to show our subjective division, because most of the time we are not whole but divided.

What are we divided by? The whole range of objects, including language or signifiers, which are public property. The bar also represents the fact that there is always something stopping the subject from getting what it wants and from being how it wants to be. A brief sketch of Freud's 'four formations of the unconscious' will demonstrate the centrality and importance of signifiers in the clinic.

Freud took on four mysterious mental phenomena as a challenge to explain. These four formations of the unconscious are: 'dreams', 'jokes', 'symptoms' and 'errors of everyday life' such as slips of the tongue and bungled actions. Towards understanding Lacan's development of Freud's four formations of the unconscious we should recall Lacan's claim that the dominant part of our minds —the unconscious— is structured like a language'.

Freud and Lacan understood these four categories: dreams, slips of the tongue, symptoms and jokes as linguistic functions, as the movement of words and letters, as a kind or reading and writing. Both called this idea 'The Agency of the Letter', because the letter seems to have a life all of its own —an autonomy— insisting on being rewritten, as the four formations of the unconscious, as signifiers in dreams, jokes, slips of the tongue and symptoms. The letters in books and on gravestones outlive the subject who was spoken by those words, providing examples of the signifier representing the subject for another signifier. 'The Agency of the Letter' is explored in the Appendix. Here are some examples:

A dream

A young woman felt tied up in her mother's problems and complained that she was having difficulty making progress in her own life. She explained that she had never known her father, and reported a dream in which she was *'being pulled by four bears'*. She produced her own reading of this dream: *'forebear means forefather'* she said. It also means *'suffer'* and *'sacrifice'*, which appears to refer to what the young woman had given up in order to continue her difficult relation with her mother.

A symptom

'[I]n the description of pathological phenomena . . . [l]inguistic usage enables us to distinguish symptoms . . .' [329]

The Fallen Woman —whom we have already met— suffered and enjoyed a phobia of open and public spaces. She had a fantasy of being viewed lying in the street. Her unconscious desire 'spoke' with a symptom that took the form of an idiom, a piece of language: 'a fallen woman'.

A slip of the tongue

> Yes, a woman must be pretty if she is to please men. A man is much better off: as long as he has five straight limbs he needs nothing more

> That Freudian slip is nothing compared to mine: I was having dinner with my mother last night, I meant to say 'Please pass the salt', but instead said 'You bitch, you've really fucked up my life'

A joke

Jokes often have the same structure as slips of the tongue, as we can see in an example of Freud's:

---

[329] S Freud, Inhibitions, Symptoms and Anxiety, *SE 20*, [1925], 1976, p87.

'A brilliant joke of Heine's, who made one of his characters, Hirsch-Hyacinth, the poor lottery agent, boast that the great Baron Rothschild had treated him quite as his equal — quite 'famillionairely'. Here the word that is the vehicle of the joke appears at first, simply to be a wrongly constructed word, something unintelligible, incomprehensible, puzzling. Accordingly it bewilders. The comic effect is produced by the solution of this bewilderment, by understanding the word. The joke depends entirely on its verbal expression.

'Are processes similar to those which we have described here already known in any other field of mental events? They are in a single field, and an apparently very remote one. In 1900 I published a book which, as its title (The Interpretation of Dreams) indicates, attempted to throw light on what is puzzling in dreams. Dreams even construct [people and things] out of words, and they can then be dissected in analysis.' [330]

Now we have established the central role for the human condition that meanings have, we should look at some ideas that restrict and limit meanings.

Objects and their Subject

'What we have lost we possess for ever.' [331]

'In man, only that part . . . is appropriate which has reference to the loss of the object.' [332]

'In my dreams I hug her naked beauty like a fragment of a lost paradise that becomes whole and entire and cosmic with wonder in the act of passionate loving. She is my last idol construed from the spirit of magic out of the wrack and ruin.' [333]

'What a man actually lacks he aims at . . . This is why lovers sometimes seem ridiculous, when they demand to be loved as they love' [334]

'Lack is graspable only by means of the symbolic' [335]

'The thing must be lost in order to be represented.' [336]

---

[330] S Freud, Jokes and their Relation to the Unconscious, *SE 8*, [1905], 1973, p16 & 28.

[331] F Nietzsche, *My Sister and I*, Amok Books, Los Angeles 1990, p221.

[332] S Freud, Inhibitions, Symptoms and Anxiety, *SE 20*, [1925], 1976, p168.

[333] F Nietzsche, *My Sister and I*, Amok Books, Los Angeles 1990, p146.

[334] Aristotle, Nicomachean Ethics, 1159 b14, section 8, book 8, trans Ross, Copyright Steve Nichols, England, 1994, *Classic Library of World Philosophy*, Actual Reality Publications, Leeds, 1996.

[335] J Lacan, Seminar on Anxiety, unpublished, trans Gallagher, 1963.

[336] J Lacan, quoted in *Introduction to the Reading of Lacan*, Other Press, J Dor, 1998, p135.

Just as there is a subject in Lacan's theory, so there are 'objects'. 'Subject and object' are a strange kind of pair that are always entangled with one another. What is an 'object' in Freud's and Lacan's theory, and how does it relate to the subject and subjectivity?

By 'object', Lacan doesn't mean a physical object such as a table or brick but something that has a special importance for a subject's desire. For any particular subject there are a variety of possible objects. But you do not collect such objects until you have a complete set. In such a theory a subject would collect all his objects and all would then be well, for he would be whole! Just as a chess set would be whole when all its pieces or objects are assembled. But Lacan does not believe that a subject can 'be whole', but rather that subjectivity and the human condition is about there being something missing.

It is 'the something missing' that is the object, in the way that an empty place setting at a table suggests a lack, or a scar on someone's face recalls an absent knife. The subject is made up above all of absences, of essential things missing and lost. This is why it is usually pleasing to be told: 'I missed you'; it tells you that your being missed —as an object— has something important to do with the other's fantasy and desire. Hence a popular erotic fantasy takes the form: 'S/he has or is my missing object and will make me whole.' Lacan argued that the idea of being one, or whole is a kind of the phallic illusion. This is connected with his theory of the image, and in particular of self-images. The phallus is undivided — one— while the subject is divided or many. This kind of consciousness is an important illusion providing us with an image of ourselves as whole, especially when we are engaged in a phallic activity that hides our subjective division. 'Self' for Lacan is part of the function of the deceptive ego, our false connections and necessary mask and is very similar to the Buddhist doctrine that rejects the concept of a stable or knowable 'self', known as 'anatman':

'All formations are transient; all formations are subject to suffering; all the things are without a self (anatman). Form is transient, feeling is transient, perception is transient, mental formations are transient, consciousness is transient. [337]

If you love someone —in whatever way— you necessarily take some aspect or ideal of him or her as an object. However much empathy or sensitivity you have, you cannot have another subject's experiences or subjectivity. You can only respond to the other's image or signifiers. If someone describes an experience — with signifiers— that you believe is 'the same' as yours, then —in this best of all cases— language stands between your experience and his.

Sympathy as the attempt to identify with another is often self-pity; it is not possible to have another subject's experiences-which are probably unique — but

---

[337] S Asma, *Buddha for Beginners,* by, Writers and Readers, 1996, p53.

only to have one's own subjectivity. Be on guard for pity as a popular form of sympathy because: *'Pity of others is a ghoulish species of self-gratification. Pity of ourselves is the lowest sort of self-degradation'.* [338]

So it is never possible to properly identify *'another subject exactly like me'*, but only an Other, a kind of object. Even in narcissism some image or signifier of the subject or his body is taken as an object. Women are objects for men: men are objects for women: men are objects for men, and women are objects for women. Each of us can only ever be an Other, object or set of objects for another subject, however much we try, because we are all separated by language. The only thing that can be a subject is that unique subject. The only access we have to other subjects is provided exclusively by their signifiers and images.

This is an important clinical issue because many non-Freudian and non-Lacanian approaches rely heavily on the idea that it is possible to gain access to some truth about the client through the clinician's identification of his own feelings as a truthful reflection of the client's feelings! Here for example in the Carl Rogers Centred approach it is claimed —in contrast— that:

'Empathy is a continuing process whereby the counsellor lays aside her own way of experiencing and perceiving reality, referring to sense and responding to the experiences and perceptions of her client. This sensing may be intense and enduring with the counsellor actually experiencing the client's thoughts and feelings as powerfully as if they had originated in herself . . . empathy is a process . . . of 'being with' the client . . . She [the counsellor] isn't just thinking about his [the client's] feelings; it is likely that she [the counsellor] will be experiencing the same general tightness, or constricted throat that precedes his crying. She is experiencing his feelings as if they were her own . . . She is able to work in this intense and feelingingful way with her client, and yet not become overwhelmed by those feelings.' [339]

The important clinical question surely is not that of articulating feelings or of sympathy, which is roughly: *'How much am I identical to some other?'*, but: 'What does it mean for an individual to be the unique subject that each of us is?' With this question in mind Freud wrote:

'I cannot recommend my colleagues emphatically enough to take as a model in psychoanalytic treatment the surgeon who puts aside all his own feelings, including that of human sympathy, and concentrates his mind on one single purpose, that of performing the operation as skilfully as possible. Under present conditions the affective impulse of greatest danger to the psychoanalyst will be the therapeutic ambition to achieve by this novel and disputed method something

---

[338] F Nietzsche, *My Sister and I*, Amok Books, Los Angeles 1990, p107.

[339] D Mearns and B Thorne, *Person Centred Counselling in Action*, Sage, London, 1988, p39.

which will impress and convince others. This will not only cause a state of mind unfavourable for the work in him personally, but he will find himself in consequence helpless against certain of the patient's resistances, upon the struggle with which the cure primarily depends. The justification for this coldness in feeling in the analyst is that it is the condition which brings the greatest advantage to both persons involved.' [340]

Lacan developed Freud's argument, claiming that the *desire* of the clinician is crucial in the ethics and practice of psychoanalysis, not his 'feelings' or 'sympathy'. If the clinician makes the mistake of sympathising with his client it is likely that the client will be comforted —in the short term— and become pleased with their new relationship. The clinician's sympathy serves as an ideal distraction from the client's suffering that had its origin in the client's relations with others. For this reason a clinical problem shared is a problem doubled. 'Sharing' is a kind of synthesis: not an analysis. When one person sympathises with another a difference or potential difference between them has apparently been eliminated from the field of analysis, at least temporarily. This elimination of difference is a synthesis, not an analysis. In the following edited transcript of a case, video recorded by Carl Rogers, Rogers can be seen synthesising a brand new relation with his client, Gloria, but only through an explicit reliance on her old father transference:

Gloria*: 'Yeah, and you know what else, I was just thinking, I feel dumb saying it, all of a sudden as I am talking . . . I thought . . . gee, how nice I can talk to you, and I want you to approve of me, and I respect you, but I miss that my father couldn't talk to me like you are, I mean I would like to say "gee, I'd like you for my father", I don't even know why that came to me'.*

Rogers: *'You look to me like a pretty nice daughter . . .'*

Because Gloria would like Rogers to be in the position of her father, and Rogers has then described Gloria as *'pretty'*, as *'nice'*, and as looking like *'a . . . daughter'* to him, Rogers has come unnecessarily and problematically to the support of Gloria's transferential fantasy by establishing her confusion of himself with her father.

If you sympathise with someone you agree with him or her. In the case of a client's suffering their demands and unconscious desire it is far from clear what the clinician's agreement actually concerns! Even the client at that point is not usually able to clearly identify the cause of their suffering! So a clinician proclaiming sympathy for a client is agreeing with something that has yet to be fully and clearly stated! Conscious identifications are usually relied upon to cover-up troublesome unconscious ones.

---

[340] S Freud, Recommendations to Physicians Practising Psychoanalysis, *SE 12*, [1912], 1976, p115.

The little object as the object of desire and the cause of desire

'I have . . . produced the only conceivable idea of the object, that of the object as cause of desire, of that which is lacking.' [341]

'The reification of bodies comes in stages in ones acquisition of language, each successive stage being more clearly and emphatically an affirmation of existence. The last stage is where the body is recognized over time, despite long absences and interim modifications. Such reification presupposes an elaborate schematism of space, time and conjectural hidden careers or trajectories on the part of causally interacting bodies . . . The very notion of object, or of one and many, is indeed as parochially human as the parts of speech . . .' [342]

'This residue . . . this object whose status is so difficult for us to articulate that it is through it that there have entered all the confusions of analytic theory, this object a . . . is the one which is at stake everywhere Freud speaks about object when anxiety is involved.' [343]

Because this is an introductory text and because the little object is a difficult topic we will not be spending much time on it although it is a vital concept in theory and practice. This little object, little other (o) or little a (French for 'autre') is remarkable for two reasons. The first is to do with the location of the little object.

The little object cannot be simply identified as residing 'within the subject', or as 'outside the subject' or residing 'within the other'. So where exactly is the little object? It is impossible to answer this question with an ordinary three-dimensional geometric understanding of space:

'In order to grasp its extent, one must abstract oneself from three dimensional space, since it is a question here only of a topological reality that is limited to the function of a surface.' [344]

Here in more detail is the same idea, note the recurring theme of the topological surface:

'Is the object of desire out in front? This is the mirage that is involved and which has sterilised everything that in analysis intended to advance in the direction

---

[341] J Lacan, *The Four Fundamental Concepts of Psychoanalysis*, trans Sheridan, Pelican, London, 1979, pix.

[342] W Quine, Structure and Nature, *The Journal of Philosophy*, vol LXXXIX, no 1, January 1992.

[343] J Lacan, Seminar on Anxiety, unpublished, trans Gallagher.

[344] J Lacan, *The Four Fundamental Concepts of Psychoanalysis*, trans Sheridan, Pelican, London, 1979, p271.

described as 'object relations' . . . this object ought to be conceived by us as the
cause of desire . . . the object is behind desire. On the other hand, there is, at
this level the explicit opposition between two terms . . . outside, and . . . inside. It
is specified that the object is no doubt to be situated . . . on the outside, and on
the other hand . . . inside of the body, it is there that it finds its . . . satisfaction.
This also tells you that what I introduced for you as a topological function
allows us to formulate in a clear fashion that what has to be introduced here to
resolve this impasse, this riddle, is the notion of an outside before a certain
interiorisation, of the outside which is situated here, a, before the subject at the
locus of the Other, grasps himself in x in this specular [imaginary] form which
introduces for him the distinction between the me and the not-me. It is to this
outside, to this locus of the object before any interiorisation . . . that this notion
of cause . . . belongs.' [345]

If this seems unnecessarily complicated bear in mind that it is no more than an
attempt to make clear Freud's discovery. If you want to understand psyche then,
Freud argued, ordinary three dimensional space is simply not sufficient:

'Now let us, by a flight of imagination, suppose that Rome is not a human
habitation but a psychical entity with a similarly long and copious past . . .
There is no point in spinning our fantasy any further, for it leads to things that
are unimaginable and even absurd . . . The same space cannot have two
different contents. Our attempt seems to be an idle game. It has only one
justification. It shows us how far we are from mastering the characteristics of
mental life by representing them in pictorial terms . . . Our psychical topography
has for the present nothing to do with anatomy; it has reference not to
anatomical localities, but to regions in the mental apparatus, wherever they may
be situated in the body . . . With the . . . topographical hypothesis is bound up
that of a topographical separation of the unconscious system and conscious and
also the possibility that an idea may exist simultaneously in two places in the
mental apparatus.' [346]

So to understand where the little object or little other is, it is necessary to rely on
an understanding of topological space rather than ordinary geometric space.

The second reason why the little object is so interesting is because it both starts
or causes desire, and is also the object of desire. According to Freud:

'The first determinant of anxiety . . . is [the] loss of perception of the object
(which is equated with the loss of the object itself). There is as yet no question of
loss of love.' [347]

---

[345] Ibid p271.

[346] S Freud, Civilisation and its Discontents, *SE 21*, [1929], 1976, p70-2.

[347] S Freud, Inhibitions, Symptoms and Anxiety, *SE 20*, [1925], 1976, p170.

Note that Freud does not start out with *'love'* but with a loss, with something missing: in Freud's and Lacan's account the loss of the object is the cause of anxiety, which in turn leads to demand or love. Below Lacan explains that the lost object, the little object or little other that has caused or started desire is necessary but not sufficient to sustain desire:

'What constitutes anxiety, is when something . . . corresponds to . . . the a, the object of desire . . . it is . . . the something which reminds us that what everything starts from is imaginary castration, that there is no —and for good reason— image of lack [lack can, at best, only be partially symbolised, but is always fundamentally in the real]. When something appears there, it is because . . . the lack is lacking . . . many things can disappear which are anomalous, this is not what makes us anxious. But if all of a sudden all norms are lacking, namely what constitutes the lack —because the norm is correlative to the idea of lack— if all of a sudden it is not lacking . . . it is at that moment that anxiety begins.' [348]

What does Lacan mean when he claims that that *'there is no . . . image of lack'*? The image is within the domain of the imaginary, while the idea of something lacking or missing is always symbolic, that is, is judged to be lacking with reference to the truth. So for example the image of a playing card such as the nine of hearts —with eight hearts— only comes to have its lack identified through reference to the concept or number nine, or some such procedure that invokes the truth. Images themselves are neither true nor false: 'the true and the false' are entirely and exclusively properties of the symbolic, or language. This is why Lacan claimed that *'Lack is graspable only by means of the symbolic'* [349]

'The real' emerges from the ongoing and impossible to eliminate leftovers and mismatches between the world of images and the world of symbols, and is often marked by anxiety.

'Cause' distinguished from 'object'

There is something necessary about the little object a —as cause— that has the effect of desire. Desire is a consequence of the little object. To try and explain this we should look at the difference between 'causes' and 'reasons'.

'Effect-cause' are one pair: 'subject-object' are another. The cause of some thing is not usually the same as the object of that thing. For instance the cause of my working slowly today is the alcohol that I drank last night: but the object of my drinking alcohol last night was not to work slowly today. Causes and reasons are

---

[348] J Lacan, Seminar on Anxiety, unpublished, trans Gallagher.
[349] Lacan, Seminar X, 1963, quoted in B Fink, *A Clinical Introduction to Lacanian Psychoanalysis,* Harvard, 1997, p184.

usually distinguished: the little object is special because it is *both* the cause and the object of desire.

Here is another example that distinguishes 'causes' from the 'reasons or rules'. Imagine that you are learning the rules of chess. It would be unhelpful to have a move explained by an appeal to causes. Bishops move diagonally because they are objects, according to conventions or rules, not as a matter of causality. We could just as well move bishops like castles, in straight lines, or move castles in diagonal lines. Of course, actually moving chess pieces does involve the body, with its causal electrical and chemical reactions, but there are no obvious causal issues of physics or chemistry in chess, only the rules of objects and their positions. We could for instance use our toes rather than fingers to move the pieces. The rules of chess can be understood as 'rule governed' that is operating on logic rather than as effects produced by causes. On the other hand, if you took your car to be fixed and the mechanic said that there were 'no mechanical issues' that caused problems with the car, 'but only logical ones', you would probably change your mechanic.

The little object is a strange kind of constant because it is something that is the same, yet different because our relation to it takes two completely different forms, the causal *and* the logical. This is one reason why desire is so complicated; there are two radically different discourse or language that govern desire. Translating from one to the other is necessarily imperfect, as a symbolic activity, and produces effects in the real.[350]

'Names of the father' or the Biggest Other

The status of this object is essential in determining whether an individual is neurotic or psychotic, so this topic is considered in Chapter Seven on psychosis.

---

[350] The two crucial properties of the little object are exactly the same two properties that two philosophers, S Haack and W Quine have relied on in order to resolve a long-standing series of philosophical difficulties. Haack's jargon for this solution is *'causical'* as a cocktail of the 'causal' and the 'logical'. This convergence of psychoanalysis and philosophy —one of many— suggests that collaborative work between philosophers and psychoanalysts would be valuable. Haack's paper is called 'Rebuilding the Ship While Sailing on the Water' in *Perspectives on Quine*, St Louis, USA, April 1988, ed. Barrett & Gibson. Her theory is detailed in *Evidence and Enquiry, towards reconstruction in epistemology* (1993, Blackwell).

The phallus again

The phallus is an important object for each of the diagnostic categories but it has a special value for perverts who confuse it with the little object a. This object is examined in the chapter on perversion.

How are objects object used to maintain subjectivity?

Some of Lacan's objects have special functions in the different diagnostic categories. In psychosis the Names of the father have a special function: in perversion the phallus and the fantasy have a special functions: in the neuroses the little object a, the little other has a special function. Symptomatic stability is aimed for in each diagnostic category through its special reliance on a particular function or the set of functions of an object. This means that some aspects of some objects will be stable, relative to other objects that are more variable. For example in paranoid psychosis the subject aims to keep the structure of his language stable by relying on the strategy of creating a persecutory Biggest Other. Why? Because in general the object or other —whatever its type— determines subjectivity, and the big Other is absent for psychotics due to the psychotic's profoundly narcissistic identification, typically with the mother. So subjectivity is absent for the psychotic because his big Other is absent.

When the ordinary neurotic language functions that many paranoid psychotics often manage to contrive become fragile, the symptom of choice is typically a Biggest Other who has a persecutory function and insists on imposing their overbearing desire on the psychotic. Such psychotics often complain that there is a particular look that they are given by a certain individual or type of person, or that *'I can tell that I'm under surveillance because of the tone of voice that man had when he asked me the time'*. Such psychotics rely on this variable function of the little object to maintain the status of their other objects more or less constant.

The Big Other, the Other of language

'The desiring human subject is constructed around a centre which is the other in so far as he [that is the other] gives the subject his unity, and the first encounter with the object is with the object as object of the other's desire. This defines, within the speech relationship, something that originates somewhere else . . . A primitive otherness is included in the object, in so far as primitively it's the object of rivalry and competition. It's of interest only as the object of the other's desire.' [351]

---

[351] J Lacan, *The Psychoses*, ed Miller, trans Grigg, Routledge, London, 1993, p39.

'The Other —with a capital O— is not a subject, it is a locus to which one strives . . . to transfer the knowledge of the subject.' [352]

'Let us set out from the conception of the Other as the locus of the signifier.' [353]

The game *'I spy with my little eye'* often played by adults with children has something to tell us about the nature of desire. What is the object that I spy with my eye? The answer to this question is determined by something within the subject's visual field. But this does not go far enough: the answer to the Other's question, the object that the Other has his eye on, is impossible to infer in advance, however detailed the child's knowledge of the adult's visual field.

The purpose of the game is to see how long the subject can ensure the frustration of submitting himself to the desire of the Other. A version of I spy with my little eye is played where a clue is given. Perhaps *'I spy something beginning with B'*. Or *'I spy something yellow'*. Here too the game is to endure desiring the Other's desire, but one aspect of the game has been made more obvious: the existence of a set of determinate rules or laws. In the simple version the subject in search of the Other's object bears the risk of frustration through selecting an object that is not the one the Other has his eye on. This frustration usually escalates as the subject repeatedly fails to discover the Other's object. The primary purpose of the game is to expose the young subject to the Other's desire.

In the version with additional rules the object of the Other's desire appears to be far less arbitrary. Of course limiting the number of possible objects to those that begin with a particular letter of the alphabet appears to be helpful, but this 'helpfulness' is an illusion; for the child to eliminate all those other objects, whose names start with the wrong letters demonstrates that the child has already submitted himself to his Other's desire; he has learnt the alphabet and how to spell the names of things. That is the child has already learnt, prior to the elimination of all those objects that have not been selected, the arbitrary conventions and rules of language, the complicated rules of spelling and pronunciation. These rules of language existed before the child.

There is something fundamentally traumatic and arbitrary about the Other's desire, however well it is determined by one or another set of rules. What do we usually seek when we are surprised by the Other's desire? A set of rules, some determinants that will somehow allow the Other's desire to appear less arbitrary through its conformity with one or another set of rules. The endless quest for a

---

[352] J Lacan, Seminar on Identification, 15. 11. 61, unpublished, trans Gallagher.
[353] J Lacan, *Ecrits*, Subversion of the Subject and Dialectic of Desire, trans Sheridan, Tavistock Routledge, London, [1966], 1980, p310.

comprehensive set of such rules of desire is a central theme in detective mysteries and love stories, questions about whodunit and why? [354]

But the search for a complete set of rules that would fully detail the Other's desire, making it determinate and so eliminating its traumatic effect is a hopeless task. When people complain of their trauma along the lines of: *'I don't understand'* or *'Why me?'* they are underlining their subjection to the indeterminate rules that govern the desires and demands of the Other. Searching for the determinants or rules of the Other's desires is an endless and necessarily incomplete task; the rule that finds the object of the Other's desire is always symbolic, a piece of language or a sequence of numbers ending in an x of the sort found in IQ tests, algebra problems and questions of science. What is the x, the object of the Other's desire? There is always yet another symbol or signifier to be written or spoken that determines the Other's desire.

I suspect that most parents would become very worried about their child if he were to merrily endure hours of frustration producing endless wrong answers in the I spy game. The point of the game is to endure the frustration of the Other's demands and desires, and then to begin to identify one's own desire through the frustration. If the I Spy game were too easy then there would be no point playing it because it would fail to allude to the Big Other of language as ultimately indeterminate, just as word meanings cannot be comprehensively determined or exhaustively defined by the contents of a dictionary.

It is impossible for the subject to exhaust the task of comprehensively establishing the determinants of the Other's desire. The closest anyone gets to this impossibility is psychosis where the subject has been so closely identified with the symbolic mother's desire that he cannot ascertain the existence of any rules that have determined the existence of his mother's desire for any other object; he is alone, The Singular Object of The mother's desire. In psychosis the subject has not been properly separated from the symbolic mother by the symbolic father; there is no third term. Instead there has been a short circuit in which the endless and ordinary neurotic task of determining the Other's desire for another object of desire, is replaced by the selection of the subject as the exclusive object of the Other's desire.

A popular complement to the I Spy game is the incessant asking of 'why questions' — why do kids — at certain stages ask why, almost without end? Presumably to test crucial hypotheses about their big Other. Perhaps including within these hypotheses are the questions: *'Is the well of language bottomless?'* or *'Are the connections within language infinite, without end?'*, or *'Will there be*

---

[354] Science constitutes a very closely related research programme, in which the object is to discover the set of rules that determine the phenomena in question. See 12 in the Appendix: *'Progress in scientific work is just as it is in an analysis.'*

a final stopping point?' And, perhaps most importantly, *'To what extent can the Other tolerate my demand?'*

The big Other is the one who listens, and whose desires and demands the subject often aims in his love, work and symptoms to place centre stage in his life. The big Other has no accent or stammer; his words denote meanings and values.

The big Other takes on board Lacan's ideas that 'desire is the desire for the other's desire', because speech is the expression of desire, and that the 'signifier represents the subject for another signifier'. Whenever anyone speaks, their desire is always presented or represented, even if it is well camouflaged. Whenever we speak and signify our desire we find ourselves in the Other's language, relying on signifiers whose use was introduced to us by our big Other.

There is a common and uncanny experience: the effect of listening to a recording of one's own voice, as if from the position of the Other. People usually comment with some embarrassment, on hearing a recording of their own voice, that they *'I did not realise that that was how I sounded'*. The focus is not on the meanings but on the grain or accent, that is on the voice as the little object.

The images we have of ourselves are always very much connected with language, with the other's signifiers, with the big Other's demands and desires. So, you may believe, for instance, that you have pretty knees, or a big nose; not simply because you decided one day, without any reference to your culture and community of images and signifiers, that *'my knees are pretty'* or *'my nose is big'*, but because, over the years, people have commented, if not on the feature that you have judged, then on one similar, or a related theme. Our own judgement and the image of our own bodies are filtered through language, through our own local and family cultures: *'Man . . . thinks as a consequence of the fact that a structure, that of language . . . a structure carves up his body, a structure that has nothing to do with anatomy.'* [355]

One dramatic bodily symptom are 'stigmata', the bleeding hands that some Christians present, especially around Easter. Stigmatics bleed from the palms of their hands, exactly where it is designated that Christ's body was pierced in paintings and sculptures. But if you were to trying to crucify a man by driving nails through his palms the nails would tear through hands and he would fall off. The Romans were not so stupid. Their nails went securely through the wrist. But is that where stigmatics bleed? No, stigmatics bleed from the place where they *imagine* Christ to have bled because of Christian symbolism. So stigmatic's symptoms are addressed to an Other, as a demand, as an appeal to the other's desire in the form of a symptom.

---

[355] J Lacan, Television, trans Mehlman et al, *October,* Volume 40, MIT, Cambridge, USA, 1987.

The subjectivity of a stigmatic has something to do with his image of Christ, and the way that it addresses what lacks in his image of his other. The object or other is always a lack, something missing, from which all subjectivity, desire and meaning arise.

What is a person?

Because psychoanalysis is a theory of the human condition you would expect it to have its own jargon instead of the ordinary language term 'person'. It does. Let's approach Freud's and Lacan's position by looking at an object relations answer from Professor Scharff to the question: 'what is a person?':

'The heart of the object relations approach is a mutual involvement of both patient and therapist as complete human beings, *each with a range of conscious and unconscious communication through which they can share complementary, resonating object relations systems.'* [356]

What is the idea of '*complete human beings*'. Does Scharff mean a physical body, complete in the sense of having legs, kidneys etc? I don't think so, because this category would then include frogs, dogs and all sorts of non-people, as well as excluding people without legs and kidneys. Towards finding an answer let's try looking in more detail at what he intends by the technical term '*object*'.

First let us briefly contrast Scharff's and Lacan's theories: Lacan argues that the idea of a 'complete human being' is a kind of fiction. The Lacanian view is that it is our very incompleteness that makes us human and creates subjectivity, although psychosis is a kind of exception to this. One picture of this completeness that most of us have of ourselves are the individual images we have of our bodies. But such an image is a type of fiction; we know from anorexics, phantom limb phenomena and a wealth of other evidence that the images people have of their own bodies are misconstructed, built in the imagination; they are not neutral and accurate descriptions of something objective in reality. Ordinary fantasies and dream reports suggest that a more fundamental image of the body is fragmented, in pieces, rather like a painting by Picasso, Bosch or Dali than an idealised 'perfectly truthful anatomical diagram' The image of a 'whole body' is fabricated by that part of the psyche responsible for deception and producing untruths, by the ego. It is part of the job of the ego to construct a 'whole body image' just as it is a magician's job to deceive. For Freud and Lacan the ego is —in crucial part— to misrepresent the body:

---

[356] D Scharff, *Refinding The Object And Reclaiming The Self,* Jason Aronson Inc, London, 1992.

'Another factor. . . seems to have played a part in bringing about the formation of the ego and its differentiation from the id. A person's own body, and above all its surface, is a place from which both external and internal perceptions may spring. It is seen like any other object . . . **The ego** *is first and foremost a bodily ego; it is not merely a surface entity, but* **is itself the projection of a surface.**' [357]

Note Freud's reliance here on the concept of 'surface', in line with Lacan's earlier in this chapter. Funfair experiences at the hall of mirrors demonstrate that Freud's *'projection of a surface'* has distorting effects. A fat person can appear thin, a thin person fat, a tall person short, etc. Projecting an image on to a surface even allows a line or a circle to become condensed [358] or 'distorted' to a point. A point can even be stretched into a line, According to Freud it is just this principle of projection that is relied on in the ego's construction of its owner's body image. Why should the image of our bodies be involved in deception, and who or what exactly is the deception aimed at? Deception is an essential part of the image and its interrogation by language, by the radically distinct world of symbols, by the world of other's desires.

The ego's deception aims to cover up the truth of a conflict. Anorexics typically believe that they are overweight, and many ordinary looking people believe themselves to be either exceptionally unattractive or exceptionally attractive. Body images have much to do with the role that others have in our lives and the role they play in our desire. The body image is always twisted, distorted and fabricated by the effects that language —the demands and desires of others as signifiers— have on the subject.

All images of the body are projected or imposed on it as a surface, just as tattoos, stigmata and circumcision are. There is no 'neutral and accurate' description of a body that somehow avoids the other's desire and the effects of their language on the body. Confirmation of this theory is even found in Leonardo da Vinci's highly detailed anatomical drawings that elaborate completely false anatomical parts that simply do not exist. One historian of medicine understates the case by claiming that 'Leonardo at times followed tradition rather than his eye' [359] Recently it was discovered that almost all

---

[357] S Freud, The Ego and the Id, *SE 19*, [1923b], 1975, p26.

[358] 'Condensation' is one of Freud's terms for a part of the dream work.

[359] R Porter, *The Greatest Benefit to Mankind, a Medical History of Humanity*, HarperCollins, London, 1997, p132. In 'Do We See through a Microscope' (Images of Science, University of Chicago Press, 1984, p132-134) Ian Hacking has answered his own question: *'I think that means we do not see, in any ordinary sense of the word, with a microscope'*. On the same subject Bergman wrote in *'Outline of Empiricist Philosophy of Physics'*, American Journal of Physics, 11, 1943: 248-58. Reprinted in *Readings in the Philosophy of Science*, ed H Fiegl and M Brodeck, New York: Appleton-Century-Crofts, 1953: *'microscopic objects are not physical things in a literal sense, but merely by courtesy of language and pictorial imagination . . .When I look through a microscope,*

medical textbooks underestimate the size of the clitoris by almost an order of magnitude. It seems that no one had actually looked, and instead had relied on culture or folklore. [360]

For 'tradition' Lacanians understand both 'culture', and 'the individual subject's history of signifiers'. It is this theory of images —in which they are understood to be entwined with signifiers— that helps explain why some problems such as anorexia are very rare in China and very common in Argentina.[361]   However in China it is considered ordinary and acceptable to present to one's medical doctor the complaint that one's 'penis is shrinking', without expecting a referral to a psychiatrist [362].

So the idea of a 'complete person' that is relied on so heavily by some clinical approaches is fatally problematic, and it is far from clear how this incoherent concept of 'the complete person' might be used to orientate and direct clinical work. Let's now turn to another problematic idea that some schools rely on in the clinic: 'mutual involvement'.

'Mutual involvement'

What can be made of this ideal of object relations? Scharff wrote of the 'mutual involvement of both patient and therapist' but unless one is in full possession of the details of the involvement of 'both patient and therapist' then it will be impossible to properly establish mutuality. No clinician is ever in such a knowledgeable position! Psychoanalysis analyses! What does it analyse primarily? The client: not the clinician. Questions regarding the 'involvement', whatever that may mean, of the 'therapist' should be pursued in the therapist's supervision or in his own clinical work. The idea of a mutual involvement is the idea of a new relationship, something mutual that has emerged between client and clinician, that is a synthesis, not an analysis.

What is meant by Scharff's claim that the client and clinician 'can share complementary, resonating object relations systems'? How could it be

---

all I see is a patch of colour which creeps through the field like a shadow over a wall'. Even 'colour', 'shadow' and 'wall' are inextricably linked with concepts. It is not possible to describe without positing objects in a theory (of perception).
[360] In another example Dorschner et al (Vol. 162, 1942-1945, December 1999, *The Journal of Urology*, 1999) report on 'The Dispute about the External Sphincter and the Urogenital Diaphragm', that '. . . *several clinical phenomena exist which are inconsistent with the description of the anatomy of the so-called external sphincter muscle and urogenital diaphragm'*.
[361] Carmen Pignotti, Reuters, *Narcissistic Argentina*
http://wedge.nando.net/newsroom/ntn/health/081597/health32_26581.html).
[362] E Showalter, Hystories, Picador, 1998.

established that the client and clinician share anything other than a few bits of language? Perhaps only through the clinician disclosing to the client information that ought to be kept private.

Scharff writes of a '*range of conscious and unconscious communication*' that the client and clinician use. But he does not provide any details or coherent theory of language or communication. Is communication achieved magically or must Scharff rely on language, that is, on words or signifiers like the rest of us? Scharff's theory of communication is absent but he would have it perform special services nevertheless, including the provision of knowledge of the '*mutual involvement of both patient and therapist*', and the sharing, between client and clinician of '*complementary, resonating object relations systems*'.

The next item relied on by Scharff that I want to criticise are 'male' and 'female' as fixed or given values.

Male and female as given values

'*The dual nature of life and its essential unity is clearly demonstrated in the sex characteristics of men and women functionally and biologically as well as mentally and spiritually, each is complimentary to, and provides the fulfilment of the other.*' [363]

Above is the thesis to which Nietzsche, Freud and Lacan demonstrate their opposition:

'*How each sex has its own prejudice about love . . . For man and woman have different conceptions of love; and it is one of the conditions of love in both sexes that neither sex presupposes the same feeling and the same concept of 'love' in the other.*' [364]

'*It is my belief that, however strange it may sound, we must reckon with the possibility that something in the nature of the sexual drive itself is unfavourable to the realisation of complete satisfaction.*'

'*One gets the impression that a man's love and a woman's are a phase apart psychologically.*' [365]

'*Love is impotent, though mutual, because it is not aware that it is but the desire to be One, which leads to the impossibility of establishing a relationship between . . . 'them-two sexes*' [366]

---

[363] H Khan, *The Secret Of Life, The Human Machine and How it Works*, Odhams, 1940, trans Rosen.
[364] F Nietzsche, *The Gay Science,* trans Kaufmann, Vintage Press, [1887], 1974, p318.
[365] S Freud, New Introductory Lectures, Femininity, *SE 22*, [1932], 1976, p134.

' . . . the nonsense of the sexual relation' [367]

'There is no sexual rapport' [368]

Why did Lacan argue that 'there is no sexual rapport', or that in sexual terms, women and men are fundamentally incompatible, and that when 'added together' a man and a woman do not make 'a whole' or 'cancel each other out, and that *'the sexual relationship . . . doesn't exist.'* [369]?

Clinical work is difficult. How much easier it would be if some positive universal values could be safely assumed and relied on. The universal values would then act as lighthouses or beacons, marking the way on an uncertain journey. For Freud and Lacan one of the most interesting facts about people is the absence or lack of fixed meanings or values. 'Woman' for example probably has as many interpretations as there are women and men. 'Woman' does not have a positive and uniform meaning that is fixed for each of us, so the clinician cannot rely on it as having a fixed and predetermined meaning in a client's speech. Yet there are many clinical schools that —without justification— assume fixed meanings for male and female, that they then use to inform their clinical work. Within this tradition of fixed meanings that Scharff relies on are also the theories of Klein and Jung.

Clinicians from different schools have described 'the object of the client' as being identified with some aspect of themselves as clinician. The very different clinical methods of Lacan and Scharff, and their different theories of the object seem to have this much in common. According to Scharff:

'Each male therapist must be able to represent the female element in relation to his own maleness, and each woman therapist the male connection. Therapists can do so because of their own internal object relations, which include themselves in relation to others, male and female, and which provide an internal universe receptive to the patient's experience.' [370]

And: *'The patient . . . deliver[s] his or her self into a nest by finally trusting the therapist enough to put the object into the therapist. The patient asks the therapist to provide the holding, and later to house the patient's internal object, allowing for the emergence from camouflage of the self that had been in hiding*

---

[366] J Lacan, *On Feminine Sexuality, the limits of love and knowledge, Book 20, Encore 1972-1973,* trans Fink, Norton, 1998, p13.

[367] J Lacan, Television, trans Mehlman et al, *October,* Volume 40, MIT, Cambridge, USA, 1987, p12.

[368] J Lacan, *On Feminine Sexuality, the limits of love and knowledge, Book 20, Encore 1972-1973,* trans Fink, Norton, 1998.

[369] Ibid. p57.

[370] D Scharff, *Refinding the Object And Reclaiming The Self,* Jason Aronson Inc, London, 1992, p18.

behind the previous description of internal objects. This reversal marks a qualitative difference between early exploratory psychotherapy that deals with problems of the self indirectly through discussion of the object, and later, more intensive work that focuses more directly on the self as it emerge.'

Here are related passages from Lacan:

'How shall I describe for you the effect of this presence of the object little a, rediscovered always and everywhere, in the movement of the transference? It is not enough that the analyst should support the function of Tiresias [who interpreted to Oedipus that he might be unaware who his parents were, and that his marriage to his mother concealed some unspecified horror]. He must also . . . have breasts. I mean that the operation and manipulation of the transference are to be regulated in a way that maintains a distance between the point at which the subject sees himself as lovable —and that other point with the subject sees himself caused as a lack by little a— and where little a fills the gap constituted by the inaugural division of the subject.' [371]

'Concerning the position called that of the analyst . . . it is the object a itself that comes to the place of the command. It's as identical with the object a, that is to say with what presents itself for the subject as the cause of desire, that the psychoanalyst offers himself as the aim for . . . a psychoanalysis, in so far as it sets out on the trace of the desire to know' [372]

'We have found a certain type of objects which, in the final resort [that is at The End of analysis], can serve no function. These are the objects little a: the breasts, the faeces, the gaze, the voice.' [373]

'The analyst makes himself the cause of the analysand's desire.' [374]

There is clearly common ground in the above, but how is it to be theorised? What is to be made of the differences between Lacan's and Scharff's theory of the object?

'The object' in question has a radically different status in Lacan's and Scharff's theories. For Scharff the object is somehow given beforehand, and has a meaning that has mysteriously been fixed by the supposedly given value of *'male'* and *'female'*. But Scharff provides no adequate justification for having fixed the meanings *of 'male'* and *'female'* that his theory rests on. In contrast, Lacan's theory of the object little a leaves open the choice of object the client

---

[371] J Lacan, *The Four Fundamental Concepts of Psychoanalysis,* trans Sheridan, Pelican, London, 1979, p269-270.

[372] J Lacan, The Inverse of Psychoanalysis, unpublished, trans Gallagher.

[373] J Lacan, *The Four Fundamental Concepts of Psychoanalysis*, trans Sheridan, Pelican, London, 1979, p242.

[374] J Lacan, The Inverse of Psychoanalysis, unpublished, trans Gallagher.

has made, from a whole universe that is far from limited to the supposedly given values of 'male' and 'female'.

Scharff also claims that *'the therapeutic relationship carries a larger potential than that of a two-person relationship'*. But he has not established what potential 'a two-person relationship' carries or even what it means to be a person.

What exactly does Scharff mean by *'male'*? A person with a beard? A postoperative female to male transsexual? Someone who has sexual fantasies in which they are active? What exactly does Scharff mean by *'male element'*? How is a 'male element' different from a 'female element'? The terms male and female cannot be relied upon as if their meanings were fixed or obvious. The idea of 'male' and 'female' elements is vague in the extreme. Scharff does not have a clearly worked out or explicit theory of sexuality or gender. In contrast Lacan has a sophisticated theory of sexuality. [375]

There are two important further problems: Scharff has written that *'therapists can do so because of their own internal object relations'*. He is making the grandiose claim that therapists have different *'internal object relations'* from non-therapists, which specifically includes an *'element'* from the other gender. What criterion or test is there for detecting the presence of this other gender element? If this knowledge could be possessed it would be useful in the problematic training of clinicians!

The second problem concerns Scharff's assumption of the receptivity of the *'internal universe'* of the therapist to *'the patient's experience'*. Given the fact that Scharff cannot possibly know in advance what any particular patient's experience has been, how might it be possible for him to know what may or may not be receptive to it? Scharff makes brave and unjustified assumptions about both clients and clinicians.

But he is not the only one. Scharff's approach to gender and sexuality have been inspired by the ideas of Melanie Klein who also made the extraordinary and unjustified assumption that infants are born fully equipped and pre-programmed with knowledge of the genitals:

'My assumption that in both sexes there is an inherent unconscious knowledge of the existence of the penis as well as of the vagina.' [376]

For Lacan objects do not straightforwardly represent a presence or something positive but a profound absence or lack: it is Scharff's belief in the existence of the object as a positive entity, rather than as a lack or absence that allows him to

---

[375] See J Lacan's, *On Feminine Sexuality, the limits of love and knowledge, Book 20, Encore 1972-1973*, trans Fink, Norton, 1998.

[376] M Klein, The Oedipus Complex in the Light of Early Anxieties, *Love, Guilt and Reparation*, Virago, [1945], 1975, p409.

claim that he has, as a clinician, the capacity to act as a sterile or cleansing container or bucket for his clients' objects:

'When patient and therapist do meet, the patient will project aspects of these prior object relationships and the anxieties they contain into the therapist, who will have the job of taking them in, containing them, and putting them back into the patient in detoxified form.

'The patient . . . put[s] the object into the therapist. The patient asks the therapist to provide the holding, and later to house the patient's internal object . . . The therapist is actually experiencing the life of the internal object because it has been thrust into him.' [377]

In the next section we will examine this bucket or container theory whose founders include Plato (in his *Republic*) and Bion. [378]

Object relations or the bucket theory of objects: numbers, breasts and penises

The bucket theory explains the individual human psyche as a bucket. Collections of people are collections of buckets. In the clinic the client and clinician get to swap the contents —the objects— of their buckets. Scharff for example (page 203), writes –in his capacity as a bucket— of his clinical work with a couple whose baby had died:

'Their mourning had begun. I noticed that I no longer felt the dead baby inside myself.' [379]

Where exactly did Scharff feel this *'dead baby'*? In his bucket. Before we elaborate this idea of a 'bucket or container for objects' let's return to the difficult question: what is an object?

In Scharff's theory of the object relations school, objects have a strange existence. For somebody using this kind of theory 'an object' is much like 'The Number 12'. No person has ever seen 'The Number 12': they may have seen 12 apples, 12 elephants or even the numeral '12' written, but they have not seen the abstract number '12'.

It is clear from the use that Klein made of the objects she theorised and worked with in her clinic, including the *'good breast'*, *'the bad breast'* and the *'father's penis in the mother'* that she intended these objects to be of a non physical sort

---

[377] D Scharff, *Refinding The Object And Reclaiming The Self,* Jason Aronson Inc, London, 1992, p137.

[378] W Bion, *Attention and Interpretation: A Scientific Approach to Insight in Psychoanalysis and Groups*, Tavistock, London, 1970.

[379] Ibid. Scharff, p203.

that have never actually been seen, smelt or physically felt. These objects of Klein's are abstract, rather like 'God', angels, devils and —for some [380]— numbers. Lacan takes an atheistic position[381] regarding the status of these objects. Aristotle, in a Lacanian moment, argued that when it comes to understanding people, objects acquire their crucially important status not from being present —from existing in a positive sense— but from their absence, by being missing:

'What a man actually lacks he aims at . . . This is why lovers sometimes seem ridiculous, when they demand to be loved as they love.' [382]

This explains why Lacanians have a special interest in the concepts of the empty set and zero; the subject is only brought into being by a lack or absence, by something crucial that is missing. For Lacanians the subject is like the number Pi, the ratio of the diameter of every circle to its circumference because Pi can never be definitively and precisely stated as a fixed quantity; computers have calculated Pi to over a million decimal places, and still Pi continues to be written, resisting comprehensive quantification and symbolisation.

For Lacan the crucial role taken by lack or absence is suggested by the role of 0 in binary mathematics. In a sense zero is a banal and contentless concept yet without it we would be without an important binary opposition or contrast for 1. The importance of this empty category, this something missing, is structural. The place it occupies allows meaning or counting to exist, yet in the history of mathematics zero is a relatively recent discovery. So it is with Freud's and Lacan's relatively recent theory of subjectivity, centred on a lack or absence, on the impossibility of a fully determinate ratio. Our lack has always been with us –and is of vital importance— but it is only recently that it has been symbolised so explicitly.

Now let's return to how Scharff explains how he thinks that these mysterious objects —with a supposedly positive existence— get put in and then pulled out of his and his client's buckets:

'When patient and therapist do meet, the patient will project aspects of these prior object relationships and the anxieties they contain into the therapist, who will have the job of taking them in, containing them, and putting them back into the patient in detoxified form . . . the patient . . . put [s] the object into the therapist. The patient asks the therapist to provide the holding, and later to

---

[380] Those who take this position are followers of Plato.

[381] Those who take this position are closer to Aristotle.

[382] Aristotle, Nicomachean Ethics, 1159 b14, section 8, book 8, trans Ross, Copyright Nichols, England, 1994, *Classic Library of World Philosophy*, Actual Reality Publications, Leeds, 1996.

house the patient's internal object . . . The therapist is actually experiencing the life of the internal object because it has been thrust into him or her . . . [383]

How might a clinician 'detoxify' someone else's 'objects', let alone 'contain' them? The only objects that we can take in, that have 'belonged' to someone else are their words or signifiers, and their image. In the Lacanian clinic the work with neurotics is exclusively with the neurotic client's signifiers, after the preliminary sessions.

Below Scharff explains the progress of his therapy with an adolescent as being due to the efficient swapping of objects as described above! But in this case, confusingly, the internal objects, those inside her bucket, have been swapped or changed for people, for her parents! Quite a trick if you can do it: *'This therapy went especially well because Tammy was ready for change and because her external objects —her parent— had had therapy . . . In this therapeutic*

situation, we can see the use and abuse of the object as a container . . . [384]

---

[383] Scharff, ibid, p137.

In this extraordinary explanation we can see that Scharff has —without warning or acknowledgement given up altogether on the abstract or Platonic idea of the object that no one can see because it's in the invisible psychic bucket and— simply substituted the ordinary term *'parents'* for the abstract term *'object'*. If we had only known that 'parents equals object' then we could do away altogether with the difficult term 'object' and simply talk about 'parents': we wouldn't have any need for anything as technical as psychoanalysis or 'object relations theory' but would be content with 'parents' relation theory'. Instead of being analysed ourselves we could send our parents!

Unfortunately the human condition is such that we not only have problems relating to each other as parents, but each of us as an individual is also likely to have problems relating to siblings, non-siblings, non-parents and above all of these conflicts, we have essential struggles between different parts of ourselves. Freud's and Lacan's theories are focused on these 'non-relations', that is, on the failures and necessary difficulties that we have with each other and ourselves. There is an extreme contrast between these vital failures and difficulties that constitute the human condition for Freud and Lacan, and the ideal of 'communication', along with the supposedly universal qualities of objects assumed by Scharff and others. With Scharff's approach it is assumed that his client above solved her problems because her parents solved theirs! Lacan and Freud understood the individual human condition as necessarily problematic and conflictual; if the child cannot identify any demands or desires or problems — that is lack— possessed by its parents or carers, then it will either become psychotic or fail to acquire even the rudiments of language, that is it will in a crucial sense fail to be a human subject.

We will return to the idea of a 'container' or bucket for objects and its close relation to what I call later in this chapter 'the sponge theory of emotions'.

The confusion of need, demand and desire, plants, people, growth and maturity

Many clinical schools produce large volumes of theoretical and clinical confusion because they fail to properly distinguish the very different categories of need, demand and desire found in Freud's and Lacan's work. Some schools, for good measure even mix in *'growth'* or *'maturity'*. I criticise one clinician's use of these terms because his use of the terms illustrates the benefits of Freud's and Lacan's theory and clinical techniques.

Below Scharff clearly confuses *'love'*, which I suspect equates with Lacan's demand, and *'need'*, which presumably equates with need in Lacan's sense, and

---

[384] Ibid, p118.

'grows in the light', which I find a difficult category to apply to clinical work, or to identify a Lacanian concept for:

'We each need the parent to love, and we need the parent to love us. And then, later as parents, husbands, wives, or lovers ourselves, we need to feel we can care for others with love-that they will grow in our holding. But it is not only later that we need this. From the beginning, the baby needs to feel that the parent grows in the light of the child's love and care.' [385]

I guess that Scharff is relying on the metaphor of a plant to explain the relation of need, demand and desire. If this is correct then Scharff is claiming that *'the baby needs to feel that the parent [regards it just as a plant does the sunlight.]'* 'If this is not correct then I am at a loss as to what it is that Scharff is claiming. This reading would also fit with Scharff's many uses of the *'growth'*, *'grows'* and *'mature'* as descriptions of progress in the clinical work, for example: *'It is the mature, resilient object relations set of the therapist that is at the leading edge of the work, available to be taken in by the patient, modified, and made the patient's own.'* [386]

How exactly does a plant regard the sunlight? And how exactly does the verb 'grow' apply to clients in psychoanalysis? How well does our understanding of plants explain human phenomena? Any clinical theory that relies on the concept of plant growth, or on any other biological theory of growth ought to take on board the important work that has already been carried out in the field, that is with reference to the work of Haeckel[387], Eldridge and Gould, [388] and others. If people are to be compared with plants then let's see it done properly, with intellectual responsibility rather than vague question begging metaphors.

---

[385] Ibid, p23.

[386] Ibid

[387] E Haeckel, *The Riddle of the Universe*, Prometheus Books, New York, Die Weltrathsel, trans McCabe, [1899], 1992.

[388] N Eldredge & S Gould, Punctuated Equilibria: an alternative to phyletic gradualism. *Models in Paleobiology*, ed Schopf, 1972, p82-115.

CHAPTER FIFTEEN

Interpretation —what do clinicians say?

'The analyst's only duty is to provide interpretations . . .' [389]

Lacan's clinical techniques were developed through his criticisms of other schools techniques, so it is only through an appreciation of the difficulties caused by the methods of other schools that Lacan's advances can be recognised: if there were no such problems with the methods of other schools then there would be no advantage to using Lacan's techniques. I elaborate some of Lacan's arguments at the theoretical level and —to avoid misrepresentation— work through case material provided by the clinicians of other schools. The central question is: how do these non-Lacanians understand and work with their client's speech and suffering?

To begin marking the differences between Lacanian interpretation and non-Lacanian interpretation, consider the strikingly similar positions taken in the first two quotes by Wittgenstein, and the two quotes of Lacan's:

*'Just because someone **sees [that is imagines]** something according to a certain **interpretation**, that doesn't mean that he experiences an interpretation.'* [390]

'All I wish to characterise was the conventions he wished to draw. If I wished to say anything more I was merely being . . . arrogant.' [391]

*'How many times have I said to those under my supervision, when they say to me 'I had the impression he meant this or that' is that one of the things we must guard most against is to understand too much, to understand more than what is in the discourse of the subject. To **interpret and to imagine** that one understands are not at all the same things. It is precisely the opposite. I would go as far as to say that it is on the basis of a kind of refusal of understanding*

---

[389] C Soler, Time and Interpretation, *Reading Seminars I and II*, ed Feldstein et al, SUNY, 1996, p62.

[390] L Wittgenstein, Vol.1, *Last writings on the Philosophy of Psychology*, Blackwell, 1982, p14.

[391] L Wittgenstein, *Lectures and Conversations on Aesthetics, Psychology and Religious Belief,* ed Barrett, Basil Blackwell, Oxford, 1978.

that we push open the door to analytic understanding.' [392]

'I often say that to people I supervise — be very careful not to understand the patient, there is no surer way of getting lost'. [393]

Their position resolves a paradox: why is understanding the client important to aim for, while remaining necessary to miss? How can understanding be unnecessary for making useful interpretations and interventions? First it is worth pointing out how distinctive the Lacanian approach is. In many schools it is common practice for clinicians to set out to provide the client's understanding in a palatable form: *'Understanding is one thing, conveying it in terms the patient can take in, is another.'* [394]

In contrast Lacan was clear: *'An interpretation whose effects one understands is not a psychoanalytic interpretation.'* [395]

How might we understand Lacan's claim, and its direct opposition to the popular goal of Alvarez and others, stated above, to convey understanding to clients? *'Understanding'* is usually taken to be the sort of thing aimed at by schools and universities, a kind of formula that can be consciously called up, and repeated to others clearly. Understanding in this sense means judging that the event in question accords with familiar rules in the discourse of the slave and master, or in the university discourse. But psychoanalysis assumes the existence of the unconscious, whose contents are necessarily unfamiliar. If you understand something about yourself in a way that you can describe clearly to others, then that something cannot be unconscious.

A common experience of clients attending Lacanian clinics is of ending a session on something that they themselves have said and are confused about. This confusion is typically not about some small or irrelevant detail, and the client is never neutral about their confusion. The client's confusion has been precipitated —in part— by the clinician's interpretation. The interpretation or ending has had unconscious effects, which helps explain the lack of understanding.

Most sessions should have at least one surprise! In practical terms this means that the client's ego —his organ of understanding— should be unsettled in some way. These unsettlings can be produced in an infinitude of ways that

---

[392] *The Seminar of Jacques Lacan, Book One, Freud's Papers on Technique of Psychoanalysis, 1953-1954*, ed Miller, trans Forrester, Cambridge University Press, Cambridge, England, 1988, p73.

[393] J Lacan, *Book Two, The Seminar of Jacques Lacan, The Ego in Freud's Theory and in the Technique of Psychoanalysis 1954-1955,* ed Miller, trans Tomaselli, p87.

[394] A Alvarez, *The Supervision Master Class 2000 brochure*, Confer, 1999.

[395] Lacan, Cahiers pour l'Analyse 3 (1966): 13, quoted from Fink's *A Clinical Introduction to Lacanian Psychoanalysis*, Harvard, 1997.

cannot be simply and comprehensively formalised [396]. Comprehensive rules
for interpretations or for clinical sensitivity are impossible to lay down, because
the rules themselves would form part of the language being interpreted, and so
subject to interpretation themselves. That is why Freud claimed that:

*'It is of course impossible to give [precise and comprehensive] instructions on
the method of arriving at an . . . interpretation.'* [397]

So it is not possible to start off with a full and ready made set of rules, when it
is those rules that are in question, and almost certainly different for each of us.
Not only is it impossible to have a comprehensive set of rules for interpretation,
but a great many successful interpretations made by the clinician will not be
understood by the clinician! The principle criterion of successful interpretation
is not understanding but the production of new material.

Sometimes clients will produce an alibi, a kind of diary or seamless story, the
telling of which is designed to eliminate difficult questions, and remove them
from the scene of their desire. It is important, sooner or later, to interrupt this
kind of speech, and by so doing, insist that your client understands that it is
their words that have meanings that demand exploration, through the raising of
questions, through the fact that you —the clinician— are listening carefully to
every word and phrase.

You can be sure that the client who insists on verbally presenting you with his
diary every session will not be free associating. In the first few sessions that the
client be clearly instructed to free associate, I explain to the client that he is
protected through confidentiality, and that nothing of practical value will take
place in the sessions. This abstention is intended to eliminate the damaging
effects of power relations that arise in the discourse of the slave and master,
and the university.

'Free association' means saying whatever comes into his head, including
philosophy, football or fashion. No issue is excluded. Whatever a client says to
his analyst speaks the truth —in a way that the client cannot yet recognise— of
his unconscious desire. True and effective interpretations can be made
whatever the topic, through a reliance on logic. After the preliminary sessions
clients should not be dissuaded from speaking about their chosen topic,
however bizarre and remote it may appear to be from his suffering.

While it is important for the clinician to try and develop beliefs or hypotheses
in his own mind concerning the client's structure, symptoms, fundamental
fantasy, little other, big Other and transference and so on, it is vital for the

---

[396] Jokes are a good way to trick the ego; by laughing at a joke the client acknowledges
its truth in relation to his life. A joke that produces such a response is usually worth
more than a 'conventional interpretation' produced by the clinician.
[397] S Freud, The Interpretation of Dreams, *SE 4*, [1900a], 1976, p97.

clinician not to pretend that he *knows* the truth of the client's unconscious; hypotheses or beliefs and knowledge are not the same: knowledge is a belief that is *both* true and justified.

Silence

Silence is a crucial part of everybody's ordinary language. Ordinarily when people speak there are silences in between most words. Usually these are short: in clinical work they sometimes last a few long minutes. There are many kinds of silence. There is the pregnant silence that accompanies an inner struggle in which the client is searching for words. Just as the one word or phrase may have very different meanings for different clients, or even for the same client —at different times— so silence can have different meanings. It is likely that silence for the hearing child of deaf parents will be different in meaning from silence for a client who was one of five children whose family frequently had loud arguments. The child of deaf parents may find that thirty seconds of silence marks the limit of what they can tolerate: the client from the argumentative family may find your speech unbearable if it lasts for more than one minute. For these reasons it is important to listen carefully and vary your tactics accordingly. If your tactics are fixed and inflexible many clients will refuse to work with you.

There is also a silence that demonstrates the client's demand to test the clinician's desire, and, in the end identify the desire of the patient. The clinician might usefully tolerate such silence for a while, but ending the session may well be more productive.

There is a silence that indicates that the client is surprised unto speechlessness at the uncovering of his trauma or unconscious meaning. This can be understood as a temporary retreat or truce. It is important to respect such a withdrawal and often useful to end a session shortly after such a discovery, since the client is usually incapable of doing any further work in the session. A withdrawal indicates a change of tactic or attempt to revalue.

The preliminary sessions

The preliminary sessions last from the point of your first clinical contact with the client, until the point at which you have become confident of both your diagnosis, and confident that the client's transference is established *and* responsive to the treatment. This can take as long as a year or as little as ten sessions.

Another way to describe the function of preliminary sessions is as the shifting of the client's demand to 'eliminate my symptom', whatever it may be, to the clear identification of the client's desire for his own knowledge of his own desire.[398] This crucial shift in orientation, from symptom to knowledge is also, in a way, a description of the shift from demand to desire. When the client accepts that his symptom or symptoms have a meaning or set of meanings —of which he *appears* ignorant but might discover through the work— the focus of the work can change from one where the client demands to be rid of his symptom, to another where he demands to know the meaning of his mysterious symptoms. This demand for knowledge persists in the transference as *'the subject supposed to know'*. This subject supposed to know is the analyst, who is supposed by his client to know some crucial thing that will allow the client to discover the meaning of his symptoms and desire.

Paradoxically it is crucial on the one hand that the client supposes that his clinician possesses this special knowledge that will help him change his relation to his suffering and ignorance, and on the other hand that the clinician makes no positive assertion of such a knowledge that does not rely almost exclusively on the client's speech. That is, the analyst must not set himself up in the position of knowledge: he must be set up in a position of supposed knowledge by the client.

So there is in fact a special knowledge that the clinician has which may allow the client to discover the hidden secrets that have governed his life, symptoms and suffering! It is that the clinician must be the subject who is supposed to know! Of course the clinician is ignorant, especially during the early part of the work; it is this ignorance that the clinician uses to shift the client's demand for relief from his symptom, to the demand for knowledge, meaning or desire. What the analyst knows is that he doesn't know, but that in a crucial sense his client does know. Freud wrote[399]:

'The dreamer does know what his dream [or symptom] means: only he does not know that he knows it and for that reason thinks he does not know it.' [400]

The preliminary sessions may last from as little as five sessions to as long as a year. Diagnosis is sometimes difficult, and may require more preliminary sessions. Many clients are skilful and effective at hiding their transference and, or their underlying clinical structure. There is an important rule here: *if you are in doubt about either your diagnosis or the responsiveness of the transference, then wait.* There is little disadvantage in doing so, and a possible catastrophe may result from your premature action in starting the clinical work proper. You could for example use the technique known as 'rectification to the real' with a psychotic client, unnecessarily precipitating a psychotic episode, causing much unnecessary suffering.

---

[398] To explain clearly, without contradiction or circularity, the desire for ones own desire would take at least a thousand words, so I don't do it here.

[399] Socrates took a version of this position. See *The Last Days of Socrates* by Plato.

[400] S Freud, Introductory Lectures on Psychoanalysis, *SE 15* [1916], 1976, p101.

Often clients will volunteer a story that explains why they decided to contact you at that particular point. If no such story is offered then you should ask for one along the lines 'Why now?' You will probably find useful clues as to the client's fantasy structure and its relation to his symptom. Why for instance did the client not consult someone six years ago when his problem started? Why you rather than an astrologer or doctor?

The preliminary sessions are amongst the most difficult for the clinician. There are a number of tasks that the clinician should carry out during the sessions, that are to some extent are in conflict with each other. These are likely to include:

1. Inviting the client to speak freely or free associate.

2. Being sufficiently responsive to a limited number of some demands in order that the client's anxiety is not unnecessarily increased.

3. Arriving at a diagnosis.

4. Demonstrating to the neurotic client that the work will not be easy by asking some challenging questions.

5. Some discussion of administrative matters such as your fee, the frequency of sessions and your policy regarding missed sessions.

It is important to allow the client to relax into the work, but the clinician should not accept at face value all the client's possible alibis, exaggerations and denials without question. Some limited interventions and interpretations should be made during the preliminary sessions, especially after the second and third sessions. Whilst all interventions and interpretations are to some extent experimental, they are doubly so during the preliminary sessions when the client's responses will provide timely information about the accuracy of your diagnosis and their transference.

Caution is required because the points three and four above are partially circular; a client's response to a challenging interpretation may help you to diagnose their structure: an interpretation that establishes an important contradiction in the client's speech is likely to produce some surprise, insight or a vigorous defence on the part of a neurotic, or, if the client is psychotic to be completely ignored, or perhaps to produce a violent response, or florid psychotic episode. Sensitivity and judgement are required.

The early sessions

There is a phase early on in the work, during the first preliminary sessions, which I call 'the early sessions'. These usually cover the first two or three sessions, and never go beyond the fifth or sixth session. I have a set of items that I always aim to discuss during the early sessions. These topics are the 'non-linearity' of the pace of the work, that is its ups and downs, the transference, the difficulty of the work, the client's autonomy, the rule of free association, payments, the frequency of sessions and missed sessions. It is all the more important to raise these topics for clients new to psychoanalytic work.

The client must have clearly explained to him the rule of free association. He is to speak whatever comes into his mind, however trivial, silly, irrelevant or offensive he might think it is. Taboos of speech are taboo. Censorship is taboo. If the client has no experience of psychoanalytic work then I sometimes justify this instruction by explaining that the sooner or later this method will lead to interesting things, to issues that have something important to say about the client's life. I explain that the client is the one who is in charge, the one who will decide the frequency of sessions, the pace of the work and the topics that are discussed.

Clients are often relieved to discover that I will not be imposing a tough regime; they already bring their own struggle. Ideally the client will make a proposal about the frequency of sessions. But if your time is restricted, or if you work in an institution with specific rules, then the amount of sessions you offer may be regulated: if they are not then allowing the client this freedom of choice often removes some of their initial anxiety. In almost all cases, where the client asks for my suggestion, I volunteer 'once a week to start with' — unless there is a crisis— in which case the frequency of sessions should be kept under review. It will often take your clients a while to discover how often they are able to attend. Sometimes they surprise themselves by finding that they have more time and more money available, when they come to attribute more importance to the clinical work. Two or three sessions per week can be overwhelming when psychoanalytic work is a new experience. It is safer from the point of view of 'client retention', or 'the negative therapeutic reaction' to build up gradually, with your client's agreement at each point, minimising the defensive response of their ego. Inviting clients to decide on the frequency of sessions demonstrates that you are not taking the position of the master; so the client will not be able to slavishly complain that he is burdened with 'too many' or 'too few sessions'.

A factor in many clients' decision about the frequency of sessions is money. For most client's money is a sensitive issue and far from being a neutral topic. If you are working in an institution, which has a policy of not charging then matters are simple: otherwise charging clients has therapeutic effects for the client, and sometimes for the clinician that should be used wherever possible. On this topic Freud wrote:

'Free treatment enormously increases some of a neurotic's resistances . . . The absence of the regulating effect offered by the payment of a fee . . . makes itself very painfully felt . . .' [401]

Clients pay me at the end of each session by cash or personal cheque only. The occasional request to accept third-party cheques are a demand to support a complicating financial transference. Being paid at the end of each session is simpler because it avoids calculations and debts, and forces an important symbolic fact. The clinical work is difficult for the clinician; the clinician pays a price, so the client pays a price. Given that psychoanalytic work takes place over years it is common for clients to have sporadic problems paying fees, for both economic and transferential reasons that are often impossible to separate with confidence. For this reason I am usually flexible, allowing clients to accumulate small debts.

Logic rules and interpretation — what part does truth play in the discourse of the analyst?

It is fashionable to discount the role or value of truth. But if there were no truth at stake for the client or for psychoanalysis then we all might as well get on with something completely different. Anyway to claim that 'there is no truth' would presumably itself be a truth, but one that leads to a clear inconsistency; disregard for truths conjoined with the attempt to promote a truth.

[401] S Freud, On Beginning the Treatment, *SE18*, [1913], 1976, p34

Truth and falsity are of course mutually supportive concepts: without one you don't get the other. Freud stressed the functions of both falsity and truth in clinical work:

'What I have in mind is an arrangement according to thought content, the linkage made by a logical thread which reaches as far as the nucleus and tends to make an irregular and twisting path, different in every case . . . By detecting lacunas in the patient's first description, lacunas which are often covered by 'false connections' we get hold of a piece of the logical thread at the periphery' [402]

And Lacan wrote that: *'What can be known is, in the analyst's discourse, requested to function in the register of truth.'* [403] And: *'My discourse . . . guarantees . . . our very instrument, namely the plane of truth.'* [404]

Because of the central role that truth plays in the clinic this section is concerned with logic because logic is the structuring of symbols or language that uniquely guarantees that truth is preserved. Truth comes in many shapes, but there is only one form that guarantees the preservation of truth: logic. Logic and truth bear on discourse. The rules of logic are vital for carrying out interpretations. It is the analysis of the logical structures in the client's speech that reveals the client's truths. There is another set of rules for arranging structures so as to discover truths that are useful in the clinic that are closely related to the rules of logic, the rules of algebra.

Algebra and interpretation

Although there are profound and complex relations between logic and mathematics, including those of topology, which there is no space to explore here, it is worth pointing out that simple algebraic methods familiar to anyone who has studied mathematics to age 16 or so can be usefully applied in the clinic.

One way to formulate a common ground between psychoanalysis and algebra is as the analysis of an unknown x. In psychoanalysis the x may be the unconscious desire of the client, but more explicitly x is the unique meaning or set of associations that the client has for a particular signifier or word, such as 'woman'. What does it mean for a client 'to be a woman'? In algebra some values are given, just as certain values are given in the client's speech.

In both the clinic and in algebraic problems we use the given values —those that are assumed to be true— that have been provided by the problem setter or

---

[402] S Freud, The Psychotherapy of Hysteria, *SE 2*, [1893], 1976, p289.

[403] J Lacan, Seminar The Inverse of Psychoanalysis, unpublished, trans Gallagher.

[404] J Lacan, Seminar on Anxiety unpublished, trans Gallagher, 12.12.62.

client to determine the value of x, of that which is not known. The 'problem setter' is a good description of a psychoanalytic client; for he who has the solution to his own problem. Typically in the clinic a number of equations are set out by the client, some of which have some variables in common, suggesting an algebraic technique called 'simultaneous equations'[405] in which the two or more equations are manipulated until both are expressed in terms of a common variable. This then allows you to substitute back into the one of the original equations, solving the original question of the value of x.

Simultaneous equations tell us two facts —as presented by a client— about two unknowns, also presented by the client. By looking at two of the facts together, we can work out what one of the unknowns is, which then enables us to work out what the other unknown is. As clinicians we can offer —in some cases— a translation or interpretation that makes such a series of substitutions. Freud, with this principle in mind, though writing on a different topic, suggested:

'But might we not change the order of things, somewhat as in an equation with several unknowns which can be solved by interchanging one or the other taking either the a or the b as the x we are seeking?' [406]

Here is a clinical example. A young man had moved many times from England to Ireland and back again during his childhood. He described bitter conflicts with both his French lover and with his mother, and complained that his accent was *'neither English nor Irish'*, and that as a result he was experiencing difficulties in being accepted as Irish in Ireland, and as English in England.

The client's French lover had ridiculed his attempts to speak French, and they continued to disagree and misunderstand each other over the long-standing debate as to whether they should live together, and if so then where. The French lover had been told by his own friends that the client *'didn't even speak English properly'*: the client's mother was able to speak fluent Irish, and expressed her wish for the client to return to Ireland, to be with her. The client spoke only a few words of Irish, and lived in England, occasionally visiting or being visited by his mother, and his lover. The client's material suggested many parallels or identifications between the following variables: linguistic fluency, national identity, love relations, and patriation, which could be regarded as algebraic variables. An interpretation relying on the algebraic technique of 'simultaneous equation' was made:

'So there are parallels between Anglo-Irish and Anglo-French relations.'

This interpretation draws simultaneously on at least three items:

---

[405] This technique is closely related to the 'and introduction' rule in the logic section of Chapter Fifteen on Interpretation.

[406] S Freud, Psychoanalysis and the Establishment of Facts in Legal Proceedings, *SE 9*, [1906], 1976, p106.

1. The long established dual histories of national conflict, conquest and attempts at unity, or reconciliation —that is ambivalence— between both the English and the Irish, and between the English and the French, suggesting that the discourse of the slave and master has been operating.

2. The conflicts that the client reported in his ambivalent relation of love and hate with his French lover.

3. The conflicts that the client reported in his ambivalent relation of love and hate with his Irish mother.

Of course, school style history lessons are not important in the clinic, but it is important to use expansive interpretations that open up questions of meaning, rather than reductive interpretations that narrow the possibilities. Here is an example of a reductive interpretation that might have been made by some class of non-Lacanian:

'Your conflicts with your lover represent your conflicts with your mother.'

Or:

'Your lover represents your mother.'

This type of reductive interpretation could be put more slyly, invoking the person or 'authority' of the clinician, rather than the client's language, making it harder for the client to object:

*'**It seems to me** that your conflicts with your lover represent your conflicts with your mother.'*

Such reductive interpretations are of course speculative and arrogant, and work to make the field of possible questions that the client can use to orientate his desire smaller rather than larger. Reductive interpretations are an attempt by the clinician to place himself in a position of superior knowledge, and so set up an impossible competition with the client to see who knows the most. Such competitions always involve some aggression and detract energy and attention from the main task: analysing the client's pre-existing conflicts.

Forcing ambiguity

Freud wrote that:

'Words, since they are the nodal points of numerous ideas, may be regarded as predestined to ambiguity' [407]

In reliance on Freud's theory of language Lacan instructed clinicians not to play the role of The discloser of secrets, of the one who knows:

---

[407] S Freud, , The Interpretation of Dreams, *SE 5* [1900], 1976, p340.

'It is the subject's refusal of this meaning [of symptoms] that poses a problem for him. This meaning must not be revealed to him: it must be assumed by him. In this respect, psychoanalysis is a technique which respects the person . . .' [408]

Deliberately interpreting ambiguities in the client's speech often leads fruitfully to new material. A woman with questions regarding her sexual identity and its consequences had stressed the importance of travel in her life, and had spent years living in foreign countries as an adult. When she repeated her wish to travel, and juxtaposed this with a question of the value of her sexual relationships with men, the clinician asked: *'A broad abroad?'* It might have been easier to wheel out a standard reductive interpretation such as: *'You are now testing our clinical relationship by threatening to leave'.* Such an interpretation may even have been the truth, but that is not sufficient reason for making it.

The truth of interpretations ought to rest on the client's speech, whether quoted or spoken by the client, not on the clinician's imagination or supposed knowledge. It is hard work carefully relying on the client's own formulations and signifiers when making interpretations. Of course such a client may well be trying to annoy or test their clinician —but this is not the point— the important question is not what —the clinician— thinks, believes or imagines the client's truth is, but how will the clinician help the client work through their pre-existing problems in their own terms, that is in reliance on their language. This modest Lacanian approach avoids colluding with the client and drawing energy away from analysing their pre-existing problems. The client should not be distracted through the fabrication of a new and unnecessary set of problems with their clinician. Of course it is often an attractive option for a client to pick a new fight with their clinician rather than face their far older and more difficult conflict with their Other. The clinician should be on the lookout for such strategies and traps, and unless absolutely necessary, should not be lured by them because of the effects of resistance that they have on clinical progress. In most cases interpreting such ploys gives them a strength and effectiveness that they would otherwise never have.

One client had been harshly treated by his father who had given himself the nickname 'King'. The client worked with 'The Royal Mail', also known as the 'Post Office'. His work there did not go smoothly. He resented taking orders from his boss, faked an accident, and then claimed compensation. The clinician asked him: *'How do you spell 'male' in 'Royal Male'?*

Another man complained that his mother had been cold towards him and that their relationship was a strange kind of economy centred on his eating food that

---

[408] J Lacan, *The Seminar of Jacques Lacan, Book One, Freud's Papers on Technique of Psychoanalysis*, 1953-1954, ed Miller, trans Forrester, Cambridge University Press, Cambridge, England, 1988, p29.

she had prepared. He described a setting in which he had been eating his mother's ice cream, *'ice cream'*. The clinician asked *'Ice Queen?'*

These interpretative techniques may appear as a kind of trick but their legitimacy relies on three criteria or questions:

1. Has the clinician's interpretation relied on an analysis of the client's speech?

2. Has the technique helped the client produce new material?

3. Does the clinician possess the desire for his client's desire? This is a question of ethics that we will explore in Chapter Sixteen.

Clients often do no more than hint at topics or ideas that are in some sense taboo. It is important for the clinician to rely on their sensitivity and intuition when such hints are made. Sometimes it is useful for the clinician to ask direct questions such as: *'Are you in love with X?'*, which might be regarded as rude in a different setting. Generally, when a client makes what I judge to be a hint or reference to suicidal ideas I ask if they have thought of hurting or killing themselves. Many people have thought of one or both. If the client admits to such thoughts I usually ask them to detail their fantasy. In particular I am looking for the identification of their Other with questions such as 'How? Where would you kill yourself?' Answers to these questions are likely to provide important clues as to who their Other is. The client might say *'Of course I would never go through with it, but I have thought that I would take a lot of sleeping pills, somewhere miles away from my father'*. So the client has hinted at the idea that her suicide would be addressed to her father. Such new material invites new explorations.

The technique of producing a fixed and standard interpretation —through the imposition of the clinician's prejudices— whenever a client reports *'low self esteem'* will reduce the chance of helping the client identify his own unique meanings and history. One popular example of a fixed clinical attitude is the *'unconditional positive regard'* of the Rogerians. There is a real risk that such a fixed or unconditional attitude will drive many clients to become increasingly demanding and difficult, as the clinician persists in being unconditionally positive, regardless of the client's impossible demands as they desperately seek a negative or impotence. Alternatives to unconditional positive regard include asking questions, remaining silent, interpreting and ending the session. If a client explained that he always demonstrated an attitude of unconditional positive regard I would tend to regard it as a symptom.

Warfare, conflict and clinical work

What is the job of the clinician? Not to befriend the client, or to be reassuring or comforting. Friends don't get paid, and —if they really are friends— they always have their own axe to grind, their own demands, and would in most cases become intolerant of a negative transference. For how many years would a real friend put up with your highly personal complaints about him? In any case it is almost certain that the clinician has no authority or knowledge with which to reassure or comfort his client. Comforting a client will —in cases where it works— distract both of you from his real underlying problem. Where a client is comforted, it will be impossible for the client to take a new position in relation to their suffering. Comforting is likely to be taken as a quick solution that short circuits the tougher job of exploring the large-scale underlying problem. As a comforter you will become identified with your client's ego, where the job of the ego is to mislead and cover over the truth. Obviously, if you are working with your client to cover up the fundamental and hidden truths of his suffering then the work is either likely to be prolonged indefinitely, or broken off prematurely. From the psychoanalytic point of view comforting a client, whether it succeeds or fails, is a waste of everyone's time. In terms of tactics, strategy and policy, 'comfort' is the attempt to avoid one particular battle, regardless of the long-term cost, even to the point of endlessly prolonging or losing the war.

There are striking parallels between love, war and clinical work, so looking at one of these can cast light on the others. In Chapter Five we asked: What form or shape do conflict, love, desire and ideas take? Freud's explanations —inspired by his clients' speech— were the myths of the Primal Horde and Oedipus as ways of understanding the human condition. These myths help explain the types of suffering seen in the clinic. The Primal Horde and Oedipus are both stories of conflict, struggle and love. War is another well structured phenomenon or form of conflict that is very human. An analysis of war informs clinical technique.

Quotes in the left column is taken from the classic *The Art of Warfare* by Sun Pin[409]; those on the right are Freud's:

'In the business of war, there is no invariable strategic advantage which can be relied upon at all times . . . Military victory can restore states that have perished and revive lines that had become extinct, but failure to gain victory can result in one's territory being pared away and the altars of one's state being put at risk.	*'. . . nearly everything still awaits definitive settlement [in the field of technique]'* [410] *'The answer to the questions of technique in analysis is never matter of course. Although there may perhaps be more than one good road to follow, still there are very many bad ones, and a comparison of the various methods cannot fail to be illuminating, even if it should not lead to a decision in favour of any particular one.'* [411] *'. . . much will be gained if we succeed in transforming your hysterical misery into common unhappiness. With a mental life that has been restored to health you will be better armed against that unhappiness.'* [412]
'For this reason, military situations must be examined with the greatest care. But, having said this, one who takes pleasure in war will perish, and one who coverts the spoils of victory will incur disgrace. War is not something to be enjoyed, and victory is not something to profit from. Move into action only after having made thorough preparations.'	*' "Wild" analysts . . . do more harm to the cause of psychoanalysis than to individual patients . . . The [wild analyst] has done himself harm and helped to intensify the prejudices which patients feel, owing to their natural resistances, against the ways of psychoanalysts. And this can be avoided'* [413] *'. . . I have secured a firm basis for deciding which of the weapons in the therapeutic armoury against the neuroses is indicated in the case concerned.'* [414] *'. . . analysis can only draw upon definite and limited amounts of energy which have to be measured against the hostile forces. And it seems as if victory is in fact as a rule on the side of the big battalions.'* [415]

[409] Sun Pin, *The Art of Warfare*, trans Lau and Ames, Ballantine Books, 1996, p129.

[410] S Freud, Future Prospects of Psychoanalytic Therapy, *SE 11*, [1910], 1976, p144.

[411] S Freud, The Handling of Dream Interpretation in Psychoanalysis, *SE 20,* [1911], 1976, p91.

[412] S Freud, The Psychotherapy of Hysteria, *SE 2*, [1893], 1976, p305.

[413] S Freud, Wild Analysis, *SE 11*, [1910], 1976, p227.

[414] S Freud, The Psychotherapy of Hysteria, *SE 2*, [1893], 1976, p266.

[415] S Freud, Analysis Terminable and Interminable, *SE 23*, [1937], 1976, p240.

It is sometimes a wise strategy to occasionally lose one or another battle, in order to win the war, whatever that turns out to mean in each client's case. We will return later to this idea of the clinician paying a price for the position he takes, and what it ultimately allows for the client, when we look at 'The End of analysis'.

To make more sense of Lacan's distinctions of tactics, strategy and policy we should look more closely at the idea of war in the clinical work because of Freud's claim of parallels between clinical work and war:

'We seek to bring this conflict to a head . . . analysis must be carried out in a state of frustration' [416]

'we have to fight against his inertia'

'Analytic experience has taught us that the better [the desire of the client] is always the enemy of the good [of the Other]'

'The rules governing the course of mental acts are different in the ego and the id; the ego pursues different purposes and by other methods. . . . Think of the difference as between 'the front' and 'behind the lines', as things were in the war. We were not surprised then that some things were different at the front from what they were behind the lines, and that many things were permitted behind the lines which had to be forbidden at the front.' [417]

War is not a simple phenomenon. It is always true to say that in each conflict or war there is always some love. I do not mean 'love' as a metaphor. The love may be a powerful attachment to an ideal, such as patriotism —the love of one's country— or the love of something possessed by an other. Perhaps a country, such as the deep love or envy that Iraq's Saddam Hussein had for the oil fields of Kuwait that he temporarily conquered. This perhaps is no different from the loves and hates that so many brothers and sisters have for one another and their parents.

One of the interesting facts about war is that the opponents often have quite different views about both the causes of the conflict, and the outcome that they would regard as ideal. One warring party may be content with some variety of mutual co-existence, while another says that he will only rest when his opponent is annihilated. These different factions can be identified for instance at various points in the conflicts between Arab factions and the Israelis, and between the Serbian and the Kosovan Albanians. [418]

---

[416] S Freud, Analysis Terminable and Interminable, *SE 23* [1937], 1976, p231.

[417] S Freud, The Question of Lay Analysis, *SE 14*, [1926], 1976, p196.

[418] Hegel's concept of the struggle for recognition, unto the death bears on this theme. See the section of Hegel's *Phenomenology of Spirit* called 'Independence and Dependence of Self Consciousness: Lordship (Mastery) and Bondage (Slavery), in the

In the clinic clients often volunteer a goal, or explain when asked, what they would like as an outcome from the clinical work. Usually clients claim that one or another symptom is the cause of much suffering in their life, and that they find their situation intolerable. Clients will sometimes even specifically ask their clinician if he is able to remove their symptoms, and ask for details of techniques that are tailor-made to address their symptoms, and for books to be recommended that can be studied and followed like a recipe. Such clients are behaving as if they were straightforward consumers who can clearly state what they want, and then get it. If psychoanalysis were a straightforward matter of questions and answers then, prior to analysis, clients could articulate their problems and desires clearly if asked. Try asking a neurotic client during the first few sessions what they desire. Their answer will go all round the houses and not end anywhere definitive or consistent. Desire is primarily unconscious, and is therefore 'spoken of' symptomatically, in ways that cannot be easily understood, as slips of the tongue, dreams, jokes and symptoms. Symptoms cannot be sold in an idealised financial exchange —without transference— for a fixed predetermined fee, or a fixed number of sessions. The discourse of the analyst is not the discourse of the consumer, that is, of the slave and master, or of the hysteric; a competent clinician will not be misled or fooled, either by such a request or by the symptoms presented; if a clinician wages war on one or another symptom, directly taking that symptom as his enemy, then he will be wasting his energy on an alibi, dummy or effigy, and it is very likely that no analysis will take place. The clinician will have squandered his efforts on fighting a counterfeit, just like the decoys, lures, masquerades and misinformation that are used in war and love. The often genuine distress and suffering that clients present is an important mask, covering the underlying conflict and problems in their life, that have caused their surface suffering and unconscious enjoyment.

Remember that the clinician is a witness to *the result* of a conflict. The conflict of interests that every client has had with their desire is a kind of war. If it were a straightforward matter for your client to follow his desire he wouldn't have consulted you. So where do you, as clinician, stand in relation to his conflict?

Initially you stand outside your client's conflict; you are not yet part of his war of love, but, if the work goes well, and the transference takes a strong grip, he will have invited you to take a key transitional role. This is a dangerous invitation: the job description he will give you will be far from simple, and will

---

chapter on 'Self Consciousness'', Oxford University Press, trans Findlay, 1977, p11-119. The Freudian and Lacanian variables of 'desire', 'enjoyment', 'mastery', 'truth' dependence' and 'consciousness' can be found here. Lacan relied on the philosopher Kojeve's reading of Hegel: *'Introduction to the Reading of Hegel'*, ed Bloom, trans Nichols, Cornell University Press. The section called 'In Place of an Introduction' may suffice.

certainly change over time, if the work progresses. What kind of role might you have in your client's conflicts that will allow him to lead his life in a different way? One of make believe, of fiction, transference or supposition of knowledge.

If you have no part of any kind in your client's imaginary conflict it will not be possible to do any clinical work. It will only be possible to carry out psychoanalytic work if your client can find a place for you in his conflict. This is a cause of tension and difficulty in psychoanalytic work: on the one hand you must allow your client to imagine that you have a special place in his conflicts: on the other hand your client may —on rare occasions— become overwhelmed by what he imagines you to represent, to the extent that he can no longer tolerate clinical work. You will have to discreetly monitor your client's perception of you so as not to take up the position that your client finds intolerable. Managing such sensitivities is sometimes referred to as 'handling transference'.

Conflictual relationships are not without love or attachment; you have two main allies in the clinical work: your client's desire —which is typically unconscious— and your client's 'positive transference', which relies on his demand, on the demand for love. You also have two enemies: your client's negative transference, which also relies on his demand, and his ego, which is often conscious. These are some of the main warring elements. There are others which we will come to later.

A simple tactical analysis of the transference suggests two kinds: a positive transference in which the client has a soft spot for the clinician which may be expressed as a kind of love or eroticism, and a negative transference in which the client experiences hostile feelings towards the clinician. Initially positive transference appears to be an ally, and negative transference an enemy.

As in any long and complex war that covers a wide territory, such as in World War II, it is not unusual for allies and enemies to change sides, especially when there is a change in the odds as to who is going to win or lose. Surprises and unmaskings are common. As the war or clinical work progresses, so the resources on each side change: one of the biggest variables or changes is transference. Allies can sometimes be difficult and demanding and occasionally enemies can be useful.

It is not unusual for positive and negative transference to develop to heights that surprise and disorientate the client. In one case a client repeatedly declared his love for his clinician, even explaining that he understood transference but declared that his feelings were 'the real thing'. Over many months of being pestered by this client the clinician finally resorted to asking: *'What should I say to my husband?'* Introducing this third or Oedipal element enabled the client to start producing new material.

Freud advised that: *'Neither the love nor the hostility reach extreme heights in the transference.'* [419]

And Lacan that: *'The operation and manipulation of the transference are to be regulated in a way that maintains a distance between the point at which the subject sees himself as loveable —and that other point where the subject sees himself caused as a lack . . . the gap constituted by the . . . division of the subject.'* [420]

Sometimes a supposedly neutral party turns out in the end not to be neutral at all — just like Switzerland— who secretly benefited from the conflict and torment of World War II, and was surely very disappointed when it all ended. Switzerland stole many thousands of trusting depositors' money, and also profited on a huge scale by knowingly exchanging the gold that the Nazis ripped out of their victims' teeth for cash, which paid for the continuation of the war. Switzerland deliberately employed professional liars to deceive the international community and her victims for many years about Switzerland's conduct, and tried to destroy any documents that might have led the way to the truth, to an unmasking of her real desire for money and gold rather than neutrality. The neutrality was a mask, a lie or alibi that allowed Switzerland to profit from suffering and to enjoy it.

Switzerland stands for the symptom or the ego in clinical work. Sometimes the client complains bitterly about his symptom, but there are nearly always symptoms or aspects of a single symptom about which the client proclaims his neutrality: 'It does not matter to me, one way or the other, I have no interest in it.' What is the client hiding and gaining with his alibi of neutrality? Jouissance, the secret enjoyment and bliss that compensates for his suffering.

For many reasons money sometimes represents the client's symptom, amongst these is the equation *'I will get rid of my symptom if I part with enough money* [421] *':'*. It is not unusual for money —as in the case of Switzerland— to represent the jouissance of the symptom, and to cover over the suffering. Just as Switzerland's project was to profit as much as possible, whilst keeping up their charade of neutrality in the theatre of war, with its secret concentration camps, so the trick of the symptom is to produce as much jouissance as possible without giving the game away, and betraying the truth of the client's desire, which is never neutral.

So there is an enjoyment, a gain, from the symptom masking the suffering. If it were not for the suffering the client would never complain to a clinician: yet

---

[419] S Freud, The Handling of Dream Interpretation in Psychoanalysis, *SE 12*, [1912], 1976.

[420] J Lacan, *The Four Fundamental Concepts of Psychoanalysis*, trans Sheridan, Pelican, London, 1979, p268.

[421] That is the equation of money and jouissance.

the symptom that is so entangled with the suffering is an important enemy in the clinical work because of the satisfaction it gives the client. The client has a major investment in maintaining his symptom. It is valuable to him, and he has paid a price for it. Be careful: if you are seen to treat the symptom in anything other than a neutral way the ego will make the work very much harder. If the clinician is seen to attack the symptom —which is an important source of satisfaction— the client will almost certainly resist. Freud warns us:

'We are reminded that analysis can only draw upon definite and limited amounts of energy which have to be measured against the hostile forces. And it seems as if victory is in fact as a rule on the side of the big battalions.' [422]

At points in the work, when the suffering is at its height, so too may be the jouissance. The jouissance will be the big battalion. As the work progresses, neurotic clients will be able to give up some of their jouissance in exchange for the truth, for the truth and meaning of their symptom and desire. This is one reason why clinical work in Lacan's tradition takes so long; it takes years to build enough support from the ally of the analyst, from the client's desire and subjectivity to overcome the demanding position of his ego or symptom. Actually the ego of neurotics is never really defeated; it is like Tom in 'Tom and Jerry'. It doesn't matter how often the lies and tricks are exposed, or how often the tactics of the ego are beaten down and flattened, the ego always bounces back, but not always to take up the same position.

It is crucial for the clinician to show relatively little or no interest in the client's symptoms, especially after the early sessions. Of course symptoms have a special place in the client's suffering, but if the client thinks that an apparently neutral item effectively disguises the painful truth of their conflict, then they will rely on it to the exclusion of other material. One client repeatedly interrupted the clinical work with complaints about his illicit use of drugs and his clichéd remarks about his status as an addict, and tried to rely on this topic as a strategy for avoiding discussion of more difficult underlying issues.

'Tactics', 'strategy' and 'policy'

'The analyst is less free in his strategy than in his tactics . . . The analyst is even less free as to that which dominates strategy and tactics, namely, his policy . . .' [423]

---

[422] S Freud, Analysis Terminable and Interminable, *SE 23*, [1937a], 1976, p240.
[423] J Lacan, *Ecrits,* The Direction of the Treatment, trans Sheridan, Tavistock Routledge, London, [1966], 1980, p230.

Just as a politician, general or marketing manager might do, Lacan categorised the actions of the analyst as: 'tactics', 'strategy' and 'policy'. These are three levels or hierarchical ways of understanding interpretations.

The clinician has almost no control over his policy because it is an ethical topic and fixed from the start. So for example the clinician always has the policy of inviting the client to free associate, to say whatever comes to mind without any censoring. Any other policy would fatally contradict the necessarily fixed policy of psychoanalysis. Can you imagine at the first session inviting a client to talk only about topic x, or to talk about anything other than y? This is exactly what many short term or 'focussed' approaches do! The trouble with such approaches is that they cannot see what is out of focus, that is those items that they have excluded.

Strategy covers the middle ground over which the clinician will exercise some control according to the idiosyncrasies of individual clients. For instance a clinician may or may not decide to invite a neurotic client to use the couch after a certain point in the work when he has become confident of his diagnosis and the client's responsiveness to transference and the treatment. If for instance the client had been sexually abused after having been instructed to lie down it might be wise to postpone inviting him to use the couch, perhaps indefinitely.

Tactics covers the smallest level of detail, over which the clinician has a high level of control. For example a clinician may choose to remain silent when the client asks a question that touches on a particular topic. Tactics are discretionary.

Psychoanalysis works by bringing into question and undermining some of the ego's tactics and strategy, but not its policy. The ego's policy of lying in order to hide conflicts of desire cannot be brought into question by psychoanalysis: the ego of a neurotic can be relied on as trustworthy when it comes to its policy of deception because its very nature and job is deceit. Freud's position is clear:

'It is obvious that this ego is not a trustworthy or impartial agency. The ego is indeed the power which disavows the unconscious and has degraded it into being repressed; so how can we trust it to be fair to the unconscious? The most prominent elements in what is thus repressed are the repudiated demands of sexuality, and it is quite self-evident that we should never be able to guess their extent and importance from the ego's conceptions. From the moment the notion of repression dawns on us, we are warned against making one of the two contesting parties (and the victorious one, at that) into being judge in the dispute. We are prepared to find that the ego's assertions will lead us astray. If we are to believe the ego, it was active at every point and itself willed and

created its symptoms. But we know that it puts up with a good amount of passivity, which it afterwards tries to disguise and gloss over.' [424]

The ridiculous idea that clinicians can somehow train clients' egos or even their own to reliably tell the truth is rather like expecting politicians to tell the truth and generals to be peace makers. The idea of the ego as *'like a politician who sees the truth but wants to keep his place in popular favour'* comes straight from Freud:

'We see this . . . ego as a poor creature owing service to three masters and consequently menaced by three dangers: from the external world, from the libido of the id [that is the love or drive of the unconscious], and from the severity of the superego . . . As a frontier creature the ego tries to mediate . . . ; it is also a submissive slave who courts his master's love. . . . it tries to remain on good terms with the id, it clothes the id's unconscious commands with its preconscious rationalisations...; it disguises the id's conflicts with reality and, if possible, its conflicts with the superego too. . . . it . . . often yields to the temptation to become sycophantic, opportunist and lying, like a politician who sees the truth but wants to keep his place in popular favour.' [425]

The policy of the Lacanian or Freudian analyst is not to be taken in by the neurotic's ego but to side step, evade and trick it. The idea — central to Ego Psychology — that the ego should be developed, made stronger, more adaptive, and an accurate mirror of reality is totally counter to Freud's and Lacan's therapeutic project. To 'strengthen the ego' would be to develop that part of the psyche that deceives. To side with the ego is necessarily to oppose psychoanalysis. The 'conflict free zone' —the ideal of 'Ego Psychology'— is, in Freudian and Lacanian terms a program for lying because life and following one's desire are necessarily conflictual. That is why, in order to survive, we must have an ego, an agency for managing conflict through lying or keeping secrets.

Just as ordinary people distrust government and politicians, Lacanians distrust the 'government' of the subject by the ego. Hardly any adult believes that it is the job of managers, politicians or parents to tell the truth. Because life is riddled with conflicts, if you don't keep secrets, you have to tell lies. This leaves the question: how should a clinician treat obstacles set up by the client's ego? The obstacles that must be worked through are not peripheral but central. It is these obstacles that actually constitute the work rather than being an irrelevant distraction. For this reason Lacan argued that resistance is on the side of the analyst. So what should a clinician do with 'the client's resistance'? Freud answers:

---

[424] S Freud, The Common Neurotic State, Introductory Lectures on Psychoanalysis, *SE 16*, [1916], 1976, p380.
[425] S Freud, The Ego and the Id, *SE 19*, [1923b], 1976, p56.

'The way to treat resistance . . . is to let it grow until it defeats itself.' [426]

And: *'One of [psychoanalysis'] rules is that whatever interrupts the progress of analytic work . . . is of course only to be taken . . . as a warning to analysts.'* [427]

This point is clarified: *'The analyst thus finds himself in the position — curious for a doctor — of coming to the help of a disease, and of procuring it its due of attention. But only those who entirely misunderstand the nature of psychoanalysis will lay stress upon this phase of the work and suppose that on its account harm is likely to be done by analysis. The fact is that you must catch your thief before you can hang him, and that it requires some expenditure of labour to get securely hold of the pathological structures at the destruction of which the treatment is aimed.'* [428]

Some psychoanalytic tactics are structurally similar to some martial arts techniques, such as those used in judo where the defensive or aggressive energy invested by the opponent is used against him. Who exactly is the opponent? Not 'the person of the client' but the client's ego and symptom. The effectiveness of many Lacanian clinical techniques relies in essential part on the driving force of the client's ego, for example the ending of a session on a client's vehement denial.

One client repeatedly introduced material about his sister. During one session the client became increasingly indignant and protested: *'I am not in therapy to waste time talking about my sister but about myself'*. The clinician asked: *'Doesn't your sister have anything to do with you?* The client replied *'no . . .'* and started to elaborate an argument. The clinician said: *'Let's end there today'*. So the client failed to engineer an argument with his clinician concerning the importance of his sister. Instead, by ending the session, the clinician left the client to focus on the value of his own denial, and at the same time avoided an unnecessary fight that he could not possibly have won. It would have been fruitless for the clinician and client to have had an argument about the importance of the client's sister. The client's ego could always easily win such a battle, and so cause the clinician to lose the whole war that he is waging against his client's ego, for the client's desire. If your clinician allows you to exercise your demand to argue with him it is unlikely that your unconscious desire will emerge. It is good to lose the battle and win the war, but it is better not to have the battle and still win the war:

---

[426] S Freud, quoted by Blanton, S. *Diary of My Analysis with Sigmund Freud*, New York, Hawthorn Books, 1971, p121.
[427] S Freud, The Interpretation of Dreams, *SE 4*, [1900a], 1976, p517.
[428] S Freud, Analysis of a Phobia in a 5 year old boy, *SE 10*, [1909b], 1976.

'A good battle is worthy of a man's mettle but . . . real heroism consists in not fighting at all.' [429]

How is interpretation in Lacanian clinical work carried out?

Most interpretations should either be true, or expressed as a question or a hypothesis. If you are in doubt as to whether you should say something or not, say nothing.

Sometimes when a Lacanian interprets he will have a clear hypothesis in mind about the meaning at stake for his client, but often he will have no idea at all. Not having any idea what your client has been imagining is fine. It is a surprising but common observation that clients often find importance in interpretations in which the clinician understands nothing.

In Scharff's version —on the left— of object relations theory the concept of truth — which is the exclusive property of symbols or language— has been subverted by a kind of metaphor of the clinician's, not the client's: on the right Lacan argues against Scharff's approach:

'Instead of the analyst as a kind of feeding breast, another version has slid in: the psychoanalyst, as an understanding object, provides a form of truthfulness that acts as the food for mental nourishment and development.' [430]	*'Of course the trap is that in interpreting you give the subject something to feed himself on, the word, even the book which is behind it, and that the word remains all the same the locus of desire, even if you give it in such a way that this locus is not recognisable, I mean that if this locus remains, for the desire of the subject, uninhabitable.* *To respond to the demand for food, to the frustrated demand in a nourishing signifier is something which leaves elided the following, that beyond any food of the word, what the subject really needs is what it signifies metonymically, it is that which is not at any point of this word and therefore that each time you introduce —no doubt you are obliged to do it— the metaphor, you remain on the same path which gives consistency to the symptom, no doubt a more simplified symptom but still a symptom, in any case with respect to the desire that it is a question of separating out.'* [431]

[429] F Nietzsche, *My Sister and I*, Amok Books, Los Angeles 1990, p154.

[430] D Scharff, *Refinding The Object And Reclaiming The Self*, Jason Aronson Inc, London, 1992.

[431] J Lacan, Transference Seminar, unpublished, trans Gallagher, 15 March 1961.

Lacan is arguing above that it is not the job of the analyst to provide the client with the meaning or meanings of his symptom as the perfectly balanced diet of therapeutic truth: it is the work of the client to discover the truth of his symptom and fantasy. Interpretation is not the mutual sharing of an understanding or idea that the clinician and client are to jointly believe, but the establishment of difference that constitutes the client's desire: not the sameness of repetition that constitutes his demand; differences are established through analysing, through the identification of similarities and differences in the speech of the client:

'Human differences are mainly differences in language. Would, then, a single language, adopted by all races and nations, solve most of our difficulties? Hardly. We need all of our differences for those eternal and fierce struggles in which our ideas and passions are refined. If we could trace the origin of all our cultural wealth we should discover that at least eighty percent of it resides in those very differences of language that appear so troublesome.' [432]

These similarities and differences can be identified by analysing the client's speech at the phonetic level, the syntactic level and the semantic level. The client's speech is the proof of his difference and desire. This Lacanian approach is the opposite of Scharff's:

' Object relations approach . . . [with its] mutual involvement of both patient and therapist as complete human beings, each with a range of conscious and unconscious communication through which they can share complementary, resonating object relations systems.' [433]

Instead of relying on this unchecked and uncheckable idea of sharing an imaginary 'object' between client and clinician, Freud and Lacan relied on the careful analysis of something symbolic and objective: the language or signifiers produced by the client because as Freud claimed, *' symptoms are . . . transcriptions . . .'* [434], in perfect accord with Lacan's observation that *'Commenting on a text is like doing an analysis.'* [435]

Categorical Interpretation

Categorical interpretation is a mainstay of Lacanian practice. Paradoxically it is both provocative —helping the client to produce new material because of its

---

[432] F Nietzsche, *My Sister and I,* Amok, Los Angeles, 1990, p133.

[433] D Scharff, *Refinding The Object And Reclaiming The Self,* Jason Aronson Inc, London, 1992.

[434] S Freud, Three Essays on the Theory of Sexuality, *SE 7* [1905d], 1976, p164.

[435] J Lacan, *The Seminar of Jacques Lacan, Book One, Freud's Papers on Technique of Psychoanalysis, 1953-1954,* ed Miller, trans Forrester, Cambridge University Press, Cambridge, England, 1988, p73.

ambiguity— and simultaneously uncontroversial because it is true. A Lacanian might say: *'In the two stories you told there was a man with a woman, and a second woman had a problem with the first woman'*. Such categorical interpretations should always be true, referring to the categories found in the speech of the client. It is not for you to say what the meaning of these categories is for the client. Meaning and interpretation are related but different concepts. In the clinician's mind there may be an Oedipal construction regarding two rivalarous women, competing for the love of one man, what you want for lunch or your own love life. There is an important point here: it doesn't matter much what you think or imagine, what you say with a categorical interpretation is demonstrably true as an analysis of your client's speech. It is commonplace for clients to find profound meanings in categorical interpretations that the clinician has made but understands little or nothing of.

The minor but necessary downside of categorical interpretation is that the interpretation will sometimes 'miss' the material that represents a conflict that the client is struggling with. But what is the alternative? If the clinician insists on trying to hit what he imagines is 'the bull's-eye of the client's unconscious conflict' with a 'complete interpretation' every time, then there will certainly be a high price to pay. Such an ambitious clinician is likely to frighten the client away, and must make many false interpretations since he must rely on material that is not within the client's speech but drawn from his imagination.

If a client asks of a categorical interpretation: 'What does it mean?' You might say 'I don't know', that it is not your job to provide meanings, or if the client's transference is well established it might be a fine point to end the session, so leaving the client with the job of finding his meanings in his speech. Categorical interpretations stress, in a highly ambiguous way something precise. For example: 'In each of the stories you told there was a man with a woman, and a second woman had a problem with the first woman'. Because this interpretation refers to a truth in the client's speech of a general form it leaves the client free to explore — in greater detail — the way in which your interpretation refers uniquely to him. Imagine instead that a different style of highly detailed interpretation was made. In this detailed interpretation far more of the client's imaginary detail is likely to be excluded, by the clinician having included so much of his own material. Here is an example of such a non-Lacanian interpretation: 'In each of the stories you told the man with a woman represented your father having intercourse with your mother. The second woman who always has a problem with the first woman is your self'. Whatever is lurking in the client's unconscious is likely to be better represented with the minimum addition of material. Lacanian clinical work helps clients discover meanings in their speech, not with a superior knowledge but with a superior ignorance, through making categorical interpretations that generalise hidden truths in their speech through following the client's *'logical thread'* [436].

How to listen to clients

Below Freud elaborates the technique of free association through examining the phenomenon of censorship, which is one of the functions of the ego:

'Let us imagine what might have happened to a book, at a time when books were not printed in editions but were written out individually. We will suppose that a book of this kind contained statements which in later times were regarded as undesirable — as, for instance . . . the writings of Flavius Josephus must have contained passages about Jesus Christ which were offensive to later Christendom. At the present day, the only defensive mechanism to which the official censorship could resort would be to confiscate and destroy every copy of the whole edition.

At that time, however, various methods were used for making the book innocuous. One way would be for the offending passages to be thickly crossed through so that they were illegible. In that case they could not be transcribed, and the next copyist of the book would produce a text which was unexceptionable but which had gaps in certain passages, and so might be unintelligible in them. Another way, however, if the authorities were not satisfied with this, but wanted also to conceal any indication that the text had been mutilated, would be for them to proceed to distort the text. Single words would be left out or replaced by others, and new sentences interpolated. Best of all, the whole passage would be erased and a new one which said exactly the opposite put in its place. The next transcriber could then produce a text that aroused no suspicion but which was falsified. It no longer contained what the author wanted to say; and it is highly probable that the corrections had not been made in the direction of truth. . . . we may say that repression has the same relation to the other methods of defence as omission has to distortion of the text, and we may discover in the different forms of this falsification parallels to the variety of ways in which the ego is altered. An attempt may be made to raise the objection that the analogy goes wrong in an essential point, for the distortion of a text is the work of a tendentious censorship, no counterpart to which is to be found in the development of the ego. But this is not so' [437]

'The technique [of psychoanalysis] . . . is a very simple one. It disclaims the use of any special aids, even of note-taking, as we shall see, and simply consists in making no effort to concentrate the attention on anything in

---

[436] S Freud, The Psychotherapy of Hysteria, *SE 2*, [1893], 1976, p292.
[437] S Freud, Analysis Terminable and Interminable, *SE 23* [1937a], 1976, p236.

particular, and in maintaining in regard to all that one hears the same measure of calm, quiet attentiveness — of 'evenly-hovering attention' . . . In this way a strain which could not be kept up for several hours daily and a danger inseparable from deliberate attentiveness are avoided. For as soon as attention is deliberately concentrated in a certain degree, one begins to select from the material before one; one point will be fixed in the mind with particular clearness and some other consequently disregarded, and in this selection one's expectations or one's inclinations will be followed. This is just what must not be done . . . It must not be forgotten that the meaning of the things one hears is, at all events for, the most part, only recognizable later on.

'It will be seen, therefore, that the principle of evenly-distributed attention is the necessary corollary to the demand on the patient to communicate everything that occurs to him without criticism or selection. If the physician behaves otherwise he is throwing aside most of the advantage to be gained by the patient's obedience to the 'fundamental rule of psychoanalysis'. For the physician the rule may be expressed thus: All conscious exertion is to be withheld from the capacity for attention, and one's 'unconscious memory is to be given full play; or to express it in terms of technique, pure and simple: One has simply to listen and not to trouble to keep in mind anything in particular.

'What one achieves in this way will be sufficient for all requirements during the treatment. Those elements of the material which have a connection with one another will be at the conscious disposal of the physician; the rest, as yet unconnected, chaotic and indistinguishable, seems at first to disappear, but rises readily into recollection as soon as the patient brings something further to which it is related, and by which it can be developed. The undeserved compliment of a 'remarkably good memory' which the patient pays when one reproduces some detail after a year and a day is then accepted with a smile, whereas a conscious effort to retain a recollection of the point would probably have resulted in nothing.' [438]

What exactly did Freud mean by this *'evenly-hovering attention'*, *'in regard to all that one hears'*? As is usual with Freud this question, in practical terms, has a complicated answer. But, put in a condensed form it amounts to no more or less than Lacan's claim that: *'the unconscious is structured like a language';* where the clinician's unconscious identifies truths and connections in the client's speech.

If you are analysing speech then there are many levels of language, and concordantly many levels of analysis. Amongst these are: the phonetic level, the syntactic level and the semantic level.

---

[438] S Freud, Recommendations to Physicians Practising Psychoanalysis, *SE 12,* [1912], 1976, p112.

The phonetic level

Many slips of the tongue are at a phonetic level. There is often just one little phoneme, one part of a word that has changed that betrays the client's unconscious desire. Here is an example. A boyfriend, on departing from his first visit to his girlfriend's family, a meeting that had not gone well said: *'Thank you for your hostility'*, instead of *'Thank you for your hospitality'*.

The syntactic level

In some cases it is a change in the position of the words, that is a change of grammar or syntax that that is interesting and says something about the truth of the client's unconscious. Here is a variation on a postcard cliché:

'The weather is here, I wish you were lovely.'

The following advertised a camping shop's wares:

'Now are the tents of our winter discount'.

The semantic level

There are times when a client will surprise herself by saying something that is perfectly correct grammatically, with all the phonemes in the right place. The surprise comes from the explicit meaning of the words! That is from a semantic analysis. It could be the realisation, after much difficult struggling and working through, that a client who has for years declared only hatred for her father, being suddenly, for first time, astonished to hear herself say: 'I love my father'.

It is often the client who makes the best interpretations. It may be a mistake to continue a session for more than a moment after such a new and different point has been reached. To continue may help the client distract themselves with other material and discount the importance of their discovery.

As you analyse your client's speech at these levels in your own mind, what analyses are you carrying out? Far too many to make a list of, or even to be fully conscious of. When you notice any similarity in two or more pieces of your client's speech, it is often best not to jump in immediately, as if to say 'snap, here are two the same'. Waiting a moment longer or perhaps for a few sessions will often provide useful clues. Clients often insist on re presenting material, until they find a new way through. Freud called this repetition 'the return of the repressed'.

So Freud's 'evenly hovering attention' covers all three levels of analysis: the phonetic, the syntactic and the semantic levels. It is as if you are fishing with three sets of nets, the first has large holes, the second medium sized, and the third small holes. You have to keep looking in all of your nets, to see if you have caught a fish. This analogy suggests that the psychoanalyst ought to check all three nets simultaneously, all over the surface of every one, before identifying a catch. Once a catch has been identified there is more work to do: you have to decide what to do with it: to keep it or throw it back in. When fishing the analyst listens out for absences and presences, for pointed references such a repetition that appears redundant from the point of view of semantics or meaning, a repeated name, a gaps or hint of material that has not been provided such as the report of a conversation without any reference to the content of the conversation. There are no comprehensive set of rules for discovering such fish: each language and subculture will have its own.

Before we look at criteria for types of different interpretation and interventions such as ending a session, let's ask if this fishing technique is a realistic demand to place on clinicians?

The task of fishing with three nets or filters requires listening to clients with the phonetic net, the syntactic net and the semantic net, and simultaneously monitoring every part of each one. Is there any evidence that ordinary people, or clinicians are clever enough to do this?

Yes. The most persuasive piece of evidence comes from an ordinary phenomenon. Within psychology it is known as 'the cocktail party problem': if you are at any gathering of chatty people you will almost certainly have noticed that if you hear your name, or some other interesting word in someone else's conversation —possibly one occurring on the other side of the room— then you will be able to backtrack to the start of the previous phrase or even the whole sentence in which the interesting word was heard.

How is it possible for us to do this? There seems to be only one plausible explanation: we must necessarily be listening to every single conversation within earshot, perhaps to as many as six or seven different conversations simultaneously, and carrying out some analysis on every one of them, most of its unconsciously.

If we are capable of this much analysis, it should be possible to monitor just three different levels or types of analysis when listening to just the one person. In practice it is, but it is hard work and takes a bit of getting used to. This magnificent ability that we all have goes some way towards confirming Freud's claim that: *'Every man possesses in his unconscious an instrument by which he can interpret the expressions of the unconscious of another . . .'* [439] and Lacan's closely related claim that: *'the unconscious is structured like a language'* [440]

[439] S Freud, The Disposition To Obsessional Neurosis, *SE 12*, [1913], 1976, p320.
[440] J Lacan, *Ecrits*, Function and Field of Speech and Language, Sheridan, Tavistock, London, 1977, p56.

It also explains why Lacan recommended —in earnest— that analysts in training should practise on crosswords. Many crossword puzzles, especially the more difficult ones can only be solved by using at least two levels of analysis simultaneously, that is with *'evenly-hovering attention'* as ought to be used with clients.[441] Here is an example of Freud's own simultaneously phonetic, syntactic and semantic crossword style analysis, carried out on the speech of his obsessional client known as 'The Ratman' in accordance with Lacan's claim that the unconscious is structured like a language:

'Our patient used to employ as a defensive formula rapidly pronouncing "aber" [German for 'but'] accompanied by a gesture of repudiation. He told me on one occasion that this formula had become altered recently; he now no longer said "a'ber" but "abe'r". When he was asked to give the reason for this new departure, he declared that the mute 'e' of the second syllable gave him no sense of security against the intrusion, which he so much dreaded, of some foreign and contradictory element, and that he had therefore decided to accent the "e". This explanation . . . was, however, inadequate; the most that it could claim to be was a rationalisation.

'The truth was that "abe'r" was an approximation towards the similar sounding "Abwehr" ['defence'], a term which he had learnt in the course of our theoretical discussions of psychoanalysis. He had thus put the treatment to an illegitimate and "delirious" use in order to strengthen a defensive formula.

'Another time he told me about his principal magic word ["Glejsamen"], which was an apotropaic against every evil; he had put it together out of the initial letters of the most powerfully beneficent of his prayers and had clapped on an "amen" at the end of it . . . when he told it me, I could not help noticing that the word was in fact an anagram of the name of his lady [Gisela.] Her name contained an "s", and this he had put last, that is, immediately before the "amen" at the end. We may say, therefore, that by this process he had brought his "Samen" [German for "semen"] into contact with the woman he loved; in imagination, that is to say, he had masturbated with her. He himself, however, had never noticed this very obvious connection . . . '[442]

What does the clinician do with his analyses? How does he implement them in his interpretations with the client? Does the clinician straightforwardly share such speculations with his client? In the above case, in the session in which the material of the second paragraph was raised a Lacanian might have —whatever he imagined— have said no more than something along the following lines:

'You appeal to God in the name of a woman.'

---

[441] See 12 in the Appendix for: *'Progress in scientific work is just as it is in an analysis.'*

[442] S Freud, Notes Upon a Case of Obsessional Neurosis, *SE 10*, [1909], 1979, p224.

Or:

'Your semen comes at the end, of a prayer.'

Alternatively:

'There is a woman's name, semen and a prayer.'

Or perhaps it would be a good time to remind him:

'You said that you repudiated your faith in God —and presumably your prayers too —when you discovered that your supposed friend intruded. He was being friendly with you only in order to gain access to a woman.'

This interpretation reintroduces material produced earlier that appears to bear on the material in hand. The relevant material is in the footnote below.[443]

Such interpretations —that rework the client's speech— but leave open the question of meaning are far more likely to provoke the client to produce new material, allowing him to change his position than cleverly informing him of your dubious insights. It is important to stress that the value of such interpretations relies on two things: their being constructed from the client's material and their meaning being forced open. The clinician's ignorance has no bearing or very little on the value of the interpretation for the client.

Some problems of translation or interpretation

What was Freud appealing to when he wrote:

'The best way of speaking about such things [sexual matters] is to be dry and direct; and that is at the same time the method furthest removed from the prurience with which the same subjects are handled in 'society', and to which girls and women alike are so thoroughly accustomed. I call bodily organs and

---

[443] *'He had a friend, he told me, of whom he had an extraordinarily high opinion. He used always to go to him when he was tormented by some criminal impulse, and ask him whether he despised him as a criminal. His friend used then to give him moral support by assuring him that he was a man of irreproachable conduct, and had probably been in the habit, from his youth onwards, of taking a dark view of his own life. At an earlier date, he went on, another person had exercised a similar influence over him. This was a nineteen-year-old student (he himself had been fourteen or fifteen at the time) who had taken a liking to him, and had raised his self-esteem to an extraordinary degree, so that he appeared to himself to be a genius. This student had subsequently become his tutor, and had suddenly altered his behaviour and begun treating him as though he were an idiot. At length he had noticed that the student was interested in one of his sisters, and had realised that he had only taken him up in order to gain admission into the house. This had been the first great blow of his life.'* S Freud, Notes Upon a Case of Obsessional Neurosis, *SE 10,* [1909], 1979, p159.

processes by their technical names, and I tell these to the patient if they —the names, I mean— happen to be unknown to her. I call a cat a cat.'

And: *'No one can undertake the treatment of a case of hysteria until he is convinced of the impossibility of avoiding the mention of sexual subjects, or unless he is prepared to allow himself to be convinced by experience. The right attitude is: 'you can't make an omelette without breaking eggs.' The patients themselves are easy to convince; and there are only too many opportunities of doing so in the course of the treatment. There is no necessity for feeling any compunction at discussing the facts of normal or abnormal sexual life with them.'* [444]

Freud was relying on words having a meaning or sense aside from those private idiosyncratic images, associations or ideas that an individual may have. I call these 'standard meanings'. Standard meanings are ethereal yet ordinary things, relied on by every language using community. So for example, for those of us who speak English there is a standard meaning for 'house'. 'House' will tend to approximate a common meaning in its actual use, although in each individual case any particular house referred to may not be a typical or average house. It is certainly possible for you and me to successfully use the word 'house' in a conversation even though I may have seen none of the houses that you have seen, and you may have seen none of the houses that I have seen. In fact there may be no such thing —in reality— as the perfectly average or 'standard house', yet language users still consistently go about using their standard meaning 'house'. 'House' is not a metaphor for a house. So the members of a language community produce a standard meaning for their words through their use, even though in any one use, the meaning may never precisely correspond to the standard meaning, it will always refer to it, just as an average may not refer to any particular object that possess that average value.

Freud was asked if it was significant, in the light of his theories of oral fixation, that he was invariably seen with a cigar in his mouth or hand. Freud famously replied that sometimes a cigar is just a cigar. That is, there is a standard meaning for cigars. 'Table' is not a metaphor for a table, but a standard meaning.

The clinician is on the lookout, amongst other things, for non-standard meanings, that is, for idiosyncratic or private associations. These divide into two types: 'over generalisation' and 'under generalisation'. What do these terms mean? The function of having one symbol stand for too many things is 'over-generalisation'; over-generalisation is the inclusion of too many members in a set. So, for example, cats and horses are over-generalised members of the set 'doggy' because cats and horses are not doggies and do not belong in the set of things properly called 'doggy'.

---

[444] S Freud, Fragment of an Analysis of a Case of Hysteria, *SE* 7, [1901], 1976, p48-9.

Along the continuum of over-generalisation and standard meaning, at the other end, is under-generalisation. Under-generalisation is the exclusion of legitimate members from a set, for example when a child claims that he has the only 'pussy cat' in the world, or when a hysteric claims to be the only person to have ever experienced 'real pain'. Over- and under-generalisation have an identical function; whether a particular item is over- or under-generalised will depend only on which set of standard meaning is being referred to. There may be words in every sentence that deviate from the standard meaning, but of course, if every word spoken was highly over or under-generalised it is very likely that nothing would be understood.

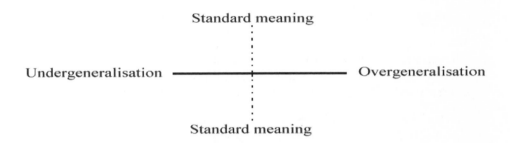

Here is a clinical example of over-generalisation: a young man reported a suicide fantasy, but made light of it, explaining that he would never carry it out. When asked for details he had said that he would take a knife to his wrists, and cut through the tendons. Later in the session the clinician —mindful of the fact that the state of wrist tendons do not determine whether you live or die— asked 'Why tendons'? The client immediately associated to his aunt, whose name sounds much like 'tendon', and to other new material that identified an important and previously unstated role that his aunt had had during his childhood. Relative to 'suicide', 'wrist tendons' are over-generalised because wrist tendons are not vital organs, that is, wrist tendons are not proper members of the set of 'vital organs' that someone seeking to take their life would specifically try to damage.[445]

There is another continuum, with jouissance at one end, and castration and desire at the other:

JOUISSANCE------------------------------------CASTRATION AND DESIRE

---

[445] For another example of over generalisation and jouissance see page 318.

The scheme below relates the two continuums. Clinicians should be on the lookout for non standard meanings, that is for over generalisation and under-generalisation —on the left of the scheme— because these often betray or point to the subject's jouissance and so are often exploited in interpretations:

Undergeneralisation ────────────────

CASTRATION

JOUISSANCE───────────── Standard meaning &

DESIRE

Overgeneralisation ────────────────

Such ambiguities are used to generate interpretations because man is the animal afflicted with language, so examining those afflictions —by testing their characteristics— seems like a good method for revealing the wounds caused and sustained by language, that is by sexuality, culture and the family.

One such ambiguity is the 'inscrutability of reference' [446] one of the one cause of over-generalisation and under-generalisation. In the best cases and the worst, and all those in between, there are vagaries of reference because the inscrutability of reference is an every sentence phenomenon, making it impossible to identify the item being referred to with certainty, without introducing new uncertainties. If I say something that refers ambiguously, the ambiguity can only be resolved at the expense of new ambiguities. It was on this problem of reference that Freud wrote:

'It quite regularly happens that a single symptom corresponds to several meanings simultaneously. We may now add that it can express several meanings in succession. In the course of years a symptom can change it's meaning or it's chief meaning, or the leading role can pass from one meaning to another. It is as though there were a conservative trait . . . which ensures that a symptom that has once been formed shall if possible be retained, even though the unconscious thought to which it gave expression has lost it's meaning.' [447]

---

[446] W Quine, *Word and Object*, MIT, Cambridge, 1960, p73.
[447] S Freud, The Sense of Symptoms, Introductory Lectures on Psychoanalysis, *SE 16*, [1915], 1976, p258.

Freud offered a partial explanation for the meaning shifts or over generalisation and under generalisations that occur in the clinic through the variable of transference. When the work goes well:

'All the patient's symptoms have abandoned their original meaning and have taken on a new sense which lies in a relation to the transference; or only such symptoms have persisted as are capable of undergoing such a transformation.' [448]

Over generalisation and under generalisation are relied on by patients as a tactic or strategy, as the patient slaves to master meaning in the process of transference or translation:

'[The hypochondriac's] voice grows more shrill and he struggles to find a means of expression. He rejects any description of his pains proposed by the physician [clinician] . . . He is clearly of the opinion that language is too poor to find words for his sensations and that those sensations are something unique and previously unknown, of which it would be quite impossible to give an exhaustive definition. For this reason he never tires of adding fresh details, and when he is obliged to break off he is sure to be left with the conviction that he has not succeeded in making himself understood by the physician [clinician].' [449]

Synonymy as Plato and Klein's supposed cure for the pandemic of over-generalization and under-generalisation

Synonymy —the establishment of identical meanings for two words— is a central issue for both clinical and linguistic theories. If synonymy could become properly established then much could be made of it. The proper and complete equation of two terms with one identical meaning would allow a clinician to make an interpretation and insist on the specific identity of a hidden meaning within the client's speech, regardless of his client's beliefs and experiences. This would be absurd; establishing synonymy is a fatally problematic project that would entail dealing with a library full of philosophical and practical difficulties. How in practical terms could you tell whether one term is perfectly synonymous with another? Only by knowing something or things that no human knows.

If *'the signifier represents the subject for another signifier'* then one signifier could never be synonymous with another, unless one subject could be equated with another subject, which it cannot. Identical twins and even identical numbers can be distinguished when in series. Desire as the desire for difference

---

[448] S Freud, Introductory Lectures on Psychoanalysis, *SE 15*, [1915], 1976, p100/1.
[449] S Freud, Studies on Hysteria, *SE 2*, [1893], 1976, p136.

insists on the unique identity of each subject. If synonymy —the sameness of meanings— cannot be established or justified then all those clinical theories and techniques that rely on fixed meanings such as Klein's are a mistaken enterprise.[450]

Who knows what about whom? Or:

'Reductive interpretation' versus 'expansive interpretation'

Interpretation is a crucially important and complex topic since it covers what the clinician says and always relies heavily on a collection of at least three different but often overlapping theories: a theory of emotion, a theory of language and a theory of what it means to be a subject. In this section we will see how the different theories of emotion that we reviewed earlier inform the different types of interpretation practised by Lacanians and others.

If for instance you believe in the sponge and bucket theory of the emotions and objects (the sponge theory is explained later in this chapter) then you are bound to 'interpret counter transference'. If you believe in fixed categories of meaning then, whenever you interpret, you will refer to one or another object within your fixed categories, whatever your client says. For example it is impossible to complete a Kleinian analysis without have pursued interpretations of the supposed objects: *'good breast'* and *'bad breast'*.

To clarify Lacanian interpretation I divide the interpretations used by clinicians of various orientations into two classes that I call 'reductive interpretation' and 'expansive interpretation'. Reductive interpretation assumes that the clinician knows the meaning of his client's speech: expansive interpretation assumes that the clinician does not know the meaning of the client's speech. Expansive interpretation is also known as 'equivocation'. Expansive interpretation is practised by Lacanians: reductive interpretation is used by Kleinians, Jungians, Adlerians and those who work in the object relations tradition.

How and why is Lacanian interpretation different? One of the most important reasons is the Lacanian reliance on the belief that 'word meaning varies according to use and is not fixed'. Lacanian interpretation is expansive and so

---

[450] The theme is taken up by Freud in papers such as 'A Note Upon the 'Mystic Writing Pad'', *SE 20* [1925], 1976.
The philosopher Quine has argued persuasively for two conclusions that are also relied on by Lacan. The two related dogmas attacked so successfully by Quine are 'reductionism' and 'analytic meanings' or put simply, synonymy. Quine's arguments can be found in Two Dogmas of Empiricism, in *From a Logical Point of View*, Harvard, 1953. page 4, and 'Synonymous Expressions' by A. White in *The Philosophical Quarterly*, Vol. 8, No. 32, July 1958. For another important point of contact between Lacan and Quine see '6. Being, being variable and language' in the Appendix.

is radically different from the reductive kind of interpretation practised by Kleinian clinicians with their fixed 'objects', and from Jungians with their fixed 'archetypes': these theorists insist that meanings are rigidly fixed by their special catalogues of objects and that their catalogues of objects exist *independently* of each individual client! Lacan argued that the object of psychoanalysis is not a singular positive presence, a thing that actually has an independent existence, but instead something that is missing, and that is likely to be different for each one of us:

'The object of psychoanalysis is not man; it is what he lacks —not an absolute lack—but the lack of an object. Even then agreement must be reached as to the lack in question —it is that which excludes the possibility of naming its object.' [451]

'For interpretation is based on no assumption of divine [Platonic or Jungian] archetypes, but on the fact that the unconscious is structured in the most radical way like a language . . .' [452]

So a very important difference between Lacan's clinical approach and the others mentioned here lies in the differences between a theory that claims that each of us is made up by a set of identical objects that have a positive existence, and a theory that argues that the most important thing is what is absent or missing for each one of us, where the identity of the missing thing is not given. Clinicians cannot justify assuming the identity of a subject's object prior to studying their speech but only by studying their unique speech, and the object exists primarily through absence, not presence.

For Lacan there is no universal catalogue of previously identified objects for every one of us; our condition is uniquely determined in each case, whatever we may have in common. To discover what has caused each of us to live our lives in the way we have can only be properly explored by studying each individual's language: it cannot be assumed to be the same thing in each and every case. We will return to question the status of objects and their relation to the subject from Lacan's view, and from the object relations school.

Here is an example illustrating the differences between reductive and expansive interpretation: a client had complained about his relationship with his father. He said his father treated him harshly, either with silence or criticism. In other sessions the client had described a pattern of difficult relationships with male bosses. The client complained yet again about the way he had been treated by

---

[451] J Lacan, February 19th, 1966, Responses to Students of Philosophy, Television, trans Mehlman et al, in *October* 42, MIT, 1987, p133.
[452] J Lacan, *Ecrits*, Direction of the Treatment and Principles of its Power, trans Sheridan, Tavistock, London, 1977, p234.

another male boss. A reductive interpretation —which would not be made by a Lacanian— might sound like this:

'Your boss stands for your father.'

Here the meanings of *'boss'* and *'father'* have been closed, rather than being left open for the client to explore: the question of meaning is forced open in the following example of expansive interpretation:

'So your boss has treated you harshly, and your father has treated you harshly.'

An expansive interpretation *does not* make any specific claim about the hidden underlying meanings in the client's speech: expansive interpretation is a way of suggesting that there may be a *question of meaning* for the client within his own speech without making any claim as to what the question or issue might be. Here the author of *Clinical Klein* provides a clear account of reductive interpretation:

' Interpretations . . . attempt to put into conscious words those ideas, emotions and relationships that are hidden, or part-hidden; in effect, to speak the unspoken [thoughts, emotions and ideas of the client].' [453]

Another clinician, Scharff, a professor of object relations theory, demonstrates reductive interpretation in his interpretation of his client's words [454]:

'I was able to respond to his blame, [I imagined that I was] now in his place as a young boy who wished to defend himself. He and I both felt vented and relieved. In defending myself, I spoke for him.' [455]

I sometimes find it difficult to speak for myself, never mind speaking for anyone else. If they are true to the stated aims of their school Kleinians, Jungians, and those who work in the object relations' tradition, who aim to speak for their clients, suppose their client to be unable to speak for himself. Here the clinician puts words —sometimes artfully— in the mouths of his clients. It is not surprising that clients who experience reductive interpretations often disagree with their clinician's idea of what their own speech really means. The reductive interpreter claims to boil down or reduce the words of his client, and then provide *'the real, proper meaning'*. Reductive interpreters assume that they possess a fundamental knowledge of their client's unconscious, which the client does not possess, and that their duty is to give their knowledge to their client. This is exactly the opposite of the Lacanian

---

[453] R Hinshelwood, *Clinical Klein,* London, FAB, 1994.

[454] Scharff also makes use here of a technique called 'interpreting counter transference' which Freud, Klein and Lacan criticised.

[455] D Scharff, *Refinding The Object And Reclaiming The Self* , Jason Aronson Inc, London, 1992.

approach. Perhaps this arrogant supposition of knowledge by Kleinians explains the following client's response:

'I began seeing a psychotherapist who told me he was a Kleinian. That was five years ago. My feelings about the treatment are mixed. I often feel irritated by his knowing the meaning of my every word and action better than I do.' [456]

Lacan identified this Kleinian attempt to monopolise meaning in Klein's case known as 'Little Dick':

'Melanie Klein . . . has the minimum of material . . . Melanie Klein . . . doesn't . . . offer an interpretation. She starts off . . . from ideas she already has . . . I won't beat about the bush, I just tell him . . . It is Melanie Klein's discourse which brutally grafts the primary symbolisations of the Oedipal situation on to . . . the child. Melanie Klein always does that with her subjects . . . more or less arbitrarily . . . [this is what she . . . calls 'gaining access to his unconscious'].' [457]

Let's look at the differences between reductive interpretation and expansive interpretation in more detail, and how these two kinds of interpretation rely on different theories about what the client knows and what the clinician knows.

Knowledge, language, truth, logic, and interpretation

One essential difference between reductive interpretation and expansive interpretation revolves around the question of knowledge. Who is it that possesses the knowledge relevant to the client's suffering? For those who work with reductive interpretation this question is relatively easy to answer: it is the clinician who knows: for those working with expansive interpretation it is the client who knows, even if she does not know that she knows.

Those who practice reductive interpretation necessarily compete with their clients to see who makes the cleverest interpretations and who knows best. This wastes much time and energy by distracting from the real work: helping the client to uncover his own unconscious beliefs, know how or knowledge through studying the client's speech with modest and honest ignorance.

The idea of knowledge being possessed by someone else —the Other— is often connected to erotic ideas as to the possession of power, especially power over the subject's enjoyment. This can be seen for instance in the relation between the powerless ignorant infant and its powerful knowing mother, where the

---

[456] Anonymous letter to *The Psychoanalysis Newsletter*, Issue No 18, Summer 1996.
[457] J Lacan, *The Seminar of Jacques Lacan, Book One, Freud's Papers on Technique of Psychoanalysis, 1953-1954*, ed Miller, trans Forrester, Cambridge University Press, Cambridge, England, 1988, p85.

mother has power or possession of know how and knowledge over the infant's enjoyment and suffering.

Reductive interpretation suggests looking at the client's words with a kind of 'meaning microscope', and seeing what meaning really lies behind or beyond them, claiming to accurately describe the client's underlying but hidden reality that has given rise to the fiction or fantasy that can be seen on the surface, within the client's words. The clinician here is the one who is supposed to possess the superior microscopic or telescopic powers of perception. Once the clinician has seen the truth he passes on his privileged vision to his client. Below are two schemes showing the different layers through which reductive and expansive interpretation claim to work:

LAYERS IN REDUCTIVE INTERPRETATION:	LAYERS IN EXPANSIVE INTERPRETATION:
4. Clinician's supposedly **conscious knowledge** of the client's unconscious thoughts, objects and fantasies	4. Clinician's **ignorance** of the client's unconscious thoughts, objects and fantasies
3. Client's language	3. Client's language
2. **Transparent veil** for clinician	2. **Opaque veil** for clinician
1. Client's unconscious thoughts, objects and fantasies	1. Client's unconscious thoughts, objects and fantasies

Bear in mind the distinctions above while reading my numbered comments on the right, which refer to Klein 's superscripted quotes on the left, where she describes her theory of language, reality and the mind:

*'But if we take the principles of adult analysis as a model and proceed first of all to get into contact with the **superficial** strata of the mind— those which are nearest to the ego and to reality— we shall fail with children in our object of establishing the analytical situation and reducing their anxiety.... The same is true of the **mere translation of symbols** [1], of interpretations which only deal with the symbolic re-presentation of the material and do not concern themselves with the **anxiety and sense of guilt** that are associated with it. An interpretation which does not descend to those **depths** which are being activated by the material and the anxiety concerned, which does not, that is, touch the place where the strongest latent resistance is and endeavour in the first place to reduce anxiety where it is most violent and most in evidence, will have no effect whatever on the child, or will only serve to arouse stronger resistances in it without being able to resolve them again. But . . .*	**1.** Klein is dismissive of *'the mere translation of interpretations which only deal with symbolic representation'.* What does this mean? It has been clearly demonstrated by the later Wittgenstein, Quine and other philosophers of language that the most profound analysis of language or symbols that we can carry out is translation or interpretation. Language, translation and interpretation are all we have in the clinic. Truth is the exclusive property of symbols or language; there are not two classes of symbols in speech, the deep and the superficial but only one, words or signifiers. **'Depth'** and **'superficial'** are themselves signifiers, and in the absence of argument do not imply any privilege [459]. Klein identifies anxiety and guilt as *'being associated'* with the speech of the client yet she fails to explain how she identifies anxiety and guilt without the mediation of 'mere symbols'.

---

[458] M Klein, The Technique of Early Analysis, p25, *The Psychoanalysis of Children*, Virago, [1926], 1989.
[459] This is also an argument against Chomsky's Platonic theory of mind and language.

these interpretations [just mentioned] by no means completely resolve the anxiety in the deeper layers of the mind, nor will the interpretations, which so soon penetrate to the deeper layers, in any way restrict the analytic work in the upper layers — that is to say, the analysis of the child's ego and its relation to reality.

It must further be remembered that children are still for the most part under the sway of the unconscious, whose language, as dreams and play show, is presentational and pictorial [2]. As we have occasion to see over and over again, children have a quite different attitude from adults to words. They assess them above all according to their pictorial qualities [3] — to the phantasies they evoke . If we want to gain access to the child's unconscious in analysis (which, of course, we have to do via the ego and through speech), we shall only succeed if we avoid circumlocution and use plain words.' [458]

2. At this point Klein wheels in an extraordinary and obviously false theory of language: she claims that language or symbols fail to represent in the unconscious or operate symbolically. Instead the words of children have direct correspondence to physical objects in a pictorial sense, rather than to each other. This is certainly not a view taken by any living linguist or psychoanalyst. Anyone who is spent time with children will have noticed that the way they play around with words and their sounds proves that they do not simply refer to things in the world. This theme is also developed in Freud's description of the fort-da episode.

3. Klein then makes the inconsistent claim that the clinician must use '*plain words*' in order to reach the client's unconscious! Yet she has only just explained that words for children are '*pictorial*' and fail to reach the items that she privileges: 'guilt and anxiety'! So on the one-hand words fail to function as symbols for children, and in the unconscious, and on the other hand they refer to the irrefutable truth of the client's guilt and anxiety that Klein can mysteriously identify, by some undisclosed and presumably non-symbolic means! So Klein wants to have it both ways; she requires language to both refer to the depths and to the superficial, yet she fails to provide any justification or criteria for distinguishing between the two.

Here is an example in which Klein reports having made the following interpretation in her third session with a young boy during World War II:

'Richard asked 'What would Hitler do to the Greeks; would he enslave them?'
Looking at the map, he said with concern that Portugal was a very small country
compared with big Germany, and would be overcome by Hitler. He mentioned
Norway, about whose attitude he was doubtful, though it might not prove to be a
bad ally after all. Mrs K[lein]. interpreted that he also worried unconsciously
about what might happen to Daddy when he put his genital into Mummy.' [460]

Note this standard interpretation of parental intercourse, wheeled out sooner or
later by every loyal Kleinian with every single client, regardless of the words
actually produced by the client. Such practices do not improve the reputation of
psychoanalysis.

Truth and Interpretation

Just because the ego exists —that is the barrier of specially constructed false
connections between language and desire— and is not clearly visible and
prevents us seeing the truth of our conflictual desires, does not mean that it is
impossible for the clinician to make true interpretations! There are techniques
that allow true interpretations to be made *without* the clinician having any
special knowledge of his client's unconscious thoughts, objects and fantasies.

What principle might these truthful interpretations —made in ignorance of the
contents of the client's unconscious— rely on? Put informally, varieties of
quotation, more formally, logic. If the clinician relies on different kinds of
quotation from the client's speech then his interpretations can be true. That is
objectively true: not 'a metaphor', or 'relatively true' or 'true for him' but one
hundred per cent true. Here is an example of an objectively true interpretation:

'My father is aggressive.' (Says client)

'I am aggressive.' (Says client)

'There is something the same about you and your father'. (Says clinician)

This is an example of an expansive interpretation. A clinician making the above
interpretation is likely to inspire his client to question. It is often useful to leave
the client with a question like this, perhaps for half a minute, until the next
session or longer. If the client persistently demands an answer from you to his
question, along the lines: *'What do you mean, 'There is something the same*
about you and your father'?' Here is one response you might give:

---

[460] M Klein, *Narrative of a Child Analysis*, third session, 17 February 1954, Virago,
[1945], 1989, p26.

'You said that your father was aggressive, and you said that you were
aggressive.'

Silence or ending the session might be better. When we use the client's speech
—without reference to the external world or anything independent from the
client's language— as to whether a client's father was actually aggressive or not,
we are relying on logic, not on our specific knowledge of what the father
actually is, or is not like.

So logic is simply the set of rules for working out what you can say that is
definitely true, based on the assumption that what the client says is true. Of
course, because you're not a policeman, lawyer or a judge you don't need to
know whether what you or your client says is true or not: but it is a necessary
part of your job to simply assume —for the sake of the therapy— that everything
your client says is true. If your client says something that you find incredible or
inconsistent perhaps you should ask a question about it?

It is the policy of the Lacanian to automatically assume the truth of whatever his
client says for the sake of analysis. He has no choice in this matter. An
alternative would be to assume that some or all of what your client says is false.
You could only make this assumption if you supposed yourself to possess the
knowledge that your client lacked! Of course the clinician need not *believe* the
assumptions he finds in his client's speech, and relies on in his interpretations.
We are all able to assume that something is true —without believing it to be
true— for a special purpose, for the sake of an argument, and in particular for
the sake of the client's development of the 'logical thread' of his argument, on
an 'if . . . then' basis.

Logic is essential when it comes to making expansive interpretations. We all
have some idea of what logic is, because we often work out things that are true,
simply on the basis of other things that we have been told, without carrying out
any other checks. Sometimes you can prove that someone is not telling the truth
because they have said contradictory things. This property of contradiction is
important in clinical technique; it guarantees that something within the
contradiction is not true, and so leads the way to new truths. *Logic or*
consistency guarantees truth —assuming the truth of what the client says—
which for the sake of interpretation you must do. There is no other guarantee of
truth.

If you do not assume that everything your client says is true, then you will be
unable to help your client explore the meanings of their speech, and
consequently you will be severely hindered in the task of helping your client
discover their unconscious desire as it emerges in their speech. For this reason I
strongly recommend that all clinicians make themselves familiar with some
elementary logic as a vital tool for studying clients' language.

Logic or truth can only be applied to symbols, for example to speech or mathematical symbols, but not to the image. An image cannot be 'true' or 'false'; it just is.[461]. Of course some images come to have symbolic values —but only once they have been taken up in symbolic discourse— such as a tick for 'correct', or a red traffic light. Beware of relying on images in your clinical work! Interpreting images of the client such as their 'body language' is likely to be regarded by them as an unwelcome, possibly aggressive or erotic intrusion, but even worse, such a strategy will distract from the project of getting your client to *speak and symbolise* their desire. In cases where clinicians make interpretations of their client's appearance, the client is likely to start dressing for the clinician. And it won't be long before the clinical work becomes a bizarre fashion show that the client uses —with the clinician's co-operation— as an efficient distraction from the difficult truth of their desire. This is one reason why Lacanians work with their client's language, not their image. Language allows objective truth: images cannot.

Over time you may note changes in your client's appearance, they may even inspire your interpretations, or perhaps suggest some important ideas about the client to you, but do not refer to your images of the client unless they are in the client's speech. Occasionally clients will ask you to look at photographs or to read something of theirs. It will probably be most helpful to ask the client to describe the photos to you, or to read his letter to you. The material will then be metamorphosed from images to symbols, which can then carry the properties of truth and falsity. You can be sure that you would have found a different set of symbolic associations or signifiers in your vision of the photos or your reading of your client's text. The battleground of psychoanalysis is the field of language, which is in the symbolic, although it draws on Lacan's other two categories of the imaginary and the real. Marking the status of this battlefield one client, commenting on his clinician's interpretation, responded:

1. *'When you said that I noticed my body language change.'*

The clinician said:

What does that mean?

The client replied, maintaining his earlier investment in an image:

2. *I moved my arms, legs like this.*

So the clinician asked:

And when you do that what does it say to you?

---

[461] There is much debate amongst neurologists, psychologists and philosophers as to the relative status of the image and the symbol, and which of the two is prior. Is one parasitic on the other? Amongst these is Peirce's iconic scheme for representing logical arguments, which is principally symbolic rather than imaginary.

The client responded:

3. *That I am being defensive.*

At this point the clinician said:

Let's finish there today.

The client had resisted speaking three times by referring or pointing to an image. When this tactic of not speaking demonstrably failed the client he clearly stated that there was some truth at stake for him, that some thing had threatened that he sought to defend himself from. For this reason the clinician, rather than escalate a difficult situation, and hopelessly pursing a hidden and well-defended truth, left the dangerous secret in the client's safe possession. By ending the session on the client's material the value or meaning of the material was left open, and the question of its value underlined.

It is not only in psychoanalysis that people tactically set out to wind each other up, the particular issue that is used to do the winding can be arbitrary, that is the object of demand. Because the clinician is unlikely to win any particular battle against the client's ego, he should not waste his time and energy, or his client's fighting the ego when there is little or no chance of victory. The clinician will generally privilege the longer-term issues, his strategy and policy, that is the whole course of the war, and the transformations it may produce, over the importance of an individual battle. One clinical strategy is to ignore or discount imaginary attempts at communication such as the client's investment in images.

The impasse constructed by the client above who offered 'to speak with his body rather than his mouth' was respected by the clinician, and the future agenda left in the hands of the client. When either the client or the clinician is without legitimate weapons, when words have been downed, the work must pause or end, a truce having been established. It is a Lacanian policy that only when the enemy is armed can he be engaged in battle.

Leaving the client with his problem —and his solution, that is with his symptom— with an invitation to return, is a way of keeping the door open, of allowing the client to review his defences on the battlefields of the analysis of his words. To find new opportunities to symbolise his suffering and traumas.

Interpreting transference

Freud and Lacan had similar positions regarding transference that stand in contrast to the majority of non-Lacanian approaches. Freud wrote:

'Transference can appear as a passionate demand for love . . . a transference is present in the patient from the beginning of the treatment and for a while is the

most powerful motive in its advance. We see no trace of it and need not bother about it so long as it operates in favour of the . . . analysis.' [462]

And: *'So long as the patient's communications and ideas run on without any obstruction, the theme of transference should be left untouched.'* [463] While Lacan wrote:

'[Freud] recognized at once that the principle of his power lay there, in the transference . . . but also that this power gave him a way out of the problem only on condition that he did not use it . . .' [464]

This principle of Freud's —of leaving *'the theme of transference . . . untouched'*— is taken even more seriously by Lacanians than it was by Freud, and far less seriously by most 'Freudians' than it was by Freud. Since the work of Heimann in the 1950's this principle of not interpreting the client's transference has been opposed by the clinicians of many schools, including those who follow Carl Rogers. These interpretations of the client's transference are nearly always guesswork, more or less. I will argue that transference interpretations are necessarily speculative and do not respect the speech of the client, but instead impose meanings imagined by the clinician to be the client's.

Clients only very rarely get stuck for long in a rut of transference because transference is the vehicle itself that allows them to free associate and produce new material. If the client does get stuck, then, when all other measures have failed to help produce new material then it may be necessary to share your speculations with the client about the nature of his transference, on a minimal basis. This should always be done with tact and caution.

Sometimes clients make explicit statements that clearly implicate their transference, but no matter how clear their transference may seem it is nearly always best not to interpret it. If for example your client shares her observation: *'Your nose looks like a penis',* how might you best respond? An interpretation of the client's transference might be: *'Do you want me to put my nose in your private business?'* or *'And what would you like to do with my penis?'*

Many clients would find this type of unfortunately common type of interpretation intrusive and aggressive, with its focus on the clinician's fiction of the 'here and now' of transference, but worse still, such clients would be efficiently distracted from the task of analysing their pre-existing relations, those that brought them to your clinic, by a focus on their relation with their clinician. So what might be said in this difficult situation? Silence is an obvious option but

---

[462] S Freud, Transference, Introductory Lectures on Psychoanalysis, *SE 16,* [1917], 1976, p443.

[463] S Freud, On Beginning the Treatment, *SE 12,* [1913a], 1976, p139.

[464] J Lacan, *Ecrits,* The Direction of the Treatment and the Principles of its Power, trans Sheridan, p236.

some clients do not respond well to silence, especially when anxious or distressed. The above client had been sexually abused and was anxious. After a pause the clinician asked slowly: *'Whose penis does it look like?'*, inviting the client to produce material that was easier to work with, so demonstrating to the client that the clinician's desire is good for the task of tolerating her working through of her demands or provocations, because the clinician's desire is for the client's desire: not her demand.

Effective tactics for dealing with material that refers to the person of the clinician is to ignore it, or to ask a question that refers to other material that the client has produced. This technique relies straightforwardly on Lacan's formulation *'the signifier represents the subject for another signifier'*; the tactic above was aimed at discovering who or what the signifier *'penis'* represented the client for, inviting the client to introduce new material, helping her to uncover a trauma that she had previously been unable to talk about.

Some clients, especially when distressed or anxious will try to provoke or antagonise their clinician. While it may occasionally be important to mark and implement limits or boundaries, it is important not to be distracted from the task of helping the client work through their demand by focusing on an analysis of their language. In some sessions clients will aim to distract you. They may ask questions whose answers they believe you cannot give, or make personal comments. If these are particularly persistent they should be recognised or acknowledged in a relaxed but respectful way. A useful technique is to refer to a different impersonal topic previously discussed by the client that has an item in common with the personal comments.

Remaining silent is sometimes interpreted by the client as an invitation to escalate their demand until it is recognised. The clinician's silence may stimulate outbursts of difficult behaviour that can lead to a profound embarrassment, or to the breakdown of the clinical relationship.

Clinical cases

In the previous section some of the differences in the theoretical approaches of different schools were explored: in this section these ideas will be applied to clinical cases to illustrate some consequences of the different theoretical positions.

Scharff reports in some detail the signifiers of a client called 'Fernando', with Scharff's own interpretations and theoretical reflections. In the left column the client's words are italicised: the other words are Scharff's theoretical comments and interpretations. The superscript numbers in the left column refer to my comments to be found in the column on the right, and those I have imposed from Freud and Lacan (also italicised):

'All the evidence, the resources are there, but I don't feel it. I don't know my own weight and form, my substance'

The client clearly identifies the existence of an unknown part of his mind, his unconscious as an essential part of himself that he does not have conscious knowledge of; he knows that he does not know! This is the admission that his unconscious exists, a good indicator that the client is therapeutically orientated:

'[The] Other is there as unconsciousness . . , and he involves my desire in the measure of **what he is lacking** *and that he does not know. It is at the level of what he is lacking and that he does not know that I am involved in the most pregnant fashion, because for me there is no other detour, to find what I am lacking as object of my desire.*

That is why there is for me not alone no access, but no possible sustentation of my desire which is pure reference to an object, whatever it may be, unless by coupling it, by linking it with the following which is expressed by the S barred, which is this necessary dependence on the Other as such . . . It is to the other as locus of the signifier.' [465] But Scharff interprets his client's identification of his own unconscious instead as:

'What had brought Fernando to treatment was his desperate need [1] *to depend on others* [2]*, on external objects, for a view of himself.'* [3]

1. 'Desperate need', when it is clear that the client has demands and desires addressed to others, rather than his physical 'needs' for food, warmth etc.

2. The alleged dependence 'on others' as 'external objects' is not coherent. Because of the topological nature of language Lacan theorises objects topologically, rather than as 'external objects'. This is crucial because the location of the subject is not simply 'within his physical body' but within the topological body of language, in relation to the Other. Topology redefines the concepts of 'internal' and 'external'.

3. The idea that Fernando was dependent on others 'for a view of himself' is of course the truth, not only for Fernando but for all ordinary neurotics because the signifier represents the subject for **another** signifier. The image we have of ourselves is always from a position that we imagine our Other viewing us. The Lacanian view is that desire is desire for the other's desire, as the client's profound material suggests.

---

[465] J Lacan, Seminar on Anxiety, unpublished, trans Gallagher.

'In the next moments of the session, Fernando gave another graphic fantasy of what I would have to supply to give him coherence.'

'*I have this image of loose atomic particles zigzagging in a defined space without co-ordination or coherence. Then you do something to that space, zap it, give it order. Then they establish an order. I feel like I'm an atom, and I've been smashed. All these particles whirling around, not knowing what to do.*'

'Here is another image that gives a clue to the sexualised longing for a penis [6], the moment of creation of a self that is an atomic 'big bang.' He needs me to give him this bang, to 'zap' his disorganised fragments. This is the form of his dream for the father who is 'a centre, a home, a father — 'a master's voice,' **an image I can feel I am coming from!'** But this desire also leads to his dread that he is issuing an invitation for this object to exploit his craving to enter him and take him over or at the core. It is here that his fight is against his father, to be not like him in refusing to be taken over by his mother as he feels his father was. He tries to be like the father he longed for, not like the one he felt he had, through being in a relationship with someone while not taken over. He told me how much **he wanted me to be firm so that he would not take me in** deceptively, and yet that he did not want to have to be like me:

'*I can't resolve the two. I can't get rid of the fear of being like him. And I can't give up on the wish for a father, for a God. That's why I go to church. It's another part of my search for something I haven't found yet.*'

'With failure came desperation and futility. But he found what he needs to begin the process of building a resilient self . . .'

6. Scharff – without support from the client's material – confidently introduces his own penis idea, and then, elaborates it with his own idea of being '*firm*'.

Here the problem of symbolising or representing the father is clear, but by now it is not clear if this material is a response to Scharff's interpretations. The problem is the client's though: not Scharff's. The 'self' is the façade, fiction or lie produced by the ego as an image of oneself. This lie is most resilient in the most troubled cases.

'I'm fighting as hard as I can with and for a father. If you're screaming and fighting with all your might against something that is supposed to be your source, what do you do? How do you stop the fighting and **acquire the source you want? All my life you try to build without him,** which you can't do! You have to accept him for what he is. You don't have to be like him. I don't have to be like him! But what do I put in his place other than the person who was naturally supposed to be there?'

Here the client appears to describe a version of Freud's and Lacan's theory of the object as lost, in which:

'[The superego] . . . **borrowed** strength to do this, so to speak, from the father, and this loan was an extraordinarily momentous act.'[466]

And:

'The subject never refunds, Freud writes, anything but **another** object that answers more or less satisfactorily to the needs in question. He never finds anything but a distinct object since he must by definition refind something that he has on loan.'[467]

How do emotions deceive? What is the exception, and what are the clinical consequences? Why is anxiety different? How do emotions deceive?

Emotions are not part of a 'fundamental structure', although they are certainly an important part of what it means to be human, of our lived experience. Emotions often deceive both their owners' —common sense or consciousness— and others. This is useful from the point of view of the ego which has produced the emotions, often in order to cover-up the difficult truth.

As I argued in the introduction, every practice incorporates and relies on theory. Is the theory explicit and honestly acknowledged —and so capable of being criticised— or is it hidden away and so supposedly immune from criticism, just like our unconscious desires? Some clinicians argue that it is possible to practice without a theoretical position. How? 'With emotion' many reply. Heimann for example has written:

466 S Freud, The Ego and the Id, *SE 18*, [1923b], 1976, p34.
467 J Lacan, *The Psychoses*, ed Miller, trans Grigg, Routledge, London, 1993, p85.

'The aim of the analyst's own analysis is not to turn him into a mechanical brain which can produce interpretations on the basis of a purely intellectual procedure, but to enable him to sustain his feelings as opposed to discharging them like the patient' [468] And:

'My thesis is that the analyst's emotional response to his patient within the analytic situation represents one of the most important tools for his work. The analyst's counter transference is an instrument of research into the patient's unconscious.' [469]

This leads to the common and arrogant practice in which a clinician reasons to himself, or even says something like the following to his client: *'I feel some anger now, I wasn't angry when we started the session; there is something that you are angry about, that is making me angry. What is that you are angry about?'* Because this technique relies on a supposed knowledge that the clinician cannot possibly possess —the unspoken emotions of the client— it functions as an abuse because the clinician poses as authoritative and knowledgeable as to the truth of the client's unconscious. In the Freudian and Lacanian tradition the clinical work is to study the speech of the client, not for the clinician to guess as to what his own emotions are and then to guess yet again on that uncertain basis about the identity and origin of his client's supposed emotions.

So *'using his emotional response as a key to the patient's unconscious'* is piling speculation on top of speculation, and then using the dubious results to 'instruct' clients about 'their truth'. Perhaps, like 'Counsellor Troi' of 'Star Trek', some of us possess some special telepathic or empathic powers: the rest of us can rely only on what our clients objectively put before us: their speech. Lacanian clinical work is the modest analysis of speech, not the divine or clairvoyant inference of the client's emotions via the clinician viewing his own emotions, whether he believes they are crystal clear, or the muddled confusion that ordinary mortals endure most or all of the time.

'Intuitions' and 'emotions'

Many clinicians claim to *'rely on my intuitions when making interpretations about my client'*. This is an interesting claim; these clinicians claim that their own intuitions actually inform them about what is important for someone else. Some aspects of this theory are considered below. We will return to other aspects of this theory of interpretation called 'interpreting counter transference' in the next chapter.

---

[468] P Heimann, Counter-transference, *Br. J Med. Psychol*, 1960, 33: p9-15.
[469] P Heimann, On Counter-transference, *Int. J Psychoanalysis*, 1950, Vol 31, p81-4.

An intuition is simply an idea that someone has, for which they are not able to identify the relevant theory or justification. If I have an intuition then I have an idea, and I do not know which set of beliefs or theory has produced my idea. All ideas and beliefs come from theories, but that does not mean that we can always properly connect our beliefs and our theories. An intuition is just a belief that has become disconnected from its theory.

For example a farmer may have the intuition that *'it will rain tonight'*, based on his observations over many years and his hidden or unconscious meteorological theories. Of course the farmer has theories about weather changes but he may not know consciously what his theories are.

Intuitions are very important in all sorts of activities, and of course we rely on them in much of what we do, especially complicated things that are difficult to articulate, such as sexual identity, catching a ball and having a conversation. To comprehensively theorise and make explicit all of these complex activities is not possible for any one of us, therefore we have intuitions, or holes in our conscious knowledge and explanations, but not necessarily in our know-how or unconscious theory.

Clinical work often necessitates interpretations and interventions being made on an intuitive basis, without having detailed conscious theoretical reasons for what one does at the time. Clinical work involves thinking and acting on your feet. These intuitive interpretations and interventions do *not* rely on the clinician's 'feelings', but on his unconscious theories. Feelings and unconscious theories are not the same. Given time, most competent clinicians would be able to theorise many or all of their earlier interventions and interpretations without reference to their emotions.

So intuition is a broad category, something that we often rely on because we don't have the time to connect an explicit or conscious theory with a particular practice, but this important fact —having to think quickly on our feet— is no excuse for 'giving up' altogether on theory.

Let us take seriously the influential claim made by Heimann that the clinician's own emotions are an accurate guide as to what is important for the client. How might this make sense? What is the underlying theory that these clinicians are relying on?

The theory such clinicians are working with are versions of what I call the 'Sponge Theory of the Emotions'. The Sponge Theory is very different from Lacan's approach and has been so influential in Anglo-Saxon clinical work that we will consider it in more detail. The sponge theory of emotions is closely related to the bucket theory of objects.

The sponge theory claims that psyche or mind, or the part of it that deals with emotions, is just like a sponge. There is, under ideal circumstances, an emotional tap that drips onto the sponge at the same rate at which the emotions dissipate into the atmosphere, so that the sponge is kept perfectly moist.

If too much emotion or moisture is prevented from leaving the sponge at a natural pace then it becomes heavy and overfilled. Or if too much emotion is put into the sponge at too great a rate, again it becomes too heavy and burdensome. According to sponge theory there are two kinds of outcome if you have a sponge that is too heavy: either a lot of emotion spills out, or the emotional tap gets turned off altogether. So sponge problems can be caused by too much dryness, perhaps in the case of trauma when the emotional tap is turned off too hard, and not turned on again because it has become stuck in the 'off' position. So carrying too little emotion, that is, being too dry, or carrying too much, that is, being too wet, cause the problems that sponge theorists report in the clinic: emotional incontinence such as rages, tantrums and weeping, and emotional constipation, or inhibited emotions, such as 'flatness of affect' and 'monotonous voice'. Here the sponge theorist uses the technical sponge theoretical terms of 'pain', 'pump' and 'contain':

'In therapy, Mr and Mrs D joined forces to pour their anger and sorrow into me, taking turns at pumping me full, then accusing me of failing to contain themselves and each other.' [470]

Clinicians of all schools are bound to notice changes in their client's emotions as the clinical work progresses, but is this emotion a by-product, that is, an effect, or a cause? Is the emotion something that leads to the truth of desire or is it a distraction or side effect? We will return to these questions. To study sponge theory more closely we must examine its theory of language or communication.

Emotional Communication and the Sponge Theory

'If the analyst can sustain feelings, they are positively useful, whereas discharging them could be damaging and certainly clouds the issue. For instance, the analyst may feel angry with the patient. He could then discharge feelings, perhaps, by having a go at the patient — giving the patient 'a piece of his mind', we might say. Or the analyst may feel overly positive, even erotic, towards the patient, and might then freeze up and perform the legendary emotionless blank screen. Alternatively, however, the analyst could hang on to those feelings, acknowledge whose they are, but understand how they have come about. This will inevitably tell something about the patient to whom the psychoanalyst is reacting. Of course it must also tell something about the analyst

---

[470] D Scharff, *Refinding The Object And Reclaiming The Self*, Jason Aronson Inc, London, 1992.

as well — provided the analyst is prepared to consider his feeling (rather than discharging it).' [471]

How do emotions get communicated? One sponge can transfer moisture to another drier sponge simply by touch. A very wet sponge communicates by rubbing or pressing against another sponge. If that person is clinically trained then their sponge will be perfectly moist, neither too wet nor too dry and so will absorb some of the excess emotion from your heavy and over burdened sponge. Alternatively if the client's sponge is too dry then it will absorb some of the clinician's moisture.

This, in rough outline, is the influential theory relied on by Heimann and others who claim that their interpretations of their clients are informed by their own emotions. Now we have a reconstructed sketch of this theory we are in a position to criticise it.

What is wrong with the sponge theory?

How exactly do the emotions get conveyed or transferred from the client to the clinician? The metaphor of emotions as moisture is too informal to be tested. It is not good enough to say that 'emotions just somehow move from one person to the other': a theory of emotional communication or movement, such as the sponge theory ought to specify the precise method. What exactly is the method by which emotions move? Where do the emotions go in to the mind? There is no direct route 'through the senses': emotions are always inferred or interpreted via signifiers or images. A metaphor is not the same as a theory.

I have not discovered any theory that explains how emotions are 'conveyed' from one person to another, without being mediated by words, that is signifiers, or via images such as the image of a person crying or speaking.. Freud's and Lacan's theories of the movement of signifiers avoid any reliance on some kind of direct emotional communication that somehow by passes signifiers or symbols. There is no known technique whereby human emotions can be 'directly communicated'. All attempts at 'communication' are via signifiers. Even non-verbal communication, such as 'body language', which many would argue is itself a symbolic language, a medium or representative rather than the emotion itself.

Freud and Lacan have explicit theories regarding words and signifiers, rather than relying on some unspecified or hidden theory that the sponge theorists rely on.

---

[471] R Hinshelwood, *Clinical Klein,* FAB, London, 1994, p153.

Freud, Lacan and emotions

There is a huge literature of scientific studies from modern psychology and social psychology experiments that support Freud's second theory of emotion and Lacan's theory, such as Schacter and Singer's influential 1962 study.[472] In 1893 Freud, a pioneer of sponge theory, clearly stated the sponge position in his first psychoanalytic paper:

'The fading of a memory or the losing of its affect depends [most importantly] on whether there has been an energetic reaction [catharsis] to the event that provokes an affect . . . If the reaction is suppressed, the affect remains attached to the memory . . . The injured person's reaction to the trauma only exercises a completely 'cathartic' effect if it is an adequate reaction — as, for instance, [in] revenge.'[473]

Compare this with his very different position, detailed in his 'Unconscious Feelings', written 22 years later:

'It may happen that an affective or emotional impulse is perceived but misconstrued [through a false connection]. Owing to the repression of its proper representative [that is the signifier] it has been forced to become connected with another idea, and is now regarded by consciousness as the manifestation of that idea. If we restore the true connection, we call the original affective impulse an 'unconscious one'. Yet its affect was never unconscious; all that had happened was that its idea had undergone repression. In general, the use of the terms 'unconscious affect' and 'unconscious emotion' has reference to the vicissitudes undergone, in consequence of repression, by the quantitative factor in the drive impulse.

We know that three such vicissitudes are possible: either the affect remains, wholly or in part, as it is; or it is transformed into a qualitatively different quota of affect, above all into anxiety; or it is suppressed, i.e. it is prevented from developing at all. . . . [B]ut in comparison with unconscious ideas there is the important difference that unconscious ideas continue to exist after repression as actual structures in the system of the unconscious, whereas all that corresponds in that system to unconscious affects is a potential beginning which is prevented from developing. Strictly speaking . . . there are no unconscious affects as there are unconscious ideas . . . The whole difference arises from the fact that ideas

---

[472] Another classic empirical study demonstrating that subjects are often helplessly confused or wrong as to their own emotional states is Schacter and Singer's 'Cognitive, Social and Physiological Determinants of Emotional State', *Psychological Review*, 69, 379-399, 1962. See also Valins, 'Persistent Effects of Information about Internal Reactions: Ineffectiveness of Debriefing', London and Nisbett, eds, *The Cognitive Alteration of Feeling States*, 1972.

[473] S Freud, On the Psychical Mechanism of Hysterical Phenomena: Preliminary Communication, *SE 2,* [1893],1976, p8.

are investments —basically of memory traces— whilst affects and emotions correspond to processes of discharge [catharsis], the final manifestations of which are perceived as feelings. . . It is possible for the development of affect to proceed directly from the unconscious system; in that case the affect always has the character of anxiety, for which all 'repressed' affects are exchanged. Often however the drive impulse has to wait until it has found a substitutive idea in the system consciousness. The development of affect can then proceed from this conscious substitute, and the nature of that substitute determines the qualitative character of the affect . . . in repression a severance takes place between the affect and the idea to which it belongs . . . the affect does not as a rule arise till the break through to a new representation in the system of consciousness has been successfully achieved.' [474]

Or put simply: *'We cannot assert the existence of unconscious affects in the same sense as that of unconscious ideas.'* [475]

So should clinicians focus on the patient's report of emotions, and make conjectures and interpretations as to their emotional states, which both they and clinicians often helplessly misconstrue? Clients may be in a uniquely privileged position from the point of view of the lived experience of the emotion, but they are not in the same privileged position when it comes to *identifying* the experience and its true connections and causes. Language goes on holiday when people report emotions. The language used to describe the experience of affect is often falsely connected to lead attention away from the underling desire; a person may be convinced that they are angry when later it turns out to be jealousy. A man may believe that he hates another man, because he is in love with that other man's wife.

Affect interpretations support the notion of the therapist as the 'subject supposed to know', as authoritative and knowledgeable with regard to the truth of the patient. It is just this type of attribution —of knowledge and mastery— that is often bound up with the client's pathology and transference, that is likely to have inspired him to seek a clinician's help in the first place.

'Complete interpretation', 'exact interpretation' and 'interpreting counter transference'

Continuing with the theme of Lacan's clinical work as the development of Freud's, consider Freud's position on the left, and Lacan's on the right:

---

[474] S Freud, *SE 14*, The Unconscious, [1915], 1976, p177.
[475] S Freud, *SE 16*, Introductory Lectures, Anxiety, Introductory Lectures on Psychoanalysis, (1915), 1976, p409.

'Suppose we succeeded in bringing a case to a favourable conclusion by setting up and then resolving a strong father transference to the doctor. It would not be correct to conclude that the patient had suffered previously from a similar unconscious attachment of his libido to his father. His father transference was merely the battlefield on which we gained control of his libido; the patient's libido was directed to it from other positions. A battlefield need not necessarily coincide with one of the enemy's key fortresses. The defence of a hostile capital need not take place just in front of its gates.' [476]

'The transference is a phenomenon in which subject and psychoanalyst are both included. To divide it in terms of transference and counter transference —however bold —however confident what is said on this theme may be is never more than a way of avoiding the essence of the matter.' [477]

The technique of 'interpreting counter transference' is precariously built on the foundations of interpreting transference, but also relies on the problematic sponge and bucket theory of the emotions and communication, and goes like this, according to Heimann who invented the technique:

'My thesis is that the analyst's emotional response to his patient within the analytic situation represents one of the most important tools for his work. The analyst's 'counter transference' is an instrument of research into the patient's unconscious.' [478]

The point of the relationship between the analyst and the patient is, according to Heimann:

'. . . the degree of feeling the analyst experiences and the use he makes of his feelings. . . The aim of the analyst's own analysis is not to turn him into a mechanical brain which can produce interpretations on the basis of a purely intellectual procedure, but to enable him to sustain his feelings as opposed to discharging them like the patient.' [479]

S Freud, Introductory Lectures, Analytic Therapy, Introductory Lectures on Psychoanalysis, *SE 16*, (1915), 1976, p456.

[477] J Lacan, *The Four Fundamental Concepts of Psychoanalysis*, London, Penguin Books, 1979, p231.

[478] P Heimann, On Counter-transference, *Int. J Psychoanalysis*, 1950, Vol 31, p81-4.

[479] P Heimann, Counter-transference, *Br. J Med. Psychol.* 1960, 33: p9-15.

So why did Lacan write that: *'The counter transference' is nothing other than the function of the analyst's ego, what I have called the sum total of the analyst's prejudices.' ?* [480]

Everybody —or more accurately every word or letter— transfers, whenever it is spoken heard, written or read. Transference is a form of life taken by language. However, by virtue of their knowledge of clinical theory and, or their 'specially trained ego', a clinician 'interpreting counter transference' also supposes that their own transference is something that they can objectively and truthfully identify. Not only do such clinicians make this immodest claim but they also supposedly identify objectively their client's transference! The clinician's supposed knowledge of the client's transference, and of their own transference apparently justifies these clinicians in making a further leap of knowledge and concluding that 'the client's transference has caused my transference to the client'. In short, interpreting counter transference involves making at least three highly speculative claims, the which proper justification for each will almost always or always be missing in part or whole. The three unjustified assumptions are:

1) Knowledge of the client's transference

2) Knowledge of the clinician's transference

3) Knowledge of how the client's transference has caused the clinician's transference, typically via sponge theory.

From the Lacanian point of view all three types of supposed knowledge are increasingly fallible. Any of the clinician's beliefs about the client's transference are uncertain. They cannot be relied upon if you are in the business of making true interpretations, because transference is imaginary, while language —the stuff of interpretation— is symbolic, and all the client shares properly with the clinician is some language. Interpreting someone's transference is an uncertain business. There is also a practical argument with the same conclusion: interpreting a client's transference is likely to upset and distract them from the already difficult task of analysing their old problems by producing new material.

Interpreting one's own transference —as a clinician— is also a risky business because the ego often deceives, and it is probably impossible for an individual to objectively check up and discover in which cases he's deceiving himself, and in which cases he's telling himself the truth. People's beliefs about themselves are notoriously unreliable, whether they are an analysed clinician or an inexperienced client.

---

[480] J Lacan, *The Seminar of Jacques Lacan, Book One, Freud's Papers on Technique of Psychoanalysis, 1953-1954*, ed Miller, trans Forrester, Cambridge University Press, Cambridge, England, 1988, p23.

Inferring the cause of the clinician's transference from the shaky basis of the supposed knowledge of client's transference, in addition to the clinician's transference is still more hazardous!

Most interpretations should either be true, or questions, but not everything that is true is an interpretation. If you have any doubts as to whether you should ask your client a particular question, or make an interpretation, then don't! Such doubts are often informed by reliable intuitions or sound ideas to which the clinician may not have easy access, but could review, perhaps in supervision. It is worth mentioning that while some 'counter transference interpretations' might be true, that is certainly not a sufficient reason or justification for making them. The truth of a client's unconscious desire can only be usefully revealed on a timely basis, when the client chooses: not when the clinician thinks that the time is right because the clinician believes that he knows the truth of his client's unconscious desire, and 'he is ready to hear me speak his truth.' In short there are three good reasons for not making counter transference interpretations:

1. Counter transference interpretations have a high risk of being false because they are founded on three false assumptions, especially relative to deductively produced, true interpretations that rely on the client's speech rather than the clinician's imagination.

2. Interpreting your client's transference with his clinician —which is the supposed cause of counter transference— is likely to disturb the client's transference with his clinician, and his continued reliance on the work. The client relies on his transference with the clinician in the production of new material.

3. Counter transference interpretations suppose that the clinician possesses a knowledge that the client lacks, but ought to have. Clients often perceive the technique to be aggressive and arrogant.

Towards exploring counter transference interpretations Etcheygoyen —who uses counter transference interpretations and other non-Freudian techniques— is quoted below:

*'However, this risk [of having increased the misunderstanding through having made transference interpretations] should not be taken as an insuperable obstacle. The analysand can always misunderstand, and **the analyst can always correct this misunderstanding** with a new interpretation . . . Wishing to be more precise, we will have to say that every interpretation will be well understood by one part of the ego (the observer), and at the same time distorted by the experiencing ego, so each time we are going to interpret we will have to weigh both possibilities. If the observing ego is sufficient (that is, if we can count on acceptable therapeutic alliance), the possibility that the interpretation will be operative is*

*naturally greater . . . However, due to its nature, **the transference***
***interpretation has better resources to correct** the perceptual*
distortion of the ego (misunderstanding) because it is directed to the
*immediate, **the given**.*

Etcheygoyen clearly believes that his position as an analyst will always allow
him to correct his client's misunderstandings! This clinician really supposes
himself to know. How can he justify this extravagant claim? He appeals to the
possibility of correction through new interpretations, yet it is easy to prove that
every new interpretation brings with it new uncertainties. What trick can
Etcheygoyen rely on to solve this problem? He redefines the ego! Suddenly the
ego has two new parts: *'the observer'* and the *'experiencing ego'*. These new
partitions have nothing to do with psychoanalysis or Freud's theory of the ego,
neither is it all clear how they might operate.

Etcheygoyen, developing his error and inconsistency, believes that attempting to
interpret the client's transference can *'correct the perceptual distortion of the*
ego', when distortion is the ego's principal function and reason of being! He
also introduces a mysterious and supposedly privileged category: *'the*
immediate, the given'. There is no category of human experience that is
immediate: all data, whether sensory or otherwise is theory laden, and can only
be perceived as images, signifiers or something missing. He compounds his
problems by explaining his theory of the 'three spheres':

*. . . a good interpretation, **a complete interpretation** has to take the three*
*spheres and show the essential identity of **what happens in the consulting room***
[1] *with **what is happening outside** [2] and **what happened in the past** [3]. If we take*
only one of these areas, whichever it be, as if the other two did not exist, then we
no longer operate with the transference.' [481]

So Etcheygoyen believes that he is capable of making *'a complete*
interpretation'. What might this be? No word, phrase or sentence in any
language represents the exhaustive interpretation of any other word, phrase or
sentence. Because the signifier represents the subject for **another signifier,** so
the chain of signifiers can never be completed. There is no such thing as a
perfect or complete translation or interpretation. Yet here is the pretence of a
recipe for just such a thing. What does this immodest clinician assume in
collecting ingredients for his all-knowing potion?

1. Comprehensive knowledge of: *'what happens in the consulting room'*.

2. Comprehensive knowledge of *'what has happened outside'*.

3. Comprehensive what has *'happened in the past'*.

---

[481] R Etcheygoyen, *The Fundamentals of Psychoanalytic Technique*, trans Pitchon,
Karnac Books, London, 1991, p424.

If Freud, Lacan and Quine [482] are correct then no clinician will have comprehensive knowledge of any one of these ridiculous criteria, let alone all three. The idea of *'a good interpretation, a complete interpretation'* taking in these *'three spheres'* is grandiose in the extreme, and appeals to a theory of word meaning or translation so ridiculous that no linguist or philosopher of language believes in it.

Within the tradition of reductive interpretation a whole literature of papers including Glover's *'The Therapeutic Effect of Inexact Interpretation . . .'* have flourished. They take *'an exact interpretation'* as the only alternative to inexact interpretation. What is an exact interpretation? A reductive one, an interpretation that Glover regards as *'accurate'* [483].

Which clinical theories interpret counter transference?

A surprisingly wide range of theories interpret the client's transference through the clinician's transference, that is, interpret counter transference. This non-Freudian technique is very widely practised, even by those who call themselves 'Kleinian', despite the fact that Melanie Klein —to her credit— was explicitly opposed to interpreting counter transference [484], although those who call themselves 'Kleinian' often practice this technique. Another surprise is provided by the followers of Carl Rogers, they too interpret counter transference, while inconsistently claiming at the same time to *'travel light'* [485] regarding theory:

'Empathy is a continuing process whereby the counsellor lays aside her own way of experiencing and perceiving reality, preferring to sense and respond to the experiences and perceptions of her client. This sensing may be intense and enduring **with the counsellor actually experiencing the client's thoughts and feelings as powerfully as if they had originated in herself** *. . . empathy is a process . . . of 'being with' the client . . . She [the counsellor] isn't just thinking about his [the client's] feelings; it is likely that she [the counsellor] will be experiencing the same general tightness, or constricted throat that precedes his crying. She is experiencing his feelings as if they were her own . . . She is able to*

---

[482] W Quine, Two Dogmas of Empiricism, *From a Logical Point of View*, Harvard, 1953.

[483] E Glover, *The Technique of Psychoanalysis,* 1955, London, Bailliere, Tindall and Cox, p354

[484] This fact is easy to establish by reading the Klein Archive at the Welcome Institute, but has generally been covered up and hidden away by 'Kleinians'.

[485] Mearns and Thorne, *Person Centred Counselling In Action*, Sage, London, 1988, pages 5 & 54.

work in this intense and feelingingful way with her client, and yet not become overwhelmed by those feelings. [486]

Is there any way of systematically predicting which clinical theories support interpreting counter transference, and which do not? Almost every clinical theory that relies either on a non-Freudian fixed vocabulary of meanings, or on a non-Freudian theory of the ego, where the ego does not cover up the conflictual truth, uses the technique of interpreting counter transference. How is it that these two apparently different aspects of theory can have the same function?

One of the principal functions of the ego —in Freud's work— is deception: non-Freudian theories of the ego make claims in the opposite direction. They argue that the ego or some part of it can be reliably trained so that it consistently tells the truth. This 'truth telling function of the ego' has the same effect as relying on a fixed vocabulary of meaning where the fixed meaning is or provides access to 'the truth'.

Reflections on a case of interpretation in the object relations tradition

In the left column Scharff, a clinician and theorist of the object relations, school describes a client's dream. In the right I comment:

---

[486] Ibid, p39.

'I had a neat little dream. You are tinkering with a car with a teen-aged boy. It was my car, and I'm there trying to tell you where to look. The car has engines at both [1] ends. I am telling you different places to look — maybe so you won't find anything?! Then I worry, 'They're experts [2] and won't they find anything?' The other person helping turns out to be me, too, only younger. You're the chief of the operation.

Adam liked the dream. He was struck by the partnership between me and the boy in a mechanical project. Adam said, 'I think I was hoping to mislead you, but I also hoped you wouldn't be fooled [3], that you and I could find out what was wrong with my car together.'

1. This material suggests the possibility of demands or desires that operate in *two* opposing directions characteristic of obsessional neurosis.	
2. Here the client identifies the clinician as 'the subject supposed to know'.	
3. This profound ambivalence is characteristic of obsessional neurosis. A competition for knowledge of the client, between clinician and client is suggested. Such competition is an inevitable result of transference interpretations.	

The dream sounds like parts of the relationship you had with your father. Did you work on cars together?' I asked.

'No,' he answered, 'but I got him to advise me on buying a used car, which turned out to be a lemon. The dream also reminds me of the summers I worked in an automobile plant to pay for college. Dad wasn't very sympathetic to the danger I felt I was in. One time I did get slightly hurt and he didn't seem to care.'

'Feeling your father gave bad advice and was unsympathetic adds something to the dream,' I said, 'In the dream you and I [4] have a partnership about fixing this car, but you are also trying to throw me off the track. Then you're worried I'll be fooled by you, so the car won't get fixed. Part of you is with me, and part of you is against me in the job.'

'I think that's the way I felt about my father,' he said. 'I wanted him to be with me, but lots of times I felt he was against me.

4. Here the clinician makes a speculative and potentially problematic transference interpretation.	

'And would you try to mislead him?' I asked.

'When I felt mad at him, I'd go to my mother, who was sympathetic,' he said. 'I'd say things to her I wouldn't tell him. So in that way I did.'

'What about the car having engines at both ends? [5]' I asked.

'It could go forward or back [6]. Or if both engines worked, it would just rev up its motors and stand still at full speed. It's a funny image, like a 'Push-me-pull-you,' the animal in the Doctor Doolittle books Dad read me as a child. You couldn't tell if it was coming or going. It had heads at both ends.'

'You haven't made up your mind whether to go forward in analysis [7],' I said. 'You're not sure if I'm a sympathetic coach or a cruel father. And you just may want to go in the other direction if things get rough, or just rev up your motors so you can stay where you are at full speed while I'm a frustrated Dr. Doolittle. But you also hope you can't fool me, so that I can help you. What about my counter transference [8] in this early stage?'

5. Here the clinician usefully hints — with his question — at the identification of a bipolar or paired structure presented in three parts of **the client's speech.** The two contrasting or opposed parts may equate with *'father'* and *'mother'* and the *'engines at both ends',* and *'I think I was hoping to mislead you, but I also hoped you wouldn't be fooled'.* **6.** The client elaborates a beautiful description of obsessional neurosis, demonstrating the opposition and ambivalence characteristic of obsessional neurosis again in his own interpretation, with the bipolar or paired structure.

7. Here the clinician produces a series of speculative and arrogant transference interpretations, which may or may not be true. The most important fact that is certainly true, is that these transference interpretations will disrupt the client's work as the client becomes embarrassed, and completes with the clinician in a scramble for knowledge.

8. Here the clinician clearly believes that his own interpretation of his feelings can reliably and usefully inform him about his client's thoughts and feelings. Not only does the clinician not understand how the client's dreams express his own, but his supervisor might not either. It is far from obvious why anybody should understand anybody else's dream, let alone expect someone else's dream to inform their own. The clinician becomes ridiculously entangled within these issues, without producing anything of value for the clinical work.

CHAPTER FIFTEEN   INTERPRETATION II

How could I know if he would support my efforts at learning car repair? Was he with me or against me? Were we on the same team or were we opponents? And how would I look to my supervisor? The dream issues could be understood as his introjection of my issues, of my transference to him, and at the same time, his own issues gave him a valency to take mine in. He worried if I would support his efforts and needs, just as I worried if he would support mine. He experienced these as problems for the growth and repair of his self, whereas I might have told myself that my own worries were about a merely professional task outside my central self. But my concerns were at the centre of my growth as an analyst. In this way, the issues were central to both of us. In the resonance between them lay the greatest intensity of our relationship, the greatest potential for mutual understanding and growth [9], the greatest potential for my becoming the analyst I wanted to be by helping him.

9. Why does this clinician believe that analysis is *about 'mutual understanding'*? The analysis should be exclusively of the client's speech in relation to his unconscious desire.

My situation with Adam was like a mother's with her baby [10]. To become a mother, a mother needs her baby's help, as I needed Adam's to become an analyst. The fate for each of us was held in our shared interaction and work. We were each becoming the other on whom our selves depended. The vehicle for our mutual evolution was the shared projective and introjective identifications that formed the transference and counter transference interplay of our work. They are the vehicle for in-depth communication in therapy and analysis, the foundation of an understanding of the relationship between self and object. [487]

10. Not only does Scharff assume the position of father (see point 5 above), but that of the mother too!

[487] D Scharff, *Refinding The Object And Reclaiming The Self*, Jason Aronson Inc, London, 1992, p59 –63.

Reductive interpretations and the sponge theory

In the following account Joseph explains how she doggedly instructed her client with her own reductive interpretations in terms of the sponge and bucket theory:

*'I had been showing my patient his way of dealing with his difficulties by trying to force despair into **me** instead of trying to contact his own depression and understand it. In this session he came in saying he was depressed. He told **me** a dream. The dream was that he was standing on the corner of a well-known central London street with someone, a woman. They were standing in the gutter, perhaps surrounded by clothes, old clothes to sell. His elder sister went past in the road with some men friends; he called to her; she nodded but went on. There was something about burglary. I briefly linked this dream with . . . how he tries to force despair into **me** . . . which then drags **me** down into the gutter . . . I am also the sister, who goes past with her own friends, her own life, and is not dragged down by despair'.* [488]

Joseph's interpretations insist on her placing herself centre stage in her client's life. Note the number of 'I's and 'me's' she inflicts on her client. Her technique is a kind of bullying, insisting on the authority of her person. An inspection of her client's speech show that she has failed to identify any reference to herself in her client's speech: she has simply imposed her own view.

Of course if clinicians insist on interpreting whatever a client says as a negative judgement that refers to the clinician, sooner or later the interpretations will acquire some truth because interpreting negative counter transference is a self-fulfilling prophecy. If I repeatedly pester a client or anyone with the suggestion 'you're talking negatively about me', whatever has been said, sooner or later something negative will be said about me, but it is unlikely to have anything to do with clinical work in Freud's or Lacan's tradition.

The idea that clients are fed *'understanding'*, required for *'mental nourishment and development'* is arrogant. Clinicians do not have a monopoly on the truth: every clinician has an ego and so is also in the untruthful position of compulsively making false connections when conflicts regarding their desire are at stake. The truth, almost certainly, is that clients, in order to encounter their own desire, must discover their own unique truths through a study of their own language, not someone else's strange views on the nutritional value of the own words for others.

In the passage below, Scharff's version of object relations theory is on the left. The concept of truth here has been subverted by a bizarre breast metaphor or myth of the clinician's, rather than being the modest discovery of truths within the client's speech: Lacan —in the right column— warns against this approach:

---

[488] B Joseph, quoted in *Clinical Klein*, R Hinshelwood, FAB, 1994, p222.

'Instead of the analyst as a kind of feeding breast, another version has slid in: the psychoanalyst, as an understanding object, provides a form of truthfulness that acts as the food for mental nourishment and development.' [489]	*'Of course the trap is that in interpreting you give the subject something to feed himself on, the word, even the book which is behind it, and that the word remains all the same the locus of desire, even if you give it in such a way that this locus is not recognisable, I mean that if this locus remains, for the desire of the subject, uninhabitable.* *To respond to the demand for food, to the frustrated demand in a nourishing signifier is something which leaves elided . . . that beyond any food of the word, what the subject really needs is what it signifies metonymically, it is that which is not at any point of this word and therefore that each time you introduce —no doubt you are obliged to do it — the metaphor, you remain on the same path which gives consistency to the symptom, no doubt a more simplified symptom but still a symptom, in any case with respect to the desire that it is a question of separating out.'* [490]

It is not the work of the analyst to provide his or her 'understanding' or knowledge to the client, who then gratefully consumes it as if it were 'nourishment'. The client ought not take the position of a hungry child —in the position of a slave— or of a pupil in relation to a teacher: it is the analyst who is primarily in the position of ignorance, not the client.

Lacan argued that clinicians should not attempt to understand everything. Understanding someone else, or more accurately, imagining that you understand someone else, has little or nothing to do with helping that person change their position in relation to their symptoms and suffering. As clinicians all we have to work with is the client's material: our attempts at comprehensive or at any specific partial understanding the client's material is, strictly speaking, irrelevant, although sometimes useful. For this reason Freud wrote: *'If knowledge about the unconscious were as important for the patient as people inexperienced in psychoanalysis imagined, listening to lectures or reading books would be enough to cure him. Such measures, however, have as much influence on the symptoms of nervous illness as a distribution of menu cards in a time of famine has upon hunger.'* [491]   And Lacan wrote:

---

[489] D Scharff, *Refinding The Object And Reclaiming The Self,* Jason Aronson Inc, London, 1992.

[490] J Lacan, Transference Seminar, unpublished, trans Gallagher, 15 March 1961.

[491] S Freud, Wild psychoanalysis, *SE 11,* [1910c], 1976, p225.

'It is necessary that the analyst should know certain things, it is necessary that he should know in particular that the criterion of his correct position is not that he understands or does not understand. It is not absolutely essential that he should not understand, but I would say that up to a certain point this may be preferable to a too great confidence in one's understanding. In other words, he should put in doubt what he understands and tell himself that what he is trying to reach, is precisely that which in principle is what he does not understand. It is in so far certainly as he knows what desire is, but that he does not know what this subject with whom he is embarked on the analytic adventure desires, that he is in a position to have in himself the object of this desire.' [492]

'It is the subject's refusal of this meaning [of his symptoms] that poses a problem for him. This meaning must not be revealed to him: it must be assumed by him. In this respect, psychoanalysis is a technique which respects the person' [493]
. . .

Dreams, interpretation and the Oedipus

Before starting let's return to a central question: 'What are the relations of loss, love and ideas within the theory of the Oedipus?'

Freud and Lacan theorised a series of subjective experiences and productions that proceed in the following order: loss, love, and then ideas. Put simply, in order to love, it is necessary first to have lost, and in order to have a value, idea or symbolisation, it is necessary to have loved, and for that love to have been ruptured or interrupted, and disappointed. Freud's theory of the relations of loss, love and ideas is his theory of the Oedipus described in a number of different papers. Perhaps one of the most important of these, *'Der Untergang Des Odipuskomplexes'*, has been mistranslated as 'The Dissolution of the Oedipus Complex': *'untergang'* is translated by my dictionary as: *'downfall, shipwreck, ruin, decline'* and *'destruction'*. A fine term for *untergang* is *'Waterloo'* as in:

'Every man meets his Waterloo at last' [494]

Given the context of the Oedipus theory, 'shipwreck' is another useful translation of *untergang* because according to Lacan:

'We are at bottom in the same boat as Oedipus, even if we don't know it.' [495]

---

[492] J Lacan, Seminar on Transference, unpublished, trans Gallagher, 8 March 1961.

[493] J Lacan, *The Seminar of Jacques Lacan, Book One, Freud's Papers on Technique of Psychoanalysis, 1953-1954*, ed Miller, trans Forrester, Cambridge University Press, Cambridge, England, 1988, p129.

[494] W Phillips, Speeches, Lecture at Brooklyn, New York, 1st November, 1859, p378 of the *Oxford Dictionary of Quotations*, London, Oxford University Press, 1972.

Ships become wrecked because of a danger encountered in their passage or journey from one place to another. Some become dismembered, others are broken up and washed up on the shore signalling the shipwreck, while others remain partially submerged. Many shipwrecks are the cause of suffering due to the enormous investment that they represented, and continue to represent. The wrecking of the 'unsinkable *Titanic*' represented the loss of a nation's ideal, of Britain's invulnerable economic, industrial, technological and expansionist superiority. This is a set of phallic values. Some shipwrecks cause the loss of an investment that becomes particularly troublesome, such as the ecological chaos caused by the wreckage of laden oil tankers.

In cases where the Oedipus complex has not been properly shipwrecked the ship's captain continues to invest some effort towards recovering his wrecked investment. What might he recover? Will the lost object be in the same state as it was when he lost it? Will it restore a lost paradise? These questions are answered uniquely in each human life and usually more explicitly, within the psychoanalysis of each neurotic. Every neurotic has some aspect, or vestiges of their Oedipus complex that have not been properly wrecked, given up or written off. Neurotics have not finished establishing the impossibility of their childish and impossible demands for love. They squander their energy in the pursuit of their impossible Oedipal demands for love, like an old and impoverished captain who repeatedly refuses all offers of work so he can devote all his energy searching the seas for the lost ship of his youth, so that he can recover its buried treasure. Does such a ship represent a treasure chest or a grave, invoking the name of a dead father? Lacan claimed that:

'The subject has to deal with as an obstacle [to his desire] . . . a reef where literally something which is profoundly fundamental about his relationship to his fantasy is shipwrecked . . .' [496]

These themes of investment and labour, change and meaning suggest that we explore further the related issues of enjoyment or jouissance and duty, in relation to meaning or expression.

Jouissance, duty and paradoxes of transgression

'The superego is the imperative of jouissance —"enjoy!"' [497]

Freud theorised that part of the ego sets itself up as a separate agency called the 'superego'. Each of the three agencies, the ego, the unconscious and the

[495] J Lacan, *The Ethics of Psychoanalysis, The Seminar of Jacques Lacan*, ed Miller, trans Porter, 1992, p309.

[496] J Lacan, Transference Seminar, unpublished, trans Gallagher, 26 April 1961.

[497] J Lacan, *On Feminine Sexuality, The Limits of Love and Knowledge, Book XX, Encore 1972-1973*, 1998, Norton & Co, p11.

superego, has conflicts of interest with the others, and each tries to exert its influence over the others. Freud categorised and diagnosed clinical problems according to the particular combination of agencies that have produced the major discord [498].

The superego concerned primarily with one thing: 'a coin with two sides', that which is forbidden or taboo, and that which is enjoyable. What does it mean to say that the forbidden is the inverse or complement of the taboo?

A simple answer is that enjoyment has an economy; the economy of enjoyment is regulated. For example if somebody with the financial means said *'I never go on holiday'*, most people would probably respond with a moral or dutiful tone along the lines *'you ought to go on holiday sometimes'*. Imagine your response to a young adult in good health, who explained that he spent at least six months of the year on holiday? Most people would have some disgust or moral revulsion. What morality is at stake here? The supposed quantity of the Other's enjoyment. That is the subject's estimation of the quantity of his enjoyment relative to the quantity of the other's enjoyment. These different quantities constitute an economy of enjoyment or jouissance. In the above examples the jouissance of the other is excessive, having the effect of disgust for the subject.

Enjoyment is regulated. *'You should have some, but not too much'*; if you came across a healthy able-bodied atheist of middle age who had never experienced a sexual relationship of the ordinary language variety, you might think that this individual *'ought to!'* The principle problem with 'recreational drugs' is that they are enjoyed *too much*. The social problem is their place in the economy of enjoyment, and the suffering that underlies and generates the jouissance, and the disgust and moral indignation it causes in others. Who regulates enjoyment? The big Other, the Other of language. One Lacanian has described this phenomenon as *'enjoy my riddle'*. Because the signifier represents the subject for another signifier an important clinical question is: Who is the Other for this client, to whom is his symptom addressed like a letter? In response to an enjoyment that has exceeded 'the proper limit' the big Other produces a taboo, 'that enjoyment of this quality or that quantity is forbidden', hence the serious joke: *'That which is not forbidden is compulsory'*. So the symptom is always addressed to the big Other as an invitation to regulate the subject's enjoyment.

When addicts complain that they are struggling to give up their addiction, they are complaining principally that their big Other is insufficiently responsive in relation to both their suffering and their enjoyment. This complaint or symptom is a demand for love. If the clinician mistakenly chooses to short-circuit the client's attempt to solve his own problem, by providing him with an 'unconditional positive regard', as Rogerians propose, or 'by loving' as Searles proposes, then the client will be held back in his attempt to properly separate,

---

[498] S Freud, Neurosis and Psychosis, *SE 19*, [1924], 1976.

identify and act on his own desire, because desire is only produced through establishing the impossibility of being demanding in relation to the Other. Only when the client can establish or prove that his Other is not able to meet his demands can the client identify what is possible for him, that is his desire.

The intertwining of enjoyment and transgression are intimately connected because expression and repression are two sides of same coin, and enjoyment is often, especially in the clinic, the simultaneous failure to clearly express and the failure to have properly repressed. That is the symptom is enjoyed by the client in ways that he is unconscious or has only partial awareness of; he fails to speak clearly with his symptom, yet he enjoys it!

This riddle of enjoyment, of something that is clearly unclear is the confusion of enjoyment and transgression, of expression and repression, and of repression and castration explain the economy and paradoxes of transgression. For example, imagine being the parent of a young child who was one hundred per cent obedient. No doubt you would become deeply concerned.

Below is a Shakespearean example of a paradox of transgression from *The Merchant of Venice* in which the following variables figure: the enjoyment of eating, the enjoyment of a Jewish woman, the inverse of enjoyment: blame or debt, money, and the big Other as racial identity, and a switching of over-generalisation and under-generalisation [499]:

'LAUNCELOT [non Jewish bachelor]: Truly, the more to blame he: we were Christians enow before; e'en as many as could well live, one by an Other. This making Christians [of Jews through conversion] will raise the price of hogs: if we grow all to be pork-eaters, we shall not shortly have a rasher on the coals for money.

JESSICA [Jewish wife of non Jewish man]: I'll tell my husband, Launcelot, what you say: here he comes.

LORENZO [non Jewish husband of Jessica]: I shall grow jealous of you shortly, Launcelot, if you thus get my wife into corners.

JESSICA: Nay, you need not fear us, Lorenzo: Launcelot and I are out. He tells me flatly, there is no mercy for me in heaven, because I am a Jew's daughter: and he says, you are no good member of the commonwealth, for in converting Jews to Christians, you raise the price of pork.'

Commonwealth, jouissance, duty free and the 'good of the Other'

What can we understand by Shakespeare's term '*commonwealth*'? Commonwealth appears to equate with the collective or 'sovereign good' identified by the philosopher Kant[500]. The collective or sovereign good is crudely and brutally contrasted with the good of the individual in trauma. Lacan, following Freud, wrote of the superego as a kind of internalisation of the Other as The Collective Good or Commonwealth.

The good of 'the collective' or Other is contrasted with the good of the individual. One expression of this contrast is the law. The law is the placing of limits on what is ordinarily called 'selfishness', or the pursuit by the individual of his own good, 'rights' or enjoyment at the supposed expense of the collective good. 'Selfishness' can only be —for our purposes— a confused ordinary language idea because the concept of 'self' necessarily relies on the demands or desires of the Other. It is this 'good of the Other' that is always aimed at by the neurotic's symptom. For example the Fallen Woman, with her agoraphobia was

---

[499] To ruin a good joke the paradox can be analysed as the sharing of pork leading to the non-sharing of pork. The over and undergeneralisation can be formulated here as the category of Christians becoming over generalised through the inclusion of Jews, the jouissance associated with this over generalisation is the illicit enjoyment of a Jewish woman by a Christian man, which may -in an undergeneralisation- remove her from the set of Jews. These variables accord with the scheme on page 282-3.

[500] I Kant, *Grounding for the Metaphysical Principles of Virtue*, Hackett, Indianapolis, trans Ellington, [1785], 1983.

acting —in her imagination— in the interests of public morality and duty, and against her own desire. Her symptom simultaneously had two values: her demands or desires, and obeying an imaginary moral policeman, or The Good of the Other. It may be that the only 'good' in the final analysis is the 'good of the Other', which can only be juxtaposed and valued against the individual subject's desire. Nietzsche [501] wrote of this theme on the moral value of the Other in relation to desire:

'You creators, you Higher Men! One is pregnant only with one's own child.

Let nothing impose upon you, nothing persuade you! For who is your neighbour? And if you do things 'for your neighbour' still you do not create for him!

Unlearn this 'for', you creators: your very virtue wants you have nothing to do with 'for' and 'for the sake of' and 'because'. You should stop your ears to these false little words.

This 'for one's neighbour' is the virtue only of petty people: there they say 'birds of a feather' and 'one good turn deserves another' — they have neither right to nor strength for selfishness!

The prudence and providence of pregnancy is in your selfishness! What no one has yet seen, the fruit: that is protected and indulged and nourished by your whole love.

Where your whole love is, with your child, there too is your whole virtue! Your work, your will is your 'neighbour': let no false values persuade you otherwise!'

Here '*work*' and '*will*' equate roughly with Lacan's 'desire' and '*whole love*' with 'demand'. In Shakespeare's paradox of the good of the commonwealth we see the tension between the good of the individual and the collective good; the good of the individual can only be comprehended in terms of the good of the collective, yet the collective denies the individual, in the same way the signifier both divides and constitutes the subject.

Kant described what the individual must do for the common good as 'duty'. This is not an ordinary category of voluntary actions but actions which must —as an imperative— be carried out. Kant's jargon for this universal to which neurotics are all submitted is the '*categorical imperative*', or 'heavy duty':

'[The superego's] relation to the ego is not exhausted by the precept: 'you ought to be like this (like your father)'. It also comprises a prohibition: 'you may not be like this (like your father) that is, you may not do all that he does; some things are his prerogative.' This double aspect of the ego ideal . . . derives from the fact that the ego ideal had the task of repressing the Oedipus complex;

---

[501] F Nietzsche, *Thus Spake Zarathustra*, Pelican, trans Hollingdale, [1892], 1961, p301.

indeed, it is to that revolutionary event that it owes its existence. Clearly the repression of the Oedipus complex was no easy task. The child's parents, and especially his father, were perceived as the obstacle to a realisation of his Oedipus wishes; so his infantile ego fortified itself for the carrying out of the repression by erecting this same obstacle within itself. It borrowed strength to do this, so to speak, from the father, and this loan was an extraordinarily momentous act. The superego retains the character of the father, while the more powerful the Oedipus complex was, and the more rapidly it succumbed to repression under the influence of authority, religious teaching, schooling and reading, the stricter will be the domination of the superego over the ego later on —in the form of conscience or perhaps of an unconscious sense of guilt. I shall presently bring forward a suggestion about the source of its power to dominate in this way— the source . . . of its compulsive character which manifests itself in the form of a categorical imperative.' [502]*

The inspiration for Lacan's famous 'Kant with Sade'[503] is almost certainly the above, and Freud's claim, in his 'Economic Problem of Masochism': *'The categorical imperative of Kant is thus a direct inheritance from the Oedipus complex.'* Notice the juxtaposition of 'economic' with 'masochism', and 'sadism' with Kant's 'categorical imperative'. What is meant by the popular idiomatic imperative: *'Don't do anything I wouldn't do'*, usually accompanied by a wink, and pronounced prior to another's jouissance? Surely a reference to Kant's categorical imperative, the fundamental moral principle where:

'The imperative of duty may be expressed thus: Act as if the maxim of thy action were to become by thy will a universal law of nature.' [504]

Money is a popular representative of jouissance; everyone requires some money and some jouissance as a minimum, just as there is universal minimum of suffering that the jouissance addresses. Yet there are great discrepancies in the amounts of jouissance and money that individuals have, and in the techniques used to produce them, both legitimate and transgressive. Many struggle with the aim of producing more money, just as clients complain of their troublesome symptoms or means of jouissance production. In both cases a key referent is the amount enjoyed by the Other.

Jouissance, beauty, duty and freedom

On one interpretation The Merchant of Venice story revolves around the enjoyment of a woman by a man, of Portia's wealth and body by Bassanio. It is for the sake of Bassanio's enjoyment of Portia that poor Antonio risks his life

---

[502] S Freud, The Ego and the Id, *SE 19*, [1923], 1976, p374.
[503] J Lacan, Kant with Sade, trans Swenson, *October*, no 51, 1989.
[504] I Kant, *Fundamental Principles of the Metaphysic of Morals*, trans Abbott, 1785.

and all his wealth. What in general are the costs of enjoyment or jouissance?
Who enjoys and how? What does Antonio get out of it? [505] What separates the
commonwealth from the foreigner, the subject from the Other? Britain is an
island, a place where the Other enjoys or pursues the good with a distinctive and
paradoxical style or method.

The paradox arises because 'commonwealth' has had its Shakespearean meaning
varied in two ways: firstly 'Commonwealth' has functioned as a proper name, as
an attempt to rescue an object lost from the shipwreck of the British Empire. In
this sense Commonwealth denotes a set of countries rather than any
fundamentally common wealth or good. Secondly the British Commonwealth, in
this parochial sense of the Falkland Islands, Australia, Jamaica, Uganda, Hong
Kong and so on, did not exist as members of the Commonwealth principally in
order to generate wealth or goods for the collective, or common good, but in
order to maintain some vestige of the mastery, of enjoyment by the British
Empire, where Britain benefited at the cost of its slaves or colonies. Any benefits
that were common to the slavish members were of a token or fictional nature:
Britain retained as much by way of goods and services as it could, minimising
that which was common. This Commonwealth, or The Common Good or
categorical imperative explains why Freud wrote:

'[Neurosis] renders the sufferer too good service in the struggle for existence'
[506]

The symptom is the compromise between the subject's desire and his demand to
present the good of the Other, or to provide the Other with service. This concept
of 'service' or servitude in Freud can be understood as referring to the discourse
of the slave and master in which the neurotic has unconsciously invested his
symptom as 'the good of the Other', and explains why hysterics wear their
affliction with honour, like a medal, flaunting their 'beautiful soul', and why
Freud wrote that:

*'Analytic experience has taught us that the better [in psychoanalytic work] is
always the enemy of the good [of the big Other]'* [507]

What implications do these ideas have for clinical work? If Freud and Lacan are
correct, and the signifier represents the subject for another signifier, then an
analysis of signifiers will reveal the underlying and often neurotic structures.
Every neurotic client complains about a problematic tension between the good of
their Other and their desire and its consequences.

---

[505] This has something in common with a minor male character in Rowling's film, *Harry
Potter and the Philosopher's Stone,* where Ron Weasly, who is without any love interest,
puts his life at risk for the main man, without gaining any obvious advantage.
[506] S Freud, Analysis Terminable and Interminable, *SE 23*, [1937a], 1976, p231-240.
[507] Ibid.

It is this tension that Shakespeare helps theorise. With a clearer theory of these competing goods, duties and desires clinicians can better understand and work with client's conflicts of interest. In particular I will argue that *The Merchant of Venice* is a clear account of the structure of phobia, of a xenophobia.

In *The Merchant of Venice* the Jew Shylock is in a paradoxical relation to the commonwealth. Without Shylock nothing in The Merchant of Venice could have happened; Shylock would not have lent Bassanio money, secured against Antonio's wealth, body and life. It is only by virtue of this wealth, goods or services that were not common, or evenly distributed —that is as the enjoyment of the Other— that allowed Bassanio to exchange his love for Antonio for his love for Portia, so that he could become free to marry and enjoy Portia. So Shylock had a crucial role as the holder of jouissance or capital that had not been invested: in stark contrast the other two characters with wealth did not have access to it because it had been invested. All of Antonio's estate was at risk, invested in his ships at sea, while Portia's wealth appears to have had the sole purpose of facilitating the will of Portia's dead father, to procure a suitable husband for his daughter. So Shylock had wealth but was without debts, while Antonio and Bassanio both became indebted.[508]

The paradoxical position of Shylock is similar to the position of the Jews in Jesus' crucifixion. Without the Jews it seems clear that Jesus would not have been crucified, so the Jews have been responsible for Christianity. Without the key role of the Jews Christianity is inconceivable. Nothing would have happened. The diabolical enjoyment of the Jew is seen as having a vital role in Christianity and *The Merchant of Venice*, causing the formation of love and ideals.

What happens after the father has allowed this vital debt? In the passage of the Oedipus the position of the Primal creditor is revalued; Shylock has everything stripped from him that marks him out as different: his wealth, his religion and his only child. There is nothing left of his outlandish identity, that we might recognise as different, but there have been consequences of this foreigner being drained of his enjoyment. The Other's profound loss of enjoyment has allowed the subject— Bassanio— to enjoy in a way that was not possible for him before. Bassanio can access or enjoy Portia and her wealth only through Shylock's surrender of enjoyment. Jesus was, beaten, crucified and deprived of life so that Christians could enjoy eternal life. Jesus, according to the Gospels clearly identified money with jouissance, ideals and images. But Christian morality emphasises not the presence of money but its lack, that is debt. However much

---

[508] There is a qualification to make here regarding Shylock's debts and assets: Shakespeare does not install Shylock straightforwardly in the position of the Primal father, as the one altogether without debts: Shylock, despite his wealth, has to borrow money from Jubal, his fellow Jew, in order to lend to Bassanio. Shylock also possessed the liability or potential debt of an unmarried daughter.

material wealth or money you have bears little or no relation to your Primal or fundamental debt to the father. To he whom you killed, to the one who died for your sake. Jesus recognised the fact that there is at least an element in most people's attempts to acquire wealth to repay their debt to their Primal Father. Just as Jesus was both loved and attacked by Jews, so Freud's phobic Little Hans subjected his father to his ambivalence:

'[Hans father challenged] 'have I ever scolded you or hit you?' Hans corrected him: 'Oh yes! You have hit me. 'That's not true. When was it, anyhow?' 'This morning', answered the little boy; and his father recollected that Hans had quite unexpectedly butted his head into his stomach, so that he had given him as it were a reflex blow with his hand . . . Hans's anxiety had two constituents: there was fear of his father and fear for his father. The former was derived from his hostility towards his father, and the latter from the conflict between his affection, which was exaggerated at this point by way of compensation, and his hostility . . . Hans deeply loved the father against whom he cherished these death-wishes; and while his intellect demurred to such a contradiction, he could not help demonstrating the fact of its existence, by hitting his father and immediately afterwards kissing the place he had hit. [509]

Is there anything more exciting to a xenophobe than a mixed race marriage? Such an event suggests the dissolution of a boundary between two economies, domains or neighbourhoods of jouissance. Marriages that appear to disregard economies of enjoyment such as those across caste, class and race are bound to be opposed by those who claim that their own investment in a particular economy has not rewarded them sufficiently, typically in reliance on 'moral justifications' such as 'what is right' and 'what is disgusting'. On this issue of the distribution of wealth or goods England, with its class structure has the highest discrepancies between wealth and poverty of all the European nations, maintained by the boundaries of jouissance.

British jouissance can be seen in the attitude to smoking. In this dramatic economy of suffering and enjoyment observe the British government's unusually high levels of tax on tobacco. Billions of pounds are raised every year. In addition to the money, suffering and death are implicated. Tobacco is the number one cause of premature death in England; some 130,000 are killed every year in Britain by tobacco. For the purposes of perspective some 3,500 people are killed every year in road traffic accidents. Smoking also causes a predictable quantity of blindness, amputations, cancers and emphysema. So there is a lot of suffering on the one hand, and there are presently 7.6 billion pounds per year

---

[509] S Freud, A Phobia in a 5 year old boy, *SE 10*, [1909b], 1976, p115.

paid to the government as tobacco tax on the other. The total of corporation taxes is only about five times this amount! [510]

Tobacco tax is governmental jouissance, collected from the minority for the common wealth. It is tragi-comic that the government takes the tiniest percentage of these massive revenues and uses it to fund anti-smoking campaigns. But smokers enjoy smoking, and the rest of the country benefits: on average smokers will be paid far less by way of pensions than non-smokers because as a group they do not live nearly as long, so smokers benefit the common wealth, not only through the tax revenues they pay, but through the many billions that they fail to claim as pension because they have died prematurely through smoking related diseases. So non-smokers can say of smokers, as Christians of Christ: *'You have suffered for us, you have died for us, so that we may enjoy'*. Non-smokers enjoy smokers. Smoking is the nation's symptom; the nation enjoys and suffers. So it is in the clinic working with individual clients. A client suffers with his symptom but he also enjoys. The non-smoker's preference for eating in segregated restaurants relies on non-smokers finding the smell of Other's jouissance too much —as an object— or objectionable. Another example is the common experience of anxiety and discomfort on entering a room to hear others' laughter. This subject of the Other's jouissance experiences his jouissance being drained by the Other. Some racists can tolerate the existence of foreigners only for as long as they are segregated: desegregation leads to accusations of 'intolerably bad smells', the sure sign of an excessive and parasitic enjoyment. Perhaps this smell operates like the smell of a small object? Sniffing one's own farts is typically enjoyable: the smell of another's, or of a foreigner's food can disgust. One popular example of the small object —around which jouissance may circulate— is shit, infamous for its smell. Disgust suggests an intolerance of the Other's jouissance.

A familiar racist claim that many enjoy making and acting on is: *'They take our jobs and our women/men.'* Standard racist behaviour aims to both eliminate and recognise the presence of the Other simultaneously. If the racist insists that the foreigner gives up their difference and jouissance, and the foreigner does give up his differences, then the racist will suffer something vitally important: the loss of a loss. The racist loves to hate, and typically hates to love. These two opposing values, which appear so paradoxical equate with the two values of the phobic object seen for instance in the case of Little Hans where the horse's two values were *'proud'* and *'fallen'* [511] and were also attributed to Shylock. Little Hans created and relied on his phobic object with its polar values in order to stage a stable economy of jouissance and desire in which he could keep his horse.

---

[510] http://www.hm-treasury.gov.uk/budget/budget_2001/budget_report/bud_bud01_repchapc.cfm

[511] They also equate with: *'. . . Hans' anxiety [which] had two constituents: there was fear of his father and fear for his father'*.

In the next section we will explore further this hypothesis that racism, and much of the production of jouissance seen within clinics as the structure of phobia, arise through the subject's failure to work through crucial aspects of his Oedipal struggle. Shakespeare's *Merchant of Venice* and *Twelfth Night* elucidate the structure and clinical phenomena of phobia and the Oedipus complex, and help explain that variety of phobia known as 'xenophobia' or racism, as a function of the Oedipus complex. This analysis of Shakespeare's texts is in some ways close to the types of analysis carried on the client's speech in the clinic.

Xenophobia and horse phobia in Little Hans and *The Merchant of Venice*

Our approach to the plays can be orientated by a series of related questions:

• Why is the Antonio, of *The Merchant of Venice*, depressed at the outset? [512]

• Why are *The Merchant of Venice* and *Twelfth Night* altogether without mothers?

• Why are the asymmetries between the pairs of sons, daughters and fathers systematically marked?

• Why do we learn nothing of Antonio's objects of love, except his incredible 'unbounded' and apparently unconditional love for Bassanio?

•Why does only one character —Antonio— risk so much, all his possessions and his life for Bassanio in order to aid Bassanio's search for a competing object of love, for Portia?

• Why is Shylock demonised, his subjectivity absent?

• Why are Shylock —and Malvolio in *Twelfth Night*— both stripped of all their distinctive powers and identity, even though they have both properly obeyed the letter of the law, and have been vital in facilitating the main characters' sexual enjoyment?

• In general which characters give up what, and who gains what?

Towards answering these questions I have grouped as pairs, the sons, daughters and fathers, making more obvious their asymmetric or opposing characteristics. Each pair can be read as constituting aspects of Lacan's subject within an Oedipal drama. A simple version of this is illustrated with a triangle[513], with the

---

[512] *'ANTONIO In sooth, I know not why I am so sad: It wearies me; you say it wearies you; But how I caught it, found it, or came by it, What stuff 'tis made of, whereof it is born, I am to learn; And such a want-wit sadness makes of me, That I have much ado to know myself.'*

[513] J Lacan, The Paternal Metaphor, unpublished seminar, trans Gallagher, 22.1.1958.

figures of the subject (in this simple case gendered as the son), symbolic father and symbolic mother occupying each point of the triangle:

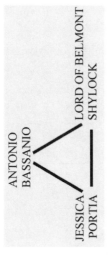

Substituting in:

SONS (AS THE MALE SUBJECT WORKING THROUGH THE OEDIPUS)

	Gender and initial status	Object of love	Wealth and its location	Obedience	Has put at risk	Has lost/gained at end
Antonio	Single depressed male	Bassanio (male)	Wealth at sea	Perfect to the law and his love for Bassanio: *'To you Antonio I owe the most, in money and love'*	All his wealth and his life	Return of ships **with goods**, that is profit, surplus enjoyment or jouissance
Bassanio	Single laughing male[514]	Portia (female)	Debts	Perfect obedience to Portia's dead father and the law	Nothing	Gained the whole estate, Portia and title 'Lord of Belmont'

---

[514] See Act 1, line 64

DAUGHTERS (AS THE SYMBOLIC MOTHER)

	Gender and initial status	Object of love	Wealth and its location	Obedience	Has put at risk	Has lost/ gained at end
Portia, the Lord of Belmont's daughter	Single daughter 'By my troth . . . my little body is aweary of this great world.' [515]	Bassanio (male)	Great wealth in the cuntry.	Perfect obedience to dead father's will: 'If I live to be as old as Sibylla, I will die as chaste as Diana, unless I be obtained by the manner of my father's will'	Marry an unwanted husband: 'But this reasoning is not in the fashion to choose me a husband. O me, the word 'choose!' I may neither choose whom I would nor refuse whom I dislike; so is the will of a living daughter curbed by the will of a dead father.'	Bassanio as beloved husband, near end of play
Jessica	Single daughter of Shylock	Lorenzo (male)	None	Perfect disobedience to father	Father's love	Father, religion, gained husband and father's money

---

[515] Act 1, Scene 2

The Madonna and the Whore

Portia and Jessica appear to jointly represent the figure of the mother. Portia respects her father's will and is concordantly in the elevated position of the virgin or Madonna:

BASSANIO In Belmont is a lady richly left; And she is fair, and, fairer than that word, Of wondrous virtues: sometimes from her eyes I did receive fair speechless messages: Her name is Portia, nothing undervalued' [that is everything about her is overvalued].

In stark contrast Jessica disrespects and disobeys her father's will, causing him to lose his paternal identity as a Jew and father, and so appears as a valueless woman, a liability who incurs debt or expense for others, and manages to marry one of the most minor characters in the play, only by relying on the lure of her stolen father's jewels and money:

JESSICA Nay, you need not fear us, Lorenzo: Launcelot and I are out. He tells me flatly, there is no mercy for me in heaven, because I am a Jew's daughter: and he says, you are no good member of the commonwealth.'

CHAPTER FIFTEEN   INTERPRETATION II

FATHERS (AS SYMBOLIC FATHERS)

	Gender and initial status	Object of love	Wealth and its location	Obedience	Has put at risk	Has lost/gained at end
Lord Belmont, Portia's father	Single father, dead	Daughter (female)	Great wealth in the cuntry	—	—	—
Shylock, Jessica's father	Single father, alive	Daughter (female) and money: '. . . my daughter is my flesh and blood.'	Great wealth in the town	To the Venetian and the Jewish law	3,000 ducats – a small part of his wealth	Lost religion, all money, and daughter

Freud wrote of

'A stage in the development of the libido which it passes through on the way from auto eroticism to object love. This stage has been given the name of 'narcissism' . . . There comes a time in the development of the individual at which he unifies his sexual drives (which have hitherto been engaged in autoerotic activities) in order to obtain a love object; and he begins by taking himself, his own body as his love object, and only subsequently proceeds from this to the choice of some person other than himself as his object. This halfway phase between auto eroticism and object love may perhaps be indispensable normally; but it appears that many people linger unusually long in this condition, and that many of its features are carried over by them into the later stages of their development.' [516]

In the following table Freud's and Shakespeare's texts are compared with a view to identifying evidence for Freud's theory above. My comments on some common elements are in the right-hand column.

Freud's case of Little Hans	Shakespeare's Merchant of Venice	Comments
'There is absolutely no justification for distinguishing a special homosexual drive. What constitutes a homosexual is a peculiarity not in the life of his drive but in his choice of an object . . . we have mistakenly imagined the bond between drive and object in sexual life as being more intimate than it really is . . . A homosexual may have normal drives, but he is unable to disengage them from a class of objects defined by a particular determinant, And in	**'BASSANIO** [to Portia] *'I thank you, madam. Give welcome to my friend. . . This is the man, this is Antonio, To whom I am so infinitely bound.'* *In my school-days, when I had lost one shaft, I shot his fellow of the self-same flight The self-same way with more advised*	Comments While Bassanio is *'infinitely bound'* to a man, Freud suggests that, homosexuality may be universal for young children. In particular this idea of homosexuality seems to rely on the idea of loving something that is 'the same', such as *'a genital organ like his own'*, or a male like himself.

[516] S Freud, *SE 12*, Analysis of a Phobia in a five year old boy, [1909], 1976, p109.

his childhood, since at that period this determinant is taken for granted as being of universal application, he is able to behave like little Hans, who showed his affection to little boys and girls indiscriminately, and once described his friend Fritzl as 'the girl he was fondest of' Hans was a homosexual (as all children may very well be), quite consistently with the fact, which must always be kept in mind, that he was acquainted with only one kind of genital organ — a genital organ like his own. ///// *He [Little Hans] has repeatedly run up to me [Daddy Hans] and bitten me.'*	*watch, To find the other forth, and by adventuring both I oft found both: I urge this childhood proof, Because what follows is pure innocence. I owe you much, and, like a wilful youth,* *That which I owe is lost; but if you please To shoot another arrow that self way Which you did shoot the first, I do not doubt, As I will watch the aim, or to find both Or bring your latter hazard back again And thankfully rest debtor for the first.'*	Bassanio describes the absence and presence of something the same that appears to describe a narcissistic love, *'the self same'*, which has two images, suggestive of Narcissus staring lovingly at the reflection of his own face in the water. Little Hans biting his father can be understood as an attempt to identify the well hidden lack in Daddy Hans by making a hole in him: *'That which I owe is lost . . .'* The repeated biting of Little Hans equates with the aggressive behaviour of some racists, such as the spitting that Shylock endured.

Sticks and stones may break Antonio's bones but words will always hurt Bassanio

These texts below develop the themes of the previous table, in particular the transformation of an imaginary relation of narcissism through symbolisation, also known as 'symbolic opposition', or binary opposition:

Little Hans	The Merchant of Venice	Comments
'Hans suddenly ran indoors as a carriage with two horses came along. I could see nothing unusual about it, and asked him what was wrong. 'The horses are so proud,' he said, 'that I'm afraid they'll fall down.' (The coachmen was reining the horses in tight, so that they were trotting with short steps and holding their heads high. In fact their action was 'proud'.) 'I asked him who it really was that was so proud.' 'He: 'You are, when I come into bed with Mummy.' 'I: 'So you want me to fall down?' 'Hans: 'Yes. You've got to be naked and knock up against a <u>stone</u> and bleed, and then I'll be able to be alone with Mummy for a little bit.' [517]	ANTONIO: In sooth, I know not why I am so sad: It wearies me; you say it wearies you; But how I caught it, found it, or came by it, that stuff 'tis made of, whereof it is born, I am to learn; And such a want-wit sadness makes of me, That I have much ado to know myself. SALARINO: Your mind is tossing on the ocean; There, where your argosies with portly sail, Like signiors and rich burghers on the flood, Or, as it were, the pageants of the sea, Do overpeer the petty traffickers, That curtsy to them, do them reverence, As they fly by them with their woven wings. SALANIO: Believe me, sir, had I such venture forth, The better part of my affections would Be with my hopes abroad. I should be still Plucking the grass, to know where sits the wind, Peering in maps for ports and piers and roads; And every object that might make me fear Misfortune to my ventures, out of doubt Would make me sad.	Sets of binary values are introduced: the two horses, that is the 'proud' and fallen, the 'sadness' of Antonio in the second line of the first paragraph, the laughter proposed by Bassanio, and Antonio's sadness: Salanio's speech sounds like a description of anxiety hysteria, the precursor of phobia in general and of the xenophobia in this particular case. In answer to the question as to who Little Hans was 'proud' of, he replied that it was his father, but that a fall and an injury to his father would allow Little Hans some enjoyment.

[517] S Freud, Analysis of a Phobia in a five year old boy, SE 12, [1909], 1976, p82 .

' . . . When he was three and a half . . . [Little Hans'] mother found him with his hand on his penis. She threatened him in these words: 'If you do that, I shall send for Dr A. to cut off your widdler. And then what'll you widdle with?'

Hans: '**With my bottom.**' [518]

SALARINO: My wind cooling my broth Would blow me to an ague, when I thought What harm a wind too great at sea might do. I should not see the sandy hour-glass run, But I should think of shallows and of flats, And see my wealthy Andrew dock'd in sand, Vailing her high-top lower than her ribs To kiss her burial. Should I go to church And see the holy edifice of _stone_, And not bethink me straight of _dangerous rocks_, Which touching but my gentle vessel's side, Would scatter all her spices on the stream, Enrobe the roaring waters with my silks, And, in a word, but even now worth this, And now worth nothing? Shall I have the thought To think on this, and shall I lack the thought That such a thing bechanced would make me sad? But tell not me; I know, Antonio Is sad to think upon his merchandise.

In both texts 'stone' is the cause of an injury that is the variable around which access to a woman is determined. The pride can also be identified in 'wealthy Andrew . . . Vailing her high-top', 'portly sail' and the pageants of the sea: the fall is identified in 'the petty traffickers', 'curtsy to them, do them reverence', 'of dangerous rocks, Which touching but my gentle vessel's side'.

This idea of trusting in *'one bottom'* may be a reference to homosexuality or narcissism.

In case you thought that Shakespeare's *'a more a swelling port'* is a straightforward reference to a penis, the issue is clarified immediately. Shakespeare makes clear that the *'chief care'*, the fall or injury, relates to a *'great debt'*, a symbolic debt. This is Lacan's notion of castration with reference to the phallus, not the penis. The symbolic debt is the debt all neurotics endure as the price for using symbols or language.

*ANTONIO Believe me, no: I thank my fortune for it, **My ventures are not in one bottom trusted,** Nor to one place; nor is my whole estate Upon the fortune of this present year: Therefore my merchandise makes me not sad.*

SALARINO Why, then you are in love.

BASSANIO 'Tis not unknown to you, Antonio, How much I have disabled mine estate, By something showing a more swelling port Than my faint means would grant continuance: Nor do I now make moan to be abridged From such a noble rate; but my chief care Is to come fairly off from the great debts Wherein my time something too prodigal Hath left me gaged. To you, Antonio, I owe the most, in money and in love, And from your love I have a warranty To unburden all my plots and purposes How to get clear of all the debts I owe.

'BASSANIO O sweet Portia . . . dear lady . . . not one vessel 'scrape the <u>dreadful touch</u> Of merchant-marring rocks?

CHAPTER FIFTEEN   INTERPRETATION II

Ambivalence, binary opposition, morality, paternity are considered in relation to phobia

LITTLE HANS AS LOVING AND VIOLENT	SHYLOCK AS KIND AND DEMONIC	ANOTHER STORY THAT ALSO STARS: AN INJURIOUS STONE, A PHOBIA, A DEBT AND THE PROBLEM OF THE ROLE OF A FATHER.	SOME COMMON ELEMENTS
'[Hans' father asked] '. . . have I ever scolded you or hit you?' Hans corrected him: 'Oh yes! You have hit me. 'That's not true. When was it, anyhow?.' 'This morning,' answered the little boy; and his father recollected that Hans had quite unexpectedly butted his head into his stomach, so that he had given him as it were a reflex blow with his hand. It was remarkable that he had not brought this detail into connection with the neurosis; but he now recognised it as an expression of the little boy's hostile disposition towards him, and perhaps also as a manifestation of a need for getting punished for it.' Later on the boy repeated his reaction towards his father in a clearer and more complete manner, by first hitting his father on the hand and then affectionately . . . he came into bed with me, whereas for the last few days he had not been	*LAUNCELOT* *. . . this Jew my master. The fiend . . .Well, the most courageous fiend bids me friend Launcelot, being an honest man's son,' or rather an honest woman's son; for, indeed, my father did something smack, something grow to, he had a kind of taste well, my conscience says 'Launcelot, budge not.' 'Budge,' says the fiend. 'Budge not,' says my conscience. 'Conscience,' say I, 'you*	*ANOTHER STORY THAT ALSO STARS: AN INJURIOUS STONE, A PHOBIA, A DEBT AND THE PROBLEM OF THE ROLE OF A FATHER.* **'FAMILY SUES BRONX ZOO AFTER GORILLA ACTS LIKE A WILD ANIMAL** [519], 'Ray Fernandez . . . became aware that his children were afraid of animals. Motivated by a determination to cure them of the phobia, he took them to one of the world's best-known zoos. But his son . . . was hit on the head by a <u>stone</u> hurled by a gorilla. He needed . . . stitches and ended up on the psychiatrist's couch. 'I had bad dreams and one-time I had a	In the zoo story there are two phobic values: 'I had a dream that the gorilla killed me' and 'gorillas are timid', and the problematic question of

[519] *The Guardian* (UK Newspaper), 20.1.99.

coming any more and had even seemed to be proud of not doing so. 'And why you come today?' I asked. 'Hans: 'When I'm not frightened I shan't come any more.' 'I: 'So you come in to me because you're frightened?' //////////// . . . this portion of Hans's anxiety had two constituents: there was fear of his father and fear for his father. The former was derived from his hostility towards his father, and the latter from the conflict between his affection, which was exaggerated at this point by way of compensation, and his hostility. ///// But Hans was not by any means a bad character: he was not even one of those children who at his age still give free play to the propensity towards cruelty and violence which is a constituent of human nature. On the contrary, he had an unusually kind-hearted and affectionate disposition: his father reported that the transformation of aggressive tendencies into feelings of pity . . . .

counsel well;' 'Fiend,' say I, 'you counsel well:' to be ruled by my conscience, I should stay with the Jew my master, . . . is a kind of devil; and, to run away from the Jew, I should be ruled by the fiend, who, saving your reverence, is the devil himself. Certainly the Jew is the very devil incarnal; and, in my conscience, my conscience is but a kind of hard conscience, to offer to counsel me to stay with the Jew. The fiend gives the more friendly counsel: I will run, fiend; my heels are at your command; I will run.

dream that the gorilla killed me and I started getting really scared'. The psychiatrist recommended a return visit. But that time the entire family was bombarded by the gorilla. The family has now filed a one million-dollar claim against the zoo. 'We are in front of the gorilla. He looked at us and started throwing stones,' Mr Fernandez said. . . . 'my first reaction was 'Who threw the rock?' Everybody started saying it was the gorilla. My son was sort of in a daze and his first words to me were: 'Daddy, am I going to die?' That was a hell of a thing to hear as a father.' The family have rejected an offer of lifetime membership of the zoo. .
.

the role of a father.

There are also two values for Launcelot: **'Budge,' says the fiend', and 'Budge not' says my conscience.'** These two values parallel yet another two: *'the Jew is the very devil'* and:

...And Hans deeply loved the father against whom he cherished these death-wishes; and while his intellect demurred to such a contradiction, he could not help demonstrating the fact of its existence, by hitting his father and immediately afterwards kissing the place he had hit. We ourselves, too, must guard against making a difficulty of such a contradiction. The emotional life of man is in general made up of pairs of contraries such as these.	**BASSANIO** [to Shylock] *This were kindness.* ///// **ANTONIO** *Hie thee, gentle Jew. The Hebrew will turn Christian: he grows* **_kind_**	*A primatologist . . . said the gorilla was just acting naturally. 'This throwing is quite normal. It's just a scared tactic, it's clearly frustration. Gorillas are <u>timid animals</u>.'*	*'***ANTONIO** *Hie thee, gentle Jew. The Hebrew will turn Christian: he grows kind'.*

Why is Shylock demonised and, why despite his suffering and protest, is his subjectivity finally absented?

The harsh superego of phobics is often quick to pronounce moral judgment of the sort seen in the case of the agoraphobic woman's disgust, in racism and in the demonising of Shylock. Why? Because

'One oppresses one's neighbour much better when one doesn't know him. The pangs of conscience disappear.' [520]

The harshness of the superego is the attempt to compensate for the weakness or absence of the paternal function, or symbolic father. This is why the aim of Shylock's famous speech aims to establish his humanity, his status as a suffering living subject through identification or pity: *'He hath disgraced me, and hindered me half a million; laughed at my losses, mocked at my gains, scorned my nation, thwarted my bargains, cooled my friends, heated mine enemies; and what's his reason? I am a Jew. Hath not a Jew eyes? hath not a Jew hands, organs, dimensions, senses, affections, passions? Fed with the same food, hurt with the same weapons, subject, to*

---

[520] G Janouch, *Conversations With Kafka*, Encounter, 1971, p114.

the same diseases? If you prick us, do we not bleed? if you tickle us, do we not laugh? if you poison us, do we not die? and if you wrong us, shall we not revenge? If we are like you in the rest, we will resemble you in that. If a Jew wrong a Christian, what is his humility? Revenge. If a Christian wrong a Jew, what should his sufferance be by Christian example? Why, revenge. The villany you teach me, I will execute, and it shall go hard but I will better the instruction.'

Shakespeare's portrayal of Freud's 'complete Oedipus complex' in *Twelfth Night*

In *Twelfth Night; or What you Will* we start with a man, Duke Orsino, who suffers with love, represented by a relation with the sea. The sea also threatened the estate and the life of Antonio in the Merchant of Venice, and it is the sea which receives and ultimately returns the narcissism of the identical twin Sebastian, the brother of Viola. So the sea is associated with absence and presence, loss and gain, death and life or profit in *The Merchant of Venice* and *Twelfth Night*:

'Receiveth as the sea, nought enters there,

Of what validity and pitch soe'er,

*But **falls into abatement and low price**,*

Even in a minute: so full of shapes is fancy

That it alone is high fantastical.'

The sea gives birth to the world of values. We will return to the fall into abatement and low price [521], and the question of price, which describes Duke Orsino's love for Olivia. Olivia is a *'virtuous maid'* (line 34) who has been mourning for her dead father and brother:

'To pay this debt of love but to a brother'

While Duke Orsino's love for Olivia pursued him like cruel hounds (lines 21 and 22), Olivia cannot tolerate the company of potential male lovers (lines 38 and 39). So far then a woman loves exclusively two dead men with whom she could not legally have sex, and a man loves a woman who cannot tolerate the idea of loving him: a fine depiction of the harmony of sex and love.

The second scene sets out with another dramatic separation and loss, again of a brother, again at sea: Sebastian and his sister, Viola —twins— who appear identical, were 'split' (line eight) apart, recalling Aristophanes' myth in which

---

[521] See Freud's On the Universal Tendency towards **Debasement** in the Sphere of Love, *SE 11*, [1912d], 1976.

humanity was once made up by eight limbed creatures with two faces that reproduced asexually, each creature cloning itself. But the gods punished humanity, splitting each creature into two. Since that time every man and woman has desperately sought their other half; when a man or woman believes that he or she has found their other half they stick together with nostalgic enthusiasm.

The triangle of paired characters appears to explain the total absence of mothers in both plays, but as Shakespeare shows the Oedipus complex is not so simple; for each 'person' in the drama is divided, ambivalent. Each possesses or is possessed by opposing demands and desires. On this theme Freud wrote that:

'[O]ne gets the impression that the simple Oedipus complex is by no means its commonest form, but rather represents a simplification or schematisation which, to be sure, is often enough justified for practical purposes. Closer study usually discloses the more complete Oedipus complex, which is two fold, positive and negative, and is due to the bisexuality originally present in children: that is to say, a boy has not merely an ambivalent object choice towards his mother, but at the same time he also behaves like a girl and displays an affectionate feminine attitude to his father and a corresponding jealousy and hostility towards his mother . . . It may even be that the ambivalence displayed in the relations to the parents should be attributed entirely to bisexuality . . . At the shipwreck [522] of the Oedipus complex the four trends of which it consists will group themselves in such a way as to produce a father identification and a mother identification.' [523]

And Lacan wrote:

'We are at bottom in the same boat as Oedipus, even if we don't know it. As far as the father that Oedipus knew is concerned, he only becomes the father, as Freud's myth indicates, once he is dead.' [524]

Freud, writing on the same topic explained that:

'The Oedipus complex would go to its destruction from its lack of success, from the effects of its internal impossibility. Another view is that the Oedipus complex must collapse because the time has come for its disintegration . . . The Oedipus complex offered the child two possibilities of satisfaction, an active and a passive one. He could put himself in his father's place in a masculine fashion and have intercourse with his mother as his father did, in which case he would soon have felt the latter as a hindrance; or he might want to take the place of his mother and be loved by his father, in which case his mother would become superfluous . . . In this conflict the . . . child's ego turns away from the Oedipus complex . . . The

---

[522] I relied on Cassell's *German dictionary* for the translation of 'untergang' as 'shipwreck'.

[523] S Freud, The Ego and the Id [1923] *SE 19,* p372.

[524] J Lacan, *The Ethics of Psychoanalysis, The Seminar of Jacques Lacan,* ed Miller, trans Porter, 1992, p309.

object-investments [objects] are given up and replaced by identifications [signifiers].' [525]

A shipwreck, or its possibility, in both *The Merchant of Venice* and *Twelfth Night* are crucial in bringing about a vital loss which then allows a love and idealisation. In The Merchant of Venice it is the whole of Antonio's estate that is at risk, against which he stakes his life in order that Bassanio can successfully woo Portia. Without the risk of the shipwrecking, and the risk of Antonio losing his life Bassanio would have been altogether without the means of successfully loving Portia. 'Portia' appears to be so named because of the relation of a ship to a port as standing for the relation of a penis to a vagina. This is suggested by:

ANTONIO Well, tell me now what lady is the same

To whom you swore a secret pilgrimage,

That you to-day promised to tell me of?

BASSANIO 'Tis not unknown to you, Antonio,

How much I have disabled mine estate, By something showing a more swelling port Than my faint means would grant continuance: Nor do I now make moan to be abridged From such a noble rate; but my chief care Is to come fairly off from the great debts Wherein my time something too prodigal Hath left me gaged. To you, Antonio, I owe the most, in money and in love, And from your love I have a warranty To unburden all my plots and purposes how to get clear of all the debts I owe.'

Further Reading

N Charraud, A Calculus of Convergence, *Drawing the Soul*, Rebus Press, 2000.

---

[525] S Freud, The Downfall of the Oedipus Complex, *SE 19*, [1924], 1976, p173-4.

CHAPTER SIXTEEN

Ethics, ends and psychoanalysis

Does psychoanalysis reduce suffering? Sometimes it does, but psychoanalysis does not claim that 'when you finally discover what you desire, all your suffering will cease and life will become good'. The function of psychoanalysis, according to Freud was to:

'transform . . . hysterical misery into common unhappiness. With a mental life that has been restored to health you will be better armed against that unhappiness.' [526]

Lacanian psychoanalysis does not offer salvation. Indeed Lacan thought that when people recognised and acted on their desire, then their life would often become difficult and conflict ridden, but in a different way. The new way is accepted by the subject as the price worth paying, so that their suffering can take a different form. Following your desire is not easy. There is often a high cost, as we saw in the case of the married father who discovered that he was homosexual. It is the fear of paying a high cost that demands that desires are kept unconscious and hidden away in relative safely. Psychoanalysis can sometimes reduce suffering, but only at the cost of the subject giving up some enjoyment, the jouissance of symptoms.

So it is not unusual for someone to complete an analysis, and then to consciously decide to keep their symptoms, as this joke illustrates: a man had been going to the same bar for a few years. One evening he urinated against the bar. The next day he did the same. The barman had got to know him well and suggested that he consult a psychoanalyst. So the unfortunate man underwent a lengthy and expensive analysis, and some years later returned to the bar, said *'Hello'* to the barman, and pissed against the bar. The barman was astonished and said *'I don't understand; you've been psychoanalysed, but you're still peeing on my bar?'* *'Yes'* he said, *'I've been analysed; now I know why I do it.'*

Psychoanalysis has no behavioural goals, so it is not a cure for difficult or antisocial people. It does not have the goal of bringing about 'better adjustment to reality', or making you nicer, more successful, less inhibited, or more inhibited. But psychoanalysis is a privileged technique for finding your essence, the division, unique lack and desire that has caused you to live your life in the way you have. What you do with this fundamental truth about yourself is not a psychoanalytic issue. Psychoanalysis has no prescriptive rules or Utopian schemes. It does not tell

---

[526] S Freud, The Psychotherapy of Hysteria, *SE 2*, [1893], 1976, p305.

you what to do, but offers a unique appreciation for each person in analysis of what it means to be that subject.

Yet there are some who have had terrible experiences and much suffering, for whom psychoanalysis has allowed revolutionary and dramatic changes in their lives, almost miracles. While psychoanalysis is uniquely privileged in its analysis of desire, it is not the only source of information on this question. It is possible to learn something about your desire through everyday life, gardening, messy love affairs or Zen meditation, although these other methods won't be as efficient or as thorough.

What does psychoanalysis have to say about the meaning of life?

In psychoanalysis there is an answer to this question that is neither grandiose nor trivial: 'meaning' is understood as a function of language, the property of words, as the passage and rewriting of the signifier. So the meaning of life is the life of meaning. Psychoanalysis aims for an understanding of the meaning of a unique subject's life, through a study of 'his signifiers', and in particular his fundamental fantasy. At The End of analysis a subject can speak clearly about the meaning of *his* life instead of having *his* symptoms speak unconsciously for him, and he can act on his desire instead of his demand.

What is 'The Good' of psychoanalysis?

'I do not think our cures can compete with those of Lourdes. There are so many more people who believe in the miracles of the Blessed Virgin than in the existence of the unconscious.' [527]

If you are analysed you will come to revalue and review your conception of what 'good' and 'bad' have meant for your Other in a way that could not have been foreseen. You will possess a knowledge of how your fantasises, symptoms and speech have been demands addressed to 'The Good' of your Other, rather than honestly following your own desire. The potential to revalue the Good that psychoanalytic work offers ought to be taken seriously; 'good' is the stuff of ethics, along with the questions and answers as to what we 'ought to do' as individuals and collectively. For this reason Lacan argued that ethical considerations can only be properly made *after* desire has been identified. Prior to identifying your desire you are compelled —or driven— to act on your demands, and demands are a kind of deceit because the subject doesn't desire the object of his demand. If the object of demand is provided the subject is driven to continually demand and demand, like Sisyphus who was condemned to roll a heavy boulder to the top of a mountain. Just before the summit was reached the

---

[527] S Freud, New Introductory Lectures in Psychoanalysis, Explanations and Applications, *SE 22*, [1933], 1976, p152.

boulder would always roll back down to the bottom again. The object that Sisyphus aimed for, but never reached, was the summit: the object of demand is that which the Other cannot provide, and if the Other does provide the object then a new and hopefully impossible object will be selected, again and again without end, until desire has been identified or death intervenes. [528]

So there are no ethical actions or interpretations made in reliance on the subject's demands. If behaviour has been motivated by demand then it has already hopelessly confused any clear consideration of ethical issues because the subject is confused about the more fundamental distinction between his desire and his Other's desire.

Before you can place a value on things, or decide what is good or bad you first have to know your desire. So the purpose of analysis is the analysis of purpose. You have to know your desires before you can begin to become clear about your values. A version of this idea is relied in the courts of law where a key question for a judge or jury is often to try and answer the question: What has been identified as the intention or desire? Imagine a defendant who has stabbed a man in the neck with a pair of scissors. What was his desire? We can imagine that in one case, where the accused's desire is identified as being murderous; he would be guilty of murder. But if his desire was of a different type, such as the desire to cut and style the man's hair, but he happened to be pushed in an accident, which led him to stab the man's neck, then the verdict would be different.

So ethical issues can only be decided *after* the prior issues of desire have been identified. The question as to what is good or bad is an ethical question, and ethical questions can only be properly considered once you have got clear about the desire at stake. And that question, the question of desire —What is it? — is the principal question that psychoanalysis seeks to answer. Psychoanalysis is ethically unique because it is unsurpassed in facilitating the reassessment of ethical judgements. Here is an illustration: it is now widely thought that much past and present legislation against homosexuals was produced by people who were themselves struggling to repress their own homosexual desires. They took what they claimed was 'an ethical platform', they argued that they were 'for the good', 'for the good heterosexuals', and 'against the bad homosexuals'. If these people had been psychoanalysed some might have come to see that 'ethical positions' were not foremost for them, but that they were instead trying, above all, to mislead themselves about their own desire, about their own repressed homosexuality; there is little doubt that many homophobes are defending against the recognition of their own homosexuality.

---

[528] At The End of analysis the drive —that which compels— takes up a different relation to the little object.

Once you can identify and, perhaps, act on your desire, then you can make ethical assessments. Prior to knowing your desire you necessarily act in ignorance, unable to make informed ethical judgements. Psychoanalysis is a technique that allows the judgment 'good' or 'bad' to be made.

One of the purposes of psychoanalysis, surprisingly some might say, is 'to change beliefs'. What would be the point of a difficult and time-consuming activity of no direct practical value —such as psychoanalysis— if it did not allow you to change your beliefs? Yet psychoanalysis is not to be found listed or described in books on the techniques of persuasion in which hypnosis and brain washing are routinely included, perhaps because the profound changes in belief that psychoanalysis brings about cannot be accurately predicted, or relied on to produce a specific attitude or behaviour.

What kind of beliefs does psychoanalysis change? Typically sexual ones. That is, 'sexual' in the broadest sense. Remember the woman who repeatedly found herself in relationships with men who beat her? Her sexual belief was that being a woman meant being hit by a man you love. For her 'man', 'woman' and 'hit' and 'being hit on' were connected sexual terms. In psychoanalysis clients discover the unique meaning that their valuations of love and sex relations have taken. In the above case the client changed her sexual beliefs about the meanings of 'man', 'woman' and 'love' through the analysis of her speech.

There are a number of positive arguments for the practice of psychoanalysis, and a more compelling negative argument. If there is some predetermined or prior notion of some service or good then psychoanalysis might be compared on equal terms with other therapies along the lines of outcome studies. I don't suppose that this approach would produce any highly persuasive arguments favouring psychoanalysis. It is certainly true that psychoanalysis can in some cases appear to work miracles, enabling previously 'unfit' individuals to work and love. But such benefits —love and work— are sometimes assumed to be ideal outcomes prior to any clinical work taking place. The practice of psychoanalysis insists that such predetermined outcomes are not assumed or aimed for by the clinician.

The most persuasive argument for being psychoanalysed is negative. It is not that psychoanalysis can be relied on to produce fantastic benefits, although in some cases it may, but, of all the alternatives, including other therapies, holidays, meditation, masturbation, religion and unanalysed neurosis, psychoanalysis is tolerated best of all by many who are giving voice to their struggling desire, as it wrestles with their taxing demand. If you are searching for the truth of your desire then psychoanalysis is the probably most efficient method, with the least surplus baggage and cost.

There is an analogy: by the time that most men and women have become sufficiently aware of their disappointment with love, perhaps in their thirties or forties, reflections can often be heard along the lines: 'my quest for the ideal man

/ woman will not provide the solution to all my problems, as I used to believe, but men / women are the best love objects that I have been able to find.'

I can imagine an objection to the above: *'But you have assumed a prior good, that of the truth of desire'*. This objection fails because the psychoanalyst should not assume that desire is good, but instead that to get clear about what is good one first must have some measure of desire. It is often those with the most to hide who proclaim the loudest that the truth must be uncovered regardless of the cost. Such proclamations are naive on the one hand and monstrous on the other. The truth can do great harm, although in some cases it may do some good. The merit of psychoanalysis is that it puts the questions of the costs and benefits of the truth of the subject's desire before him or her with sufficient clarity for that individual to choose how to act and live with the consequences of their desire, at their own pace. There is no activity outside psychoanalysis as efficient at offering the subject the timely opportunity to recognise and act on his desire. For many this opportunity for responsibility is judged 'unwelcome'. No doubt there is some wisdom in an individual's choice not to pursue the truth of their desire, however parochial it may appear to those who suppose themselves to know better.

What are 'The Ethics of Psychoanalysis'?

The ethics relied on by doctors are inappropriate for psychoanalysts; doctors are paid to provide their clients with benefits based on their positive beliefs or knowledge: psychoanalysts are paid for their persistent ignorance, which they rely on to study the speech and beliefs of their clients. The standard sets of professional ethics produced by professional organisations may be of some benefit to some clients but their principal function is to protect clinicians as a profession and help them make money. No amount of professional ethics of the sort found in professional charters will be of significant help when it comes to working as a Lacanian.

What is so special about Lacanian ethics? Their focus on the desire of the analyst. The desire of the analyst is relied on fundamentally in every interpretation because: *'The analyst says: "I am possessed by a stronger desire".'* [529] What does this mean? If a client misses six consecutive sessions, or repeatedly criticises the clinician's appearance or spends years complaining *'I am wasting my time and my money here'*, then, if your desire is stronger than your client's demands, psychoanalysis may take place. If your desire is weaker, psychoanalytic work is unlikely to take place because you risk being distracted by the demand of your client's symptoms.

The idea of 'one person's desire being stronger than an other's' should be clarified because desire is always fundamentally the *'desire for the Other's*

---

[529] J Lacan, Seminar on Transference, unpublished, trans Gallagher, 8 March 1961.

desire'. That is the desire of the clinician is for his client's desire, which can only emerge from the working through of the client's demand. Clinical work is difficult for both clinicians and clients. Only if the clinician can tolerate his client's demands does the client have a chance of working through them and reaching their desire. This is why the identification by the analyst of his own desire —as the desire for the other's desire— is a fundamental ethical foundation stone for all his clinical work with others. Lacanian ethics are not a set of rules reached for only on the occasion of an emergency: every single interpretation relies on the clinician's desire as distinct from their pity, sympathy or identifications with the client.

No comprehensive list of prohibited actions or interpretations could ever be substituted for the continual pursuit of the ethical principal of the clinician's desire for difference. For this reason supervision is necessary to support ethical practice, however experienced the clinician is, and there may well be good reasons for an experienced clinician who has previously gone to The End of analysis, to be further analysed.

Symptoms or demands are attempts to establish or prove the limits of the subject's phallic function, that is the domain of his power. Until the subject can properly establish —through the elaboration of a series of demands or proofs— the relation of his power and castration relation to his Other, the subject will continue to demand. That is, he will continue to apply his proof procedure, his attempts to identify the truth of his power and its lack. Only when the subject of demand has identified his castration or investment can he identify and act on his desire. Only when the subject of demand establishes what is impossible for his Other is he able to discover what is possible for himself as his desire.

This equation of the limits of the subject's power, marked out by 'the good of the Other' invokes Nietzsche's profound equation of 'power' with 'goodness'. Nietzsche argued that any analysis of 'the good' could always be reduced to, or understood in terms of power. [530]

The beginning and the middle of analysis

Freud had argued that there were two phases in clinical work, or three, depending on how you count:

---

[530] A unique *'Beyond Good And Evil'* is established in the completion of each individual's analysis, as the subject's desire can go beyond of the good of the Other, and evil is exhaustively identified as *'our eternal inability to find what we seek.'*, F Nietzsche, *My Sister and I*, Amok Books, 1990, p103. *'The subject never refinds'*, Freud writes, *'anything but another object that answers more or less satisfactorily to the needs in question.'* So we can deduce, if the two quotations above are true, that every ordinary subject is evil, because the loss of the object is universal in neurosis.

'All the libido, as well as everything opposing it, is made to converge slowly on the relation with a doctor [clinician]. In this process the symptoms are inevitably divested of libido. In place of his patients true illness there appears the artificially constructed transference illness, in place of the various unreal objects of the libido there appears a single, and once more imaginary, object in the person of the doctor . . . **Thus our therapeutic work falls into two phases**. *In the first, all the* **libido is forced from symptoms into the transference** *and concentrated there; in the second,* **struggle is waged around this new object and the libido is liberated from it**.*' [531]

Lacan argued that there are three phases in the analysis of neurotics. This claim is related to two Lacanian innovations: a new theory of The End of analysis, and a big increase in the amount of time that Lacanians take to complete analyses, typically some ten to fifteen years compared to anything between a few months to three and a half years for Freud [532]. Lacan's three phases of analysis are:

1. The rectification of the subject's relations with the real.
2. The development of the transference.
3. Interpretation.

'[There is order in the] direction of the treatment . . . According to a process that begins with the rectification of the subject's relations with the real, and proceeds first to the development of the transference, then to interpretation.' [533]

We will now look at each stage in more detail.

'Rectification of the subject's relations with the real'

This technique is the sensitively carried out deduction of contradictions and inconsistencies found in their speech of neurotics. Rules for carrying out these deductions are in the section called 'Logic Rules' in Chapter Ten on Obsessional Neurosis. The rectification of the subject's relations with the real is likely to have the following effects:

a. A deepening of the client's transference with the clinician.

---

[531] S Freud, Introductory Lectures on Psychoanalysis, Analytic Therapy, *SE 16*, [1917],1976, p454-5. In this quote we can see a description of Lacan's little object, and of the drive that is released at The End of analysis.
[532] See for example, *Sigmund Freud and Lou Andreas-Salome Letters*, ed Pfeiffer, Hogarth Press, 1972, p80.
[533] J Lacan, *Ecrits*, The Direction of the Treatment, trans Sheridan, Tavistock Routledge, London, [1966], 1980, p237.

b. The client's awareness of their contradictions, producing a shift from their demand for help or relief from their symptoms, especially if they are hysterical, to a demand for knowledge of their desire that will explain their symptoms.

c. The production of new material.

Rectification of the subject's relations with the real is not suddenly given up as the work progresses but becomes used increasingly rarely as the client actively searches out and identifies tensions and contradictions in their own speech.

On happy and unhappy returns —the *'Development of the transference'*

Pythagoras believed that whatever is happening now, will happen again, exactly as it is now, an infinite number of times. The whole course of history and of the future too is just a series of identical repetitions, going round and round. So you will read this sentence, just as you are now, an infinite number of times. On your second, third and nth such reading you will have no new criticism or understanding: everything will be just as it is now. This is Pythagoras' theory of eternal recurrence.

Psychoanalysis of course has nothing to contribute towards ascertaining the truth or falsity of this grand theory, but it is clear that repetition and return in psychoanalysis —over the course of clinical treatment— are not of this Pythagorean variety.

The middle stage of analysis is characterised by having passed the point of no return. One client explained: *'It is like I am swimming: I cannot see the shore ahead, and I have lost sight of where I set out from.'*

Paradoxically, The End of Analysis is marked by a return to the point of origin, that is to the problem/s or question/s that the analysis started out with. This return is not a pure return of the Pythagorean sort, without any change in the subject's resources or his ability to organise change, but a return in which the subject has —for the first time— a unique freedom to do something different with his life. A freedom to give up the repetitions of demand that formed his symptom, and do something else instead with the drive or energy that his symptom had greedily consumed. At the start of analysis the subject has some kind of repetition or symptom that he complained about: by the middle stage he cannot innocently return to his symptom because he possesses some coherent and conscious knowledge of its meaning: at The End he can return knowingly to the problem of his symptom, in possession of sufficient knowledge of its meaning and his fundamental fantasy to make changes and allow something novel, through a giving up of the repetition of symptomatic demands:

'We shall not cease from exploration
And the end of all our exploring
Will be to arrive where we started
And know the place for the first time.' [534]

This work is only carried out through transference, claimed Lacan: *'The transference becomes the analyst's security, and the relation to the real, the terrain on which the combat is decided. The interpretation, which is being postponed until consolidation of the transference now becomes subordinated to reduction of the transference.'* [535] This accords with Freud's assertion that: *'The transference becomes the battlefield on which all the mutually struggling forces should meet one another.'* [536]

How does transference change? By the end of the first phase of analysis the transference is well established. But transference is not a stable constant: in the second phase the silence, and the deductions or interpretations ought to take on a different character; in reliance on the transference, and the establishment of a unique linguistic subculture between client and clinician, interpretations can become more enigmatic and expansive, that is more equivocal. Ending a session on a highly equivocal interpretation early in the first phase is likely to frighten the client away: but the same technique used later is more likely to stimulate the client to produce new material. What has occurred in the movement from first to second phase that explains this? A shift from a demand for help or relief from their symptoms to a demand for knowledge, a knowledge that the client comes to believe they alone possess, or the means to possess.

Where else is the imperative —frustrate— observed? Why is it that many negotiating the early stages of courtship set out to be sexually attractive, and yet will not allow the one in whom they are sexually interested to have sex with them? It is usual for women to carefully set out to sexually frustrate their hoped for long-term partner because they fear —no doubt with good reason— that allowing their partner to have this jouissance would be to risk ending the relationship prematurely. What justification is there for this practice? What is the theory that these women are relying on? Perhaps a version of Freud's and Lacan's theory of demand and desire? It is only through the progressive exhaustion of demand that desire emerges. To some extent sexual activity early in a relationship, and the likelihood of a long-term relationship are seen as mutually exclusive. Many women and most mothers know that to create the best conditions

---

[534] T.S. Eliot, Little Gidding, *Four Quartets*, 1943.

[535] J Lacan, *Ecrits*, The Direction of the Treatment, trans Sheridan, Tavistock Routledge, London, [1966], 1980, p235.

[536] S Freud, Introductory Lectures on Psychoanalysis, Analytic Therapy, *SE 16*, [1917], 1976, p454-5.

for desire, some demand must first be worked through, as frustration and or castration, just as Lacanians must work with the client, through his demand, in order to isolate his desire:

'If I frustrate him [the client] it is because he asks me for something. To answer him, in fact. But he knows very well that it would be mere words. And he can get those from whom ever he likes . . . It's not these words he's asking for. He is simply asking me, from the very fact that he's speaking: his demand . . . carries no object with it.' [537]

'Thus the analyst is he who supports the demand, not, as has been said, to frustrate the subject, but in order to allow the signifiers in which his frustration is bound to reappear.' [538]

'The importance of preserving the place of desire in the direction of treatment necessitates that one should orientate this place in relation to the effects of demand, which alone are . . . conceived as the principle of the power of the treatment.' [539]

Silence and the ending of a session are useful techniques for deepening the transference. During this second phase much of the 'working through' takes place. Working through is the elaboration of themes and material introduced earlier, the approaching of the same field of problems from a number of different perspectives until a path through can be found.

'Interpretation'

Why did Lacan claim that the last phase of analysis is distinguished by 'interpretation'? Distinguishing the last phase of analysis by 'interpretation' is surprising because interpretation will have been taking place from the outset. What will have changed is the type of interpretation. In the first phase interpretations were characterised by rectifying the subject's relations with the real: in the second phase interpretation became more equivocal or expansive: in the third phase interpretation is still more equivocal or expansive as the clinician invites the client to locate him in the position of the little other or little a. How in more general terms can The End of analysis be understood?

---

[537] J Lacan, *Ecrits*, The Direction of the Treatment, trans Sheridan, Tavistock Routledge, London, [1966], 1980, p254.
[538] Ibid p255.
[539] Ibid p269.

The End of Analysis

'Anyone who hopes to learn the noble game of chess from books will soon discover that only the openings and end games admit of an exhaustive systematic presentation and that the infinite variety of moves which develop after the opening defy any such description. This gap in instruction can only be filled by a diligent study of games fought out by master hands. The rules which can be laid down for the practice of psychoanalytic treatment are subject to similar limitations.' [540]	*'In the analytic discourse the fantasy can emerge [and] tells us a bit more about how the foundation of the master's discourse is.'* [541] *'It's by what the truth of the discourse of the master is masked that analysis derives its importance.'* [542]

What is 'The End of analysis'? Because this is an introductory text, and The End of analysis is a difficult idea and takes many years to achieve, I haven't spent much time on it here. If you're talking about what happens at the end of clinical work in different schools, such as in Ego Psychology, then that's a very different thing from what happens at The End in the Lacanian tradition. In Ego Psychology the aim of the work is *'adaptation to reality',* and the establishment of a *'conflict free zone in the ego'* so, as the clinical work progresses, the ego of the client will supposedly become 'better adapted', and his ego increasingly identical to the clinician's ego. So with this approach the progress of clinical work is described by a kind of polishing. At the end the client has finished polishing his ego. It has become bright and shiny, and is supposed to clearly reflect an accurate image of the world outside, as well as 'the whole person' inside! This ideal is very different from The End of Lacanian work: the establishment of difference as the condition of desire. To understand The End of analysis in Lacanian terms is not straightforward; there are many ways of explaining it.

It is as if the client has the project of producing a highly detailed map of an area through which they have passed, and on which they wish to gain a perspective, in order to become free so as to move, perhaps on to a new location off the map. The terrain is complex. There are obstacles, mountains, paths that disappear and reappear, impasses and so on. Whenever the client speaks the same landscape is referred to, travelled along and described but from a different perspective. With each apparent repetition is a revaluation of that which came before it. Just as triangulation is a technique relied on by map makers, so the unique co-ordinates

---

[540] S Freud, Further Recommendations in the Technique of Psychoanalysis, *SE 12*, [1914], 1976, p147.
[541] J Lacan, The Inverse of Psychoanalysis, unpublished seminar, trans Gallagher, 11 March, 1970.
[542] Ibid, 18 February 1970.

of each subject's place in the Oedipus become better identified and symbolised in the context of his place in the family and its romances, demands and desires. For a more detailed and accurate account of this simplified idea of 'triangulation' see Chapter Ten on obsessional neurosis, and the section on Shakespeare in Chapter Fifteen.

Another related way of looking at this problem was described by Empedocles, the Ancient Greek philosopher who influenced Freud [543]. Empedocles identified conflict or strife and love as an entangled pair, symbiotic, mutually perpetuating and mutually destructive. With this theory in mind we can lean on an analysis of the outcomes of war to clarify The End of analysis.

What is the ideal outcome of war? What is the good of war? For some the surrender of the enemy is sought. What might this entail? Sometimes surrender is unconditional, at other times surrender simply insists on rituals of submission or humiliation, the giving up of certain claims or the payment of damages. The victor sometimes insists on a regular tribute or tax from the one he has conquered. In other cases the ideal outcome of war is the complete elimination of the enemy. What parallels are to be found in the end of war and The End of analysis?

Within Ego Psychology the end is characterised by a singular and specific ideal. The client is to identify his ego with his clinician's ego! The clinician's ego is 'ideal'. The victor of this struggle suddenly has an ally who is —in part— identical to himself! 'If you can't beat them join them' has been a popular option for those on the losing side. At the end of war the vanquished can clearly recognise the identity of their master or Other, who they have become a slavish part of: in Lacanian analysis there is no sameness aimed for, no straightforward uniformity, instead the opposite is sought: difference because:

'It is in as much as the analyst's desire, which remains an x, tends in a direction which is the exact opposite of identification, that the crossing of the plane of identification is possible, through the mediation of the separation of the subject . . . The analyst's desire is not a pure desire. It is a desire to obtain absolute difference . . . ' [544]

In contrast 'synthesis', the opposite of analysis, exampled by love and symptoms usually involves the glossing over and ignoring of difference. When freshly in love people often claim that *'this or that thing about my lover is exactly the same for both of us'.* The appearance of 'agreement' is usually far easier to achieve and manage than confident disagreement or difference. Properly establishing a few points of vital difference —through a painstaking analysis of words— is much harder work than imagining huge fields of agreement. In shocking contrast to

---

[543] S Freud, Analysis Terminable and Interminable, *SE 23,* [1937], 1976.

[544] J Lacan, *The Four Fundamental Concepts of Psychoanalysis,* trans Sheridan, Pelican, London, 1979, p273-6.

Lacan's policy of obtaining *'absolute difference'* one clinician[545] has confessed to falling in love with every one of his clients and to telling them so, believing that: *'The patient's self esteem benefits greatly from his sensing that he (or she) is capable of arousing such responses in his analyst'.*

This potentially injurious technique is founded on a number of false assumptions. Analysis is primarily of unconscious desire, not of *'self esteem'*, which is often a conscious function, and always a function of the ego: not the unconscious. Secondly the patient is always driven to carry out their difficult clinical work because of their historical problems: the placing of new complications before the client, such as the clinician declaring his love for the client is nothing to do with the analysis of problematic relations whose origins are in the past, but the tragically misguided attempt to synthesise a new relation that is likely, at best, to cover up the old ones. Searles goes on to argue that neurosis and psychosis could be avoided —if only parents would mutually renounce their desire for their children— instead of coldly pushing them away. As if it were a simply voluntary act of consciousness to 'renounce ones desire'! This idea totally ignores the existence of the unconscious, the home of most, or all of our desires, and the fact that:

'symptoms are supported by the ego . . . Because they [symptoms] have a side with which they offer satisfaction to the repressing purpose of the ego.' [546]

Given this clear position of Freud's, how then are we to understand his claim that:

*'. . . settling the [above] conflict by constructing a symptom is the most convenient way out and one most agreeable to the pleasure principle . . . there are cases in which even the physician [clinician] must admit that for a conflict to end, a neurosis is the most harmless and socially, tolerable solution. **You must not be surprised to hear that even the physician may occasionally take the side of the illness he is combating**. It is not his business to restrict himself in every situation in life to being a fanatic in favour of health. He knows that there is not only neurotic misery in the world but real, irremovable suffering as well, that necessity may even require a person to sacrifice his health; and he learns that a sacrifice of this kind made by a single person can prevent immeasurable unhappiness for many others.'* [547]

Isn't it surprising to find Freud suggesting that the clinician should sometimes side with the symptom? Surely this contradicts Lacan's ethical principal that the

---

[545] H Searles, Oedipal Love in the Countertransference, 1959, *Int J Psychoanalysis*, 40, p180-90.
[546] S Freud. Further Recommendations in the Technique of Psychoanalysis, *SE 12*, [1914], 1976, p47.
[547] S Freud, The Common Neurotic State, Introductory Lectures on Psychoanalysis, *SE 16*, [1915], 1976, p383.

analyst desires difference rather than identification with the symptom? How might this apparent contradiction be resolved?

A good warrior doesn't always fight and a good psychoanalyst doesn't always psychoanalyse. The psychoanalyst waits —sometimes actively influencing conditions— until the right conditions exist and only then does he allow psychoanalysis to take place. The setting of the battle scene is likely to have a very important bearing on the outcome. Warring against guerrillas for instance may well not result in victory for a conventional force. In ordinary social settings and some common clinical situations psychoanalysts ought not to practise psychoanalysis. These situations include the preliminary sessions, cocktail parties, work with psychotics and to some extent work with clients who are extremely distressed or freshly traumatised good psychoanalyst knows when not to psychoanalyse.

There is a fixed Lacanian policy of insisting that the client determines the point at which the analysis stops. This policy is a necessary consequence of the analyst failing to suppose that he knows the essential truth about his client: the client is in the uniquely privileged position of seeking his own knowledge. The extent to which the client completes this journey, and the resources he calls on to do so are best determined by him in his struggle with the indeterminacy of his desire.

Freedom and *'Desire [as] the very essence of man . . . determined to do something by . . . some modification of itself'*

At The End of analysis, having exhausted the impossibility of his Other the subject has become free to identify and act on the opposite: what is possible for himself. Prior to this proof or exhaustion it was necessary for him to devote much of his energy or libido to his demand or symptoms, to what was impossible for his other. This freedom at The End of analysis is the unique realisation of the determinants of one's being as a desiring subject, realised when the subject's demand —as that which is impossible for the subject's Other.

It is ironic that the essence of the human condition, where, for Spinoza *'desire is the very essence of man . . . determined to do something by . . . some modification of itself. . .'* [548] has a compulsory ideal, the retrospective imperative where, through a novel return to the object of his cause, the subject establishes the impossibility of following *both* the causal and the logical paths of the little object as the cause of desire. When demand as the impossible is identified it becomes necessary to act on the possible, that is to act on desire.

---

[548] B Spinoza, *Ethics*, Origin and Nature of Emotions, Everyman Library, trans Boyle, [1660], 1910, p128.

This theory of freedom —Spinoza's, Freud's and Lacan's— has nothing at all to do with the kind of 'freedom' in which it is possible for the 'free subject' to carry out any particular acts or identifications at random, where it is equally possible to be a prostitute or policeman, a man or woman, 80 years old or three years old, or all of these simultaneously. Identifying desire as the exhaustion of demand would not be possible under such conditions: 'freedom' here is not the freedom to do all that is demanded, but only to pursue that which is desired. Until the subject has exhausted his demand, that is until he has established the cause and object of his desire as the impossibility of his Other, he will struggle in vain, his libido entangled with his Other, rather than being recognised as his own impossibility. Once the impossibility of reconciling the causal and objective aspects of the little object a have been realised at The End of analysis the subject is free because he has finally recognised his essence as the uniquely irreconcilable, as the incommensurable, as the real that is necessarily determined to do something by some modification of itself.

Confusing the little object a with the demand of the Other; subjecting cause and effect to topology

A necessary consequence of Spinoza's definition of desire is the discontinuity or interruption of any attempt to impose a linearity, such as that of an ordinary chronological account of time, in which causes always precede effects. Discontinuity or interruption, caused by something effecting itself, as a symptom of the imposition of an ordinary three-dimensional geometric understanding or scheme onto a topological phenomenon appears to explain the experience of the little object. The human condition is an affliction resulting from the necessary compulsion to carry out a series of proofs —as demands or impossible goals— producing the deduction that the topology of the little object cannot be reduced to the demands of the Other in our three dimensional world of goods and services. This impossibility of reducing or comprehensively translating the topology of the little object to the often geometric demands of the Other without error is our essence and reality, uniquely established as a necessary task in each ordinary, neurotic human life.

To understand where the little object or little other is it is necessary to rely on an understanding of space as topological rather than as ordinary geometric space: *'In order to grasp its extent, one must abstract oneself from three dimensional space, since it is a question here only of a topological reality that is limited to the function of a surface.'* [549] The little object is a very strange kind of constant because it takes two completely different forms, the causal *and* the logical. This is

---

[549] J Lacan, *The Four Fundamental Concepts of Psychoanalysis*, trans Sheridan, Pelican, London, 1979, p271.

one reason why desire is so complicated; there are two radically different discourses or languages that govern desire, and translating from one to the other is necessarily problematic, producing the uniquely human effects of trauma, of that which cannot be symbolised. That which cannot be symbolised is within Lacan's category of 'the real'. The real includes trauma, as well as being an every sentence phenomenon and covering quantum phenomena in physics.

'Back To The Future Stories' and the 'Return of the Repressed'

There are a set of time travel stories including 'Twelve Monkeys' [550], 'Back to the Future' [551] and the 'Terminator' series that I call 'Back To The Future Stories'. These have in common 'the re-turn' of an individual to an earlier time, but with the psychic state or memory that he possessed, or will possess in the future. It is hard to decide which tense to use to describe such events. This complicated return always leads to uncannily strange yet seemingly familiar consequences in which some effects precede their causes. So 'a son' may 'travel' to an earlier time in order to protect the woman —who will become his mother— from some threat or problem, at the time when she had had no contact with the 'son's father'. A clear case of an effect preceding its cause, of a sort that Oedipus might have prayed for. How widespread are these stories? What criterion distinguishes Back To The Future Stories from other stories?

In the Oedipus story the Oracle predicted that Oedipus would kill his father and marry his mother. The object of this prediction was also the cause of the prophecy. That is the killing and the marrying —in the future— caused the prophecy to exist in the past, prior to the killing and marrying! So Oedipus Rex, or as Woody Allen spells it, 'Oedipus Wrecks', qualifies as a Back To The Future Story; the prophecy went back to the future.

This inclusion suggests that all our stories that refer to desire be regarded as within the Back To The Future genre because desire is necessarily 'forward looking' —abstracted from three dimensional space as a topological reality— and desire is determined to do something by some modification of itself.

Lacan's psychoanalytic theory of the little object a, déjà vu; and Hadley's Einsteinian theory of the sub-atomic particle

Hadley's Einsteinian theory[552] of the sub-atomic particle helps characterise the topological aspects of Lacan's psychoanalytic theory of the little object a. It may

---

[550] Gilliam, 1995.
[551] Zemeckis, 1989.
[552] There is a large speculative literature on connections between quantum theory, neurology and consciousness.

seem inappropriate to compare quantum physical phenomena with trauma but I hope to justify the parallel. In both cases there is a failure to symbolise. A vital characteristic of the little object is that it cannot be straightforwardly or comprehensively symbolised, that is they are within Lacan's category of the real. This failure of symbolisation is established in time travel stories and Hadley's Einsteinian theory of the sub-atomic particle.

If a son travels back in time to save his mother to may be in order that she may meet his father to may be, then the hero must come too, to exist in the future. But, if the mother to may be does not meet the father to may be, then the hero would not exist, and then he would not be able to go back in time! The paradox can be put more concisely: if the past is comprehensively written, in such a way that it may be 'visited' then presumably it will not be possible to rewrite any of it? The same applies to the future: if the future is written, then it will not be possible to rewrite it.

Lacan and Hadley go some way towards dissolving this paradox. Their solution is simple: from our ordinary standpoint of chronological or clock time, and of our three dimensional geometric understanding of space, the paradox or contradiction cannot be resolved, but if effects can precede causes, because the underlying nature of psychic and physical time and space are topological rather than geometric then the paradox is dissolved, with consequences for our understanding of the human condition and physics.

Both Hadley's development of Einstein's theory of space and time and Lacan's theory of little object a rely on topological theories of space and time, and the associated theory of knots. Einstein was also a determinist, that is he believed that chance or probability had no part to play in theories of space and time [553]. In contrast, currently popular quantum theories insist on probability as a fundamental property of physical things. In quantum physics it is standard for a prediction to be made, based on detailed calculations, and for that prediction to either be correct to 20 decimal places —that is for an extremely accurate prediction to be confirmed— or for the prediction to be totally wrong! There is an important sense in which quantum physicists have not been able to understand or symbolise 'the fundamentals of quantum physics' prior to Hadley's work because of quantum theories' reliance on probability theory and indeterminacy; indeterminate or probabilistic events are something which cannot be determined, by thought or formulae, because their causes cannot be comprehensively grasped: neither can the effects [554]. Einstein's theories aimed at deterministically grasping

---

[553] See his letter in Popper's *The Logic of Scientific Discovery*, Hutchinson, London, 1980, p457-460.

[554] '[Quantum physics] has remained an impenetrable mystery, to its creators, on their own admission.' H Thirring, Die Wandlung des Begriffssystems der Physik, (essay in Krise und Neuauf bau in den exakten Wissenschaten, Finf Wiener Vortrage, by Mark,

the structures and relations of physical things in a way that quantum physics systematically gives up on. Here is Hadley's development of Einstein's account:

'My work offers an explanation for quantum phenomena in terms of classical general relativity. Far from being incompatible the two great theories of the 20th century are shown to be closely related. Quantum theory gives clues to the small scale structure of space and time . . . general relativity can account for the strange effects seen in quantum theory. The crucial link is a relaxation of the strict causal structure that is normally imposed upon Einstein's theory, but which forms no part of the mathematical structure.' [555]

Before looking at Hadley's development of Einstein's theory it is worth stressing Einstein's monism, that is his reliance on the idea there is only one kind of stuff:

*'We may therefore regard matter as being constituted by the regions of space in which the field is extremely intense . . . **There is no place** in this new kind of physics **for both** the field and matter, for **the field is the only reality'.*** [556]

A monist system —a system with just one type of stuff— allows difference; the stuff plus its structured absence, or its modification by absence allows difference, as in the binary code of computers composed exclusively by '1' and it's absence '0'. So in answer to the two questions: What is a particle?, and What is an object? Einstein's single answer is a field of variable intensity: for Lacan the intensity of the field of desire is in relation to its cause and object.

In subjecting the notion of causality —the concept of cause and effect— to a topological analysis Hadley has developed Einstein's theory. If there are loops or tunnels, knotted in space-time, then the future can influence the past, because effects can 'precede' causes. Einstein's general relativity theory viewed particles as distortions in the topology of space alone, kinks of a limited kind, rather than as a wholesale distortion in the time of cause and effect too: Hadley argues that particles are distortions in space-time, not just space, and has proposed that a sub-atomic particle is a region of space-time that is so dramatically warped —because of the intensity of the field— that it has become knotted. Such knots contain a 'closed, time-like curve' — a loop or tunnel of time. *'This is the crucial ingredient which enables [Einstein's] General Relativity [theory] to reproduce the effects of quantum theory'*, writes Hadley. [557]

Time loops enable a particle to interact with other particles not only in its past but in its future too. In the illustration Hadley offers of a billiard ball rolling across a table, its path is ordinarily fully determined by the conditions at the start, such as

---

Thirring, Hahn, Nobelling, Menger; Verlag Deuticke, Vienna, 1933, page 30. Quoted in P opper's *The Logic of Scientific Discovery*, Hutchinson, London, 1980, p216.
[555] M Hadley, PhD thesis, Warwick University: *www.warwick.ac.uk/~phsem/thesis.html*
[556] A Einstein, *Matter, Space and Motion*, Sorajbji, Duckworth 1988, p40.
[557] M Hadley, PhD thesis, Warwick University: *www.warwick.ac.uk/~phsem/thesis.html*

its initial speed, direction and so on. But strange things happen if a time loop crosses its path. For instance, if a space-time tunnel connects two of the billiard pockets, then the ball can be deflected —through its interactions with itself— by having entered one pocket, and materialized from the other pocket, at a point earlier in time.

Hadley explains that this particular outcome is only one of many possibilities: *'Where there was only one outcome, suddenly there are many'* [558]. It is this lack of a single determinate effect —along with the lack of a parallel set of comprehensive set of causes— that explains the phenomena of indeterminacy in quantum physics. Hadley explains that *'the properties of a fundamental particle are determined by measurements that can be made on it in the future. If those measurements are mutually incompatible, the particle's properties will be ill-defined.'* Hence the indeterminacy of quantum phenomena.

Making a quantum measurement has an effect on the outcome because the particle has already been affected by causes that will take place in the future because *'for a classical particle [such as a regular billiard ball on a regular table] . . . everything is determined: for a quantum particle . . . not everything is determined.'* [559]

Back to a conclusion

Freedom for Spinoza, Freud and Lacan is a clinical, epistemological and metaphysical ideal [560], the unique realisation of the determinants of one's being as a desiring subject. This subjective freedom is realised when the subject's demand —as that which is impossible for the subject's Other— has been worked through and identified. Back To The Future Stories can be understood as the subject — perhaps the sympathetic viewer or writer —working through his demand, where demand is formulated as 'being impossible for the other'. In radical contrast desire is that which is possible for the subject. This helps explain why the time traveller is always in a position of demand; he appears as the impossibility, as the unintelligible paradox of the other, that is what he has become: he has yet to discover what is possible for himself, as his desire. Questions of the time traveller's desire are systematically suspended until his formulation of the impossibility of the other has been worked through. At the End of analysis, having exhausted the impossibility of his Other, the subject is free to identify and act on what is possible for himself. Prior to this proof it was necessary for him to

---

[558] M Chown, *New Scientist*, All the world is a time machine, 7 March 1998, vol 157, No 2124, p38-41.
[559] Ibid, p34.
[560] The consequences of freedom from the point of view of the subject's action are detailed by Lacan in his unpublished seminar 'The Psychoanalytic Act'.

devote much of his energy or libido to his symptoms, on what was impossible for his Other.

It is ironic that the essence of the human condition has a compulsory ideal, the retrospective imperative where, through a novel return to the effects of his cause, the subject establishes the impossibility of following both the causal and logical knots of the path of the little object a.

Until the subject has exhausted his demand, that is until he has established the cause and object of his desire as the impossibility of the other he will struggle in vain, his libido invisibly entangled with the impossibility of the Other, rather than being visible as his own impossibility. Once the impossibility of reconciling the causal and objective aspects of the little object a have been realised at The End of analysis the subject is free because he has recognised his essence as the irreconcilable, as the incommensurable, as the real that is determined to do something by some modification of itself. This *'modification of itself'* is part of Lacan's theory of the little object, where: *'... in order to grasp its extent, one must abstract oneself from three dimensional space, since it is a question here only of a topological reality . . . '* [561] and in the identical topology of Hadley's analogy for sub-atomic particles, where a billiard ball rolling across a table has a space time loop crossing its path. If the space time loop connects two of the billiard pockets, then the ball can be deflected —through its interactions with itself— by having entered one pocket, and materialized from the other pocket, at a point earlier in time, that is through some *'modification of itself'*.

A necessary consequence of Hadley's object's interactions with itself, and of Spinoza's desire is the discontinuity or interruption of any attempt to impose a linearity, such as that of the ordinary chronological account of time, in which causes always precede effects. Discontinuity or interruption caused by something effecting itself, as a symptom of the imposition of a geometric understanding or scheme onto a topological phenomenon appear to explain both the indeterminate phenomena of quantum physics and the experience of the little object a.[562] The human condition is an affliction resulting from the necessary compulsion to carry out a series of proofs —as demands or impossible goals— producing the deduction that topology cannot be reduced to geometry. This impossibility of reducing or comprehensively translating topology to geometry without error is our essence and reality, uniquely established as a necessary task in each ordinary, neurotic human life. Déjà vu is one symptom of this impossibility.

---

[561] J Lacan, *The Four Fundamental Concepts of Psychoanalysis*, trans Sheridan, Pelican, London, 1979, p271.

[562] I am not suggesting that theories of quantum phenomena have anything positive to offer psychoanalysis besides their importance in the history of indeterminacy and science, marking the indeterminacy of human sexuality, and the topological account of cause and effect.

Psychoanalysis as the height of culture

Being psychoanalysed is learning how to speak properly. Prior to analysis the ordinary neurotic subject is spoken by language and their clumsy, repetitive and dominating symptoms. So at the start, clients cannot clearly explain their symptoms and suffering: at The End of analysis the subject can act and speak, clearly and actively instead of being spoken:

*'The ideal of analysis is not complete self-mastery, the absence of passion. It is to render the subject capable of sustaining the analytic dialogue, to speak **neither too early, nor too late.**'* [563]

Speaking and acting on one's desire on a timely basis does not imply mastery: there are two different discourses suggested by The End of analysis. The discourse of the analyst will be taken up by some of those who go to The End of their analysis. The other discourse which has a far greater profile in the provision and consumption of goods or services is that of the hysteric, which is also used by obsessional neurotics.

Is this a good time to conclude?

No. It is not yet possible to properly assess Lacan's ideas and their implications for clinical work. Much of his huge volume of work has yet to be published, translated and studied. But it is also too soon to comprehensively assess Freud's poorly translated work; it is only since Lacan's reading of Freud, and the study of psychoanalytic questions alongside the history of science and mathematics, immunology and other topics that we have started to understand some of the formal theories —both implicit and explicit— within Freud's writing. Lacan's theories and clinical innovations have been responsible for a massive advance in both clinical and non-clinical psychoanalysis, and have had an enormous influence on a wide range of topics. It is certain that Lacan's theoretical and clinical work has been a major contribution to our understanding of all that is human, ensuring that he will be regarded as one of the most resourceful and creative of those who have practised and theorised psychoanalysis.

---

[563] J Lacan, *The Seminar of Jacques Lacan, Book One, Freud's Papers on Technique of Psychoanalysis, 1953-1954*, ed Miller, trans Forrester, Cambridge University Press, Cambridge, England, 1988, p3.

Why do Lacanians end on a question?

Why shouldn't they?

APPENDIX

1. Desire, guilt and The Law

This is the final word . . . that passes through all of Freud's work. From beginning to end, from the discovery of the Oedipus complex. . . . Freud only ever asked himself, personally, one question—how can this system of signifiers without which no incarnation of either truth or justice is possible, how can this . . . have a hold on an animal who has no need of it and who doesn't care about it—since it doesn't at all concern his needs? It's

'Unfortunately our laws are not generally known: they are the secret of a small group of noblemen who govern us. We are convinced that these ancient laws are scrupulously adhered to, but all the same it is exceedingly distressing to be governed according to laws that one does not know. I am not thinking here of the various ways of interpreting the laws, or of the disadvantage involved when only a few individuals and not the whole people are allowed to take part in their interpretation. These disadvantages are perhaps not so very great. For the laws are very ancient, centuries of work have gone into their interpretation and by now this has probably become law itself; there does indeed still remain a certain possible latitude of interpretation, but it is very limited. Besides, the nobility have obviously no call to let their personal interest sway them into interpreting the laws to our disadvantage, since these were drawn up in the interests of the nobility from the very beginning: the nobles stand above the law, and that seems to be the very reason why the law has been given over exclusively into their hands. Of course, there is wisdom in that —who doubts the wisdom of the ancient laws ? —but equally there is distress for us; probably that is unavoidable.

Moreover these apparent laws are really no more than a matter of conjecture. There is a tradition that they exist and are entrusted as a secret to the nobility, but this is not and cannot be more than an ancient tradition to which age lends authority, for the character of these laws requires that their very existence be kept secret as well. But if we common people have been following the actions of the nobles since the earliest times, and possess records of them made by our forefathers which we have conscientiously continued, and if among the myriad facts we think we can detect certain tendencies which permit us to conclude this or that about our

---

[564] J Lacan, *The Psychoses*, ed Miller, trans Grigg, Routledge, London, 1993, p242.

APPENDIX

nevertheless this very thing that causes neurotic suffering. Man is in fact possessed by the discourse of the law, and he mortifies, punishes himself with it in the name of that symbolic debt which in his neurosis he keeps paying for more and more. How can this have taken hold, how does man enter into this law, which is foreign to him and which as animal he has nothing to do with? It's to explain this that Freud constructs the myth of the murder of the father . . . Man must make himself take part in this as guilty.'.[564]

historical destiny; and if we then, on the basis of these most carefully sifted and sorted conclusions, try to put our lives into some kind of order for the present and the future – then all that is in the highest degree uncertain, and perhaps no more than a game, for perhaps these laws which we are trying to guess at in this way do not exist at all. There is a small party which really is of this opinion, and which seeks to prove that if any law exists, it can only run thus: What the nobility does is the law. This party sees nothing but arbitrary acts on the part of the nobility, and it rejects the popular tradition, which according to them is only beneficial in minor and incidental ways, while being for the most part seriously harmful, since it gives the people a false and deceptive sense of security and disposes them to recklessness in the face of coming events. This harmful effect cannot be denied, but it is attributed by the overwhelming majority of our people to the fact that the tradition is still far from being sufficient, that it needs to be much more fully studied, and indeed that even the material available, immense though it appears to us, is still far too meagre, and that centuries must pass before it will become adequate. This prospect, so gloomy as far as the present is concerned, is lightened only by the belief that one day the time will come when both the tradition and our study of it will arrive, almost with a sigh of relief, at their conclusion, when all will have become clear, when the law will at last belong to the people, and the nobility will vanish. This is not said with any hatred for the nobility; not at all, not by anyone; rather we are inclined to hate ourselves because we cannot yet be judged worthy of the law. And this is the real reason why the party which believes there is no law –in some ways such an attractive party – has remained so small, for it too fully recognizes the nobility and its right to existence. One can only really express the matter in a kind of paradox: Any party which would repudiate, not only belief in the laws, but the nobility as well, would instantly have the whole people behind it; but such a party cannot arise, for no one dares repudiate the nobility. It is on this razor's edge that we live. A writer once summed it up in this way: The one visible and indubitable law that is imposed upon us is the nobility, and could it really be our wish to deprive ourselves of this solitary law?'.[565]

[565] F Kafka, *Parables and Paradox*, The Problem of our Laws, Shocken Books Inc, New York, 1961.

APPENDIX

2. On the technique of frustrating demand in the name of The Law or the symbol

'We clear the ground in front of the door, but as regards the door, I believe that we are not very competent.' [566]

'If I frustrate him [the client] it is because he asks me for something. To answer him, in fact. **But he knows very well that it would be mere words.** And he can get those from whom ever he likes for. . . . It's not these words he's asking for. He simply asking me, from the very fact that he's speaking: his demand . . . carries no object with it.' [567]

'Of course the trap is that in interpreting you give the subject something to feed himself on, the word, even the book which is behind it, and that the word remains all the same the locus of desire,

'Before the Law stands a doorkeeper on guard. To this doorkeeper there comes a man from the country who begs for admittance to the Law. But the doorkeeper says that he cannot admit the man at the moment. The man, on reflection, asks if he will be allowed, then, to enter later. . . 'It is possible', answers the doorkeeper, 'but not at this moment'. Since the door leading into the Law stands open as usual and the doorkeeper steps to one side, the man bends down to peer through the entrance. When the doorkeeper sees that, he laughs and says: 'If you are so strongly tempted, try to get in without my permission. But note that I am powerful. And I am only the lowest doorkeeper. From hall to hall keepers stand at every door, one more powerful than the other. Even the third of these has an aspect that even I cannot bear to look at.' These are difficulties which the man from the country has not expected to meet, the Law, he thinks, should be accessible to every man and at all times, but when he looks more closely at the doorkeeper in his furred robe, with his huge pointed nose and long, thin, Tartar beard, he decides that he had better wait until he gets permission to enter. The doorkeeper gives him a stool and lets him sit down at the side of the door. There he sits waiting for days and years. He makes many attempts to be allowed in and wearies the doorkeeper with his importunity. The doorkeeper often engages him in brief conversation, asking him about his home and other matters, but the questions are put quite impersonally, as great men put questions, and always conclude with the statement that the man cannot be allowed to enter yet. The man, who has equipped himself with many things for his journey,

---

566 J Lacan, Seminar on the Psychoanalytic Act, unpublished, trans Gallagher, 21 February 1968.

567 J Lacan, Ecrits, The Direction of the Treatment and the Principles of its Power, trans Sheridan, Routledge, London, [1966], 1980, p254.

568 J Lacan, Transference Seminar, unpublished, trans Gallagher.

parts with all he has, however valuable, in the hope of bribing the doorkeeper. The doorkeeper accepts it all, saying, however, as he takes each gift 'I take this only to keep you from feeling that you have left something undone'. During all these long years the man watches the doorkeeper almost incessantly. He forgets about the other doorkeepers, and this one seems to him the only barrier between himself and the law. In the first years he curses his evil fate aloud; later, as he grows old, he only mutters to himself. He grows childish, and since in his prolonged watch he has learned to know even the fleas in the doorkeeper's fur collar he begs the very fleas to help him to persuade the doorkeeper to change his mind. Finally his eyes grow dim and he does not know whether the world is really darkening around him or whether his eyes are only deceiving him. But in the darkness he can now perceive a radiance that streams immortally from the door of the Law. Now his life is drawing to a close. Before he dies, all that he has experienced during the whole time of his sojourn condenses in his mind into one question, which he has never yet put to the doorkeeper. He beckons the doorkeeper, since he can no longer raise his stiffening body. The doorkeeper has to bend down far to hear him, for the difference in size between them has increased very much to the man's disadvantage. 'What do you want to know now?' asks the doorkeeper, 'you are insatiable'. 'Everyone strives to attain the Law,' answers the man, 'how does it come about, then, that in all these years none has come seeking admittance but me?' The doorkeeper perceives that the man is at the end of his strength and that his hearing is failing, so he bellows in his ear: 'No one but you could gain admittance through this door, since this door was intended only for you. I am now going to shut it.' [569]

even if you give it in such a way that this locus is not recognisable, I mean that if this locus remains, for the desire of the subject, uninhabitable.

To respond to the demand for food, to the frustrated demand in a nourishing signifier is something which leaves elided the following, that beyond any food of the word, what the subject really needs is what it signifies metonymically, **it is that which is not at any point of this word** *and therefore that each time you introduce - no doubt you are obliged to do it - the metaphor, you remain on the same path which gives consistency to the symptom, no doubt a more simplified symptom but still a symptom, in any case with respect to the desire that it is a question of separating out.'* [568]

[569] F Kafka, *Parables and Paradox*, Before The Law, Shocken Books Inc, New York, 1961.

3. The agency of the letter

'Seeing. . . that we are no great wits, I think that we had better adopt a method which I may illustrate thus: suppose that a short-sighted person had been asked by someone to read **small letters** from a distance; and it occurred to someone else that they might be found in another place which was larger and in which the **letters were larger** —**if they were the same** and he could read the larger letters first, and then proceed to the lesser —this would have been thought a rare piece of good-fortune.

Very true, said Adeimantus; but how does the illustration apply to our inquiry?

. . . the subject. . . is . . . **an individual and . . . a State.**'[570]

'BASSANIO O sweet Portia, . . . dear lady, you shall see How much I was a braggart. When I told you My state was nothing, I should then have told you That I was worse than nothing; for, indeed, **I have engaged myself to a dear friend,** Engaged my friend to his mere enemy, **To feed my means. Here is a letter,** lady; **The paper as the body of my friend, And every word in it a gaping wound, Issuing life-blood.**'[571]

' . . . may the Lord make an example of you among people in adjurations and in swearing of oaths by bringing upon you miscarriage and untimely birth; and this water **that brings out the truth** enter your body; bringing upon you miscarriage and untimely birth.' The woman shall respond, 'Amen, Amen.' **The priest shall write these curses on a scroll and wash them off into the water of contention; he shall make the woman drink the water that brings out the truth, and the water shall enter her body.**'[572]

---

[570] Plato, The Republic, trans Cornford, Oxford, 1941 Book II, p55.

[571] W Shakespeare, The Merchant of Venice, act 3, scene 2

[572] God, The Old Testament, Numbers 5, 6 Israel in the Wilderness of Sinai.

APPENDIX

'. . . then the voice which lies open in the hand of the angel standing on the sea and on the land.' I therefore ask the angel to give me the little book, and he said to me: "take, and eat it, it will fill your entrails with bitterness, but in your mouth it will have the sweetness of honey, in my mouth it had the sweetness of honey but when I had eaten it, it filled my entrails with bitterness.'[573]

'So I studied law . . . I was positively living . . . on sawdust, which had, moreover, been chewed for me in thousands of other people's mouths.'[574]

'Witness : I do not live: I write.'[575]

'I am nothing but literature.'[576]

[573] Book of Apocalypse
[574] F Kafka, Letter to His Father, *Wedding Preparations in the Country and Other Stories*, Penguin, 1958, p63.
[575] F Nietzsche, *My Sister and I*, Amok Books 1990, p97.
[576] F Kafka, *The Diaries of Franz Kafka*, ed Brod, Penguin, 1972, p230.

APPENDIX

4. A popular metaphysical myth of pornography

If clinicians had some kind of privileged knowledge of reality or the external world and, if the external world were also of central importance in the client's suffering, then clinicians would be in a privileged position to reduce their clients' suffering. But the two assumptions in the last sentence are nearly always false: there is no reason to think that clinicians will generally have any special knowledge or privileged view of reality, and there is no reason to think that the external world has any straightforward or simple relation to the suffering of clients. Yet these two assumptions above —which cannot be justified— are commonly believed to be true, and acted upon by those clinicians in the object relations tradition and Kleinians. Melanie Klein for instance claimed that genitals are equated with reality, so she was able to practise therapy in virtue of her knowledge of genitals, which she shared with clients when she interpreted their play and speech: *'In the play of normal children these latter processes testify to the stronger and more lasting influence of identification originating on the genital level.* **In proportion as the imagos [images] approximate to the real objects** ^{D} **a good relation to reality characteristic of normal people becomes more marked.'** ^{577}

In a shocking pornographic aesthetics Klein also equated and reduced wholesale *'every kind of performance'* —encompassing the whole universe of music, film and theatre— with the child's viewing of its parents' sexual intercourse (that is the *'primal scene'*): *'I have found the equation of theatre, cinema and every kind of performance with the primal scene . . .'* (A) So in Klein's work there is a grand equation with six terms:

'primal scene' ^{A} = *'reality'* ^{B} = *'penis'* & *'vagina'* ^{C} = *'real objects'* ^{D} = *'interpretation'* ^{E} = *knowledge* ^{F}

Her pornographically grandiose variables in this equation are identified in the two quotes above and three below:

'. . . my assumption that in both sexes there is an inherent unconscious knowledge of the existence of the penis ^{C} *as well as of the vagina* ^{C}*.'* ^{578}

---

^{577} M Klein, Personification in the Play of Children, Virago, *Love, Guilt and Reparation*, 1988, p207.
^{578} M Klein, The Oedipus Complex in the Light of Early Anxieties, *Love, Guilt and Reparation*, Virago, [1945], 1975, p409.

And: *'Even the quite small child*, which seemingly knows nothing about birth, **has a very distinct** *unconscious knowledge* [F] *of the fact that the children grow up in the mother's womb.'* [579]

And: *'This task [of interpretation* [E] *] . . . was bound up and in step with the development of their ego and the growth of their adaptation to reality* [B] *. The* **sexual enlightenment** *follows gradually by removing the unconscious resistances which work against it.* **Full sexual enlightenment, therefore, like a full adaptation to reality** [B] *, is one of the consequences of a completed analysis.'*

Note Klein's claim that *'interpretation'* is equated with *'reality'*, which is equated with *'full sexual enlightenment'*. It is not possible to practise Kleinian clinical technique without relying on this immodest equation, or a version of it. The belief that makes Kleinian clinical practice possible is this theory of porno-metaphysics and knowledge, supposedly possessed by the clinician. The clinician 'knows' the details of the real objects and the genitals in the above equation, so all the clinician has to do is to substitute in whatever material the client brings, in order to draw the relevant genital and real objects into correspondence. Unfortunately Klein also demonstrates a confusingly variable use of the word 'reality'. It seems for example in the following phrase that Klein intends by the term 'reality' no more than experience: *'The child's earliest reality is wholly phantastic . . .'* In contrast, a little further on in the same article it seems she has a totally different second meaning for 'reality' where it is used to refer to either or both the external world and what she calls 'real objects': *'As the ego develops, a true relation to reality is gradually established out of this unreal reality.'* By 'unreal reality' I guess Klein to be referring to the child's early experience and its lack of correspondence with reality, that is with her 'real objects' which are the 'real objects'. This is rather surprising given her assumption that ' *. . . in both sexes there is an inherent unconscious knowledge of the existence of the penis as well as of the vagina.'* [580]

Lets look at how Klein's theory of reality and its relation to symbolism and the ego has implications in the clinic, in Klein's case of a psychotic child known as 'little Dick'. Below Lacan (17 February 1954) commented on Klein's: 'The importance of symbol-formation

---

[579] M Klein, Criminal Tendencies in Normal Children, *Love, Guilt and Reparation*, Virago, [1927], 1975, p173.
[580] M Klein, The Oedipus Complex in the Light of Early Anxieties, 1975, *Love, Guilt and Reparation*, Virago, [1945], 1975, p409.

APPENDIX

in the development of the ego', (1930), in *The Writings of Melanie Klein*, vol 1. pp. 219-32. My comments are on the right:

KLEIN	LACAN	COMMENTS
'But [Little Dick] was interested in trains and stations and also in door-handles, doors and the opening and shutting of them. *The interest in these things and actions had a common source: it really had to do with the penetration of the penis into the mother's body. Doors and locks stood for the ways in and out of her body, while the door-handles represented the father's penis and his own. Thus what had brought symbol-formation to a standstill was the dread of what would be done to him (particularly by the father's penis) after he had penetrated into the mother's body. // I took a big train and put it beside a smaller one and called them 'Daddy-train' and 'Dick-train'. Thereupon he picked up the train I called 'Dick' and made it roll to the window and said*	**'She slams the symbolism on him with complete brutality,** *does Melanie Klein, on little Dick! Straight away she starts off hitting him large-scale interpretations.* **She hits him a brutal verbalisation of the Oedipal myth, almost as revolting for us as for any reader**	Note Klein's serious use of the term 'really', suggesting a clinical correspondence between reality and the objects 'penis' and 'mother's body'. In Klein's theory 'reality' is what the clinical work aims for. Klein introduces both these terms: 'Daddy-train' and 'Dick-train' herself and then her own interpretations. There is not much left for the client to do! Klein's text is without any justification or support for her claim that 'door handles' and 'doors and the opening and shutting of them . . . really had to do with the penetration of the penis'.

581 M Klein, Virago, London, *Love, Gratitude and Reparation*, [1930], 1975, p21.

'Station'. I explained: '**The station is mummy; Dick is going into mummy.**' He left the train, ran into the space between the outer and inner doors of the room, shut himself in, saying 'dark' and ran out again directly. He went through this performance several times. I explained to him: 'It is dark inside mummy. Dick is inside dark mummy.'

// The desire to make himself intelligible, which was lacking before, is now in full force. Dick tries to make himself understood by means of his still meagre but growing vocabulary which he diligently endeavours to enlarge. There are many indications, moreover, that **he is beginning to establish a relation to reality.**

/**It has been possible to get into contact with him with the help of quite a few words** . . . I would emphasise the fact that in Dick's case I have modified my usual technique. In general I do not interpret the material until it has found expression in

—*You are the little train, you want to fuck your mother* . . . .
You will have noticed the lack of **contact that Dick experiences. That's where the defect of his ego is. His ego isn't formed.** *Moreover Melanie Klein differentiates Dick from a neurotic, by his profound indifference, his apathy, his absence. In fact, it is clear that, for him,* **what isn't symbolised is reality. This young subject is completely in reality, in the pure state, unconstituted. He is entirely in the undifferentiated.** *Now, what constitutes a human world? — if not the interest brought to bear on objects as distinct entities or as equivalent ones. The human world is an infinite world as far as its objects are concerned.* **In this respect, Dick lives in a non-human world.** . . *The theory of the ego is incomplete here* . . . **Dick cannot even engage in the first sort of identification,** *which would? already bean essay in symbolism.* **He is, paradoxical as it may seem to say it, eyeball to eyeball with reality, he lives in reality.**

The idea of '**contact**' appears to be that of Lacan's 'Big Other', the other of language, who speaks.

In Lacan's theory '**reality**' is something that simply exists: people and language on the other hand are very different. People use language to symbolise reality and to differentiate it: in the same way it is only symbols or language that can be 'true' or 'false'. Reality itself cannot be false, or true. It is these qualities of the endless permutations of language, of the infinite diversity of such polarities as 'true-false', 'metaphor-literal', of all the 'maybes', and so on that are —through language- applied by people to reality.

Because Little Dick has a psychotic relation to language and symbolism he has no ego as such, and concordantly, no unconscious either.

		For Lacan the ego is constructed through the relation with the Other of language: the ego has no direct access to reality. But for neurotics, rather than psychotics like Little Dick, 'reality' is as variable as the meanings within language, which all depend on one another and shift about. Symbols and language with their ability to shift meanings can covey change or movement: reality cannot change its meaning. For Lacan language only comes to dominate the human condition through the 'real', that is through the attack that language makes on the fixity of reality of the sort that Little Dick lives in.
various representations. In this case, however, where the capacity to represent it was almost entirely lacking, I found myself obliged to make my interpretations on the basis of my general knowledge, the representations in Dick's behaviour being relatively vague. Finding access in this way to his unconscious . . . [581]	**In Melanie Klein's office, there is neither other nor ego for him, just a reality pure and simple . . . The trains and all that is doubtless something, but something which is neither nameable nor named.** *It is at this point that Melanie Klein...dares to speak to him —to speak to a being who nonetheless allows himself to be apprehended as someone who, in the symbolic sense of the term, does not reply.* **He is there as if she didn't exist, as if she were a piece of furniture. And yet she is speaking to him. She literally gives names to what doubtless does indeed partake in the symbol,** *since it can be named immediately; but which was, up to that moment, for this subject, just reality pure and simple . . . Now,* **for Dick, reality is clearly fixed,** *but that's because he cannot undertake . . comings and goings . . the problem of the relation between the symbolic and the real . . . [is] the function of destructionism in the constitution of human reality.'*	

APPENDIX

5. Pity and The End of analysis

'**Pity** of others is a ghoulish species of self-gratification. **Pity** of ourselves is the lowest sort of self degradation.' [582]

"O you higher men, it was of your distress that old prophet prophesied to me YESTERDAY MORNING, he tried to seduce and tempt me to your distress: O Zarathustra said to me, I have come to seduce you to your **ultimate sin**. 'To my ultimate sin?' cried Zarathustra and laughed angrily at his own words. 'What has been reserved for me as my ultimate sin?' and once more Zarathustra became absorbed in himself – **Pity! Pity!** for the higher man!' he cried out, and his countenance was transformed into brass. 'Very well! THAT -HAS HAD ITS TIME! 'my suffering and my **pity** -what of them! for do I aspire after happiness? . . . I aspire after my work! Zarathustra has become RIPE, MY HOUR HAS COME!'" [583]

' . . . access to desire necessitates crossing not only all fear but all **pity**, and especially not before the good of the Other, because all this is experienced in THE TEMPORAL UNFOLDING OF THE STORY, that the subject learns a little more about the **deepest level of** himself than he knew before . . . for him who goes to The End of his desire, all is not a bed of roses.' [584]

'The ideal of analysis is . . . to render the subject capable of sustaining the analytic dialogue, to speak NEITHER TOO EARLY, NOR TOO LATE.' [585]

' . . . much will be gained if we succeed in TRANSFORMING your hysterical misery into common unhappiness. With a mental life that has been restored to health you will be better armed against that unhappiness.' [586]

582 F Nietzsche, *My Sister And I*, Amok Books, Los Angeles 1990, p107.
583 F Nietzsche, *Thus Spoke Zarathustra*, Penguin, 1969, Trans Hollingdale, p336.
584 J Lacan, *The Ethics of Psychoanalysis*, Routledge, 1992, p319.
585 J Lacan, *Book One, Freud's Papers on Technique of Psychoanalysis, 1953-1954*, ed Miller, trans Forrester, Cambridge University Press, Cambridge, England, 1988,p3.
586 S Freud, Wild Analysis, *SE 11*, [1910], 1976, p227.

APPENDIX

6. Being, being variable and language

Quine's criterion of being or of 'ontological commitment': 'To be is to be the value of a variable' is concordant with Lacan's criterion of subjectivity where 'the signifier represents the subject for another signifier'. Here the signifier is the variable of the subject's being. The subject's existence is within language, both as divided and as constituted by signifiers. To be 'a male' or 'a female' is to be a variable in a complex equation of suffering and enjoyment.

'To be . . . is . . . to be . . . the value of a variable.' [587]	'The signifier represents the subject for another signifier.' [591]
'Language is where **intersubjectivity** sets in.' [588]	'Speech is the founding medium of the **intersubjective** relation . . . ' [592]
'The concept of a living **being** has the same indeterminacy as that of language.' [589]	'I always speak the truth. Not the whole truth, because there's no way, to say it all. Saying it all is literally impossible: words fail.' [593]
'Language is born out of the process of its own degeneration.' [590]	

Both Lacan's and Quine's formulations accord with Peirce's: 'A sign . . . is something for something else in some respect or capacity.' '[The sign] addresses somebody, that is, creates in the mind of that person [a] . . . sign.' '[T]he object as the sign itself represents it, and whose being is thus dependent upon the representation of it in the sign.' [594]

---

587 W Quine , From a Logical Point of View, On What There Is, Oxford University Press, 1953, p13.
588 W Quine, Three Indeterminacies, Perspectives on Quine, ed Barratt and Gibson, Blackwell, 1990, p4.
589 L Wittgenstein, Zettel, 2nd edition, Basil Blackwell, 1981, number 326.
590 J Derrida, Of Grammatology, The John Hopkins University Press, 1974, p242.
591 J Lacan, Subversion of the Subject and Dialectic of Desire, Ecrits, trans Sheridan, Tavistock, London, 1977, p316.
592 J Lacan, Freud's Papers on Transference, The Seminars of Jacques Lacan, Book I, ed Miller, trans Forrester, p274.
593 J Lacan, Television, Dossier on the Institutional Debate, trans Mehlman, October, Number 40, MIT, Cambridge, USA, p7.
594 2.228 & 4.536, Collected Works of Charles Sanders Peirce, Hartshorne et al, Harvard University Press, 1930-1958.

APPENDIX

Sartre claimed that *'existence precedes essence'*: Lacan developed Freud's argument, claiming that absence **is** man's essence, leaving open vital questions regarding the status of non existent things such as unicorns, a field to which Meinong [1904] made an important contribution. See Lambert's *Meinong and the Principle of Independence*, Cambridge University Press, 1983.

7. Jouissance, Pleasure, Pain and Consciousness

'We remain in complete ignorance both of the origin and of the nature of the sexual tension which arises simultaneously with the pleasure when erotogenous zones are satisfied. . . The problem is how can it come about that an experience of pleasure can give rise to a need for greater pleasure? [595]	*'Sensual Pleasure - but I will fence my thoughts round, and my words too: so that swine and hot fanatics shall not break into my garden!'* [596]	*' . . . [the] hysterical attack is designed to take the place of an auto-erotic satisfaction previously practised and since given up . . . The loss of consciousness, the absence in a hysterical attack is derived from the fleeting but unmistakable lapse of consciousness which is observable at the climax of every intense sexual satisfaction, including auto-erotic ones . . . The so called 'hypnoid states' absences during day dreaming - which are so common in hysterical subjects, show the same origin. The mechanism of these absences is comparatively simple. **All the subject's attention is concentrated to begin with on the course of the process of satisfaction; with the occurrence of the satisfaction, the whole of investment of attention is suddenly removed, so that there ensues a momentary void in her consciousness.'** [597]	*' . . . the cycle of pain is longer in every respect than of pleasure, since a stimulation provokes it at the point where pleasure ends.'* However prolonged one supposes it to be, it nevertheless has, like pleasure, its term: **the fainting of the subject.'** [598]

---

[595] S Freud, Three Essays on the Theory of Sexuality, *SE 7*, [1905d], 1976, p212.

[596] F Nietzsche, *Thus Spake Zarathustra*, Penguin Classics, trans Hollingdale, p207.

[597] S Freud, Some General Remarks On Hysterical Attacks, *SE 9*, [1908], 1976, p233-4.

[598] J Lacan, Kant with Sade, *October*, trans Swenson from 3rd edition 1971, p62.

8. A note on the 'Übertragung' of Freud —German for both 'translating' and 'transference'

'A failure of translation —this is what is known clinically as 'repression'.' [599]

If it were easy to talk about one's problems and traumas in a direct way, without going all round the houses, and talking about all sorts of things that are metaphors or symbols for their problems, then clinicians would have no work to do. This suggests that clinical work is principally with language and its meanings. One of the consequences of Lacan's theory of language is that there could be no perfect translation of Freud's German, simply because all translation is, by its nature, necessarily imperfect[600]   However admitting this does not allow just any translation! Just because all translations are necessarily problematic does not mean that all translations are equally good. Just as it is true to claim that:

1. No complete manual or method could be provided with comprehensive rules for translation.

2. All translations are necessarily problematic.

3. Not all translations are equally good.

So it is equally true to make the equivalent claims of clinical technique:

1. It is not possible to provide a comprehensive rulebook for clinical technique or interpretation.

---

[599] S Freud, *The Complete Letters of Sigmund Freud to Wilhelm Fliess* (1985 [1887-1904]), trans Masson, The Belknap Press, London, Letter from December 6, 1896, p208.

[600] *'The question whether it is possible to interpret every dream must be answered in the negative.'* S Freud, The Interpretation of Dreams, *SE 7*, [1901], 1976, p525.

APPENDIX

2. All clinical techniques and interpretations are necessarily problematic.

3. Not all clinical techniques and interpretations are equally good.

Sadly there are important obstacles in the way of an English reader of Freud's work. For an elaboration of this theme see Oriston's *Translating Freud* (1992). Many of Freud's terms are badly translated, making nonsense of some of his key ideas. For example *'trieb'* —the German for *'drive'*— is currently mistranslated by almost all English texts as *'instinct'*, which is a completely different idea from drive! I believe that Freud intended 'instinct' only when he used the German *'instinkt'*. In fact there are only a very few occasions when he used instinkt, and a great many when he used trieb. 'Drive' and 'instinct' have been correctly translated in this book. Because this is an introductory text and the drive is a difficult topic we will not be spending much time on it, although it is a vital concept in Lacanian theory and practice.

For similar reasons I have translated Freud's ordinary German word *'besetzung'* as *'investment'*. This is a standard translation and so is preferable to *'cathexis'*, a confusing technical term unnecessarily invented by Strachey, Freud's translator.

9. Kafka and Lacan on reality

'Many complain that the words of the wise are always merely parables and of no use in daily life, which is the only life we have. When the sage says: 'Go over', he does not mean that we should cross to some actual place, which we could do anyhow if the labour were worth it; he means some fabulous yonder, something unknown to us, something too that he cannot designate more precisely, and therefore cannot help us here in the very least. All these parables really set out to say merely that the incomprehensible is incomprehensible, and we know that already. But the cares we have to struggle with every day: that is a different matter. Concerning this a man once said:

'Why such reluctance? If only you followed the parables you yourselves would become parables and with that rid of all your daily cares.'

Another said: 'I bet that is also a parable.'

The first said: 'You have won'.

The second said: 'But unfortunately only in parable.'

The first said: 'No, in **reality**: in parable you have lost.' [601]

'You never thought of that. It is nevertheless because of this that we are required to introduce into our operation this something that takes account of this . . . element that we are going to be able to grasp, of course, through a logical articulation. Because, if you expect to catch it in **reality**, like that, in a corner, you will always be swindled because, precisely, reality, as everyone knows, is constructed on your I, on the subject of knowledge, and it is precisely constructed so that you will never find it. Only for us as analysts, it is our role. We, for our part, have the resources for it.' [602]

[601] F Kafka, *Parables and Paradox*, Shocken Books, New York, 1961.
[602] J Lacan, Seminar 11, unpublished, trans Gallagher, 28 February 1968.

APPENDIX

10. Shylock's Phobia

There are two further pieces of evidence for the phobia theme in the Merchant of Venice: the first is Shylock's explicit list of three phobias, marked A, B & C in the table below. The second is the mysterious identification of phobias —with their *'harmless'* objects— as a generic response, given when *'there is no firm reason to be rendered.'*. Shylock's ironic alibi here is in place of a reason for his pursuit of his debt of a pound of flesh rather than the alternative offer of 3000 ducats. Shylock's response is surprising: how does a single phobic signifier, a pig, cat or bagpipe solve the mystery of Shylock's behaviour? Freud and Lacan answer this question. Freud describes phobia as disposing of *'aggressive impulses'*, and invisibly abolishing an *'affectionate . . . investment'*. This description corresponds perfectly to Shylock's: *'So can I give no reason, nor I will not, More than a lodged hate and a certain loathing'*.

SHYLOCK 'You'll ask me, why I rather choose to have a weight of carrion flesh than to receive Three thousand ducats: I'll not answer that: but, say, it is my humour: is it answered? What if my house be troubled with a rat and I be pleased to give ten thousand ducats To have it banned? What, are you answered yet? Some men there are love not a gaping **pig** *[A]; Some, that are mad if they behold a* **cat** *[B]; and others, when the* **bagpipe** *[C] sings i' the nose, Cannot contain their urine: for affection, Mistress of passion, sways it to the mood Of* **what it likes or loathes. Now, for your answer: as there is no firm reason to be rendered,** *why he, he cannot abide a gaping pig; why he, a* **harmless** *necessary cat; Why he, a woollen bagpipe; but of force must yield to such inevitable shame As to offend, himself being offended,* **So can I give no reason, nor I will not, More than a lodged hate and a certain loathing** *I bear Antonio, that I follow thus A losing suit against him. Are you answered?' . . .' [603]*	*'The formation of his phobia had the effect of abolishing his affectionate object investment of his mother . . . though the actual content of his phobia betrayed no signs of this . . .* **His phobia disposed of the two main impulses of the Oedipus complex -the aggressive impulses towards his father and his over fondness for his mother.'** *[604]*

---

[603] W Shakespeare, *The Merchant of Venice*

[604] S Freud, Inhibitions, Symptoms and Anxiety, *SE 20*, [1925], 1976, p106.

APPENDIX

In Lacan's explanation of phobia as a solution anxiety emerges at the point when the subject's lack —the real— disappears because the symbolic —on which the real depends— has become unstable or fragile. Phobia is a singular defence against a nihilistic attack on the whole of the subject's language, an attack that itself also causes there to be *'no firm reason to be rendered'* for the defence, because providing firm reasons presumes that the whole foundation or structure of language is itself firm:

'Here . . . with little Hans, the universal signifier that the phobic object realises is that, and nothing else. Here it is at an advance post . . . well before one approaches the hole, the gap realised in the interval where the real presence threatens that a unique sign prevents the subject from approaching. This is why the role, the mainspring and the reason for the phobia is not, as people who have nothing but the word 'fear' on their lips believe, 'a vital danger' or even 'a narcissistic one'. It is very precisely, according to certain privileged developments of the position of the subject with respect to the big Other (in the case of little Hans, to his mother) this point where what the subject dreads meeting is a certain sort of desire of a nature to make return into the previous nothingness the whole of creation the whole signifying system.' [605]

The phobia is what holds things together for the phobic. It is his symptomatic solution to the problem of his subjectivity.

11. Jouissance and arithmetic: subjective division and multiplication

'The whole is only the ghost of the part . . .' [606]

The replacement of the suffering of the subject, or of subjective division with jouissance is in accordance with an economy or arithmetic. The subject is usually symbolised by Lacanians with an S with a diagonal bar through it because the subject is nearly

[605] J Lacan, Transference seminar, unpublished, trans Gallagher.
[606] J Lacan, Seminar 11: Wednesday 28 February 1968, p8, trans Gallagher

always divided. So this is an unusual convention as we can see in the more widespread mathematical practice of writing numbers on their own, such as one, or five as: '1' and '5'. But ordinary numbers such as these are also divided as:

$$\frac{1}{1} = 1 \qquad \frac{5}{5} = 1$$

Numbers may appear to be isolated but they never are; all numbers are divided, that is their nature. Equally all numbers are multiplied. There are though some numbers that have special status when it comes to multiplication and division. The numbers zero, one, infinity, and certain imaginary numbers such as the square root of minus one have special consequences for theories of jouissance; there is an arithmetic and mathematics of the different diagnostic structures seen in the clinic. One popular fantasy relied on to eliminate division is multiplication: multiply two subjects in the bliss of simultaneous orgasm to produce zero, the infinite or one, depending on your subjective mathematics, that is on your clinical structure. Or put one mystic into divine union with God. Feminine jouissance for instance is associated with the infinite in Lacan's seminar Encore. Just as the signifier represents the subject for another signifier [607], so the number represents the set or function for another number. Numbers do not exist in isolation, just as the subject, undivided and without language does not exist.

When the neurotic subject has jouissance there is a multiplication, a brief elimination of the subjective division. At the point of jouissance the subject is not divided but, for a moment is whole, one and undivided, zero or infinite. The temporary disappearance of the subject's division and the subject's consciousness are simultaneous: they are one and the same event. The subject of jouissance is the transitional subject. In the moment of jouissance the subject is in transit, that is in between two subjective states of division or suffering since he is temporarily a being without consciousness. The so-called subject of jouissance is not a subject properly speaking because 'the subject of jouissance' has efficiently forgotten their subjectivity by eliminating their division.

[607] J Lacan, *Ecrits*, a selection, trans Sheridan, Tavistock Routledge Publications, London, 1977, p316.

APPENDIX

The subject's unique division is always responded to with a specific technique or set of techniques that they use to produce jouissance, which temporarily removes the division. One useful approach towards understanding the subject's relation to jouissance is to look at the subject's big Other because the big Other determined our subjectivity, and therefore set the stage for the jouissance that we use to cover-up our subjectivity.

So in psychosis the subject does not exist in the same way as it does in neurosis because the division is in one sense more variable, and in another less: the neurotic subject is divided by signifiers in a largely variable manner. The exceptions are The names of the father. The division of the neurotic subject by The names of the father is fixed: in psychosis there is no such fixed division. It is the absence of the fixed division that is the cause of the fragility of language functions in psychosis.

12. *'Progress in scientific work is just as it is in an analysis.'*

'. . . Science has succeeded extraordinarily well, by and large, by our standards of empirical evidence. The best model of those standards is not, as much recent epistemology had assumed, a mathematical proof, but a crossword puzzle. The clues are the analogue of experiential evidence, already completed entries the analogue of background information. How reasonable an entry in a crossword is depends upon how well it is supported by the clue and any other already completed intersecting entries; how reasonable, independently of the entry in question, those other entries are; independently of the proposition in question; and how much the relevant evidence includes.' [608]	'Do crossword puzzles (Advice to a young psychoanalyst)' [609]	'Progress in scientific work is just as it is in an analysis.' [610]

[608] S Haack, *Manifesto of a Passionate Moderate*, Chicago, 1998, p95.
[609] J Lacan, *Ecrits*, Function and Field of Speech and Language, trans Sheridan, Tavistock Routledge, London, [1966], 1980, p56.
[610] S Freud, New Introductory Lectures, *SE 22*, A Worldview, p174.

13. Woman, sensations, distance and words

'Bridegroom 'How beautiful you are, my dearest, how beautiful! Your eyes behind your veil are like doves, your hair like a flock of goats streaming down Mount Gilhead. Your teeth are like a flock of ewes just shorn which have come up fresh	'Dromio. Do you know me, sir? Am I Dromio? Am I your man? Am I myself? Antipholus. Thou art Dromio, thou art my man, thou art thyself. Dromio. I am an ass, **I am a woman's man and besides myself.** Antipholus. **What woman's man? and how besides thyself?** Dromio. Marry, [an oath], sir, besides myself; **I am due to a woman**; one that claims me, one that haunts me, one that will have me. Antipholus. What claim lays she to thee? Dromio. Marry, sir, **such claim as you would lay to your horse**; and she would have me as a beast not that, I being a beast, she would have me; but that she, being a very	'The loneliness of a deserted womb! I once saw a photograph of a street in an American city which grew up during a gold rush in that part of western United States, and was completely abandoned as soon as the mining possibilities of the terrain had been exhausted. The photograph I saw must have been taken quite a few years after the last of the street's inhabitants had vanished. The wild brush had conquered all paths leading into it and away from it, it reached in height the highest of its houses, the loftiest of its roofs. No	'Always get rid of **the private object** in this way: assume that it constantly changes but that you do not notice because your memory deceives you.' 'Why can't my left hand give my right hand money? —My right hand can put it into my left hand. My right hand can write a deed of gift and my left hand a receipt. —But the further practical consequences would not be those of a gift. When the left hand has taken the money from the right, etc, we shall ask: 'Well, and what of it?' **And the same could be asked if a person had given himself a private definition of a word; I mean, if he has said the word to himself and at the same time has directed his attention to**	'A doctor, consulted ten years before because she was suffering from shortness of breath, had spoken of hypertrophy, and ever since, **the word, whose meaning she hardly understood, had fixed in her head.** She was constantly insisting on

[611] Solomon, Song of Songs 4,15, Old Testament, *The New English Bible*, Oxford University Press, 1970, p797.

[612] W Shakespeare, *The Comedy of Errors*, act III

APPENDIX

from the dipping; each ewe has twins . . . Your neck is like David's tower, which is built with winding courses; a thousand bucklers hang upon it, and all are warriors' shields. Your two breasts are like two fawns,

beastly creature, lays claim to me.

Antipholus. What is she?

Dromio. A very reverent body; aye, such a one as a man may not speak of, without he say, 'Sir-reverence.' I have but lean luck in the match, and yet is she a wondrous fat marriage.

Antipholus. How dost thou mean a fat marriage?

Dromio. Marry, sir, she's the kitchen-wench, and all grease; and I know not what use to put her to but to make a lamp of her and run from her by her own light. I warrant her rags and the tallow in them will burn a Poland winter; if she lives till doomsday; she'll burn a week longer than the whole world.

window was left unbroken or unbent, no door secure on its hinges, no single beam was left with any of the pride with which it is first taught to uphold a house. Even those ruins did not create an image of loneliness comparable to that of a deserted vagina.'
613

a sensation.'
'. . . What about the language which describes my inner experiences and which I myself can understand? **How do I use words to stand for my inner sensations?** *—As we ordinarily do? Then are my words for sensations tied up with my natural expressions of sensation? In that case my language is not a 'private one'. Someone else might understand it as well as I. -But suppose I didn't have any natural expression for the sensation, but only had the sensation? And now I simply associate names with sensations and use these names in*

the Baron, Jeanne and Rosalie feeling her heart, which no one could in fact owing to the puffiness of her breast; but she absolutely refused to let another doctor examine her, fearing that he might discover

613 F Nietzsche, *My Sister and I*, Amok Books, 1990, p32.
614 Ibid.
615 F Nietzsche, *The Gay Science*, trans Kaufmann, Vintage Books, 1974, p124
616 Ibid p249-250.
617 L Wittgenstein, *Philosophical Investigations*, Basil Blackwell, 1958.
618 G Maupassant, *A Woman's Life*, Penguin, 1965, p22.

twins fawns of a gazelle.

Groom . . . You have **stolen** my heart, my sister, you have stolen it, my bride,

with one of your eyes, with one jewel of your necklace. . . . Your two cheeks are an orchard of pomegranates, an orchard full of rare fruits . . .

Antipholus. What complexion is she?

Dromio. Swart, like my shoe, but her face nothing like so clean kept: for why she sweats; a man may go over shoes in the grime of it.

Antipholus. That's a fault that water will mend.

Dromio. No, sir, 'tis in grain; Noah's flood could not do it. . . .

Antipholus. Then she bears some breadth?

Dromio. No longer from head to foot than from hip to hip: she is spherical, like a globe; I could find out countries in her.

Antipholus. In what part of her body stands Ireland?

Dromio. Marry, sir, in her buttocks: I found it out by the bogs.

Antipholus. Where Scotland?

"Is it true that God is present everywhere?" a little girl asked her mother. "I think that's indecent" — a hint for philosophers!

One should have more respect for the bashfulness with which nature has hidden behind riddles and iridescent uncertainties. Perhaps truth is a woman who has reasons for not letting us see her reasons? Perhaps her name is —to speak Greek— 'Baubo'?

[Baubo: A primitive and obscene female demon (Oxford Classical Dictionary, a personification of the female genitals]

---

descriptions. Let us imagine the following case. I want to keep a diary about the sign 'S' and write this sign in a calendar for everyday on which I have this sensation. —I will remark first of all that a definition of the sign cannot be formulated. But still I can give myself a kind of ostensive definition. How? Can I point to the sensation? Not in the ordinary sense. But I speak, or write the sign down, and as it were, point to it inwardly. But what is this ceremony for? For that is all it seems to be!" A definition surely serves to establish the meaning of a sign. —Well, that is done precisely by the concentration of my attention; for in this way I impress on myself the connection between the sign and the sensation.

---

some other complaint, and she talked of her hypertrophy on every possible occasion, so often that it seemed that **this condition was something peculiar to her and belonged to her as a private possession, to which no one else had any right.**

My sister, my bride, is a garden close-locked, a fountain sealed.

. . .

Bride: The fountain in my garden is a spring of running water pouring down from Lebanon

. . .

Bridegroom: You are beautiful, my dearest, . . . lovely as **Jerusalem**,'611

Dromio. I found it by the barrenness; hard in the palm of the hand.

Antipholus. Where France?

Dromio. In her forehead; armed and reverted, making war against her heir.

Antipholus Where Spain?

Dromio. O, sir! upon her nose, all o'er embellished with rubies, carbuncles, sapphires, declining their rich aspect to the hot breath of Spain, who sent whole armadoes of caracks to be ballast at her nose.

Antipholus. Where stood Belgia, the Netherlands [The Lowlands]?

Dromio. O, sir! I did not look so low

612
. . .

'**Women are the only private property** that has complete control over its owner.'614

'The magic and the most powerful effect of women is, in philosophical language, action at a distance . . ; but this requires first of all and above all —distance.615

'My dog. - I have given my name to my pain and call it 'dog'. It is just as faithful, just as obtrusive and shameless, just as entertaining, just as clever as any other dog -and I can scold it and vent my bad mood on it, as others do with their dogs, servants and wives.'616

But 'I impress it on myself' can only mean: this process brings it about that I remember the connection right in the future. But in the present case I have no criterion of correctness. One would like to say: 'whatever is going to seem right to me is right'. And that only means that we can't talk about 'right'. It might be said that if you have **given yourself a private** definition of a word, then you must inwardly undertake to use the word in such-and-such a way. And how do you do that? . . .617

---

*The Baron spoke of '**My wife's hypertrophy**', and Jeanne of '**Mama's hypertrophy**', as they might have mentioned her dress or her hat or her umbrella.'618*

D

INDEX

BIBLIOGRAPHY OF WORKS CITED

Asma S, *Buddha for Beginners,* Writers and Readers, 1996.

Aristotle, Nicomachean Ethics, trans Ross, on CD, copyright Steve Nichols, England, 1994, *Classic Library of World Philosophy*, Actual Reality Publications, Leeds, 1996.

Atkinson J, *Primal Law,* Longmans, Green, and Co, London, 1903.

Bagemihl M, *Biological Exuberance: Animal Homosexuality and Natural Diversity,* 1999, St Martins Press, New York.

Baron-Cohen S, *Mindblindness, An Essay on Autism and Theory of Mind*, Cambridge, MA, MIT Press, 1997.

Bergman, *Outline of Empiricist Philosophy of Physics*, American Journal of Physics, 11, 1943: 248-58. Reprinted in *Readings in the Philosophy of Science*, ed H Fiegl and M Brodeck, New York: Appleton-Century-Crofts, 1953

Bhagavad-Gita, Penguin, 1962.

Bhugra D et al, Schizophrenia and African-Caribbeans: a conceptual model of aetiology, *International Review of Psychiatry*, 1999, 11, p145—152.

Blackmore S, *The Meme Machine,* Oxford University Press, 1999.

Bion W, *Attention and Interpretation: A Scientific Approach to Insight in Psychoanalysis and Groups*, Tavistock, London, 1970.

Bigge M and Hunt M, *Psychological Foundations of Education,* 2nd ed., New York, Harper & Row, 1968.

Burgoyne B, Autism and Topology, *Drawing the Soul*, Rebus Press, 2000.

Carnap R, *The Unity of Science*, Kegan Paul, London, 1934.

Chaitin G, Information-Theoretic Computational Complexity and Gödel's Theorem and Information, *New Directions in the Philosophy of Mathematics*, ed Tymoczko, Princeton University Press, 1998).

Chown M, *New Scientist*, All the world is a time machine, 7 March 1998, vol 157, No 2124, p38-41.

Charraud N, A Calculus of Convergence, *Drawing the Soul*, Rebus Press, 2000.

Cioffi F, Was Freud a Liar? *Unauthorised Freud*, ed Crews, Viking, 1998, p34.

Crow T, Schizophrenia as the price that homo sapiens pays for language . . . *Brain Res Res Rev,* 2000 Mar 31 (2-3) 118-29.

Daniels D, Jenkins P, Therapy with Children: Childrens Rights, Confidentiality and the Law, Sage Publications, 2000.

Dawkins R, *The Selfish Gene*, Oxford University Press, 1976.

Day M, *New Scientist* 11.7.98, p13.

Derrida J, *Of Grammatology*, The John Hopkins University Press, 1974.

Dorschner et al, The Dispute about the External Sphincter and the Urogenital Diaphragm, Vol. 162, 1942-1945, December 1999, *The Journal of Urology*, 1999

Eldredge N & S Gould, Punctuated Equilibria: an alternative to phyletic gradualism. *Models in Paleobiology*, ed Schopf, 1972, p82-115.

Einstein A, quoted in *Matter, Space and Motion*, Sorajbji, Duckworth 1988.

Einstein A, *Physics and Beyond: Encounters and Conversations,* New York: Harper and Row, 1971.

Einstein A, in Popper's *The Logic of Scientific Discovery,* Hutchinson, London, 1980, p457-460.

Einstein A, quoted in *The Sickening Mind, Brain, Behaviour, Immunity and Disease*, P Martin, HarperCollins, 1997, p165.

Ellis A & Dryden W, *The Practice of Rational-emotive Therapy*. New York: Springer, 1987.

Etcheygoyen R, *The Fundamentals of Psychoanalytic Technique*, trans Pitchon, Karnac Books, London, 1991, p424.

Eliot TS, Little Gidding, *Four Quartets*, 1943.

Freud S, The Psychotherapy of Hysteria, *SE 2*, [1893], 1976.

Freud S, On the Psychical Mechanism of Hysterical Phenomena: Preliminary Communication, *SE 2,* [1893], 1976.

Freud S, Studies on Hysteria, *SE 2*, [1893], 1976.

Freud S, The Interpretation of Dreams, *SE 4*, [1900a], 1976.

Freud S, Fragment of an Analysis of a Case of Hysteria, Pelican Freud Library, *SE 7*, [1901], 1976.

Freud S, Psychopathology of Everyday Life *SE 6,* [1901], 1976.

Freud S, Jokes and their Relation to the Unconscious, *SE 8*, [1905], 1973.

Freud S, Three Essays on the Theory of Sexuality, *SE 7,* [1905d], 1976.

Freud S, Psychoanalysis and the Establishment of Facts in Legal Proceedings, *SE 9*, [1906], 1976.

Freud S, Some General Remarks on Hysterical Attacks, *SE 9,* [1908], 1976.

Freud S, Notes Upon a Case of Obsessional Neurosis, *SE 10*, [1909], 1979.

Freud S, Analysis of a Phobia in a five year old boy, *SE 12*, [1909], 1976.

Freud S, The Future Prospects of Psychoanalytic Therapy, *SE 11*, [1910], 1976.

Freud S, Psychoanalytic Notes on an Autobiographical Account of a Case of Paranoia, *SE 12*, [1910], 1976.

Freud S, The Handling of Dream Interpretation in Psychoanalysis, [1911], 1976.

Freud S, Wild Analysis, *SE 11*, [1910], 1976.

Freud S, The Future Prospects of Psychoanalytic Therapy, *SE 11*, [1910], 1976.

Freud S, Recommendations to Physicians Practising Psychoanalysis, *SE 12*, [1912], 1976.

Freud S, The Handling of Dream Interpretation in Psychoanalysis, *SE 12*, [1912], 1976.

Freud S, Totem and Taboo, *SE 13*, [1912], 1976,

Freud S, The Dynamics of Transference, *SE 12*, [1912b], 1976.

Freud S, On the Universal Tendency towards Debasement in the Sphere of Love, *SE 11*, [1912d], 1976.

Freud S, The Disposition to Obsessional Neurosis, *SE 12*, [1913], 1976.

Freud S, On Beginning the Treatment, *SE 12*, [1913a], 1976.

Freud S, Further Recommendations in the Technique of Psychoanalysis, *SE 12*, [1914], 1976.

Freud S, Observations on transference-love, *SE 12,* [1915], 1976.

Freud S, Introductory Lectures to Psychoanalysis, Fixation to Traumas, *SE 16*, [1915], 1973.

Freud S, The Common Neurotic State, Introductory Lectures on Psychoanalysis, *SE 16*, [1915], 1976,.

Freud S, Introductory Lectures, Anxiety, Introductory Lectures on Psychoanalysis, *SE 16*, (1915), 1976.

Freud S, The Sense of Symptoms, Introductory Lectures on Psychoanalysis, *SE 16*, [1915], 1976, p258.

Freud S, Introductory Lectures on Psychoanalysis, The Technique of Interpretation, *SE 15*, [1916], 1976.

Freud S, Introductory Lectures, Analytic Therapy, Introductory Lectures on Psychoanalysis, *SE 16*, (1915), 1976.

Freud S, The Paths to Symptom Formation, Introductory Lectures on Psychoanalysis, *SE 16*, [1915], 1976.

Freud S, The Unconscious, *SE 14*, [1915], 1976.

Freud S, Introductory Lectures on Psychoanalysis, Psychoanalysis and Psychiatry, *SE 16*, [1915], 1976.

Freud S, Instincts and their Vicissitudes, *SE 14,* [1915c], 1976.

Freud S, Mourning and Melancholia, *SE 14*, [1915], 1976.

Freud S, Introductory Lectures on Psychoanalysis, *SE 15*, [1916], 1976.

Freud S, Transference, Introductory Lectures on Psychoanalysis, *SE 16,* [1917], 1976.

Freud S, The Common Neurotic State, *SE 16*, Introductory Lectures on Psychoanalysis, [1916], 1976.

Freud S, General Theory of the Neuroses, Transference, *SE 16,* [1917], 1976.

Freud S, Introductory Lectures on Psychoanalysis, Analytic Therapy, *SE 16*, [1917], 1976.

Freud S, Lines of Advance in Psychoanalytic Therapy, *SE 17*, [1918], 1976.

Freud S, Introductory Lectures on Psychoanalysis, Analytic Therapy, *SE 16*, [1917], 1976.

Freud S, A Child is being Beaten, *SE 17,* [1919e], 1979.

Freud S, Turnings in the Ways of Psychoanalytic Therapy, *SE12*, [1919], 1976.

Freud S, *Sigmund Freud and Lou Andreas-Salome Letters*, ed Pfeiffer, Hogarth Press, [1919] 1972.

Freud S, The Ego and the Id, *SE 19*, [1923b], 1975.

Freud S, *SE 19*, Neurosis and Psychosis, [1924], 1976.

Freud S, *SE 19*, The Downfall of the Oedipus Complex, [1924], 1976.

Freud S, On Transformations of Drive as Exemplified in Anal Eroticism, *SE 7*, [1924], 1976.

Freud S, Resistances to Psychoanalysis, *SE 19*, [1925], 1976.

Freud S, Inhibitions, Symptoms and Anxiety, *SE 20*, [1925], 1976.

Freud S, A Note Upon the 'Mystic Writing Pad, *SE 20* [1925], 1976.

Some Psychical Consequences of the Anatomical Distinction between the Sexes [1925j], *SE 19*.

Freud S, The Question of Lay Analysis, *SE 14*, [1926], 1976.

Freud S, Fetishism, *SE 21*, [1927], 1973.

Freud S, Civilisation and its Discontents, *SE 21*, [1929], 1976.

Freud S, On the Acquisition and Control of Fire, *SE 22,* [1932a], 1976.

Freud S, New Introductory Lectures, Femininity, *SE 22*, [1932], 1976.

Freud S, New Introductory Lectures in Psychoanalysis, Explanations and Applications, *SE 22*, [1933], 1973.

Freud S, Civilisation and its Discontents, *SE 21*, [1929], 1976.

Freud S, *SE 22*, New Introductory Lectures in Psychoanalysis, Explanations and Applications, [1933], 1976, p152.

Freud S, Analysis Terminable and Interminable, *SE 23*, [1937a], 1976.

Freud S, Moses and Monotheism, *SE 23*, [1939a], 1976.

Freud S, *The Complete Letters of Sigmund Freud to Wilhelm Fliess* [1887-1904], 1985, trans Masson,

Freud S, New Introductory Lectures, *SE 22*, A Worldview.

Freud S, *A Phylogenetic Fantasy —Overview of the Transference Neuroses*, The Belknap Press of Harvard University Press, 1987.

Gallie W B, *Pierce and Pragmatism*, Penguin, London, 1952.

Gershwin I, Lyrics from Porgy and Bess, 1935.

Glover E, *The Technique of Psychoanalysis,* 1955, London, Bailliere, Tindall and Cox.

Grey S, *Swimming to Cambodia*, Theatre Communication Group, 1988.

Guimaraes L, From Autism to Psychosis, *The Clinical Florilegium of the year 2000*, World Association of Psychoanalysis, 1994.

Haack S, Rebuilding the Ship While Sailing on the Water, in *Perspectives on Quine*, St Louis, USA, ed. Barrett & Gibson, 1988.

Haack S, *Evidence and Enquiry, towards reconstruction in epistemology*, Blackwell, 1993.

Haack S, *Manifesto of a Passionate Moderate*, Chicago, 1998.

Harlow H, reported in *Principles of General Psychology*, John Wiley and Sons, 1980.

Heisenberg W, *Physics and Philosophy,* Harper, 1958.

Hadley M, PhD thesis, Warwick University: *www.warwick.ac.uk/~phsem/thesis.htmlHutchinson* Hinshelwood R, *Clinical Klein,* London, FAB, 1994.

Heimann P, Counter-transference, *Br. J Med. Psychol*, 1960, 33: p9-15.

Hegel G, *Phenomenology of Spirit*, Oxford University Press, trans Findlay, 1977.

Heimann P, On Counter-transference, *Int. J Psychoanalysis*, 1950, Vol 31.

Haeckel E, *The Riddle of the Universe*, Prometheus Books, New York, Die Weltrathsel, trans McCabe, [1899], 1992.

Hacking I, Do We See through a Microscope?, Images of Science, University of Chicago Press, 1984.

Janouch G, *Conversations With Kafka,* Encounter, Quartet Books 1971.

Kafka F, Letter to His Father, *Wedding Preparations in the Country and Other Stories*, Penguin, 1958.

Kafka F, *The Diaries of Franz Kafka*, ed Brod, Penguin, 1972.

Kafka F, *Parables and Paradox*, Before The Law, Shocken Books Inc, New York, 1961.

Kant I, *Grounding for the Metaphysical Principles of Virtue,* Hackett, Indianapolis, trans Ellington, [1785], 1983.

Kernberg O, Further Contributions to the treatment of narcissistic personalities, *International Jrnl of Psychoanalysis 55*: 216-240, 1974.

Kline M, *Mathematics —The Loss of Certainty*, OUP, New York, 1980.

Klein M, The Technique of Early Analysis, *The Psychoanalysis of Children,* Virago, [1926], 1989.

Klein M, *Narrative of a Child Analysis*, third session, 17 February 1954, Virago, [1945], 1989.

Klein M, Personification in the Play of Children, Virago, *Love, Guilt and Reparation,* 1988.

Klein M, Criminal Tendencies in Normal Children, *Love, Guilt and Reparation*, Virago, [1927], 1975.

Klein M, The Oedipus Complex in the Light of Early Anxieties, *Love, Guilt and Reparation,* Virago, [1945], 1975.

Klein M, *Love, Gratitude and Reparation*, Virago, London, [1930], 1975.

Khan H, *The Secret Of Life, The Human Machine and How it Works*, Odhams, 1940, trans Rosen.

Lacan J, Kant with Sade, *October,* no 51, trans James Swenson from 3rd edition 1971.

Lacan J, Subversion of the Subject and Dialectic of Desire, *Ecrits*, trans Sheridan, Tavistock, London, [1966], 1980.

Lacan J, *Desire and Interpretation of Desire in Hamlet, Literature and Psychoanalysis,* ed Felman, Baltimore and London, Johns Hopkins University Press, 1982.

Lacan J, *The Seminar of Jacques Lacan, Book One, Freud's Papers on Technique of Psychoanalysis, 1953-1954*, ed Miller, trans Forrester, Cambridge University Press, Cambridge, England, 1988.

Lacan J, Geneva Lecture on the Symptom, *Analysis* No 1, 1989, trans Grigg, p9.

Lacan J, Note to Jenny Aubrey, Note on the Child, *Analysis*, Number Two, 1990, p7.

Lacan J, *The Ethics of Psychoanalysis, The Seminar of Jacques Lacan*, ed Miller, trans Porter, 1992.

Lacan J, *The Seminar of Jacque Lacan, The Psychoses,* trans Grigg, Routledge, London, 1993.

Lacan J, *The Seminar of Jacques Lacan, Book Two, The Ego in Freud's theory and in the Technique of Psychoanalysis 1954-1955,* ed Miller, trans Tomaselli, Cambridge University Press, England, 1988.

Lacan J, Presentation of the Memoirs of President Schreber, (1975), trans Lewis, *Analysis* no 7, 1996.

Lacan J, *On Feminine Sexuality, The Limits of Love and Knowledge, Book XX, Encore 1972-1973,* 1998, Norton & Co.

Lacan J, Summary of the Seminar of 1966-1967, *The Letter*, Spring, 1999, trans Gallagher, p92.

Lacan J, The Paternal Metaphor, 22.1.1958, unpublished seminar, trans Gallagher.

Lacan J, Seminar on Transference, unpublished, trans Gallagher, 8 March 1961.

Lacan J, Seminar on Identification, unpublished, trans Gallagher, 15 November 1961.

Lacan J, Seminar on Anxiety, unpublished, trans Gallagher, 16 January 1963.

Lacan J, Seminar on the Psychoanalytic Act, unpublished, trans Gallagher, 21 February 1968.

J Lacan, The Inverse of Psychoanalysis, unpublished seminar, 11 March, 1970, trans Gallagher.

J Lacan, Television, Dossier on the Institutional Debate, trans Mehlman, *October*, Number 40, MIT, Cambridge, USA, 1987.

J Lacan, quoted in *Introduction to the Reading of Lacan*, Other Press, J Dor, 1998.

J Laplanche, *Essays on Otherness*, ed Fletcher, Routledge, 1999.

Lefort R & Lefort R, *The Birth of the Other*, Urbana and Chicago, Illinois University Press, 1999.

Lemmon E, *Beginning Logic*, Thomas Nelson and Sons, London, 1969.

London and Nisbett, eds, Internal Reactions: Ineffectiveness of Debriefing, *The Cognitive Alteration of Feeling States*, 1972.

Lohser and Newton, *Unorthodox Freud*, New York, Hawthorn Books 1996.

Multimedia Encyclopaedia, on CD, Helicon Publishing Ltd, 1996.

Monty Python's Previous Record, The Famous Charisma Label, 1973, Phonogram Ltd.

Mearns D and Thorne B, *Person Centred Counselling in Action,* Sage, London, 1988.

McCourt F, *Angela's Ashes*, Flamingo, 1997.

Maupassant G, *A Woman's Life,* Penguin, 1965.

Masood E, Howzat! Why the best players don't always watch the ball, *New Scientist,* 25.11.2.

Margulis L, Mehos D, and Kaveski S, There is no such thing as a one celled animal or plant, *Science Teacher* 50:34-36, p41-43

Mathelin C, *Lacanian Psychotherapy with Children -the broken piano*, Other Press, New York, 1999.

Nietzsche F, *Thus Spake Zarathustra,* Pelican, trans Hollingdale, [1892], 1961

Nietzsche F, *The Gay Science*, trans Kaufmann, Vintage Books, [1887], 1974.

The New Shorter Oxford English Dictionary on CD-ROM, Oxford University Press, 1996.

Nietzsche F, *My Sister And I*, Amok Books, Los Angeles 1990.

Nietzsche F, *Beyond Good And Evil, Penguin Classics,* trans Hollingdale, [1886],1973.

http://www.hm-treasury.gov.uk/budget/budget_2001/budget_report/bud_bud01_repchapc.cfm

Thirring H, Die Wandlung des Begriffssystems der Physik, (essay in Krise und Neuauf bau in den exakten Wissenschaten, Finf Wiener Vortrage, by Mark, Thirring,

Hahn, Nobelling, Menger; Verlag Deuticke, Vienna, 1933, quoted in Popper's *The Logic of Scientific Discovery*, Hutchinson, London, 1980.

Palomera V, The Fragmentation of Identity in the Psychotic Experience, *Analysis, No 7*, 1996, p5.

Pignotti C, Reuters, Narcissistic Argentina
http://wedge.nando.net/newsroom/ntn/health/081597/health32_26581.html

Popper KR *The Logic of Scientific Discovery*, Hutchinson, London, 1980.

Porter R, *The Greatest Benefit to Mankind, a Medical History of Humanity,* HarperCollins, London, 1997.

Plato, *The Republic*, trans Cornford, Oxford, 1941.

Plato, *The Last Days of Socrates*, Penguin, trans Tredennick, 1965.

Peirce C S, *Collected Works of Charles Sanders Peirce*, Hartshorne et al, Harvard University Press, 1930-1958.

Quine W, *From a Logical Point of View*, On What There Is, Oxford University Press, 1953.

Quine W, Two Dogmas of Empiricism, *From a Logical Point of View*, Harvard, 1953.

Quine, *Word and Object*, MIT, Cambridge, 1960.

Quine W, Structure and Nature, *The Journal of Philosophy*, vol LXXXIX, no 1, January 1992.

Quine W, Three Indeterminancies, *Perspectives on Quine*, ed Barratt and Gibson, Blackwell, 1990.

Roudinescu, E *Jacques Lacan & Co, A History of Psychoanalysis in France,* 1928-1985, FAB, 1990.

Rosenhan D L, On Being Sane in Insane Places, *Science*, vol 179, 1973.

Rodriguez L, The Position of the Analyst with Children in Psychoanalysis: the Lacanian contribution compared with other perspectives, *Analysis*, Number Three, 1991, Centre for Psychoanalytic Research.

Ragland-Sullivan E, The Limits of Discourse Structure: Obsession and Hysteria, *Papers of the Freudian School of Melbourne*, 1988.

Scarman, Lord, House of Lords. 1986 House of Lords, *Hansard*, vol. 502, No.7, Col.488.

Searles H, Oedipal Love in the Countertransference, 1959, *Int J Psychoanalysis*, 40, p180-90.

Schacter and Singer Cognitive, Social and Physiological Determinants of Emotional State, *Psychological Review*, 69, 379-399, 1962.

Scharff D, *Refinding The Object And Reclaiming The Self,* Jason Aronson Inc, London, 1992.

Scharnberg, M The Non-Authentic Nature of Freud's Observations. *Uppsala Studies in Education*, Vols. 47-48. 1993, Uppsala: University of Uppsala, Vol II, p64-5.

Shakespeare W, *Twelfth Night,* Oxford University Press, London, 1911.

Shakespeare W, *The Merchant of Venice*, Oxford University Press, London, 1911.

Shakespeare W, *The Comedy of Errors*, Oxford University Press, London, 1911.

Soler C, Time and Interpretation, *Reading Seminars I and II*, ed Feldstein et al, SUNY, 1996.

Solomon, Song of Songs 4,15, Old Testament, *The New English Bible*, Oxford University Press, 1970.

Showalter E, *Hystories,* Picador, 1998.

Spinoza B, *Ethics*, Origin and Nature of Emotions, Everyman Library, trans Boyle, [1660], 1910.

Sun Pin, *The Art of Warfare*, trans Lau and Ames, Ballantine Books, New York, 1996.

Von Neumann J, On the Presentation of the Albert Einstein Award to Gödel, 1951; Tribute to Gödel, Foundations of Mathematics, *Symposium Papers Commemorating the Sixtieth Birthday of Kurt Gödel*, ed Bullof et al, Springer Verlag, Berlin, 1969.

White A. Synonymous Expressions, *The Philosophical Quarterly*, Vol. 8, No. 32, July 1958.

Wittgenstein, L., *Philosophical Investigations,* Basil Blackwell, 1958.

Wittgenstein L, *Lectures and Conversations on Aesthetics, Psychology and Religious Belief,* ed Barrett, Basil Blackwell, Oxford, 1978.

Wittgenstein L, Vol.1, *Last writings on the Philosophy of Psychology*, Blackwell, 1982.

Wittgenstein L, *Zettel*, 2nd edition, Basil Blackwell, 1981.

Young R, *The Culture of British Psychoanalysis* www.human-nature.com

Zeigarnik B, Das Behalten erledigter und unerledigter Handlungen, *Psychol. Forsch.,* Vol. 9, p1-85.

First published 2002 by **Press for the Habilitation of Psychoanalysis**
36 Stanhope Gardens, London, N6 5TS   © Philip Harry Fenton Hill

ISBN 1-903859-00-X